POLAND IN THE SECOND WORLD WAR

POLAND
IN THE
SECOND WORLD WAR

Józef Garliński

MACMILLAN

First published 1985

Published by
THE MACMILLAN PRESS LTD
Houndmills, Basingstoke, Hampshire RG21 2XS
and London
Companies and representatives
throughout the world

Printed and bound in Great Britain by
Anchor Brendon Ltd, Tiptree, Essex

British Library Cataloguing in Publication Data
Garliński, Józef
Poland in the Second World War
1. Poland—History—Occupation, 1939–1945
I Title
943.8'053   DK4410
ISBN 0-333-39258-2

To my wife, Eileen, a soldier of the Home Army

Contents

Contents

Lists of Maps and Illustrations

MAPS

ILLUSTRATIONS

Abbreviations

Abwehr	German military intelligence
Anna	Communication base in Kowno, later in Stockholm
AK	*Armia Krajowa* (Home Army)
Alek	Communication base in Cairo
BBC	British Broadcasting Corporation
BCh	*Bataliony Chłopskie* (Peasant Battalions)
Bey	Communication base in Istambul
Bolek	Communication base in Bucharest
BUND	Jewish Socialist Organisation
ChD	Chrześcijańska Demokracja (Christian Democrats)
Comintern	The Soviet Organisation established in 1919 to foster world revolution
COP	Centralny Okręg Przemysłowy (Central Industrial District)
Die Rote Kapelle	The Red Orchestra, Soviet spy-ring in Western Europe
Die Schwarze Kapelle	The Black Orchestra, German anti-Hitler underground organisation
DR	*Delegatura Rządu* (Government Delegacy)
Einsatzgruppe	German police formation for clearing the countryside of elements dangerous to the occupants
Enigma	German ciphering machine
F	Communication station in Marseilles
Fall Weiss	Code name of secret plan for the German invasion of Poland in 1939
Gestapo	*Geheime Staatspolizei* (secret state police)
Grzegorz	Communication station in Athens
H	Communication station in Madrid
Janka	Communication station in Paris
Jodoform	System of secret signals in connection with dropping and landing operations, sent by the Polish Radio in Britain through the BBC
Kedyw	*Komenda Dywersji* (Diversion and Sabotage Command of the Home Army)

KON	*Konwent Organizacji Niepodległościowych* (Convocation of Organisations for Independence)
KOP	*Korpus Ochrony Pogranicza* (Frontier Guard Corps)
KOP	*Komisja Oświecenia Publicznego* (Commission for Public Education)
KRN	*Krajowa Rada Narodowa* (Polish National Council)
KRP	*Krajowa Reprezentacja Polityczna* (Polish Political Representation)
KWC	*Kierownictwo Walki Cywilnej* (Directorate of Civil Resistance)
KWK	*Kierownictwo Walki Konspiracyjnej* (Directorate of Clandestine Resistance)
KWP	*Kierownictwo Walki Podziemnej* (Directorate of Underground Resistance)
Maginot Line	French fortifications on the French–German frontiers
Marta	A secret Polish radio station in London
MD	'Mining and diversionary' equipment
Most	Bridge, two-way operation with a plane landing in Poland and returning to its base in Allied territory
NIE	*Niepodległość* (Independence, a new underground organisation under the second Soviet occupation)
NKVD	*Narodny Komissariat Vnutrennich Dyel* (People's Commissariat of Internal Affairs: used for Soviet secret police)
NOW	*Narodowa Organizacja Wojskowa* (The National Military Organisation)
NPR	*Narodowa Partia Robotnicza* (National Labour Party)
NSZ	*Narodowe Siły Zbrojne* (National Military Forces)
ONR	*Obóz Narodowo Radykalny* (National Radical Camp)
OPW	*Obóz Polski Walczącej* (Fighting Poland Camp)
OW	'Fighting area' equipment
OZN	*Obóz Zjednoczenia Narodowego* (The Camp of National Unity)
P	Communication station in Lisbon
PIST	*Państwowy Instytut Sztuki Teatralnej* (National Theatrical Institute)
PKP	*Polityczny Komitet Porozumiewawczy* (Political Advisory Committee)

PKWN	*Polski Komitet Wyzwolenia Narodowego* (Polish Committee of National Liberation)
PPR	*Polska Partia Robotnicza* (Polish Workers Party)
PPS	*Polska Partia Socjalistyczna* (Polish Socialist Party)
RJN	*Rada Jedności Narodowej* (The Council of National Unity)
Romek	Communication base in Budapest
Regina	Secret Polish radio station in Paris
RSHA	*Reichssicherheitshauptamt* (state security headquarters)
S	Communication station in Bern
Sanacja	Piłsudski's party after his death
Siegfried Line	German fortifications in the West
SL	*Stronnictwo Ludowe* (Peasant Party)
Sława	Communication station in Belgrade
SN	*Stronnictwo Narodowe* (National Party)
SOB	*Socjalistyczna Organizacja Bojowa* (Socialist Combat Organisation)
SOE	Special Operations Executive
SOS	*Społeczna Organizacja Samoobrony* (Self-defence Organisation)
SP	*Stronnictwo Pracy* (Labour Party)
SS	*Schutzstaffel* (German political–military protection units)
Światpol	The World Union of Poles Abroad
SZP	*Służba Zwycięstwu Polski* ('In Service of Poland's Victory')
Tempest	Local mobilisation of the Home Army units against the retreating Germans
TON	*Tajna Organizacja Nauczycielstwa* (Secret Teachers' Organisation)
Volkslist	Declaration of option to the German nation
Wachlarz	Fan, diversionary organisation of the Home Army in the East
Wehrmacht	German Armed Forces
Żegota	Council for Aid to Jews
ZWZ	*Związek Walki Zbrojnej* (Union for Armed Struggle)
ŻOB	*Żydowska Organizacja Bojowa* (Jewish Fighting Organisation)

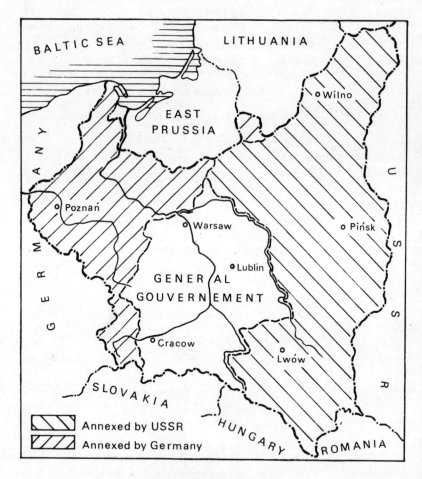

Poland in October 1939

Preface

Before the Second World War Poland was a poor country which, after over a hundred years of partitions, returned to independent political life in 1918. Seven years of fighting had ruined the country's economy. The unification of the three parts which had been so long under foreign rule created a serious problem as did the fact that about 30 per cent of the population were minority groups. The young state had also to decide on her foreign policy in the face of aggressive German revisionism and constant Soviet diversionary actions. But the Polish nation, connected by historical and cultural ties with the West, was determined to join the large family of the free European countries.

In theory, in 1939, there had originally been several options open to Poland, but long years of partition made any compromise impossible. So the Polish Government had to reject all Hitler's demands when he came to power and set aside the Treaty of Versailles. The Poles had also to decline the Soviet proposition to allow the Red Army to enter Polish territory in order to encircle the Third *Reich*. The Red divisions would never leave Poland voluntarily. There was also a possibility of rejecting the German demands, and also refusing the guarantee offered by Britain, thus remaining strictly neutral. Yet the Polish nation, determined to fight in defence of its freedom, had accepted the British guarantees, although it was clear that Hitler would consider this to be provocation and that Poland would be the first victim of German aggression.

As the result of the war Poland lost its independence, although the Western Allies were victorious in the struggle against Hitler. Unfortunately they decided that Poland should remain in Soviet Russia's sphere of influence, which meant that our country would have a communist government, installed by force, Red Army garrisons and complete Soviet domination.

Some people believe that if Poland had been more co-operative and had accepted compromise propositions, the final result would be better and the Polish nation would enjoy more freedom. Definitely not. Soviet Russia would not have honoured any obligations and would have compromised only under physical pressure which the Western Allies were not prepared to exert. We are proud that our Government resisted colossal pressure during the war and did not accept the Curzon Line. Nothing would have stopped Soviet Russia from dominating Poland, but Polish capitulation would have gone down in history as our consent to the Russian aggression.

Of course, we made many mistakes and we must admit that our quarrels and blunders helped our enemies to regain control over our country. But the fact remains that even if we had acted faultlessly, we could not have prevented it. The Western Allies left Poland alone at the mercy of her powerful Eastern neighbour. Thanks to her resistance and to her ties with the West, Poland is today on the map of Europe, but her cultural and economic development is severely limited and politically she is not a free country.

In my work I have relied on archival sources and on many published books and articles as well as on unpublished statements. I have based my research on Polish, English, French, German and Vatican sources, as well as on some available Soviet documents. For help shown to me I am grateful to the Polish Library, to the Polish Underground Study Trust and to the General Sikorski Historical Institute, all in London.

I am indebted to the individual help of many people, above all to Rafał Brzeski, Jerzy Budkiewicz, Halina Czarnocka, Jerzy Cynk, Colonel Roman Garby-Czerniawski, Wojciech Fibak, Jarosław Garliński, M. B. Grabowski Fund, Dr Rosemary Hunt, Dr Zdzisław Jagodziński, Jerzy Kulczycki, Ronald Lewin, Colonel Tadeusz Lisicki, Rev. Jerzy Mirewicz, Dr Alicja Moskalowa, Orbis Books London Ltd, Dr Antony Polonsky, Colonel Antoni Rawicz-Szczerbo, Nina Taylor, Comandor Bohdan Wroński and Tadeusz Zawadzki.

London
August 1984   JÓZEF GARLIŃSKI

Introduction

In the second half of 1938 Poland covered an area of 389 000 square kilometres. She shared borders with seven neighbour states and one protectorate: 2000 km with Germany; 1500 km with Soviet Russia; 600km with Czechoslovakia; 450km with Lithuania; 250km with Romania, 220km with Hungary and 120 km with Latvia. With the exception of the chain of the Carpathians in the south and the marshes of the River Pripet in the east, these were all completely open frontiers. Warsaw, the capital, counted 1 289 000 inhabitants.[1]

The population then exceeded 35 million, a figure that includes about 30 per cent of national minorities. The last national census in 1931 showed that the largest minority groups numbered 3 222 000 Ukrainians; 3 113 000 Jews; 1 219 000 Ruthenians, 989 000 Byelorussians and 741 000 Germans.[2]

The country was economically poor and about 70 per cent of the population were country-dwellers. Industry was only just beginning to develop, more strongly in the Western parts. The Central Industrial District (COP) planned in south-central Poland was in the process of being constructed. A port had been built in Gdynia, which offered competition for Gdańsk, where Poland had only limited rights. Silesia was a strong economic asset with its coal deposits, as was the oilfield of Borysław. Polish exports relied mainly on coal and food produce, sold at very low prices to win foreign markets and earn strong foreign currency.

Poland's poor industrial potential is well illustrated by the figures for 1937. Coal extraction amounted to 36 million tonnes annually. At the same time, the USA produced 448 million, Great Britain 245 million, Germany 185, Soviet Russia 123 and France 44 million tonnes. Half a million tonnes of crude oil were extracted annually from the Borysław oilfield, while the USA extracted 173 million and Russia almost 28 million. Germany extracted no more crude oil than Poland and France was dependent on her colonies in this sector. Poland produced only 1.5 million tonnes of steel per annum, while the American production amounted to 51 million tonnes, Germany

19.8 million, Russia 17.8 million and France 7.9 million tonnes. In the field of motor-car production, statistics did not list Poland, when USA were producing almost 5 million cars annually, Great Britain 493 000, Germany 327 000 and France and Russia almost 200 000 each.[3]

In view of its weak economic situation, Poland was unable to achieve a modern and well-equipped army, even though in the last years before the war almost one third of the entire national budget was spent on the army.

In 1939 Poland had 2 million trained soldiers, of whom the bulk belonged to the reserve. The army comprised thirty divisions of infantry, eleven cavalry brigades and one armoured motor brigade. The air force had fifteen fighter squadrons with obsolete planes, eleven bomber squadrons, partially equipped with modern gear of home production, and twelve reconnaissance squadrons. Some 400 planes were suitable for fighting. A small navy consisted of four destroyers, five submarines, six minesweepers, one mine-layer and a dozen or more small units.[4]

Poland's poverty was principally the result of the long period of partitions and the seven-years of fighting on Polish territory during both the First World War and the Polish–Russian war of 1919–20. The reconstruction of the ruined country was the task of greatest importance. The old partitioned sectors, which for the best part of 150 years had existed within separate different political, cultural, social and economic conditions, had to be unified. A completely new state administration was needed. This task was complicated by the great number of national minorities, which had their own political aspirations.

A year before the outbreak of the Second World War, Poland maintained regular relations with all her neighbours. The arbitration pact signed in 1925 had not completely smoothed relations with Germany. Aggressive German propaganda kept up a volley of revisionist slogans. There were few who remembered that the land to which Germans laid claim had been taken over from Poland in an unprecedented manner at the time of the partitions. In the first phase of Hitler's rule, the new chancellor tried to emphasise that he had peaceful intentions. On 26 January 1934 the Polish–German non-aggression pact was signed for a ten-year period. It brought about a decrease in German anti-Polish propaganda and led to co-operation in various fields of interest to both sides.

Poland had won the war with Soviet Russia and in March 1921, had signed the peace treaty in Riga. Later, in July 1932, a non-aggression pact had been signed, extended to 1945. A trade agreement was also concluded. Despite this Russia tried constantly to weaken the young Polish state by means of underground diversion and propaganda. The Polish Communist Party collaborated with Soviet Russia in these machinations. History had taught Poland always to expect aggression from Russia, so Poland's defence plans between 1921 and 1938 were based mainly on such an assumption.

The Polish relationship with Czechoslovakia was cold, and co-operation was restricted to intelligence. Lithuania did not even maintain diplomatic relations with Poland as Lithuanians could not forgive the annexation of Wilno, but in 1938 relations were renewed and the Lithuanian Government declared that in the event of a German–Polish conflict it would remain neutral, and it kept its promise.

The relations with Romania, Hungary and small Latvia were excellent. With Romania Poland had a guarantee treaty concluded in 1926 and binding until 1941. There was no formal treaty with Hungary, but the two countries were bound in a friendship of several centuries.

France, though she had no common frontier with Poland, was greatly interested in her fate, being connected by numerous historic, political and cultural ties. In February 1921, just before the Treaty of Riga, Poland concluded an alliance with France, to which a military convention was appended. The basic condition of the alliance was that if either country were attacked, the governments would jointly agree on a course of action.

The military convention was far more specific and distinctly formulated mutual obligations with regard to Germany and the Soviet Russia. 'In the event of German aggression against one of the two countries, both are equally bound to provide support for the other, according to their mutual understanding. In the event of Poland being threatened with war by the Republic of Soviets, or in the event of attack on the part of the latter, France undertook to act both on land and on sea in order to ensure Poland's safety on the German side as before and to bring help in her defence against the army of the Soviets.'[5]

The other country with which Poland had no common frontiers, but which was interested in Poland towards the end of the 1930s was Great Britain, although she shared little historical or cultural past with the Polish nation. For many years after the First World War

Great Britain had not been interested in Central Europe. A trade exchange was undertaken with Poland, but little happened in the political and military arenas. When Hitler began to present *faits accomplis* counter to the decisions of Versailles, the British protested but considered these to be internal German affairs. However, when on 11 March 1938, Hitler walked into Austria and two days later annexed her to the *Reich*, the British recognised this as an act of aggression. Britain continued to hold the view that a new world conflict could be avoided by means of further concessions, yet the need to form a common anti-German front began to crystallise. Accordingly Britain turned to Poland and diplomatic contacts became more intense.[6]

In this decisive period Poland was ruled by the political party of Józef Piłsudski who came to power by a coup in 1926. Before this, Poland had gone through a very difficult period of party discord. The impossibility of forming a government which could effectively manage the exceptionally tricky affairs of state had, in some ways, justified his action. Until his death in May, 1935, Piłsudski ruled the country in partly dictatorial manner, but it was not a dictatorship of the German, Soviet or Italian type. In Poland there existed full freedom of religion, language, culture and schooling, but just before the death of Piłsudski, the ruling people introduced a new constitution that, practically speaking, excluded free elections.[7] The head of state was then Professor Ignacy Mościcki (1867–1946) and the Premier was General Felicjan Sławoj-Składkowski (1885–1962), a professional soldier and a doctor of medicine, but not a politician. The function of Commander-in-Chief was performed by Marshal Edward Śmigły-Rydz (1886–1941). The strongest opposition to the rule of Piłsudski's camp known as *Sanacja*, came from the four most important political parties: the Christian Democrats (ChD), the Peasant Party (SL), the Polish Socialist Party (PPS) and the National Party (SN). The right-wing National Radical Camp (ONR), consisting mainly of the younger generation, was making itself increasingly heard. The communists were weak and played a very small part in the political life of the country.

Despite considerable internal difficulties and a harsh political struggle, the Polish nation showed decided unanimity in defending its frontiers and its sovereignty. This was made particularly manifest when the Government launched a collection for the National Defence Fund. Contributions came pouring in from millions of people, and the opposition parties joined the general fund-raising committee.

Unfortunately, the government camp refused to allow other parties to participate in making political decisions. In the spring of 1939, when the opposition parties saw that war was unavoidable and suggested creating a Government for National Unity, they were refused.[8] That decision was to weigh fatally on the subsequent actions of the Polish nation during the Second World War.

In the twenty-four chapters of this book the fate of Poland and Poles during the Second World War is presented against the background of the wide panorama of the global conflict.

A century and a half of subjection, ended by the regaining of independence after the First World War, precluded any compromise by the Poles. So the Polish government had to reject all Hitler's demands, after he had come to power, abrogated the Treaty of Versailles and was threatening a new war. Neither was there any question of allowing the Red Army on to Polish territory which together with the Western democracies would surround the German *Reich*. The Polish nation, deciding to fight in defence of its freedom, accepted the guarantee offered by the West in the knowledge that it would thus become the first victim of the German attack.

The book begins with the situation in Europe before the German aggression, the efforts made to preserve the peace and the outbreak of war. Later on we have the Polish–German September Campaign, the Soviet attack in the East and the Polish defeat and division into two zones of occupation; further on the creation of the Polish underground resistance movement, the new Polish government in France and the re-formation of the Polish Army. Further chapters deal with the fall of France, the Battle of Britain, the fighting at sea and in other theatres of war, with Poles taking part almost everywhere.

Much of the book is devoted to presenting the efforts of the Poles in trying to gain the support of the Western Allies, seeking agreement with Soviet Russia and building up an underground state, as well as their own internal difficulties.

Later in the book, when the Western Allies decided to leave Poland within the orbit of Soviet Russia, the tragic fate of the Poles is presented, their efforts to gain their freedom, the Warsaw Uprising and the decisions of the great powers taken at Teheran and Yalta. The matter of the Roman Catholic Church and the question of the Jews are presented in separate chapters.

1   The Outbreak of War

THE PARTITION OF CZECHOSLOVAKIA

The occupation of Austria in March 1938 was proof that Hitler would defy the Versailles treaty and turn to external aggression, but because Austria was inhabited by German-speaking people, France and Great Britain continued to hope that peace would be maintained and they refrained from any action which might suggest that it was time to prepare for war.

The governments of both great democracies continued their peace efforts even when Hitler, immediately after seizing Austria, turned his gaze towards Sudetenland. This mountainous country belonged to Czechoslovakia and contained about 3.5 million Germans. The Czechs naturally rejected this demand. Not only would it mean a significant material loss, but it also would completely expose them to Germany, for it was in Sudetenland that the Czechs possessed their modern fortifications.[1]

The German demands were clearly contrary to the Treaty of Versailles, France was tied to Czechoslovakia by a mutual assistance pact, yet once again the Western democracies did not resolve on a more decisive response. The British Government in July sent Lord Runciman to Prague to attempt to arbitrate. Nothing came of this and his proposal to arrange a plebiscite in the disputed territory coincided with Hitler's own intentions. So the British Prime Minister, Neville Chamberlain, tried to make personal contact with Hitler, but this proved fruitless. The Italian dictator, Benito Mussolini, also tried to intervene.

Czechoslovakia also had a mutual assistance treaty with Soviet Russia, which had been signed on 15 May 1935. It was difficult to foresee how Moscow would react to German aggression, so France put the question directly to her and was told in reply that she would honour her treaty obligations if France did likewise. In response to the further question as to how this would actually be achieved, it was stated that Soviet divisions would have to march through either

1

Polish or Romanian territory and that France, allied to both these countries, must obtain agreement for this. Naturally Poland and Romania refused, Russia did not insist and her treaty obligations remained in abeyance.[2]

By every principle of political and strategic logic Poland ought to have striven for a lasting agreement with Czechoslovakia. They had a common border 600km long, Czechoslovakia had superior economic potential and was able to raise a modern army, and German revisionism threatened both countries. However, despite some concerted efforts, neither friendship nor agreement were achieved. The traditional pro-Russian attitude of the Czechs, the Teschen affair (Czechoslovakia had taken Teschen, in Silesia, in 1919, when Poland was fighting desperately against Russia) and the Polish minority living in Czechoslovakia continued to outweigh everything.

During the Sudetenland crisis, when a definite stance was required, Poland at first tried to remain neutral, to avoid annoying the Germans. When it became clear that Hitler would take Sudetenland, Poland adopted a hostile attitude towards Czechoslovakia. The Polish government informed the French that Poland had no obligations towards Czechoslovakia. Moreover, when Hungary made claims of her own, Poland demanded the return of Teschen (Trans-Olza).

On 29 September 1938 a conference took place in Munich, in which the participants were the British Prime Minister, Neville Chamberlain; the French Premier, Edouard Daladier; the German dictator, Adolf Hitler and the Italian dictator, Benito Mussolini. It was unanimously decided that Czechoslovakia must cede Sudetenland to Germany, in exchange for which her frontiers would be guaranteed; Hitler himself made this assertion.

Forty-eight hours later, on 1 October 1938, the Czechs caved in under this collective pressure and German units marched onto Sudeten territory. On the same day Czechoslovakia accepted the Polish ultimatum and the Polish army began occupying Trans-Olza. On 5 October the President of Czechoslovakia, Edward Beneš, resigned and the following day Slovakia and Transcarpathian Ruthenia were granted autonomy. On 2 November 1938 Hungary annexed Southern Slovakia.[3]

Poland's participation in the dismemberment of Czechoslovakia created a very bad impression and harmed her greatly. Poland, which had herself endured the very harsh experience of partition, was now taking part in a similar act against one of her neighbours, in the company, moreover, of Germany, which had for years been directing revisionist slogans against Poland. There was even suspicion that the Poland–German non-aggression pact contained a secret clause dealing with the partition of Czechoslovakia.[4] To Hitler's satisfaction, Poland had fallen out with the Western democracies. With Soviet Russia and her treaty obligations towards Czechoslovakia looming ominously, Poland found herself completely alone.

GERMAN PROPOSALS TO POLAND

Hardly a month had passed after the Munich conference when the nature of Hitler's further plans became clear. On 25 October the German Foreign Minister, Joachim von Ribbentrop, in conversation with the Polish ambassador, Józef Lipski, raised the question of Gdańsk and its incorporation into the Reich and also its transport links with East Prussia through Polish Pomerania. To Hitler's mind these were very restrained demands and he expected the Poles to accept them, the more so as he was supporting the creation of a joint Hungarian–Polish border by handing over Transcarpathian Ruthenia to the Hungarians. During these months the German dictator hesitated and it appeared that he was intending to direct the cutting edge of his diplomacy first against the West, and was seeking security in the East. An agreement with Stalin had not yet crystallised in Hitler's mind and he wanted Poland at least neutralised in order to screen him from Soviet Russia.[5]

Then, during the last months of 1938, Poland's attitude and her political and military response to the changing situation began to emerge. Everything suggested that the opportunity should be seized to accept Hitler's proposals and attempt to ensure that his gaze turned westward first. No-one at that time in Poland, nor indeed elsewhere, imagined that France, in alliance with Great Britain, would collapse so quickly under the onslaught of the German divisions. The *Blitzkrieg* had not yet been tried out, and long and heavy fighting, similar to that of the 1914–18 war, was expected, as were great losses on both sides and Germany's eventual defeat. In such an event Poland would survive and might even emerge with honour if she entered the fray at a moment favourable to her, when the West's success would be assured. This could be interpreted as political cynicism, but the great powers subsequently used the same reasoning.

But events turned out differently. In 1938 the Polish nation was coming to the end of its first twenty years of independence, after almost 150 years of bondage. The new state, uniting the three partitioned areas, was experiencing great difficulties and the unification process continued. Economically Poland was among Europe's poorest countries, no common ground was found with the ethnic minorities and internal political relationships were tense. However, in the realm of the defence of their rights and land, all Poles were united and uncompromising. The Polish nation was incapable either of compromise or of subtle diplomatic manoeuvring and the Polish government recognised and respected this attitude. Whoever stretched out a hand for Polish land could expect to encounter armed resistance and the Polish reply to the first German proposals was in this spirit. Even the seizure of Gdańsk, then a free city, would have been a *casus belli*. These preliminary Polish–German talks in the autumn of 1938 were conducted in extreme secrecy, but Hitler had already received the first indications of Polish reactions.[6] Perhaps it was then that he adjusted his political plans and turned his eyes to the East.

Before undertaking any further political initiatives, the Third Reich set about clearing up the Czechoslovak problem and it was then that the real value of Hitler's guarantees and the West's optimistic hopes became apparent. Continual German subversion stimulated Slovak separatism and encouraged the Hungarians to annex Transcarpathian Ruthenia, placing Czechoslovakia in a quite hopeless situation. Beneš was succeeded by Emil Hacha, as President of this mauled country. Hacha was elected on 30 November 1938 and had no room for manoeuvre, as the Western democracies gave him no support.

Finally, in mid-March 1939 Czechoslovakia's political independence ended. On 14 March the Slovak parliament endorsed the independence of the puppet state, at whose head was the priest, Joseph Tiso, premier of autonomous Slovakia for several months. The same day Hitler summoned Emil Hacha to Berlin and in brutal conversation, during which the President suffered a heart attack, he forced him to accept German 'protection'. The following day German tanks entered Prague and the Protectorate of Bohemia and Moravia was proclaimed. A certain semblance of Czech independence remained: the office of President was retained, as was the government of General Alois Eliáš, but the real power was in the hands of the Protector nominated by Hitler, Constantin von Neurath. Barely a day passed before the Hungarians entered Transcarpathian Ruthenia.[7]

The end of independent Czechoslovakia changed Poland's southern border and enabled Germany to extend her frontier further round the Polish state. Admittedly, the changes gave the Poles a 200km frontier with Hungary, but the former Czechoslovak border was lined with German divisions. Now Poland had about 250km of common frontier with Slovakia, which was ready to carry out Hitler's every instruction, while a remaining 150km divided Poland from the Protectorate of Bohemia and Moravia.

On 21 March 1939, a few days after the occupation of Prague, Hitler seized Memel from Lithuania and on the same day von Ribbentrop had formal talks with ambassador Lipski in which he repeated the detailed German proposals, which were intended to regulate relations between the two countries. Gdańsk was to be incorporated into the Reich, the Poles were to agree to an ex-territorial motorway and railway line across Pomerania and in exchange the Germans were to extend the non-aggression pact to twenty-five years.[8] Hitler continued to believe that these proposals were very mild and that they ought to be accepted, but within five days the Polish side gave a categorical rejection. Ignoring the psychological dimension, who could now trust the Germans after Czechoslovakia?

BRITISH GUARANTEES

That country's fate finally aroused the Western democracies. Great Britain addressed a very discreet question to Poland. The British government, after consultations with France, intended to make a declaration guaranteeing Poland assistance in the event of aggression and asked whether this was what Poland in fact wanted. There were still a number of options: Poland could re-examine the German Chancellor's proposals; she could consider the idea of allowing Soviet troops across her territory; she could thank the British and request complete silence so as not to annoy the Germans. The Polish government, backed by public opinion and its own views, recognised the need to create bonds with the West and gave London a positive response. It contained a proposal for a bilateral pact. Forthwith, on

31 March, the British Prime Minister, Neville Chamberlain, made his historic declaration in the House of Commons guaranteeing Poland's independence and promising aid.[9] A fortnight later similar guarantees were offered to Greece and Romania with their agreement, while Yugoslavia was not mentioned, since she had not accepted this offer.

The British declaration, in concert with France, dispelled any illusions which Hitler might have had about Poland. If in the autumn of 1938 he had still been undecided, his gaze now turned definitely towards his Eastern neighbour. On 28 April in a great speech in the *Reichstag* he annulled the German–Polish non-aggression pact and less than a month later, on 23 May, had secret discussions in the Chancellery with his senior commanders. He had taken the final decision and was presenting his plans:

> The mass of eighty millions Germans has solved the ideological problems. The economic problems must also be solved ... Further successes without invasion of foreign countries or attacking the property of others are not possible ... Danzig is not the object at stake. We are concerned with expanding our living space in the East and securing our food supplies ... The question of sparing Poland can therefore no longer be considered and we are left with the decision to attack Poland at the first suitable opportunity. We cannot expect a repetition of the Czech solution. This time there will be fighting ... The war with England and France will be a life-and-death struggle.[10]

There could no longer be any doubt: Poland had called down on herself the German dictator's fury and was to be the first object of his military aggression.

MUTUAL ASSISTANCE PACT BETWEEN GREAT BRITAIN AND POLAND

After Chamberlain's declaration, relations between Poland and Great Britain gained a new lease of life. By 3 April the Polish Foreign Minister, Józef Beck, was in London and the terms of the British–Polish mutual aid agreement were drawn up. It had not yet been signed, when a joint communiqué was issued on 6 April. A week later, on 13 April, the French press published a statement by Premier Daladier accepting the British–Polish agreement and mentioned the

Franco–Polish mutual aid pact. British–Polish and Franco–Polish consultations and military discussions began. Poland also sought loans for armaments and in the course of the following months London offered £8 m.[11]

The clarification of the Polish position was considered in London to be a diplomatic success; the pragmatic British did not take into account Polish emotional and psychological motivation and were afraid they might come to some agreement with the Germans. Nevertheless London knew, as did Paris, that Poland was a poor country without heavy industry and thus without a modern army. Therefore Russia had to be secured for a joint, anti-German front. By the middle of April preliminary negotiations on a mutual-aid pact begun in Paris between representatives of Great Britain, France and Russia. These negotiations were somewhat disrupted when, on 4 May, Russia recalled her pro-Western and well-known Commissar of Foreign Affairs, Maxim Litvinov, and replaced him with the almost unknown Vyacheslav Molotov, but the negotiations did continue. At the end of June they were moved to Moscow.

The Western Allies were right to seek an alliance with the Soviet Union, but their discussions in Moscow created a very difficult situation for Poland. Her eastern neighbour was historically an enemy. For London and Paris it was clear that Moscow must be able to move her divisions into Polish territory, to surround the Germans. No Polish government could accede to such a request arguing justifiably that the Red Army would never leave Poland voluntarily. Once again, as in her relations with Germany, the lessons of history did not allow Poland to compromise even though a Franco–Russo–British agreement was of fundamental importance to her. Such an agreement would preclude the fatal threat of a Berlin–Moscow pact.

Hitler was convinced that Poland would be an easy victim for him and that – as in the case of Czechoslovakia – the Western democracies would not come to her assistance. Nevertheless, he could not discount intervention, and therefore sought an agreement with Russia. Such an agreement was seemingly unlikely in view of the great ideological differences, yet several earlier Soviet statements suggested that Russia was also aware of such a possibility. Of particular significance had been a statement by the Soviet government on 20 May, during some trade negotiations, that there was a need to create an essential political framework between the two countries.[12] So the Soviet dictator was also aware of the need to negotiate with his ideological adversary. Both now knew that war was inevitable. Hitler wanted to secure his rear while fighting in the West; Stalin wanted the fighting to last as long as possible and to lead to the mutual exhaustion of both sides. Then his hour could come and with it the opportunity of lighting the fire of revolution in the West.

During these negotiations Poland's military leaders took a step which had great influence on the course of the Second World War. In 1931, under the auspices of Military Intelligence, a cipher department had been set up to try to break the secret of the German cipher machine, called *Enigma*, which had been introduced into the *Reichswehr*, the German skeleton army limited by the Treaty of Versailles. Thanks to several outstanding Polish crypto-analysts and help from French Intelligence, *Enigma*'s secret had been broken right at the end of 1932. A copy of the German machine and additional equipment which helped to discover the *Enigma* setting were built. These were essential for reading the radio signals intercepted by monitoring stations.

The Chief of the Polish General Staff decided that the secret should be revealed to the Western Allies as an initial contribution towards joint victory, and this was done at a secret conference near Warsaw in July 1939.

The French made only partial use of the information since the Western front collapsed quickly, but the British built a secret cryptological centre and throughout the whole war were able to read the Germans' most secret radio signals.[13]

RIBBENTROP – MOLOTOV PACT

The Franco–Russo–British talks went badly, partly because of Polish refusal to permit the transit of Soviet divisions. The Russians continually made new difficulties and meanwhile, in the greatest secrecy, talks were taking place between Berlin and Moscow. Suddenly, on 22 August, when it seemed that the Western powers were close to success, von Ribbentrop went to Moscow and on the following day the stunned world discovered that the Third Reich and Soviet Russia had signed a non-aggression treaty. It has gone down in history as the Ribbentrop–Molotov pact. Its secret and then quite unknown contents contained a clause dealing with the fourth partition of Poland.[14] On the same day that his minister landed in Moscow, Hitler, quite confident of success, had a meeting with his senior military commanders at which he said:

Annihilation of Poland in foreground. Goal is elimination of the vital forces, not the attainment of a specific line ... I shall provide the propaganda pretext for launching the war, no matter whether it is credible. The victor is not asked afterwards whether or not he has told the truth. What matters in beginning and waging the war is not righteousness, but victory. Close heart to pity. Proceed brutally. Eighty million people must obtain what they have a right to ... The stronger is in the right. Supreme hardness.[15]

On 25 August the German dictator issued the order that the attack on Poland was to begin the following morning, but that same evening he received information which caused him to reflect: a mutual assistance pact between Poland and Great Britain had been signed in London.

It was a very wide-ranging agreement, which bound both partners to render each other assistance in the event of direct and indirect aggression and even economic pressure. It was up to the injured party to decide whether to call on its partner for help. The agreement did not guarantee frontiers, although it was understood that since the contracting countries had frontiers, any violation of them constituted aggression. A secret protocol was appended, clearly indicating the Third Reich as a 'European power', which could be an aggressor. In the pact, aggression by any other country was treated differently from possible German aggression and would initiate only consultation on the part of the signatories and only some joint action.[16]

The signing of the pact was immediately announced, since part of its effect was to be a deterrent to Hitler. This aim was achieved for Hitler wavered, understanding that he had failed to isolate Poland. He called off the attack to gain some time for further diplomatic manoeuvring. This was a pretext, since, despite appearances, the dictator vacillated and hesitated and was not a man who made up his mind quickly.

There were attempts at German–Polish talks; there was an exchange of letters between the French Premier and the German dictator; there was a similar exchange of views between London and Berlin; there was an attempt at mediation by Mussolini, who was not ready for war, but the course of events could not be stopped. On 29 August Poland announced general mobilisation, but postponed it after a frenetic intervention by Western ambassadors and military *chefs de mission*, who at this late hour were still trying to maintain the peace.

GERMAN ATTACK

At about midday on 31 August Hitler finally made up his mind. Late that evening a fake attack by Polish soldiers on a radio station at Glivice took place. It was carried out by political prisoners from Sachsenhausen concentration camp dressed in Polish uniforms.

In the early hours of 1 September, without a formal declaration of war, the German armed forces crossed the Polish frontier.

2 The September Campaign in Poland

POLISH AND GERMAN FORCES

For nineteen years the Poles had been preparing first of all for war in the East; they had built fortifications there, expecting an attack from that direction, but when Hitler began to threaten from the West, this orientation changed decisively. As a poor country with long, open frontiers, Poland could not even contemplate a war on two fronts against powerful neighbours and once the decision to stand up to Hitler had been taken, the concept of an Eastern threat had to be dropped. It was simply hoped that, in the event of hostilities with Germany, Soviet Russia would remain neutral. This might have been reasonable if, immediately after a German attack on Poland, France had honoured her treaty obligations and made an effective attack in the West, supported by the RAF. Such an attitude, however, had all the hallmarks of 'wishful thinking', yet was not without certain psychological justification. Without it all the preparations for war with the Germans and the hope of holding them up for some time, would have been pointless.

The initial plans dealing with the possibility of war with the Germans assumed that the main burden of conducting hostilities would fall on France, which would be attacked first. Poland would then honour her obligations and commence hostilities against Germany. This had been the opinion of Marshal Piłsudski with which the French had concurred.[1] Such a view of things enabled the Poles to avoid having to build defensive fortifications in the West.

Only in 1936 was a start made on fortifying Silesia where a continuous defensive line was to be built. After the fall of Czechoslovakia the frontier there was fortified, but mainly with barbed-wire entanglements and anti-tank traps. Poland's eventual decision to reject the German demands and join the West produced a need to reverse her offensive plans, which even in 1936 still formed the basis

11

of all staff studies. Since it was now clear that the first German blow would be aimed at Poland, there was a need to think not of attack but of defence from which emerged the need for the rapid construction of fortifications. It was however already 1939, little time remained and so major concrete emplacements were completed only on the north-east sector of the Polish–German frontier, near Augustów. In all other sectors a series of field emplacements were built by the army assisted by reservists and the civilian population.[2]

General mobilisation, announced on 30 August, revoked and then announced again within twenty-four hours, was something without precedent in modern warfare. Chaos arose, which was only controlled with the greatest difficulty. Not every unit managed to complete full mobilisation, not every man managed to reach his unit, not every piece of equipment, drawn from stores already under German attack, reached the right hands. For example, of the fifty-four infantry battalions assigned to Łódź army, only thirty-four were in position; of the forty-five cavalry squadrons only twenty-nine; of the 316 cannons, only 168.[3] On 1 September there were about 1 million under arms in thirty-seven infantry divisions, eleven cavalry brigades, two armoured brigades (one incomplete) and in a dozen or so lightly-armed National Guard battalions. The Frontier Guard Corps (KOP) – stretched out along the Soviet, Lithuanian and Latvian borders – mustered a combined strength of three divisions. There were available more than 300 medium and light tanks, deployed for the most part in the motorised armoured brigades, there were also 500 light reconnaissance tanks attached to divisions and brigades. Ten armoured trains and 100 armoured cars also took part in the fighting. Altogether Poland had about 4000 field guns, of which only 1154 were in front-line divisions and brigades; the rest protected strong points or were assigned to KOP. The Air Force possessed forty-three combat flights, of which sixteen were bombers (four of *Łoś* aircraft and twelve of *Karaś*) and twenty-seven fighters (fifteen flights of P–7 and P–11, as well as twelve of *Lublin* and *Czapla* aircraft). In addition there were twelve postal-liaison groups with forty RWD–8 aircraft. Altogether about 400 aircraft were ready for combat, but of these only thirty-six Polish-produced *Łoś* aircraft were comparable to German machines. Polish fighters' speed was about 300k.p.h., while *Karaś* bombers were a little faster. Only the new *Łoś* bomber could fly at 445k.p.h. and carry 3000kg of bombs. The Germans used the *Messerschmidt–109* fighter with a speed of 470k.p.h. and the *Heinkel He-111* bomber with a speed of 350k.p.h. and 2000kg bomb-load, and

diving *Junkers 87 (Stuka)* with a speed of 405k.p.h. The Navy
consisted of four destroyers, five submarines and six minesweepers.[4]

Since Poland had about 1 500 000 trained soldiers, mainly reservists, under the age of 39, and a further 600 000 who had served in the
armies of the partitioning powers or in the Russo–Polish war – older
men, but still capable of bearing arms – a very difficult situation
arose. Spirit in Poland was such that thousands of men who had not
been mobilised trailed behind the units pleading to be given weapons
and enlisted.[5] This further complicated an already very difficult
situation and increased chaos.

Six armies were created from the large units and were deployed as
follows: 'Modlin' army in the area to the North of Modlin; 'Pomorze'
army in the area of Bydgoszcz; 'Poznań' army in the area of Poznań;
'Łódź' army to the south-west of Łódź; 'Kraków' army in the Kraków
region; 'Karpaty' army in the region of Nowy Sącz-Sanok. In addition
there was also an independent operational group 'Narew' in the area
of Łomża-Suwałki. There were also reserve groups: 'Warszawa',
'Kutno', 'Tarnów' and 'Wyszków', but they were not very large.[6]

This order of battle clearly shows that almost the entire mobilised
army was geared towards fighting the Germans. In accordance with
the hope that Russia would remain neutral, only the KOP remained
on her frontier. Even anti-aircraft defences were deployed in such a
way that there were almost none in the east.[7]

In 1939 the Third Reich was not yet fully prepared for a war which
Hitler had anticipated starting only in 1942 or 1943. The treaty of
Versailles had established that the German state could possess an
army of only 100 000 with a truncated navy and no air force. The new
Chancellor repudiated these restrictions, introduced compulsory
military service, began to re-create the air force and enlarge the fleet.
The army's weaponry was the very latest, but even the fastest
preparations for war needed time. Nevertheless in operation *Fall
Weiss* the Germans threw against Poland forty-two infantry divisions,
four motorised divisions, seven armoured divisions, one cavalry
brigade and two Slovak divisions. These forces had 2700 tanks, 6000
field guns and 1900 aeroplanes. The total number of German soldiers
slightly exceeded 1.5 million, but their battalions' firepower was
frequently four times greater than that of the Poles and in the
quantity and quality of their tanks, guns and aircraft the Germans
possessed crushing superiority.[8]

The invader's land forces were deployed in two army groups:
'North' and 'South'. Army group 'North', 630 000 strong, was

commanded by Colonel General Fedor von Bock and its task was rapidly to unite East Prussia with the rest of Germany and then drive South to join up with German units approaching from that direction. Army group 'South', with 886 000 men and under Colonel General Gerd von Rundstedt, was to head for Warsaw, smash the Polish forces defending it, seize the Vistula river to the north and south of the capital and, of course, link up with the northern forces.[9]

THE CAMPAIGN

The great German superiority became apparent almost at once during the first days of the war, despite stiff Polish resistance. The field fortifications did not provide enough support for the Polish divisions stretched out along the extensive front, Polish artillery firepower was unable to contain the German offensive and the panzer divisions advanced, tearing open the front and biting deeply into the Polish positions.

In the north the German third army attacked 'Modlin' army from East Prussia and in a couple of days greatly weakened it. The Polish commander, although pushed south, tried to launch a counter-attack with reserve group 'Wyszków', so as to fight the deciding battle further to the north, but the Germans did not lose the initiative and within a few days threatened Warsaw from the eastern bank of the Vistula. Further to the east on this sector of the front, for the only time during the whole campaign, on 4 September, Polish troops found themselves on German soil. 'Podlaska' cavalry brigade carried out a raid for several hours into East Prussia.[10]

Pomerania was attacked from two sides. In the West along a broad front, from Chojnice to Koronowo, the Fourth Army attacked, in the east a corps from the Third Army was deployed. Within two days the Germans had broken the Polish defence, joined East Prussia to the Reich and cut off Polish forces to the north. The fighting there continued for several days, but only a small number of these Polish forces managed to break through the German lines. Units of 'Pomorze' army which lay to the south of the German thrust were ordered to withdraw rapidly in the direction of Bydgoszcz. It was there that on 3 September events took place which the Germans exploited in their worldwide anti-Polish propaganda campaign. Retreating Polish units entering the town encountered some of the German inhabitants shooting at Polish troops and supply columns.

After the German forces took the town, they carried out bloody reprisals against the Polish inhabitants, shooting about 500 people and sending off about another 1000 to concentration camps.[11]

On the central sector of the front, which extended furthest West and was defended by 'Poznuń' army, there was no major fighting in the first few days, since after German successes in the south, as early as 2 September the army received an order to withdraw in the direction of Kutno and achieved this almost without making contact with the enemy.

To the south of the Poznań-Kutno axis lay 'Łódź' army which was attacked by two German armies, the Eighth and the Tenth, with two panzer and two motorised infantry divisions. After two days the Polish units withdrew in good order and the Germans headed further south where, between 'Łódź' and 'Kraków' armies lay a poorly defended area about 80kms wide. A rapid German advance in this region forced 'Łódź' army to retire to the line of the Warta river incurring heavy losses.[12]

Right in the south all-important Silesia was defended by 'Kraków' army which was attacked by the German Fourteenth Army with very heavy armoured formations. 'Kraków' army at once found itself in a critical situation and already on the first day began to withdraw, the commander throwing his reserves into the battle. The reserve consisted of the single large Polish unit capable of matching a similar German one: the 10th Motorised Armoured Brigade. It clearly demonstrated that, in addition to exposed frontiers, it was a lack of modern equipment which prevented the Poles from making an effective stand.[13]

Within a few days it was perfectly clear that, despite stubborn and often heroic Polish resistance, no defence line had been held. An attack without a declaration of war increased an already superior German position, based on modern equipment and very favourable start lines, enabling the Germans to outflank the Poles on three sides. A certain number of Polish aircraft were destroyed on the ground, while surprise was achieved at many frontier posts. Moreover, thanks to a 'fifth column' (the term was first used in 1936 during the Spanish Civil War) composed of the many Germans living in Poland, together with paratroopers, there was much sabotage disrupting communications and hindering mobilisation which had to be completed during hostilities. Additional problems were caused by the great columns of civilians fleeing before the invaders. Over the whole country now rose German planes, the airmen flying low to attack columns of refugees with machine guns. Poland became the first target for German fury.

Within a few hours the whole world found out about the German attack and Polish resistance and everywhere it made a deep impression. The First World War had ended barely twenty one years before and those countries which had taken part in it remembered the terrible trench warfare and the millions of young people killed. Now those who had managed to survive those years were at the helm of their countries and realised only too well the need to protect the world from further madness.

Despite Hitler's dreadful record, despite Austria, Czechoslovakia and the current onslaught on Poland, there remained fond illusions that the threat of this new war could still be averted by means of conferences and talks, and so France immediately recalled Mussolini's initiative. On 31 August Mussolini had proposed that a conference of the great powers should be called for 5 September, at which the Polish problem would be settled and all international issues resolved. The British also agreed to this idea, but both countries made the condition that Poland must participate in the talks, and France immediately approached the Polish government to this end.[14] The President of the United States, Franklin D. Roosevelt, also undertook a peace initiative.

Warsaw, however, saw things differently. The war was already in progress, German divisions were advancing and the most important thing for Poland now was not talks, but action. Poland expected both the great democracies to honour their treaty obligations and in the early hours of 1 September the Polish ambassadors in both Paris and London immediately took appropriate steps.

GREAT BRITAIN AND FRANCE DECLARE WAR ON GERMANY BUT REMAIN INACTIVE

A difference at once appeared between French and British behaviour. The French government announced general mobilisation and presented its case to parliament, but it continued to hope that Mussolini's initiative might save the peace; in London it was not rejected, but the situation was viewed more realistically. The conference proposed by the Italian dictator required Germany's participation and her acceptance of the need to withdraw from Poland. The French harboured the illusion that Hitler would agree to this, while the British, although handing in an appropriate note together with the French, did not share their illusions.

On 2 September the parliaments of France and Great Britain met, but while in Paris there was a general despondency, which could be felt during the debate, in London the atmosphere was resolute and in the House of Commons all three parties spoke out clearly for honouring treaty responsibilties, to the great applause of MPs. The following day, after final night-time talks, at 11 o'clock in the morning, the British Prime Minister informed the House that the country was in a state of war with Germany. Several tense hours passed during which Paris came under great pressure from London and finally, at 5 o'clock in the afternoon, the French ambassador in Berlin, Robert Coulondre, informed von Ribbentrop that France would honour her obligations towards Poland. The two decisions immediately ran round the world and caused despondency, fear and anxiety. Even Hitler felt ill at ease, since he had hoped to be able to deal with Poland without the West's intervention. The only leader to be pleased was Joseph Stalin, since his policies were already beginning to bear fruit. In Poland naturally the decisions of her Western allies produced an outburst of great enthusiasm. Poland no longer felt alone in her struggle with a powerful opponent now that the world's two greatest powers were at her side.[15]

Meanwhile, Hitler continued methodically to go about realising his political plans. He immediately incorporated Gdańsk into the Reich and began highly secret talks with Russia which commenced on 3 September. He was eager for Russia to come out openly as his ally and to carry out the details of the pact's secret clause which had foreseen the partitioning of Poland. An advance by Soviet forces into Polish territory would suit the Germans very well, but the Russians preferred caution and on 5 September, Molotov informed Berlin that there would be Russian action, but a little later. A premature attack on Poland could only unite the German and Soviet enemies. Simultaneously the Soviet ambassador in Warsaw was inquiring why Poland was not implementing a trade agreement and turning to Russia for supplies of raw materials and military equipment.[16]

Before Great Britain even declared war on Germany, the decisions governing her military co-operation with Poland had been taken. They dealt above all with the Polish navy, which had no chance in a battle with the Germans, but which could be very useful in any subsequent naval engagements. As early as May 1939 the appropriate agreement was made, the orders were drawn up in August on the basis of which three Polish destroyers, *Błyskawica*, *Burza* and *Grom* left Gdynia on 30 August and by 1 September were in the Scottish port of Rosyth. It was after the outbreak of hostilities that the submarine *Wilk* joined them and a little later *Orzeł*, which had slipped out of the Estonian port of Tallinn, where it had been interned, and had made a daring escape sailing without navigational instruments and eluding the Germans in pursuit. Three more submarines, *Ryś*, *Sęp* and *Żbik*, sailed for Swedish ports where they were interned. Almost the whole Polish merchant fleet of about 140 000 tonnes had got out of the Baltic in August.[17]

In the afternoon of 8 September the first patrols of motorised infantry of the German Sixteenth Corps appeared near Warsaw from the south-west. By the evening the city found itself already under harassing artillery fire. The Germans had occupied some towns due west of the capital.[18]

Already, on 3 September, when the Germans broke through the front near Częstochowa occupying the town, the Polish Commander-in-Chief issued the order to prepare to defend the capital and instructed the Prime Minister to order the evacuation of the government and its offices. This began during the night of 4 and 5 September. In the night of 6–7 September the threat to Warsaw became so grave that the Republic's highest authorities – the President, the Government and the Commander-in-Chief – left. The whole diplomatic corps followed them.

After the government's departure, the city mayor, Stefan Starzyński (1893–1944) who had also been nominated as civilian defence commissioner, remained at his post. He assumed full moral responsibility for continuing the struggle, did not shirk it and set up around him a committee composed of representatives of the leading political parties and established the closest possible co-operation with the command of the defence of the capital.

Parallel to the preparations in Warsaw which were meant to thwart the Germans' hope of quickly capturing the city, on the Bzura river near Kutno, about 100kms to the west, the chance of a Polish counter-offensive appeared. In this area lay 'Poznań' army, which had hitherto suffered only light losses and still represented a significant strike force. To its north was 'Pomorze' army, which was withdrawing under enemy pressure, much weakened, but not broken. The German Eighth Army, after shattering 'Łódź' army, was heading quickly for Warsaw and had seriously extended its lines of communication in the area of Łęczyca, Ozorków and Łowicz. The commander of 'Poznań' army contacted the Chief of Staff in Warsaw, received permission from him for the planned offensive, got in touch with the commander of 'Pomorze' army, assumed overall command and on 9 September struck the German lines in the direction of Łęczyca and Łowicz. The German 30th Division was broken and other units repulsed to the south. The Polish attack might have been even more effective, had not 'Pomorze' army been so far away that it was only able to enter the fray on the third day and capture Łowicz from the Germans. Similarly the great exhaustion of the soldiers deprived them of the speed so necessary in attack.[19]

The Polish action surprised the Germans who were already outside Warsaw. They had to regroup their forces, weaken their pressure on the capital and throw into battle some of the reserves of army group 'South'. The battle only culminated on 16 September when the Germans introduced about 800 tanks and 300 aircraft as well as most of The Tenth Army's divisions. The attack, which brought the Poles success, had to turn into defence. The surrounded Polish forces had to head for Sochaczew to try to break the German ring and reach Warsaw. The battle was exceptionally bloody and during it the tired Polish soldiers displayed the very highest valour. Commanders of major formations personally led their men into battle and three generals were killed.[20]

By the second week of the fighting there could no longer be any doubt as to its eventual outcome, but Polish units retreated as slowly as possible, every day expecting an offensive in the West, honouring treaty commitments. The need for such an offensive arose also from political and strategic circumstances. Great Britain had not yet sent her Expeditionary Corps to France, but she did have a strong bomber force of around 600 aircraft capable of reaching at least the western part of Germany.[21] In Poland an immediate aerial offensive by the French and British was expected in reprisal for German attacks on town and roads, in fact the French made no sorties, while the British flew over the Reich only to drop leaflets calling on Germany to stop the war. Only one raid was made, on the German naval base on the island of Heligoland, with great losses.

After the announcement of mobilisation France had the equivalent of 110 divisions under arms. Some of them manned fortifications, others had old-fashioned equipment and were not at full strength, but there was a mobile and well-armed force of sixty-five divisions ready for action. This figure consisted of fifty-seven infantry divisions, five cavalry divisions, two motorised divisions and one armoured division.

The very considerable number of 3000 tanks was deployed in battalion strength. The French air force had about 300 bombers and an equal number of fighters, many of them modern and in no way inferior to their German counterparts. The French had to keep some of their forces in North Africa and on their southern borders to prevent any possible Italian attack, but the equivalent of about eighty-five divisions manned the German frontier.[22]

This major force the Germans could match only with thirty-three infantry divisions, of which a certain number were still not at full strength.[23] They were shielded by two air armies with several hundred aircraft. Almost all the panzers and two-thirds of the air force had been launched against Poland, for Hitler was attempting the fastest possible victory and counting on the slowness of the Western democracies. The justification for the wholesale deployment of armour in the East was the *Siegfried Line*, which was intended to halt a French attack and the Germans did not anticipate any offensive action in that area during this phase of the war. This German fortification was constructed between 1936 and 1939, stretching 600km from Kleve in the north to Basel (Switzerland) in the south. It consisted of a series of fortresses, such as Wesel, Cologne, Koblenz, Mainz and more that 15 000 strong-points. The defences were in two zones, each 10km wide. In September 1939 these fortifications were not yet completed. The French could outflank the German fortifications in the north, but this would mean violating Belgian neutrality.

Unfortunately, the one and only chance of throwing everything against the still unprepared Germans, who had their hands full fighting Poland, was wasted. There each day of resistance was paid for with huge losses, while in the West the French dawdled with their mobilisation. By the terms of the treaty and Franco–Polish staff consultations in May 1939, limited offensive operations were to commence three days after the start of mobilisation and a full offensive within fifteen days, but reality was different. During the night of 6–7 September French units carried out very limited offensive operations and within two days had occupied a dozen or so abandoned German villages in front of the *Siegfried Line*. On 12 September, the French Commander-in-Chief, General Maurice Gamelin, ordered them to return to their original positions and to restrict themselves to reconnaissance work. The French air force carried out no operations at all for fear of a German counter-attack which might create chaos in the slowly-moving mobilisation.[24]

It turned out that the France of the First World War was no more.

The terrible carnage wreaked by trench warfare, the loss of a generation which fell under German machine gun and artillery fire, the political confusion of the last few pre-war years and cleverly exploited and propagated pacifism, which was really only defeatism, all contributed to a situation in which the French nation was incapable of moral or physical effort and was unable even to contemplate the idea of attack. But the most serious reason for such a state of affairs was the *Maginot Line* mentality breeding a sense of complete security. The famous French defensive line, built between 1929 and 1934 on the instigation of a special commission, got its name from André Maginot, Minister of Defence in 1930–4. It cost 9 million francs in gold for every kilometre. It was 450 km long from Belgium to Pontarlier by the western Swiss frontier; it needed 55 000 tons of steel and 3000m³ of concrete.

At the beginning of the third week of hostilities the Germans, coming from the North and the South, were already to the east of the Vistula river. The battle on the Bzura river was continuing, Hel was still holding on, the fortress at Modlin was holding out as was 'Lublin' army, Lwów was preparing its defences, but organised resistance on a common withdrawal line was by now impossible. However, Warsaw above all continued to hold out. It was an improvised defence, based mainly on units withdrawing east under German pressure. It was led by military men, but its real leader was the city mayor, Stefan Starzyński, who had become a symbol of fighting Poland. The whole country listened to his radio broadcasts.

At the same time the country's leaders, knowing that the Germans had already crossed the Bug river, decided to leave for the south-eastern tip of Poland. Their immediate future was now under discussion. The possibility of defending the south-eastern corner with Romania at their backs was mooted. This would require major units and well-motivated and disciplined troops, not demoralised stragglers. A further difficulty was posed by German-inspired Ukrainian acts of sabotage. Roads were blocked, Polish country estates attacked, Polish soldiers disarmed and killed.[25] The leadership also discussed the possibility of approaching the Romanians for permission to pass freely through their country to go to France, where it could continue to lead its country.

THE SOVIET ATTACK FROM THE EAST

These discussions continued to ignore Russia's attitude and it was indeed there that the decision which eventually doomed Poland to defeat at the hands of the Germans was taken. At 3 o'clock in the morning of 17 September, Molotov's deputy, Vladimir Potiemkin, summoned the Polish ambassador, Wacław Grzybowski, and read him a note from his government. It dealt with the collapse of the Polish state, the disintegration of the Polish government and capital and the need to protect the life and property of the peoples of Western Ukraine and Western Byelorussia. Under the circumstances the Soviet government had ordered its forces to cross the Soviet–Polish frontier. The ambassador refused to accept the note and made a formal protest. By 4 o'clock that morning divisions of the Red Army were on Polish soil.[26]

In planning the war with the Germans the Poles had not anticipated Soviet intervention and so the KOP units, the only ones on the Polish–Soviet frontier, had no instructions and did not know what to do. Some resisted, some surrendered without a fight. Moreover no-one knew the reason for the Soviet advance. It was even thought that they were coming to help, although the Ribbentrop–Molotov pact contradicted this. Only their continued penetration into the country and leaflets dropped from planes clarified the issue. There was no longer any doubt as to the reasons for the Red Army's advance into Poland and individual Polish commanders, both on the border and deeper in the country, tried to organise resistance whenever they saw an opportunity, but the Soviet forces, supported by armour, had such an advantage that there was no chance of success. The Red divisions headed for Warsaw, some crossed the Bug, but quickly retired. It was clear that they were operating to a plan, which, as it later transpired, was based on a secret clause of the Ribbentrop–Molotov pact:

> On the occasion of the signature of the Non-Aggression Treaty between the German Reich and the Union of Soviet Socialist Republic, the undersigned plenipotentiaries of the two Parties discussed in strictly confidential conversations the question of the delimitation of their respective spheres of interest in Eastern Europe. These conversations led to the following result:
> 1. In the event of a territorial and political transformation in the territories belonging to the Baltic States (Finland, Estonia, Latvia, Lithuania) the northern frontier of Lithuania shall represent the frontier of the spheres of interest both of Germany and the USSR. In this connection the interest of

Lithuania in the Wilno territory is recognised by both Parties.

2. In the event of a territorial and political transformation of the territories belonging to the Polish State, the spheres of interest of both Germany and the USSR shall be bounded approximately by the line of the rivers Narew, Vistula and San. (On 28 September it was decided that the frontier would go alongside the Bug and San rivers.)

The question whether the interests of both Parties make the maintenance of an independent Polish State appear desirable and how the frontiers of this State should be drawn can be definitely determined only in the course of further political developments. In any case both Governments will resolve this question by means of a friendly understanding.

3. With regard to South-Eastern Europe, the Soviet side emphasises its interest in Bessarabia. The German side declares complete political *désintéressement* in these territories.

4. This Protocol will be treated by both parties as strictly secret.

Moscow, 23 August, 1939

For the Government of   With full power of the
the German Reich: Government of the USSR:

v. Ribbentrop   V. Molotov[27]

POLISH GOVERNMENT CROSSES THE ROMANIAN BORDERS

News of the Soviet note and of the Red Army's advance onto Polish territory reached the Polish leadership on the same day and hastened its decision to cross the Romanian frontier. Earlier the Polish government had been in touch with the Romanian authorities about transit through their territory and had received verbal assurance that the unofficial and relatively speedy passage of the President and his government to the Black Sea port of Constanţa would be facilitated. In these assurances no mention had been made of passage for military personnel nor had it been specified where the Polish politicians would go, once they had left Romania. This country's situation was very difficult, since it found itself under great pressure from both the Germans and the Russians. The Germans were very interested in the Ploesti oilfields, while the Soviets had their eye on Bessarabia which had belonged to Russia under the Tsars. Strictly speaking, by the terms of the treaty with Poland, Romania ought to have declared war on Russia on 17 September, when the Red Army crossed Poland's borders, but this was clearly out of the question and the Poles did not insist. They did, however, count on simplified transit and a speedy passage to France.

Talks were also held with the French ambassador to the Polish government, Leon Noël, who stayed with the government on Polish soil to the very last. At issue was French agreement on hospitality for the Polish authorities and assurances that they could continue to function. France was already at war with Germany and was linked to Poland by a treaty, so there was no question of a refusal. However difficulties in such an agreement produced a situation in which a clearly defined French attitude was not received.[28]

Just before midnight the President and other senior Polish officials arrived in Romania. Gold from the Polish Bank, to the value of 325 million zlotys, was also brought over. A little later the Commander-in-Chief, Marshal Śmigły-Rydz and the General Staff crossed the same bridge.[29]

The departure of the President and the government was completely justified, since Soviet units were so very close, however the Commander-in-Chief's departure was another matter. The campaign had already been lost, but fighting continued and was to do so for another fortnight. The Commander-in-Chief was a symbol of armed resistance, he was also the senior commander and the fighting units expected to receive orders from him. He may have listened to bad advice, the fact remains, however, that his departure from the country before the end fo the battle was a major psychological error, which could not be corrected later. It further weakened the authority of the political camp to which he belonged.

Despite the Russian invasion and great German superiority, the fighting in Poland continued. Hel fought on, Modlin fought on, Lwów fought on, Warsaw fought on, major fighting continued to the north of Lublin. It was now known everywhere that Soviet Russia had remained faithful to tradition by exploiting Polish misfortune, but this did not weaken the determination to continue to resist.

On 22 September Lwów surrendered to Soviet forces, but only on 28 September, after much heavy bombardment and great civilian losses, did Warsaw capitulate. Modlin fell the following day and Hel surrendered on 2 October. The last battle of the campaign took place between 2 and 5 October near Kock, to the East of the Vistula river.

LOSSES

It is extremely difficult to determine just what losses both sides suffered, particularly since there was also a third side: Soviet. There are no final and accurate figures, only approximations, partly dating from the actual fighting and partly calculated later. The combatants, for purposes of propaganda, usually lessened their own losses and inflated those of their opponents. Bearing this in mind, the best thing to do is to give the Polish and German figures without comment.

According to Polish estimates, made many years after the war, in the September Campaign the country lost about 200 000 men killed and wounded. One hundred aircraft flew to Romania and were interned, the rest, about 300, were destroyed in the fighting. All the tanks were destroyed with the exception of a small number which, together with the 10th Cavalry Armoured Brigade, ended up in Hungary. A certain amount of light weaponry was buried, but it is quite impossible to establish just how much. The rest was destroyed in the fighting.[30]

Polish figures on prisoners and internees raise no doubts. The Germans captured about 400 000 Polish soldiers, the Russians about 200 000 and about 85 000 were interned in Romania, Hungary, Lithuania and Latvia. Many managed to reach France quite quickly, a few – mainly airmen and other specialists – went straight to England.[31]

According to Polish figures, the Germans lost 45 000 dead and wounded; the Germans themselves claim 10 572 dead, 30 322 wounded and 3409 missing, so the discrepancy is minimal. The Poles calculate that the Germans lost, through damage and breakdown, 993 tanks and armoured cars, 300 aircraft (150 shot down by the Polish air force, 150 by anti-aircraft fire), 370 guns and mortars as well as 11 000 mechanical vehicles.[32] German figures are only one third of these.

We do not know how many Polish soldiers lost their lives fighting the Red Army, all we do know is the figure of 200 000 prisoners already mentioned. Russian losses can only be gauged from their own sources. On 31 October 1939, at a session of the Supreme Soviet of the USSR, the Commissar for Foreign Affairs, Vyacheslav Molotov, said in a speech that in its fighting with the Poles the Red Army had lost 737 men killed and 1862 wounded.[33] According to British historians, Russia lost 734 men killed while occupying Eastern Poland.[34]

3 The Partition of Poland

POLAND UNDER TWO OCCUPANTS

On 28 September 1939, at the very moment when German divisions entered Warsaw, the Third Reich and Soviet Russia entered into 'A Borders and Friendship Treaty', which sanctioned Poland's fourth partition. The secret document signed by Ribbentrop and Molotov established the German–Russian border along the Bug and San rivers.[1]

The treaty had been preceded by earlier talks between Germany and the Soviet Union regarding Poland, which was now occupied almost entirely. Hitler had been hesitant, not yet having a clear picture of how he should proceed. He had been contemplating the establishment of a rudimentary state of Poland, the eastern border running along the line Grodno-Przemyśl, and the western along the 1914 German frontier with Russia, which would have 12 or perhaps 15 million inhabitants. Such a plan would have brought pressure to bear on the Western powers and, according to Hitler, might have made it easier for them to back away from a needless war. Mussolini was in favour of this, but Stalin opposed it quite categorically. He was of the opinion that it was essential to 'avoid anything which might in the future create friction between Germany and the Soviet Union. Taking this point of view, he considers it mistaken to allow an independent state of Poland to continue to exist'. During the course of further negotiations, intent on taking possession of Lithuania which he had previously offered to Hitler, he agreed in exchange to move the demarcation line back from the Vistula and San rivers to the Bug and the San. It was this border that was eventually ratified by the secret protocol of the treaty of 28 September.[2]

Having achieved his first military victory, Hitler naturally could not deny himself the satisfaction of taking the salute at the parade on 5 October through conquered Warsaw. Although secretly he agreed with the Soviet view, he was interested in finding out what the reaction of the West would be to his plans for creating an 'independent Poland'. Next day therefore, at a solemn session of the Reichstag[3], he mentioned such a possibility. Great Britain reacted immediately: the very same day it rejected all German offers of 'peace'. France did the same, via its prime minister, Edouard Daladier, on 10 October. Thus Germany finally understood that the war could not be localised and that an exceptionally hard and probably lengthy engagement with the West awaited it. The concept of 'the Polish state' finally disappeared from its political programme, and the sorting out and absorption of war conquests began.

WESTERN TERRITORIES ANNEXED TO THE THIRD REICH

On 8 October Hitler issued a decree determining which provinces of Poland were to be incorporated immediately into the Reich: the whole of Polish Silesia, all of Polish Pomerania, the second largest town in Poland, Łódź, and the area to the south and west of Łódź, with a border running only 25km north-west of Warsaw. The area covered nearly 92 000km^2, equivalent to a quarter of the entire country, and was almost twice that which had formerly been annexed by Prussia. The border of the German state was pushed 150 to 200km to the east of the 1914 border. The region annexed was inhabited by more than 10 million Polish citizens, including nearly 9 million Poles, 600 000 Germans, a somewhat greater number of Jews, 11 000 Ukrainians, and 21 000 of other nationalities.[4]

The formal annexation was preceded by a time of terror which began immediately after the German troops invaded. Prior to the attack on Poland, five operational units (*Einsatzgruppe der Sicherheitspolizei*) had already been formed from SS men and police officers, and assigned to each of the armies prepared for combat. These units had in their possession lists containing the names of political activists, those who had taken part in the Silesia and Wielkopolska uprisings, and others who represented the stratum that generated the leaders in Poland; those listed were seized and shot without trial, a few hours after the area was occupied. The operation received the code-name *Unternehmen Tannenberg*, and during its course more than 16 000 people were executed in Pomerania, Wielkopolska and Silesia.[5] These preliminary murders were an expression of German fury, engendered by German propaganda and unfounded slogans that Poles active in the western provinces and in particular those who had fought for them after the First World War, were traitors, for these provinces had belonged to Germany twenty years previously.

No-one in Germany, even amongst the educated, chose to recall that they had been annexed to their country in an unprecedented seizure of land – the three partitions of Poland. If, following this initial reflex action, near-normal relations had come to prevail, the situation would not yet have become intolerable, but the Germans were incorporating these territories into the Reich with a view to their complete Germanicisation. They entrusted this task to men who were ruthless: Albert Forster became Gauleiter of Pomerania; Arthur Greiser, Gauleiter of Poznań, and Fritz Bracht, Gauleiter of Silesia. They did not have to wait long to show their mettle. It was on 6 September, immediately following the taking of Kalisz, that Greiser told the German colonists in a speech 'In ten years there will not even be a peasant smallholding which will not be held in German hands'. On 27 September, in Bydgoszcz, Forster declared:

> I was appointed by the Führer to represent German interests in this country, with the clear instruction to Germanicise the land again ... to eradicate within the next few years any manifestations of the Polish nationality, of no matter what kind ... whoever belongs to the Polish nation must leave this country.[6]

This announcement forecast the resettlement to central Poland; the first sweep aimed to evacuate about 2 million Poles, principally the landowners, businessmen and intellectuals. It was begun at the start of the very severe winter of 1939–40; entire families were transported in goods wagons, allowed to take with them only 20 – 50kg of personal belongings and a few hundred zloty in cash, and having to leave behind businesses, estates and homes, without any compensation. These were to be taken over by Germans from the Baltic countries, Rumania, and the eastern borders of Poland. The evacuation was carried out in an exceptionally cruel manner: several minutes were given to collect one's belongings, and the state of health of the evacuees was not taken into account at all. Those who still remained were subjected to great moral and economic pressure which was imposed by a variety of regulations. Poles were compelled to put their names down on a *Volkslist*.[7] Every sign of Polish life was suppressed, and all Polish institutions of higher education, schools, publications, theatres, museums, libraries, publishers and bookshops were closed down, and the government of Polish provinces incorporated into the Reich changed hands, passing to the Gestapo and the Nazi administration.[8]

German orders were of a different nature in the case of Polish nationals of Jewish descent. On 21 September the head of the Central Office of Security of the Reich (RSHA), Reinhard Heydrich, had issued an instruction to the commanders of the special operations units, advancing close behind the Wehrmacht detachments, to make an immediate attempt to gather all the Jews in the larger cities. Murder and looting could not be avoided. On 30 October, after the annexation of the western provinces of Poland to the Reich, the head of the SS, Heinrich Himmler, issued an order that all Jews were to be resettled in central Poland within four months. This deportation was similar in nature to the deportation of the Poles, but it was even more brutal and severe. At the beginning of the first winter of the war, 1939–40, about 100 000 Jews from Wielkopolska alone were evacuated to the areas surrounding Cracow, Kielce, and Lublin.

Besides the deportation, a system of isolation from the rest of the community was introduced: in Febrary 1940 a ghetto was established in Łódź in which more than 160 000 people were crowded into an area of barely 4km^2. They were transported there from the surrounding towns.[9]

GENERAL GOUVERNEMENT

On 12 October there was another decree from Hitler: this established the office of governor general for further Polish territories which had fallen into German hands, but which had not been annexed to the Reich, the eastern boundary of these being the Ribbentrop–Molotov demarcation line. This date marks the day on which external expression was given to the German decision that an administrative creation was to come into being on a tiny patch of Poland which would be subjected in all respects to the Third Reich, and where Poles would be treated a little differently from those in areas annexed to the German state. The *General Gouvernement* came into existence in fact on 26 October, when the governor himself, Hans Frank, issued a proclamation to the Poles, notifying them that he was assuming the post, promising that Poles would be able to live there according to their custom, under the protection of the great German Reich, and threatening reprisals for the smallest gesture of insubordination.

The *General Gouvernement* covered a considerable area, and included Warsaw, Kraków, Lublin, Kielce, Radom, and Częstochowa. It contained more than 96 000km^2, with over 12 million inhabitants, and the Germans divided it into four districts: Kraków, Lublin, Radom and Warsaw. Frank took up residence at the Wawel castle, and the German headquarters and the offices of the so-called government of the *General Gouvernement* were also to be found in Kraków.[10]

GERMAN RULE

Only at the very beginning of the occupation did the Germans behave correctly in the territories assigned by Hitler for the Poles, and which were not incorporated into the Reich. In Warsaw Stefan Starzyński was allowed to remain in his post as Lord Mayor. The German City Commissioner, Dr Alfred Otto, conducted conferences in French, and negotiations on the subject of the reopening of the university and the Central Commercial College were initiated. In Kraków a Citizens' Committee was formed, which was granted recognition by the Germans, and headed by Cardinal Adam Sapieha (1867–1951). The university was preparing for a new academic year, theatre performances began, and the *Illustrated Daily Courier* started to appear. The commandant of the city, General Eugen Höberth, went to the Józef Piłsudski crypt at Wawel castle and paid a visit to the rector of the university, Professor Tadeusz Lehr-Spławiński; the Lord Mayor, Dr Stanisław Klimecki, continued in his post. In Lublin, without asking the Germans for their consent, the university and the secondary schools were opened, the theatre began performances, and the publication of the *Lublin Express* was resumed.[11]

This period lasted for a very short while – to the day, exactly, on which Hans Frank assumed the office of governor and issued his proclamation. The very next day the Lord Mayor of Warsaw, Starzyński, was arrested. On 6 November the professors of the Jagiellonian University and the Academy of Mines, and other teaching personnel – a total of 183 people altogether plus the Lord Mayor, Klimecki – were arrested in Cracow. On 9 November the first of the street round-ups took place in Lublin, and two days later German police closed down the university and arrested fourteen professors. During the course of the same few days several dozen more distinguished citizens, headed by the mayor, were arrested in Częstochowa.[12]

Following Hitler's edict that created the office of governor general, and following Frank's proclamation, there came further instructions which defined explicitly what the adminstrative absurdity in the territory of central Poland was to be like. All the universities and secondary schools were shut, as were all the museums, archives, libraries, book and newspaper publishers; radio receivers were confiscated; a list was drawn up of Polish books to be destroyed, and the playing of musical works by Polish composers was prohibited. The battle against Polish culture and the attempt to stifle and obliterate it from history extended to such lengths that monuments were destroyed, works of art were removed, and every expression of Polish national identity was hunted down. Even the preliminary, equally far-reaching plan for German-occupied Poland to become an auxiliary country (*Nebenland*) of the Reich was never realised. The Germans decided that Poland was to become a country consisting solely of slaves, and treated as a colony where Polish culture, the intelligentsia, and anyone with an apparent sense of national belonging would be wiped out. The conquerors wanted to carry out their plan quickly, and therefore reached for an instrument which they considered infallible, namely terror.[13]

By January of the following year a plan had already been created for a concentration camp at Oświęcim (Auschwitz) in which about 3 million people were to die, and which was to become a symbol of Nazi rule and the Nazi philosophy.[14]

The Jews who were living in central Poland, and those who had been deported to the *General Gouvernement* from territories annexed to the Reich, found themselves in an even worse situation than the Poles. In the first months of the year about 2 million Jews were to be found on Polish soil within reach of German hands. Almost from the beginning of the occupation they had been ordered to wear armbands with yellow stars. Later there came orders to deprive them of property and some of their goods; Jews were removed from jobs in public institutions and were forbidden to move about freely. On 26 October 1939, on the same day that Governor Frank made his proclamation to the Poles, he issued an order enforcing mandatory labour for all Jews aged 14–60. This ruling, which gave oppression legitimate status, led to many excesses and facilitated the ill-treatment of many defenceless people. At the beginning of 1940 the Germans created the first labour camps for the Jews, which differed little from concentration camps.[15]

During the short period in which the different alternatives were being considered and the idea of an 'independent Polish state' was being manœuvred in a diplomatic game with the West, the question of political representation emerged. Hitler of course had in mind Polish puppets, far worse than Quisling,[16] but from the Polish point of view it might have looked different had there been any possibility of German brutality being considerably reduced and the substance of the nation rescued. Of course, without using the title 'Polish Government' or entering into political commitments – and had there been a suitable candidate, Władysław Studnicki might have been one. He was a politician from the period of the First World War, an advocate of co-operation with the Germans during the twenty years of Polish independence, who sought contact with the occupying powers as long ago as the time of the September campaign. The Germans became interested at first in his suggestions, which reached the Ministry of Foreign Affairs, but when it turned out that the Western powers were not going to allow themselves to be misled by Hitler's 'peace' initiative, he ceased to be of interest to them.[17]

'ELECTION' IN THE EASTERN TERRITORIES AND THEIR ANNEXATION TO USSR

Conditions were different to the east of the Bug and San rivers in the Polish territories that found themselves under the rule of Soviet Russia and that encompassed 196 000km^2 including Wilno and Lwów, with 13 million inhabitants, amongst them 5 million Poles. Whereas Hitler announced openly that he was fighting for the spoils of war and for the hegemony of Germany, in Europe at least, Stalin, in a most cunning and deceitful way, was attempting to create an illusion of honesty and law-abidance. The Red Army invaded Polish soil under the pretext of spreading protection to Western Ukraine and Western Byelorussia, and it was now necessary to create a *fait accompli* by incorporating these territories into the Soviet empire. Hitler operated simply by means of decrees, while Stalin turned to the 'wishes' of the local inhabitants, so that the whole world could marvel at Soviet justice, and so that the requirement of international law could be satisfied. Acting in this way, he safeguarded himself against the accusation of land seizure and created a legal position difficult to challenge from a formal point of view.

Putting this scheme into action, the Soviet authorities immediately set about organising elections in the regions they had taken. On 6 October 1939, before the Soviet civil authorities had been appointed, the Commander-in-Chief of the Ukrainian Front ordered that elections should be held for the 'West Ukrainian National Assembly'. The Soviet War Council in the Ukraine issued a similar order. However, keeping up appearances mattered a great deal to the Soviets, and they did not wish the elections to take place at the suggestion of the army, so, five days later, on 11 October, *Izvestia* published a despatch quoting the text of a proclamation by the provisional administration of Lwów to the people, calling upon them to appoint a 'West Ukrainian National Assembly' in a fair and secret general election. The following day *Izvestia* published a similar despatch about a proclamation issued by the provisional administration of Białystok on the subject of elections to the 'West Byelorussian National Assembly'.[18]

Their haste was so great that the elections were fixed for 22 October, which ruled out any semblance of preparation for them, but this was of no significance, for, according to usual Soviet practice, it was possible to vote for only one candidate in each constituency. These candidates were put up by election committees in Lwów and Białystok appointed by the provisional administrations of the Soviet occupying authorities which consisted of officers of the army and the NKVD. Naturally, nearly all those proposed for these committees were either local communists recruited mainly from ethnic minorities, or Soviet state officials, delegated by the Councils of the Ukrainian and Byelorussian republics. According to the usual Soviet pattern, the voting turnout was extremely high: nearly 97 per cent in Lwów, and almost 93 per cent in Białystok. The election was for 2410 delegates, and all were voted in; amongst them were not only local people, but also many Soviet citizens.

The 'National Assemblies' of Western Ukraine and Western Byelorussia came into existence thus, and were in theory capable of deciding that separate states, with the same names, should come into being. The purpose of this whole procedure was achieved. Both Assemblies, in Lwów on 27 October and in Białystok on 29 October, resolved unanimously to request the Supreme Council of the Soviet Union to take the occupied Polish territories within their boundaries. The request was granted, and on 1 November the Council decreed that Western Ukraine be incorporated into the Ukrainian Soviet Socialist Republic. The following day, the same distinction was bestowed on Western Byelorussia: it became absorbed by the Byelorussian SSR.[19] At the same session of the Supreme Council of the USSR, on 31 October, Molotov summed up the attitude of his country to Poland and sealed the fate of the seized provinces, saying, 'After one quick blow, first from the German, and next from the Red Army, nothing remained of the misshapen monster created by the Treaty of Versailles.'[20]

SOVIET RULE

At the same time as the political formalities were being concluded, the territory was being prepared for immediate Sovietisation. In this respect, Soviet methods did not differ overmuch from Hitler's, except that they were based on different motivations. In the west, immediately after invading, the Germans set about murdering the Poles, seeking out the leaders and using as pretext their anti-German activities; in the east the invading Red divisions scattered leaflets designed to arouse class hatred towards the owners of the larger estates and factories, officers, judges, magistrates, priests, and politicians. The leaflets fell in part on fertile ground, for the country included numerous ethnic minorities with whom the young Polish state had not yet managed to establish the foundations of harmonious coexistence. As early as October, there were systematic arrests, particularly of the higher, managerial, strata of society. The provisional Soviet administration, assisted by the NKVD, began an operation aimed at setting the Poles against all the minorities and at setting-up groups which would struggle to eliminate each other. In this respect the Soviet occupation was significantly more treacherous then the German, as it divided the community by class and nationality. Joint resistance immediately became impossible, even from the Poles alone.

The main thrust was directed against religious beliefs, which had generated the strongest resistance during attempts to impose a foreign ideology. The persecution of religions and clergy became more systematic. Churches, monasteries and convents were either closed or had imposed on them such high taxes that they were forced to close themselves. Religious seminaries and schools run by religious orders were shut down and a great many priests arrested. In all about 4000 churches, not only Catholic, but also Protestant and Greek Orthodox, suffered closure, destruction or suppression.[21]

However, at the same time, the Soviets attached great importance to creating a semblance of liberty and freedom in the sphere of cultural activities, as they had done in the political arena. In contrast to the Germans, they permitted universities, schools, theatres, and other institutions of a similar nature to reopen. Arts organisations like the Literary Association underwent a revival, and its committee was elected on the basis of a list prepared in advance, and consisted of several Ukrainians and a few Polish communists. Such bodies have a serious role to play in the Soviet system, for, on the one hand, they create the semblance of cultural liberty and bring together serious writers and artists, and on the other, they are used as passive instruments in the hands of the authorities, who manipulate them whichever way they choose. They keep up the pretence that free public opinion and the liberty to express one's thoughts and ideas exist in the Soviet Union.[22]

The reopening of universities and schools, except those run by religious orders and cultural associations, was also related to the process of Sovietisation. The academic curriculum was altered completely; the teaching of Polish language, history and geography, and of religious instruction was forbidden, and all Polish textbooks were withdrawn. The two universities, the Jan Kazimierz in Lwów and the Stefan Batory in Wilno, were deprived of theology departments and numerous arts faculties. The teaching staff was decimated, and many lecturers were arrested and deported. New publications came into being with specific functions, and similar restraints applied to theatre and radio.[23]

The Soviet authorities' methods of creating a semblance of cultural freedom were particularly treacherous for the intelligentsia. Many Polish writers, scientists and artists driven out of western and central Poland by the German offensive arrived in Lwów only to find themselves cruelly deluded. They were given studios and offered university chairs; newspaper columns were made available to them and halls opened where they could present their works and exhibit sculptures or paintings – but at the same time they were subjected to moral and physical pressure to embrace Soviet ideology. No formal renunciation of nationality was required as such, but the obligation to reflect in their work the spirit of Soviet internationalism, glorifying the country of workers and peasants as the cradle of freedom, would stifle completely the reconstruction of the Polish state. It was a delusion that only the strong survived – and they soon wandered into prison. Even Polish communists of the pre-war era had the carpet pulled from beneath them; they adjusted to the new conditions with difficulty and were unable to understand their Soviet colleagues who had lived under the same system for years. The situation was complicated further by Stalin's pact with Hitler, completely incomprehensible to those who saw the communist party as a symbol of the struggle against fascism.[24]

The formal annexation of eastern Poland to the Soviet empire did not, however, dispose of the matter once and for all, since over 5 million Poles lived there as well as a number of ethnic minorities who remained loyal subjects of the Polish state. These people – above all the intelligentsia, the landowners, the clergy, officers, civil servants, ex-army settlers, policemen and all those who were connected in any way with serving the Polish state – had to be removed, and the Soviet authorities prepared a large-scale plan to deport them into the interior of their vast country.[25]

The first deportation took place on 10 February 1940, and included over 200 000 people, mostly entire families, who were sent to the northern part of European Russia. They were allowed to take with them their personal belongings, some kitchen utensils, and provisions for several weeks – since that was how long the journey would take by goods wagon. The majority were unloaded in the middle of nowhere or in out-of-the-way villages, where they had to save themselves from death by starvation by means of very hard labour. The fathers of these families, if they were officers, businessmen or landowners, were separately transported to concentration camps, following sentencing by summary courts.[26]

The second deportation, carried out on 13 April 1940, was primarily of women and children, since the menfolk had already been arrested, sentenced and transported to labour camps in Siberia. Over 320 000 people were deported to the southern part of Asiatic Russia, mainly to Kazakhstan. This country was so poor that even if the local populace had been well-intentioned, they hardly had any resources with which to help. The mortality amongst the displaced, especially the children, was extremely high.

The third wave of deportations took place towards the end of June and in July 1940, and included over 240 000 people, who were sent to Siberia.[27] Apart from the mass deportations, which were carried out as an administrative procedure, tens of thousands of people found themselves in prison as a consequence of individual arrests. These, as already mentioned above, were tried by provisional courts which sentenced them to a dozen or so years' imprisonment for a great variety of offences they had never committed. In the eyes of the Soviet authorities, every official, soldier, legal practitioner and policeman who served the Polish state deserved a heavy sentence.

The offender could also be a writer who had published a book inconsistent with Soviet ideology, or a theatre producer who had put on a play not popular with the Soviet authorities.[28] They all found themselves in Siberian prison camps in the far north.

Because Hitler had given up Lithuania to Stalin in return for a slice of Poland between the Vistula and Bug rivers, all the Baltic states there found themselves within the orbit of Soviet influence. Russia extorted their consent to the establishment of its military bases on their territories and entered into agreements with all of them in turn which diminished their sovereign rights. The agreement with Estonia was signed on 28 September, with Latvia on 5 October, and with Lithuania on 10 October 1939.[29] After these formalities were concluded Red army divisions began crossing the frontiers into all three countries, although the operation differed from the Russian invasion of Poland on 17 September. This time it continued to keep up appearances and outwardly acknowledged the independence of the tiny republics.

As part of their agreement with Lithuania, and by prior arrangement with Germany, the Russians undertook to hand back Wilno and the surrounding area, and on 27 October they left the city, and Lithuanian detachments entered. Wilno, which during the twenty years of Poland's independence had been a part of it, was a bone of contention between two nations who shared so much of the historical greatness. The Lithuanians had felt animosity towards Poles for many years, but the takeover of the city by them brought a great relief to all. True, the Poles suffered changes for the worse: the Stefan Batory university was closed, street names were altered, Lithuanian became the official language and they were frequently humiliated by the Lithuanian police – but the nightmare of nocturnal arrests and threat of deportation had gone. This state of affairs, however, was not long-lived.[30]

RUSSO-GERMAN CO-OPERATION

Sharing the spoils increased even further the co-operation between Hitler and Stalin. The Soviet dictator, whose objective was a war in the West between Germany and the Franco-British coalition, tried to support the Third Reich in every possible way. German industry was manufacturing many precision instruments and a great variety of military equipment, but it was short of raw materials and petroleum.

Its window on the world was Soviet Russia, which moreover owned raw materials in unlimited quantities and was eager to avail itself of German-made goods. On 10 February the two countries signed a trade agreement on a very grand scale. In the course of the following twelve months the Russians were to supply 900000 tonnes of petroleum, 100000 tonnes of cotton, 500000 tonnes of phosphates, 100000 tonnes of chromium ore, 500000 tonnes of iron ore, 300000 tonnes of raw steel, 2400kg of platinum, and 100000 tonnes of feed, not counting smaller items. In exchange, the Germans undertook to supply radio, telephone and telegraph equipment, many precision instruments, ship construction tools, aircraft models, plans for the 42000 tonne battleship the *Bismarck* and for tanks and many different machines. Deliveries began straight away, and Soviet zeal in fulfilling the undertaken commitments significantly exceeded German.[31]

Stalin, however, did not confine himself to merely supply raw materials. His alliance with Hitler caused great consternation among communists all over the world, who completely lost their heads. For this reason Moscow issued a special communiqué on the subject, which advised communist parties in all countries to struggle against and sabotage the actions of the Western allies, since they had entered the war only in pursuit of their imperialist purposes. That was not all. Soviet pandering to the Nazis went so far as to denounce German communists to the Gestapo. Many of them had taken refuge in Russia after Hitler's rise to power but later, at the time of Stalin's great purge, they found themselves in labour camps or prisons. At the beginning of 1940 in Brześć-on-Bug, around 150 of these unfortunate individuals were handed over to the Germans by the NKVD.[32]

All outward signs pointed to a final conquest of Poland, which the two victors had divided up between them, and which would no longer disturb their peace. The occupying powers were however aware that this was not the case, and co-operated between themselves in every way so that their conquest would not add to their troubles. Collusion between the Gestapo and the NKVD came about for this reason. In March 1940 a secret conference took place in Cracow, attended by German and Soviet specialists who exchanged their experiences in the field of coping with every kind of attempt by the Poles to put up resistance.[33]

The development of events in Poland and in the Baltic states clouded the brows of French and British politicians. Their hopes for curbing Hitler's spirit of conquest shattered, but they still did not lose the belief that Stalin would behave with moderation and that he would not become further entrenched on the side of the German dictator. It is true that by not attacking when Poland was defending itself, the West thus weakened its international authority, but it still represented colossal strength, particularly in the economic sphere, and Russia had to take account of this. Especially disadvantageous to the West was the German–Soviet economic agreement, because to a large extent it wiped out the effects of the blockade, but it was expected in Paris and in London that this was the last step Stalin was to take in Hitler's direction.

Unfortunately, that was not to be the case. On 30 November 1939, without formally declaring war, the Red army crossed the borders of Finland at many points.

4 The Underground under German and Soviet Occupation

'IN THE SERVICE OF POLAND'S VICTORY'

Despite being interned in Romania, Marshal Śmigły-Rydz managed to send an order to beleaguered Warsaw to start underground activity. The order was received by General Michał Karasziewicz-Tokarzewski (1893–1964) who had received over 1 million zlotys from the military authorities and the mayor of the city, Stefan Starzyński.[1]

General Tokarzewski had a previously prepared plan; he also had underground experience from the First World War and so on the first day he immediately gathered a group of fifteen officers. One of these was Lieutenant-Colonel Leopold Okulicki of whom there is more later. They received orders for immediate action: to secure and hide arms, ammunition and technical equipment, put the money in a safe place, prepare for 'legalisation' (in other words, forge documents) and establish techniques for mutual communications. The plan envisaged that the whole of Poland would be divided into areas and districts, which was a complex problem, since the country was under two occupations and, moreover, the Western territories had been incorporated into the Reich and the Eastern ones into the Soviet Union. Nevertheless, immediate efforts were made to man those areas where it was easiest to operate – Cracow, Lublin and Radom.[2]

During the earliest days of this work General Tokarzewski, who had adopted the pseudonym *Torwid*, worked out a blueprint of the constitution for the organisation which he called 'In the Service of Poland's Victory' (*Służba Zwycięstwu Polski* – SZP). This constitution was designed on a large scale, setting up a framework for an organisation, which was not simply military, but politico-military and which was meant to embrace the whole nation and the whole of

Poland. At the head of the SZP was to be an overall commander who was also to chair a political body: the Supreme Council of National Defence. The resolutions of this Council could be vetoed by the chairman if he felt that they were harmful for the country or contrary to the constitution. The plan also presented a detailed outline of the organisation's staff, as well as an administrative division of the country from areas coinciding with the provinces right down to small units and outposts. The plan included guidelines on underground work, which were too specific for such a document, which ought to have been more conceptual.[3]

In mid-October, when the organisation's main framework was already prepared, Colonel Stefan Rowecki (pseudonym *Grabica*) joined as Chief of Staff and in him General Tokarzewski gained an officer of the highest calibre. The most pressing task was to get into the field and begin work in all the areas and districts. However, this turned out to be very difficult in the territories incorporated into the Reich. Deportations had already begun, the Polish population was terrorised and had been deprived of its places of work and freedom of movement, new identity documents had been introduced and all the frontiers were watched. At this stage only in the Łódź area was anything achieved.

Realising that a military organisation must have political backing, General Tokarzewski began immediate talks with representatives of the political parties which before the war had belonged to Poland's opposition. They proved to be sympathetic and supportive and a few days later the 'Chief Political Council' was established and held its first meeting on 10 October 1939. It was composed of the three parties which had undoubtedly been the strongest in pre-war Poland: the Polish Socialist Party (*Polska Partia Socjalistyczna* – PPS), the Peasant Party (*Stronnictwo Ludowe* – SL) and the National Party (*Stronnictwo Narodowe* – SN). The parties' leading representatives were in the Council: Kazimierz Pużak (PPS), Maciej Rataj (SL) and Leon Nowodworski (SN). Although the SZP outline had proposed that the overall commander would chair the Council, the post was eventually filled by a politician, a member of the PPS, Mieczysław Niedziałkowski, who also acted as Civil Commissioner for General Tokarzewski. Although himself a member of the Piłsudski camp which had been in government at the outbreak of the war, he realised full well that it was essential to set up the Council with the opposition parties. The rapid defeat in the September Campaign, the refusal to establish a government of national unity and the bitterness of defeat, all made it impossible to turn to the representatives of the party which was at least partly responsible for all these things.[4]

On approximately 15 October General Tokarzewski sent abroad his first report containing details of the SZP's structure and aims. It was carried out secretly by the Hungarian military attaché who had instructions to hand it over to the Polish Commander-in-Chief. Officially this was Marshal Śmigły-Rydz who was in Romania and so it was to him that the Hungarian officer went. This had tragic consequences for General Tokarzewski's subsequent fortunes.[5]

OTHER UNDERGROUND ORGANISATIONS UNDER THE GERMAN OCCUPATION

The initiative and order leading to the creation of 'In the Service of Poland's Victory' were not isolated impulses. Immediately after the Germans' arrival local people in many towns and villages, without any orders from national or local authorities, took the decision to set up small cells, which rapidly grew into secret organisations. Their primary task was to raise local morale, propagate optimistic radio news and encourage resistance. These were usually military-style organisations, but in addition people of similar professions or interests, such as scouts, teachers, agricultural workers, parishioners and others, got together. The number of these organisations very rapidly reached one hundred and in the early stage the vast majority were not related to political movements and indeed, provoked by the Nazis' brutality, had arisen spontaneously, calling for national resistance and survival.

THE POLITICAL PARTIES

Parallel to the rise of underground military organisations secret political life was also developing. The leadership of the three main political parties in Warsaw supported the underground army, setting up with it the 'Chief Political Council', but their organisation in the field had been partially destroyed by the war and by the division of the country into two zones of occupation and required rebuilding.

It was the National Party which had been strong in Wielkopolska, now incorporated into the Reich, which had suffered relatively the hardest. Some of the older members, who had already been active at the start of Independence, had fallen immediately into the hands of the *Einzatzgruppen*; a great many younger ones were picked up later and deprived of their freedom of action. The party tried to get its own people into those posts which were able to operate legally in the *General Gouvernement* and thus gain some influence on the course of events.[6]

The Polish Socialist Party quickly began to rebuild and operate in the field, since it had a great many active members with resistance experience from the days of the struggle for independence, yet who were little-known and were therefore not in the occupation authorities' files. The moment the factories were started up, particularly in the *General Gouvernement*, informational and educational work began to proceed on a large scale.[7]

The Peasant Party, based mainly in the country, encountered greater difficulties, for the Germans tried to win over the peasants by paying well for farm produce. Also the effects of the war were felt less in the country than in the ravaged and starving towns. The older generation of peasants felt at first that it would be better to lie low and wait and see what would happen next, but the younger, more dynamic men, especially those who had returned to the country from the army, immediately got down to organising things. Their efforts embraced the whole German zone of occupation, but mass deportations from the Western lands weakened them there considerably.[8]

The extreme right-wing, organised before the war in the National Radical Camp (*Obóz Narodowo Radykalny* – ONR), also began to operate very rapidly. It adopted the underground code-name *Szaniec* and began a propaganda action aimed at changing people's attitudes towards an almost Italian fascism with a strong anti-communist element. It operated primarily in the urban areas and from the end of 1939 published its journal, *Szaniec*. Its attitude towards the central authorities being set up underground was negative, but this did not signify any tendency to collaborate with the occupiers.[9]

The Camp of National Unity (*Obóz Zjednoczenia Narodowego* – OZN), which had been the political instrument of those who had been governing Poland at the outbreak of the war and was popularly known as the *Sanacja*, had disintegrated completely. Most of its leaders were abroad, the people held them and the whole camp responsible for the defeat and conditions did not exist for rebuilding it in the underground. Nevertheless a number of little groups appeared, who hoped to gain some influence through advocating extreme violence in the struggle with the German occupiers and criticising the Western Allies and the new Polish authorities.[10]

The Communists showed almost no activity. Their organisation, the Polish Communist Party, had been wound up in 1938 by the executive committee of the Comintern[11] for allegedly having been penetrated by the Polish police and it had not been reconstituted. Stalin's pact with Hitler had completely disorganised the Communists, although Moscow tried to explain it to them; they were the Nazis' formal allies and so had no need to go underground, since no-one was persecuting them. The faction least critical of Moscow published a bulletin, which tried to justify Stalin's pro-Nazi policy, but no-one wanted to read it and this faction's influence was minimal.[12]

Although the three great political parties supported the military underground, this did not mean that it had their full confidence. In its leadership they saw many of those who had refused to form a government of national unity and, having no faith in them, began to set up their own underground military organisations not only to fight the invaders, but also to have forces when the war ended and the battle for power began. The PPS had already set up workers' battalions during the defence of Warsaw and now all that was needed was to expand them and set up equivalents in other towns. They were given a name – The Socialist Combat Organisation (SOB). The Peasants Party began to set up military units called Peasant Battalions (*Bataliony Chłopakie* – BCh). The National Party started to set up a military structure called the National Military Organisation (*Narodowa Organizacja Wojskowa* – NOW).[13]

The same thing, only on a much greater scale, applied to the extreme right-wing *Szaniec*, which also began to set up its own military organisation under the name *Związek Jaszczurczy*.[14] It operated mainly in urban areas and was totally opposed to any co-operation with the SZP with which it competed – at least in its own opinion – as equal.

THE UNDERGROUND UNDER SOVIET OCCUPATION

Conditions of underground work turned out to be completely different under the Soviet occupation. The Germans, by the use of general terror, united every social class and themselves brought about a united front of resistance; the Russians proved to be much more subtle. Profiting from the large number of ethnic minorities in the occupied territories, proclaiming misleading slogans of equality and social justice and taking advantage of local communists who were more loyal to the party than to their own country, they rapidly succeeded in splitting the people into rival groups. Informers, arrests, deportations, loss of jobs, all this terrorised even the genuine patriots and deprived them of the desire and the will to undertake anti-Soviet underground work. Anything set up was almost immediately destroyed and the whole network had to be set up again.[15]

LWÓW, BIAŁYSTOK, WILNO

The largest city in the Soviet zone of occupation was Lwów and it was there that the largest number of eminent people, who preferred to avoid the Germans and had left their zone were to be found; so it was in Lwów that the most intensive underground work was undertaken. In the first few weeks of the occupation several military organisations were set up there by professional army officers who were aware that a superior underground military organisation had been established in Warsaw, but had not subordinated themselves to it, although they occasionally invoked its mandate. Representatives of the three main political parties (PPS, SL, SN) gathered round them and with the greatest difficulty were setting up a network in the field, which was being disrupted by continual arrests. It was easier for those few groups to contact Bucharest and Budapest, where there were Polish diplomatic missions, than to contact Warsaw. From Bucharest and Budapest they received certains sums of money which allowed a moderate increase in manpower and the setting up of intelligence-gathering nets. In addition to arrests a serious threat to this work was Soviet penetration, which was made all the easier since these groups did not want to combine and therefore competed with one another.[16] There was a clear need to subordinate them to headquarters in Warsaw, but General Tokarzewski's attempts met with initial failure.

The second city in this zone of occupation in which a military underground had also been spontaneously formed was Białystok, but the occupying forces soon broke that organisation. For a time Polish partisans operated not far from the town, but were also speedily destroyed.

Wilno was in quite a different position, since the fact that it had several times changed hands, had influenced its secret initiatives. The Russians' initial entrance on 18 September was a great shock for the town and the bewildered population did not know how to adjust, especially since the occupiers retained the appearances of liberality, permitting the university, the schools and the theatre to open. Repression and arrests were not long in coming, but before any serious resistance work could be undertaken, the Russians handed over the city to the Lithuanians.

The Lithuanian occupation was not pleasant for the Poles, but there was no comparison with Soviet rule. During the first months of the new state of affairs it was difficult to organise any Polish–Lithuanian co-operation, but at the same time there was no need for an underground as the Lithuanians permitted the publication of Polish journals and a Polish Committee was formed to represent the Polish inhabitants to the authorities in Kowno.[17]

The future, however, was somewhat unclear and experience taught that a return by the Russians was to be expected so the nucleus of an underground army needed to be prepared. The seeds of future larger groupings were sown, their task for the present being spiritual, social and intelligence matters. Sabotage and diversionary activity were not advisable, since it was better not to upset the Lithuanians needlessly. As in Lwów the resistance maintained communications with Budapest and Bucharest, this being easier than with Warsaw. From Wilno the underground routes led to Kowno. Irrespective of the short distance there was a contact there, for after the closing of the Polish legation, Professor Adam Żółtowski was in residence. He had no diplomatic status, but was recognised by the Lithuanians.[18]

The SZP sent a number of officers to Wilno, but during this initial phase it was almost impossible to arrange any collaboration between Wilno and Warsaw. This was true of the whole Soviet zone of occupation.

In addition to the military underground in the Soviet zone there were other organisations whose aim was the protection of Polish assets. The political parties also operated, but these efforts were very weak, continually broke down and things were a far cry from the German zone where, despite the terror, hundreds of groups were active. The NKWD had so infiltrated the population that the more active people crossed the border and set off for France by way of Romania and Hungary.[19]

5 Polish Government and Army in France

THE INTERNMENT OF POLISH AUTHORITIES IN ROMANIA

The Polish political and military authorities' optimism that Romania would help them to reach France quickly was soon dispelled. Inadequately armed and poor, under pressure both from the Germans and the Russians, Romania was unable to honour the obligations of her pact with Poland and interned the Polish President, Government and Commander-in-Chief. A very complex situation then arose. This internment hindered all communications and, with the war continuing, the Polish authorities were unable to carry out their duties. Poland had powerful allies in the West and the nation was in need of continued political leadership, based on the constitution of April 1935. Article 13 stated that one of the President's powers, in time of war, was to nominate a successor, while article 24 stated:

> In case of war the President's term of office shall extend until three months after peace has been concluded; in the event of his office falling vacant before peace is concluded, the President should by a special act, published in the government newspaper, nominate a successor.[1]

President Ignacy Mościcki understood the situation and realised that on him alone depended the upholding of Polish legality in the face of German and Soviet threats, so he decided to resign his office, handing it over to a suitable person who had freedom of action.

Meanwhile General Władysław Sikorski (1881–1943) had arrived in France. He had not been detained by the Romanians, having held no office in Poland before the outbreak of war. He was a former Prime Minister, Chief of the General Staff and Minister of War, but

47

he belonged to Józef Piłsudski's opponents and, after the *coup d'état* of May 1926, had been relieved of command of a corps in Lwów, although remaining on the active list. He had then spent several years in France where he had excellent contacts. He was also one of the founders of the opposition Morges front. This was formed in 1936 on the initiative of the centrist parties: the *National Labour Party* (NPR) and the *Christian Democrats* (ChD), using the authority of the famous pianist and former Prime Minister, Ignacy Paderewski (1860–1941). Sikorski had been not given command in September and had found himself in Romania. In the company of the French ambassador to the Polish government, Léon Noël, he had left for Paris which he reached on 24 September, and immediately made contact with ambassador Juliusz Łukasiewicz and the French authorities, assumed the role of leader of the opposition to Poland's last government and became a figure to be reckoned with.[2]

Ambassador Łukasiewicz, knowing local conditions and French attitudes, accurately assessed Sikorski's position. Having to act independently and fast, and after consultation with Polish politicians on the spot, as early as 28 September he entrusted the General with the command of the new Polish army forming in France. The General accepted and the French authorities endorsed the choice, which was important, since they were to equip and supply this army.

RACZKIEWICZ NEW PRESIDENT

Two days later, on 30 September, a message came from Romania in which President Mościcki resigned from office and nominated as his successor Władysław Raczkiewicz (1885–1947), a former provincial Governor, Minister of the Interior, Marshal of the Senate and President of the World Union of Poles Abroad (*Światpol*). Some other candidates had been considered, among them the Polish Primate, Cardinal August Hlond, and Ignacy Paderewski.

The same day the new President took the oath in the Polish embassy in Paris and a few hours later the news arrived from Romania that the government of General Składkowski had resigned in order to 'remove from the conscience of every citizen of the Polish republic any possible doubt as to the legality of the transfer of power'. Not a day passed before the new President carried out the first act within his powers, namely he entrusted the formation of a new government to General Sikorski.[3]

GENERAL SIKORSKI NEW PRIME MINISTER AND C-IN-C

Within the space of two days the General had concentrated in his hands the most important positions, both political and military. He managed to form a Government of National Unity, including representatives of *Front Morges*, PPS, SL, SN, NPR and even *Sanacja*, and this was immediately recognised by France and Great Britain. On 2 October the USA recognised it as also did a number of neutral countries later, although some of them, frightened by Germany and the USSR, preferred not to show it.

General Sikorski wanted first of all to tackle the problem of rebuilding the armed forces on Allied soil, but quickly changed his mind as problems in Poland herself took first place. Whatever happened in France and whatever appointments were received there, everything depended on the mandate received from the Polish nation. Every experienced politician realised that its activities abroad must depend on a mandate from the occupied country.[4]

In October General Sosnkowski arrived in Paris and, in a decree of 16 October, President Raczkiewicz appointed him his deputy. During the time of the Polish Legions in the First World War the General had been Józef Piłsudski's chief of staff; during the critical months of 1920 he had raised a reserve army, and in independent Poland had held various prominent posts. However, after the *coup d' état* of May 1926, when he had feigned suicide, he had lost the Marshal's full trust. He had not been tarnished with blame for the September defeat and was on good terms with the leaders of the opposition parties, so General Sikorski, although not a political friend, decided to offer him a place in the government and entrust domestic Polish affairs to him. He hoped by doing this to remove a number of difficulties, to regain control over the affairs of the occupied country and to weaken party in-fighting. Sikorski further strengthened his position, for by a decree of 7 November, the President relieved Marshal Śmigły-Rydz of the post of Commander-in-Chief and entrusted it to the General.[5]

UNION FOR ARMED STRUGGLE

On 13 November the Prime Minister issued a decree based on a cabinet decision of 8 November, setting up a Committee of Ministers for the Occupied Country with, at its head, General Sosnkowski, who had also been appointed Commander of the 'Union for Armed Struggle' (*Związek Walki Zbrojnej* – ZWZ).

This announcement overturned everything that had hitherto been achieved within Poland and heralded the end of the SZP and its replacement by the ZWZ, directed from France and entirely under the control of the government and Commander-in-Chief. By 15 November the Committee of Ministers for the Occupied Country had approved initial orders which were sent to Warsaw by various couriers, while General Sosnkowski had also begun to prepare instructions formally establishing the structure of the ZWZ. On 4 December these instructions were ready and twenty days later were taken to Warsaw by special courier. General Tokarzewski continued to be the head of the SZP, but the instructions were addressed not to him, but to his chief of staff, Colonel Stefan Rowecki.[6]

LIAISON WITH THE OCCUPIED COUNTRY; BASES

The most characteristic and least justified feature of these instructions was the establishment of the ZWZ's command in France, with orders to control underground operations in Poland, with which communications would be maintained by means of slow couriers, since a radio link was still only being established. A further serious failing was the lack of knowledge of conditions in Poland, which appeared in the further absurdity of dividing Poland into six areas – Warsaw, Białystok, Lwów, Cracow, Poznań and Toruń. The boundaries of these areas were not clearly defined and their commanders were directly responsible to General Sosnkowski. A positive feature of the instructions was the clear segregation of the military from politics, in which the ZWZ clearly distinguished itself from the SZP. They also contained organisational guidelines, an order to dissolve all other military organisations, rules of communication and an oath of allegiance.[7]

Such an approach, liquidating the SZP and depriving General Tokarzewski of his achievements, was still not enough for General Sikorski, who was uncertain whether, even with General Sosnkowski's authority, these instructions would be heeded. They were moreover clearly unjust towards the founder of the SZP. Sikorski was also worried by the group of Piłsudski's followers surrounding Tokarzewski in Warsaw and so he decided to move the latter from the capital. He designated him commander of area no. 3 in Lwów, while area no. 1 (Warsaw) was entrusted to Rowecki. This decision not only compounded the injury already done to him, but exposed Tokarzewski to almost certain loss of freedom and even of his life, since he was widely known in Lwów and there could no doubt that the NKVD would seize him.

It was very quickly realised in Paris that the direct subordination of the six area commanders to General Sosnkowski in France was impracticable and order no. 2, sent to Rowecki on 16 January 1940, set up command structures for the two zones of occupation: the German zone, based in Warsaw with Rowecki (*Grabica*) as commander and the Soviet zone with its headquarters in Lwów, if necessary in Wilno, with Tokarzewski (*Stolarski*) in charge. This changed the tone of the first order and put Tokarzewski on an equal footing with Rowecki. However, it did get rid of him from Warsaw with the possibility that he might quickly fall into the hands of the Soviets. Indeed that was what happened. The General obeyed the difficult order and set out for Lwów, but he never got there, for on the night of 6–7 March, while crossing the demarcation line between the two zones of occupation, he was arrested by a Soviet patrol.[8]

The speedy, regular contact with occupied Poland was important and since radio communications were still only developing with several months work still ahead,[9] the whole load had to be borne by emmissaries and couriers as well as by bases in neighbouring countries. There were three such bases: no. 1 in Budapest (code-name *Romek*), no. 2 in Bucharest (code-name *Bolek*) and no. 3 in Kowno (code-name *Anna*). There were also two stations: *Sława* in Belgrade and *Bey* in Istambul.

These three bases were linked to Polish diplomatic facilties with the essential difference that in Budapest and Bucharest diplomatic representation operated openly, since neither Hungary's nor Romania's neutrality were in doubt, while Hungary's neutrality was extremely favourable towards the Poles. In Kowno the situation was somewhat different, for although Lithuania was not at war with Poland, her anti-Polish co-operation with Soviet Russia led to the occupation of Wilno and the surrounding area by the Lithuanian army and to the closure of the Polish legation in the small republic's capital. However, an unofficial representative of Polish affairs operated there, as well as some officials of the closed legation. The Lithuanians turned a blind eye to Polish activities and so it was relatively easy to set up a secret base there.

The initial chaos made difficulties, the underground in Lwów was in contact with Budapest and Bucharest, the underground in Wilno with Kowno and only the emergence of the ZWZ tidied up every-thing. This eventually took place on 29 February 1940 when General Sosnkowski issued special instructions for the bases. Before the German attack in the West, the average journey from Paris to Warsaw lasted several weeks while the delivery of mail to Budapest or Bucharest caused no great difficulty, since diplomatic immunity was used and only the actual crossing of the Polish frontier caused a serious problem.[10]

The slowness of courier communications made it imperative that radio links be established as rapidly as possible and this problem was tackled at both ends: in Poland and in Paris. In Warsaw the first secret radio station was set up as early as December 1939 and in Paris in January of the following year. Despite apparent appearances, this was not an easy problem, for at that time the French treated the Poles with some disdain and were not eager to facilitate such independent action. Moreover, various details of the radio traffic had to be agreed and thus in January 1940 a special courier was sent from Warsaw to Budapest. From 25 January 1940 the Paris radio station, concealed by the code name *Regina*, began to call its correspondents and on 19 February for the first time caught a signal from Budapest. Finally, on 5 April, Warsaw was heard and Budapest received five messages for General Sosnkowski. An attempt was made to establish a direct Warsaw–Paris link, but it was unsuccessful. Nor did Paris' efforts to receive signals direct from Lwów meet with any success. For several months Budapest and Bucharest had to be used as intermediaries.[11]

THE GOVERNMENT DELEGACY AND POLITICAL PARTIES

Together with the liquidation of the SZP and the conversion of the military underground to the ZWZ, the structure of political repre-sentation in Poland also changed. The Chief Political Council gave way to the Political Advisory Committee (PKP), which came into being on 26 February 1940. It consisted of the same parties which had belonged to the Political Council: PPS, SL and SN. Later, in the autumn of 1940, the Labour Party (SP) also joined. The chair-manship was assumed by Kazimierz Pużak (PPS).

However, the Political Advisory Committee continued to be only a co-ordinating body and General Rowecki, who was hoping to raise the importance of the underground fighting in Poland, considered a plan to set up a 'Council of National Defence', which would be still no more than an advisory body attached to the ZWZ. He was of the opinion that during war the most important thing was unity of action and that political factors should be subordinated to the military commander. For this reason in his plans the position of Civil Commissioner, who was to represent the government in occupied Poland, was to be subordinate to him.[13]

An exchange of views on this subject between Poland and Paris began and it at once became clear that the politicians in France did not share the opinions of General Rowecki, who was to some extent supported by the political parties operating underground. The government in Paris, reasoning according to the principle recognised in the West that politics should be separate from the military, which is only an agency of government, was reaching a different conclusion. The government, however, was not subject to the ceaseless pressure of life under the occupation; furthermore, in the early months of 1940 there was widespread belief that Hitler would be defeated in the West and that the war would end quickly. The battle for influence and for who would govern Poland after the war had begun.

On 16 April the Committee of Ministers for the occupied country passed a resolution calling for the appointment of a Government Delegate in occupied Poland, independent of the ZWZ and with control of its budget. The following day a further resolution established guidelines for the Delegate's relationship with the political parties: he would be their link with the government, but they would not be subordinate to him.[14] The resolution was not specific and spoke once of a Delegate, then of Delegates, for indeed there were meant to be three of them: one for the *General Gouvernement*, one for the lands incorporated into the Reich and one for the territories seized by the USSR. The political parties were meant to propose candidates.[15]

In May the government sent to Poland an emissary in the role of temporary delegate who was to help to find candidates for the posts of delegates. This was not an easy task and took some time to achieve.

THE NATIONAL COUNCIL IN FRANCE

Of all these important problems there still remained one to be solved, so that the new Polish political structure in the West could be finalised. On 9 December 1939 President Raczkiewicz issued a decree setting up a National Council and nominated twenty-two of its members from among representatives of political parties currently in France and from various well-known personalities. Ignacy Paderewski became President of the Council, whose task was partially to replace parliament and to provide the government with advice and assistance.[16]

NEW POLISH ARMY IN THE WEST

Alongside such critically important internal matters within Poland, General Sikorski directed his energy towards the problem of raising Polish armed forces abroad. Above all this concerned France and her dependent territories in the Near East, as well as Great Britain where there were several Polish naval vessels and the bulk of the Polish merchant navy, and where it was hoped to rebuild the Polish air force with the support of the RAF.

The whole question had two aspects: the formal one, involving suitable agreements with both allies, and the purely human one that rebuilding an army required soldiers.

The Polish–French Pact, signed on 4 September 1939, but drawn up before the war, did not, of course, deal with raising Polish units on French soil, so on 9 September an additional agreement was signed, which envisaged the creation of only one large formation. More extensive plans for rebuilding the armed forces required a new agreement and so, after negotiations, a Polish–French military agreement was signed on 4 January 1940 by General Sikorski and Prime Minister Daladier.[17]

An important problem was the question of authority and the agreement therefore established that Polish units would be under Polish command, but that during hostilities they would be operationally under the French Commander-in-Chief. The agreement referred in detail to the issue of recruitment of Poles resident in France as well as to the questions of supplies, weaponry, training and finance. All expenditure on the Polish units in France was to be funded by the French exchequer with the proviso that this was only a loan.

On the same day an air agreement was signed with France. Polish units were to be raised according to French regulations, it was hoped to be able to form two fighter squadrons, two joint liaison flights, as well as some cadre units.

The Polish–British pact, concluded on 25 August 1939, was first of all political in nature, and thus on 18 November of the same year an agreement was signed which dealt with the Navy, formalising the operation of Polish vessels within the structure of the Royal Navy. Air Force matters grew more complicated, for General Sikorski wanted to rebuild it in France, while senior Air Force officers maintained that it would be better to use the RAF for support. On 25 October 1939 a Polish–French–British conference took place in the French Air Staff during which a compromise solution was reached to send half the Polish Air Force personnel to Great British and the other half to France. There now ensued protracted negotiations with the British, who were unwilling to accept General Sikorski's demand that the Polish Air Force should have complete autonomy: eventually a compromise was reached and the agreement signed. This took place on 11 June 1940 when France had already fallen and by which time a great number of Polish airmen had been in the British Isles for some time. The agreement envisaged the formation of two bomber squadrons with a Polish inspectorate as a liaison with the British, the airmen were to take two oaths, both Polish and British, were formally to be volunteers, were to be subject to British Air Force law and officers' promotions were to be agreed with the Polish Commander-in-Chief. For the time being the British were to cover the costs, but in the form of a loan.[18]

Alongside all this formal activity, efforts increased to extricate the Polish soldiers from those countries where they had taken refuge after the unsuccessful September campaign. The greatest number – around 40 000 – was in Hungary, amongst them 5500 officers, and almost the entire modern motorised armoured brigade, as well as valuable air force personnel, about 900 strong. In Romania there were about 30 000 personnel most of whom came from various base and rear areas, as well as the whole High Command, the Ministry of Defence and, of course, many older officers. Almost one third of them were air force personnel of various descriptions, comprising 9276 men, of whom 1491 were officers. They were really valuable and a speedy evacuation needed to start with them. There were a further 20 000 civilian refugees, amongst whom were many men with military training and of the right age. There were 13 800 Polish soldiers in Lithuania and 1315 in Latvia. Altogether this amounted to around 85 000 men who, after passage to France and, in some cases, to Great Britain, could immediately man the newly-formed regiments, batteries and squadrons.[19]

Evacuation was a very complicated matter, for the soliders were kept in internment camps, from which they had to escape, obtain civilian clothes and documents and find some sort of transport. Of great help were Polish diplomatic posts as well as French and British embassies and consulates. From Hungary and Romania the escape route ran through Yugoslavia and Italy, which, although allied to Hitler, showed the Poles sympathy and respected the Polish embassy. The sea route to Marseilles and the Near East was also used, for in Syria (a French mandate) a Polish brigade was being raised within the army commanded by General Maxime Weygand (1867–1965). Things were somewhat different in Lithuania and Latvia, since the Soviet Union's hand lay heavy on them. The sea route to Sweden and Norway was used. It is calculated that by 15 June 1940 22 000 men had been evacuated from Romania, 21 000 from Hungary, but barely 500 from the Baltic states: 60 per cent by sea, 40 per cent overland.[20]

Poles who had settled in various parts of the world constituted a very large reservoir of potential soldiers. This was most obvious in France where the Polish community was almost 500 000 strong, many of whom were still Polish citizens. With the agreement of the French authorities it was possible to carry out mobilisation of the suitable age groups and, despite various exemptions – particularly of miners – this produced about 44 000 recruits. The small Polish colony in Britain supplied 900 men. The potential of the United States, with more than 5 million Poles, and Canada, with about 170 000, was enormous, but only for volunteers and not in the short term.

The final reservoir was Occupied Poland herself, which admittedly was already organising an underground army, but this was not attractive to everyone and a great many young men decided on the journey to France, dreaming of a Polish uniform and open fight. These men usually went through Hungary and Slovakia, breaking out over the mountains; some fell into German hands and some reached their goal. It is quite impossible to calculate this supply of manpower, even in the most approximate terms. At this stage of the war it was reasonable to anticipate that the Polish army in France would be able to muster a minimum of 185 000 men.[21]

SOVIET RUSSIA ATTACKS FINLAND

These optimistic forecasts were not realised and the Polish armed forces in France came to barely 82 000 soldiers. Furthermore, there arose the need to change already prepared plans as a result of the

Soviet attack on Finland. This time Russian aggression aroused a reaction. On 14 December 1939 the League of Nations expelled the Soviet Union and appealed to the world to provide Finland with assistance. A scheme was devised to send out an expeditionary force. France and Great Britain took up this initiative, began to send military supplies and discussed the rapid preparation of suitable units. The Polish Government joined in these plans and at breakneck speed began to prepare a Fusilier Brigade with a strength of about 5000 men. It was estimated that the expeditionary force would consist of 50 000 men. If it were ever sent and became involved in fighting with Red forces, a completely new situation would arise, for the Western Allies, already at war with the Germans, would then find themselves in open conflict with Soviet Russia, a situation which, after her attack on Poland, they had hoped to avoid.

Any military aid for Finland was conditional on her agreement and formal request for assistance; however, the Finns continued to fight alone and their defence aroused the admiration of the whole world. A small nation of barely 4 million people was putting up effective resistance to powerful Russia, whose attack was a classic example of Red imperialism. Soviet forces continued, however, to penetrate into the heart of the country and Finland proposed a cessation of hostilities, signing peace with Russia on 12 March 1940 and relinquishing part of Karelia with the town Vyborg.[22] The expeditionary force was never sent and the Polish Brigade remained in France.

It was by now the spring of 1940 and the 'phoney war' continued in the West. Patrols operated beneath the walls of the Maginot Line, Allied planes appeared over Germany to drop leaflets, both sides stalked each other, but perceptive observers knew already that it would be the Germans who would launch an attack. Only at sea did the real war continue.

THE NORWEGIAN CAMPAIGN

Suddenly, on 8 April 1940, the Germans attacked Denmark and Norway. Denmark was occupied within less than twenty-four hours without offering any military resistance, but Norway resolved to resist and the Western Allies decided to help her. The Supreme Allied Military Council took a binding decision and the British fleet entered the fray, supported a little later by the French fleet. Three Polish destroyers, *Błyskawica*, *Burza* and *Grom*, operated with the

British, as did the submarine *Orzeł*. The British were already prepared, since, together with the French, they had planned to occupy Norway in view of her strategic location and the priceless Swedish iron-ore mines, so on 14 April they landed their forces on the island of Hinnöy in Northern Norway. On 8 May on the same island the Polish *Podhalańska* Brigade was landed and together with the British 24th Guards Brigade, two French battalions and one Norwegian battalion, prepared to attack Narvik, which was already in German hands. Further British and French battalions were landed near Trondheim and were to attack the town from two sides.

The Germans had committed to Norway five infantry divisions, two mountain divisions, about 1000 planes and almost the entire fleet. The Norwegians had mobilised about 50 000 men and the Allies landed five French, four Polish (*Podhalańska* Brigade) and five British battalions. The Allied navy, mainly British, protected convoys, attacked German sea transport and supported land operations with naval gunnery. The British air force took on the Germans who had a decided advantage in the air.[23]

ORDER OF BATTLE OF THE POLISH ARMY IN FRANCE

Meanwhile in France further units of the rebuilding Polish armed forces were being speedly trained and organised. At the moment of the *Podhalańska* Brigade's entry into Norway the Polish order of battle in France was as follows:

— 1st Grenadier Division, strength about 16 000
— 2nd Fusilier Division, strength about 16 000
— 10th Armoured Cavalry Brigade, strength about 5000, 2000 ready for combat
— 3rd Infantry Division, strength about 8000 in the process of forming
— 4th Infantry Division, strength about 3000 in the first stage of organisation

The Polish Air Force in France, formed around a nucleus evacuated from Romania and Hungary, began to organise at the beginning of 1940 and underwent training on French aircraft at the Polish Air Force Training Centre at Lyon-Bron as well as at several French centres. In command of it, as well as of the anti-aircraft artillery, was General Józef Zając (1891–1963), with 1449 officers, 2836 NCOs and

2578 men under his command. In May 1940 the order of battle was as follows:

— I/145th Warsaw Squadron, trained and organised; 34 Morane-Saulnier MS-406 and Caudron C–714 Cyclone aircraft and in June Bloch MB–152
— II Cracow/Poznań Squadron of which one half, the 'Montpellier Flight', equipped with Morane-Saulniers, was ready for combat, and the other half was trained, but awaiting aircraft
— III Squadron, which had barely begun flying training.
— IV Squadron, which had begun training.

Furthermore, the fighter formations had five small detachments guarding key areas. Each such detachment normally had seven aircraft. Reconnaissance and bomber formations had not yet been trained and were not ready for combat. Altogether, Poles had eighty-six aircraft.[24]

Outside France herself, in Syria, there was one other Polish formation, the Independent Carpathian Fusilier Brigade formed form soldiers extricated from Romania and sent to the Near East, since sea travel was easier than rail transport to France.

The first contingent of several hundred men arrived in Beirut towards the end of April 1940, to be followed by others. The Brigade also received volunteers in the form of Poles who had escaped from Poland on their own initiative, as well as many others who lived abroad, wanted to fight for Poland and for whom Syria was nearer than France. By May the Brigade was not yet completely organised and its complement was about 4000 men.[25]

The only part of the Polish armed forces which was involved in action from almost its first days abroad, was the small Polish navy. The three Polish destroyers, *Błyskawica*, *Burza* and *Grom*, were in the Scottish port of Rosyth on 1 September 1939 and by the 6 September were taking part in their first combat patrol; later they went to Plymouth and in November they entered Harwich. Each one carried a British signals officer with codes, radio operators and yeomen. Operationally they were under British command, but retained Polish uniforms, colours and naval regulations. Two submarines, *Orzeł* and *Wilk*, joined them later. The German attack on Norway threw the Polish vessels into further action.[26]

Such were the Polish armed forces abroad when on 10 May 1940, just before dawn and without any declaration of war, German divisions began a massive attack in the West, invading France, Belgium, Holland and Luxemburg.

6 The Church

THE CATHOLIC CHURCH UNDER GERMAN OCCUPATION

The partition of Poland between the two invaders, the destruction of its national structure, the replacement of its own administration by one imposed by the occupying powers did not in any way alter the fact that the Catholic Church, with almost 1000 years of history, continued to exist. In Poland Catholicism was the religion of the majority of the people; 65 per cent of the whole population professed it and it was thus considered to be the state religion. The Church's organisation was ubiquitous and well-disciplined; the clergy enjoyed universal respect. Moreover, the Church was an organisation allied to Rome and the Papacy which gave it a strong international position and a certain influence on the country's fortunes. Both the occupying powers knew this and had to take it into account, but each responded to the situation in a different way.

Nazism had resolved to destroy the Polish nation and turn its remnants into slaves. It thus had no option but to attack the Church, particularly on territory incorporated into the German Reich. This embraced the archdiocese of Gniezno-Poznań, the dioceses of Chełmno, Katowice and Włocławek as well as parts of the dioceses of Częstochowa, Kielce, Cracow, Łomża, Łódź, Płock and Warsaw. In this region, which was to be completely Germanised, there was no room for a Polish Church structure or clergy, although the Catholic Church itself would continue to exist, for there were Germans there who professed it.[1]

On the face of it the Germans would solve this problem in the same way that they dispatched the Polish upper classes by mass arrests, shootings and forcible resettlement. However, it transpired that the Polish Church's thousand-year link with Rome afforded it a certain protection. The German Reich contained 30 million Catholics, who recognised the Pope's authority, while the German nation still retained the great traditions of the Holy Roman Empire and each new ruler of the country, however strongly opposed to Rome, had to

60

take account of this. To be sure the new Pope, Pius XII, who ascended the throne of Peter in March 1939 and who had previously been Papal Nuncio in Germany for many years, retained an affection for the country, and yet he could react strongly if the Church's affairs in Poland were handed over exclusively into the hands of the SS and the Gestapo. A firm Papal condemnation of Nazism would have placed German Catholics in a terrible moral dilemma, their loyalty to their country and system might be undermined and even Hitler could not take that risk. Moreover, in 1933 the Vatican had established a concordat with Nazi Germany. Therefore, despite great brutality, the struggle with the Polish Church and clergy retained a certain semblance of legality on the territory incorporated into the Reich.[2]

It immediately became clear that the entire Polish clergy ought to remain in its own diocese, parish or seminary, for although this entailed great personal risk, it was a cause of some embarrassment to the German authorities. The overwhelming majority of bishops and priests maintained a solid front. There were nevertheless several exceptions producing unfortunate consequences. Under pressure from the Polish Government, the Primate of Poland, Cardinal August Hlond, left the archdiocese of Gniezno-Poznań, Bishop Stanisław Okoniewski the diocese of Chełmno-Pelplin and Bishop Karol Radoński the diocese of Włocławek. The Germans immediately exploited this situation, permitting no replacements and it was in those areas that the swiftest and most painful blows were struck against the Polish Church and its clergy.[3]

POMERANIA

During the first weeks of the occupation in Pomerania almost all the Polish churches were closed and turned into storehouses, garages and stables, while Church property was looted. Only after a long time were they reopened, but by then there were few Polish priests left and mainly only those who had signed the *Volkslist*.[4] Most of them were sent to the concentration camps of Dachau and Stutthof where many of them ended their lives. Seminaries were also closed. At the same time, towards the end of 1939, the Vatican entrusted the administration of the orphaned diocese of Chełmno-Pelplin to the ordinary of the diocese of Gdańsk, the German Bishop, Carl Maria Splett.[5] To replace the Polish clergy who had been deported Bishop Splett sent over 100 Germans and *Volksdeutsch* and he banned the use of Polish in churches, even at confession, a move which was criticised by the Vatican. He also ordered that all signs of Polishness be removed from the churches and cemeteries and diligently executed the demands of the German administration. He gained its recognition and yet did not lose the Vatican's, and historians do not agree in their assessment of his actions. After the war he was imprisoned in Poland, but it must be admitted that, to a certain extent, he did ensure the survival of the Church's possessions within his dioceses.[6]

WARTA

In the Warta region the first months of German rule were as difficult for the Polish Church as in Pomerania, with the difference that there was no improvement with time. The immediate closure of Polish churches began at once and during the course of the war the sum of these closures, including chapels, reached 1300. Moreover about 500 churches were turned into storehouses and a certain number were handed over to the Evangelists. The basilica in Gniezno suffered grieviously, as did the cathedrals of Poznań and Włocławek, which were stripped of their works of art and devastated. As in Pomerania all Polish seminaries were closed.

The initial onslaught on the Polish clergy took place at the end of 1939 when mass arrests and resettlement to the *General Gouvernement* were carried out. These attacks were later renewed and a great wave of arrests took place in the autumn of 1941. Then about 500 priests were taken to concentration camps. This process of continually weakening Polish Catholicism can best be illustrated by the following figures: out of 2500 Polish priests working before the war in the Warta region, 752 lost their lives, mainly in concentration camps, and a further 800 were sent there, but managed to survive; out of the six bishops in the region only one remained – Walenty Dymek, whom the Vatican nominated Apostolic Adminstrator for the Polish Catholics of the region; in the diocese of Poznań alone, by 1943, of the 800 priests working before the war, only 34 remained in their parishes and only 30 Polish churches were open.[7]

The Catholic Church's great losses in the Warta region were caused by the exceptionally aggressive politics of the Gauleiter, Arthur Greiser, who went much further than did the Gauleiter of Pomerania, Albert Forster. There losses were smaller, since the authorities were not trying to isolate the Polish Catholics from the Germans at once, hoping instead that under pressure many of the Poles, together with some of the clergy, would accept the *Volkslist*. Moreover in Pomerania, in the interests of Germanisation, use was made of German priests, who nevertheless felt themselves to a certain extent to be servants of the Church and formed something of a buffer between the Nazi authorities and the Polish population. Greiser ignored all this, since his aim was the complete and speedy elmination of the Polish Catholic Church on the territory under his control. In his eagerness his instructions began to threaten German Catholicism and even the Evangelical Church. At that junction Cardinal Adolf Bertram of Wrocław (Breslau), Chairman of the Conference of German Bishops at Fulda, spoke out informing Pius XII of the situation and asking for assistance.[8] This was not easy to provide, for even ignoring the Poles completely and raising only the issue of the rights of the German Catholics could easily arouse Hitler's anger. He was at that moment at the height of his power, took little notice of anything and could decide on a break with Rome and the formation of a National Church. Such an outcome would be the worst possible and the one that the Vatican feared the most, for in the history of the Church there had already been similar situations which had had a fatal effect on the Church's unity (for instance, Henry VIII's Reformation in England). It was for this reason that Pius XII restricted himself to a private correspondence with the Bishop of Berlin, but made no open criticism of the behaviour of the Nazi authorities in the Warta region.[9]

SILESIA

The least painful blows fell on the Catholic Church in Upper Silesia and this was mainly due to Bishop Stanisław Adamski, who was at the head of the diocese of Katowice and who put the affairs of the Church in first place, even above the attitudes adopted by the whole nation. When in December 1939 the German authorities ordered a census to be taken, he advised Poles to sign the *Volkslist* and issued a similar instruction to the clergy, since this gave them a greater chance of remaining in their parishes. 954 priests followed this advice. He suggested to monasteries and convents that they might admit a number of German monks, who could then represent the community to the German authorities. He sought contacts with the German military authorities and when Bishop Juliusz Bieniek, Suffragan of the diocese of Katowice, was forced to resign at the end of 1939 from his post as Vicar-General, he appointed a German in his place. He introduced German into the churches, even in prayers. He declared himself a Pole and in this respect retained his personal integrity, not seeking any protection for himself.[10]

At that time, during this period of brutal German rule, most Poles adopted an inflexible attitude and considered as treachery any attempt at co-operation with the occupiers. The Polish underground authorities also took this line and the High Command of the Home Army judged Bishop Adamski's actions very critically. They did to some degree protect the Polish population from persecution, yet at the same time provided the Germans with an excellent propaganda weapon. The census showed that there were few Poles in Silesia and thus that the German revisionists had been correct in declaring at the end of the First World War that the Poles had taken wholly German land. Moreover, signing the *Volkslist* produced positive benefits only in the first phase of the war, when it allowed many Poles to remain in their factories and places of work. Later, when the Reich was in desperate need of soldiers, hundreds of thousands of Silesian *Volksdeutsch* were conscripted into the Wehrmacht and died fighting for an alien cause. Unfortunately it was impossible to wage total war without a great many victims and survival alone could not be an adequate contribution to the final victory.

However, if one examines this problem exclusively from the point of view of the Church, Bishop Adamski's policy brought a great deal of benefit. In Silesia there was no separation of the Polish Catholics from the Germans, and the German clergy – representing about 11 per cent of the total – behaved correctly towards the Poles. No churches were closed and only monasteries were touched by repression: sixty were closed in the diocese of Katowice. Losses amongst the Polish clergy were also comparatively light: forty-three died in camps and gaols, two died as a result of belonging to the Resistance, thirteen were resettled to the *General Gouvernement* (among them two bishops: Adamski and Dymek) and a dozen or so were relieved of their duties.[11]

THE CATHOLIC CHURCH WITHIN THE *GENERAL GOUVERNEMENT*

In the *General Gouvernement* where, nevertheless, the Poles' position was easier than in the lands incorporated into the Reich, the Catholic Church also found itself in a better position than in Pomerania, Wielkopolska and Silesia. Nazism recognised it as an enemy, but on the territories in which it had allowed Poles to live, it did not want to undertake an open battle with it, since it hoped to be able to exploit it to its own ends. Despite his pact with Stalin, Hitler was an opponent of Communism and was planning an attack on the Soviet Union and he hoped that when he announced an anti-communist 'crusade', he would find an ally in the Church. Counting on the Vatican's cautious policies, one of whose main aims was the protection of the Church's position, he hoped that the Polish clergy would show a certain understanding and support the German author-ities on forced labour transports to Germany, food quotas and even the resistance movement.[12]

It was for this reason that in the *General Gouvernement* churches were not closed and only in a few instances were they requisitioned by the Army for its own religious purposes. Similarly the Church administration was not attacked nor were the bishops hampered in the administration of their dioceses. The Archbishop of Cracow, Adam Sapieha, in constant proximity to the German Governor, Hans Frank, was treated in a manner which, in the light of Nazi methods, could be termed courteous. Yet even here many religious organisa-tions were wound up, their assets confiscated, many seminaries and monasteries closed and there were round-ups in front of churches. There was no frontal assault on the clergy as on the territories incorporated into the Reich, but a general terror, with the taking of hostages and the arrest of thousands of priests and monks, several hundred of whom died for participating in the resistance movement. In the diocese of Warsaw 212 priests lost their lives; in Cracow, thirty; in Kielce, thirteen; in Lwów (after the German attack in the East), eighty-one; in Wilno, ninety-two.[13]

Amongst the clergy arrested or interned throughout the whole of Poland occupied by the Germans there were also a great many heads of diocese and their closest advisors. Four of them: Bishops Nowo-wiejski, Góral, Kozal and Wetmański died in camps.[14]

The Evangelical Church also became an object of attack in the territory incorporated into the Reich and in the *General Gouverne-ment*, although it did gravitate partly towards the Third Reich. However, many pastors of German descent retained their loyalty to the Polish state and its religious authorities in Warsaw and they also suffered various forms of repression. They were deprived of their parishes and some of them were arrested and sent to concentration camps. In the *General Gouvernement* the Evangelical Church was in an even worse position than the Catholic Church, since it was completely pro-Polish and the occupiers had condemned it to extermination. First of all they separated the German element from the Polish and then set about liquidating the latter. Its Superintendent, Juliusz Bursche, died in a concentration camp, the Consistory was wound up and a quarter of the pastors, under strong pressure, joined the German Church. For its size the losses of the Polish part of this Church were serious: seventy-six pastors were thrown out of their parishes, forty-six were arrested, about thirty were sent to concentration camps and half of them died there.[15]

THE CATHOLIC AND UNIATE CHURCHES UNDER SOVIET OCCUPATION

The position of the Catholic Church in the Eastern part of Poland, which had been incorporated into the USSR, was different since Russia's attitude to the Church had been different for many centuries. In 988 the Kiev prince, Vladimir the Great, accepted Christianity from Byzantium and so began the rivalry between the Byzantine East and the Roman West. The Orthodox Church became the national church in the lands round Kiev and later acquired similar status in the Russian state and the religious and cultural dissonance between the East and West increased with each century. Catholicism was tolerated, but regarded as heresy, while Tsarist Russia never distinguished itself for religious toleration. It showed particular aggression towards the Uniate Church (Greek Orthodox Catholics) who, as a result of the Union of Brest-Litowsk (1596), became Catholic, but retained Eastern ritual and who, after the partitions of Poland found themselves under the sway of Moscow. The Revolution, in accordance with the view of Lenin (1870–1924), who regarded religion as the 'opium of the masses', became a great threat to all religions and Churches, but if it did make any concessions for political motives, then it was to the Russian Orthodox Church, which could be of some use. So the Patriarch remained in Moscow, as head of the Church, but now stripped of any power or significance and completely dependent on the political authorities. Simultaneously, Orthodox churches were being closed and changed into cinemas and museums and the clergy was being persecuted and deported *en masse* to camps, mainly on Solovetski Islands. The position of the Catholic Church was much worse, since Moscow did not recognise Rome and had no relations with the Vatican. There was a wholesale closure of churches and the Catholic and Uniate clergy were persecuted without mercy. In 1924 there were in Russia about 1 600 000 Catholics and barely 200 priests, whereas in 1921 it had been calculated that there were 900.[16]

Before the outbreak of the Second World War Catholicism in Russia continued to be under the ceaseless pressure of anti-religious and particularly anti-Vatican propaganda, churches were closed and the clergy for the most part in prisons and camps. The sole Catholic bishop able to work was the Apostolic Administrator in Moscow, the Frenchman Eugène Neveu, who was simultaneously parish priest of the single Catholic church open in the Russian capital. When, however, for health reasons, he returned to France, he was not allowed back and his duties were assumed by the American, Father Leopold Braun, who belonged to the American embassy. His functions were purely theoretical, since the Soviet authorities persecuted and provoked him at every step, quite preventing him from work.[17]

The Red Army's advance onto Polish soil on 17 September 1939 could not fail to arouse long-term fears for the fate of the Catholic and Uniate Churches.

Yet things turned out somewhat differently. Naturally the Soviet authorities, proclaiming atheism and anti-religious propaganda, could not but be associated with the struggle against religion, but it was not aimed solely at the Catholics and Uniates. There began an onslaught on each belief, each religion, and therefore on Catholicism, but without extreme brutality. The initial restrictions were directed at monasteries and seminaries, ordering them to vacate their buildings and justifying this by the Army's needs. A few seminarists were arrested, but on the whole both they and the monks were allowed to seek new accommodation. Churches and monasteries were deprived of their schools, which were nationalised, religious education in them was suspended and replaced by lessons in Marxism, crosses were removed from classrooms. All religious publications were banned and replaced by anti-religious propaganda, Priests were not arrested, except in isolated incidents, but when the great deportations to the East began, hundreds of them were among the deportees.[18]

All these directives and repressions hurt the Uniate Church more than the Catholic, since Russia had some long-standing scores to settle with the Uniates. In this instance old hatreds became more pressing than political considerations. The occupying power wanted to woo the Ukrainians, who were for the most part Uniate, and to demonstrate to them that Soviet rule was very much better than Polish, from which they had been liberated, and yet these anti-religious repressions achieved quite the opposite effect.[19]

On the Polish Eastern territories there were six Catholic dioceses: Lwów, Łomża, Łuck, Pińsk, part of Przemyśl and Wilno, together with 6.5 million faithful, not just Poles. Alongside them were three Uniate dioceses: Lwów, Przemyśl and Stanisławów – embracing more than 3 million faithful – and one Armenian diocese. Contrary to fears, the Soviet authorities did not attack them and did not aim at a speedy destruction of their organisational framework, but simply nationalised them, depriving them of their former status and imposing very high taxes. All the bishops remained at their posts and were allowed to carry out their pastoral duties, although there were occasional local difficulties. They were also allowed to remain in touch with the Vatican, although here there were some problems.[20]

This state of relative toleration, departing quite considerably from normal Soviet methods, had to have some motive and indeed it did. The first one probably derived from the assumption that a frontal assault on the Church and religion could wait, for political issues were more important, especially the rapid assimilation of occupied Polish territory and all the accompanying problems and difficulties. However, the second motive was related to the fact that both Churches, Catholic and Uniate, were subordinated to the Vatican which maintained diplomatic relations with all the great powers and which within many of them had millions of faithful. Both Hitler and Stalin regarded religion as their enemy and its representative churches as rivals for the control of souls, but they could not ignore them. Finally the third motive was political caution which suggested a certain care when taking on the Church and the Vatican in order not to make of them effectively allies of the Third Reich. Stalin had made a pact with Hitler and gave him every possible assistance, but he knew that the Chancellor was anti-communist and that he had a powerful army which could sooner or later turn against Russia. Before the fall of France it was still possible to hope for a general blood-letting in the West, but after June 1940 these hopes were shaken. The Vatican feared Communism and had suffered great losses at its hands; it might therefore out of necessity take the side of Hitler who was preparing an attack on Russia if antireligious excesses in the style of Nero [21] were to begin in territories conquered by the Soviets – Eastern Poland, the Baltic States, Romanian Bukowina and Bessarabia.

Since Moscow had decided that, for political reasons, the Vatican would retain some of its possessions in the territories incorporated into the Soviet empire, it had to be sure that the Russian Orthodox Church was represented there as well. Just opportunity had arisen and it was for this reason that there was an Orthodox Patriarch in Moscow. He was given instructions and in the spring of 1940 he nominated an Orthodox Metropolitan with his seat in Łuck and with authority extending over all the lands taken from Poland. His main task was to try to take over the three Uniate bishoprics and the 800 Uniate parishes and bring them back into the Orthodox fold. The NKVD offered its services and drew on its rich arsenal of well-tried measures to destroy the Uniate church and detach it from Vatican.[22]

With the passage of time pressure on the Catholic and Uniate Churches in the Eastern part of Poland grew, the obstacles increased as did the number of closed churches, but the Soviet authorities retained a semblance of religious freedom. However, just before the German attack in June 1941 and just after it had begun, when the Soviet authorities were evacuating in panic, they murdered thousands of prisoners, amongst them many priests arrested in the previous few weeks.[23]

THE VATICAN'S PROBLEMS AND ATTITUDES

On the eve of the outbreak of the Second World War the Vatican found itself in a very difficult situation. In February 1939 Pope Pius XI died, to be succeeded in March by Cardinal Eugenio Pacelli (1876–1958) who took the name Pius XII. This change occurred at an exceptionally difficult time and at the very moment when Hitler was marching into Czechoslovakia, having previously taken control of Sudetenland and assimilated Austria. A new war was very likely and feverish attempts were being made to avert it; the Vatican had to contribute to them, but it was unclear which line it should adopt. Naturally it had to be anti-Soviet, since Communism preached atheism, attacked every religion and thus was enemy number one for the Church. Moreover, the Church had already suffered at the hands of the Soviet Union, and this country as Orthodox, had for many centuries preached a different creed.

Two political camps were formed: on the one side Great Britain and France with Poland, which was to be the object of Hitler's next attack; on the other the Third Reich. Despite the most careful maintenance of neutrality it was necessary, of course in the greatest internal secrecy, to come down on one of two sides, since this would govern its outward behaviour. While the Vatican was reviewing this difficult dilemma, an unexpected complication arose: in May the British and the French sent a mission to Moscow to seek some kind of alliance before the impending storm. What should be done now? If the Vatican came to the conclusion that it should take the side of the Western democracies and they managed to come to an agreement with Russia, it would automatically become an ally of Communism. If it inwardly came to the conclusion that the German side was better, it would have the Western democracies, the guarantors of freedom, and ultra-Catholic Poland as its adversaries; and Hitler with his methods as an ally. The choice was difficult, for there was little difference between Communism and Nazism, each system attacked religion, both denied freedom and the victory of either would be a defeat for the Church.[24]

The only solution which could save the Vatican from the inevitability of taking one of the two sides, since complete neutrality was impossible, and which would also be beneficial for the whole world, was to avert the approaching conflict and from May Pius XII undertook a series of political initiatives. In the same month he sent an invitation to Great Britain, France, Poland and Italy for representatives of these countries to meet and discuss the most pressing current issues. It was not clearly stated, but the reason for the invitation was the view that there was some justification in the German demands towards Poland and that, perhaps, they should be met over the issue of Gdańsk (Danzig) and communications through Pomerania. The conference never came to anything, since the British, French and Poles did not agree to it. The Vatican would have liked the Poles to give in to Hitler for then, at least for a time, there would have been no need for Germany to attack Poland nor for Western intervention. After this failure the Pope tried three times, with Mussolini as intermediary, to influence Hitler not to go to war over Poland. These interventions took place on the 6 and 30 June and 29 August, just before the German attack. Furthermore, the Vatican tried by various means to persuade the German dictator to treat the British and French undertakings seriously, since both Great Britain and France would certainly declare war on Germany if he attacked Poland.[25]

Suddenly, on 23 August, the news broke that Hitler had signed a pact with Stalin and for some time the Vatican's diplomacy lost its bearings. Thus the greatest enemies of religion and the Church had become allies and if this alliance continued, the world would be faced with a threat to Western civilisation and Christian morality.

Several days later the German army was on the soil of Catholic Poland; and after two weeks the Red Army moved west in the direction of the Vistula. So it was the Nazis, who had been going to. crush Communism, who had themselves facilitated its Western expansion. Worse: by entangling themselves also in a war with the West they had created a situation in which there would be a great bloodbath between themselves and France and Great Britain, while godless Russia would calmly await the day on which it 'would deal Christian Europe the final blow'.[26]

Naturally the Vatican attempted to break the German–Soviet pact by trying to head off any further fighting in Europe and in December 1939 it prepared a five-point peace plan, but nothing came of it and the Vatican was forced to accept that Catholic Poland was under occupation by the two powers, who were treating the conquered country like a colony, while the Church there found itself in a very difficult position.

From the first weeks of both occupations the Vatican received from them precise information, since the Church's organisation continued to operate. Information about German-occupied territory went by means of Archbishop Cesare Orsenigo, the Papal Nuncio in Berlin – not the happiest of arrangements, since he had at the same time to protect the Church's interests in Poland and to improve relations with the Reich, which was quite impossible. Moreover he was fascinated by Germany's power and during the first years of the war this attitude greatly influenced his reactions and reports. Unfortunately, Archbishop Filippo Cortesi, the Papal Nuncio in Poland, had left Warsaw with the diplomatic corps, a step of which the Vatican had been critical, but there did exist secret Polish channels for sending information to Rome. The Polish Primate, Cardinal Hlond, who was already there, kept his eye on these matters. From the area of Soviet occupation information was sent by the bishops still working there and this channel of communication was quite efficient.[27]

The Vatican took one step which, in the current European situation, was of some significance. In January 1940 it named its plenipotentiary to the Polish Government in France, Monsignor Alfredo Pacini, Papal Nuncio in Romania. This was a symbolic act, but it did prove that the Holy See had not recognised the partition of Poland.[28] There were further steps. After their victory in the West, the Germans demanded that the bishoprics on the territory of the Protectorate of Bohemia and Moravia and in Poland should be given to German bishops. The Vatican refused claiming that it did not recognise the new boundaries and that only after a peace treaty had been signed, could it accept the state of affairs then obtaining.[29]

These were important actions, but they lacked real impact in comparison with what was actually happening in occupied Poland. A struggle was taking place there for the life of a nation, a resistance movement was already in existence, the occupiers were using the most brutal methods, there were mass deportations and the Polish nation, overwhelmingly Catholic, expected a firm stance on the part of the Holy See. This took place on 20 October 1939 in the papal encyclical *Summi pontificatus*, which attacked the war as anti-Christian, but the passage on Poland contained only the remark that thousands of families were enduring hard times.[30] There was no direct mention of the aggressors and their methods; they were not condemned. An act, which could be construed as such, took place for the first time when, after the German attack in the West, the Pope sent expressions of support to the heads of state of Belgium, Holland and Luxemburg, but this was a purely diplomatic move. The Polish nation, which had been faithful to Rome for so long, had not allowed schism to spread in its country and had retained Catholicism as its national religion, now felt abandoned and left to its fate. The atmosphere in Poland was such that it had been expected that the Vatican would throw a curse on the aggressors, although it was difficult to imagine that either Hitler or Stalin would find themselves in the role of the German emperor, Henry IV, who in 1077 had to go to Canossa to abase himself before Pope Gregory VII.

The German attack on Russia in June 1941 was greeted in the Vatican with great relief, since the alliance of the two hostile powers had collapsed and there now appeared a real chance that Communism might be defeated and pushed out of Eastern Europe. On the other hand it was reasonable to assume that now that the West would seek an alliance with the Soviet Union to prevent Hitler's victory and would thus save Stalin and his system. The best outcome would have been a German Victory in Russia and the destruction of the world base of Communism, to be followed by the subsequent defeat of Hitler by the West; but such an outcome, dreamed in of Poland, was too ideal to be possible.

The German onslaught almost ended in victory, but the Soviets caught their breath, which gave them the opportunity for some intensive diplomatic activity. One of its aims was the improvement of relations with the Vatican, since Russia was benefiting from the enormous aid being sent from the West and wanted to be seen there as a democratic country of religious toleration. These efforts did not bring results, for although the Vatican ceased attacking the atheistic Soviet state, it did not attack German aggression and explained this to the West by saying that Russia was only pretending to acknowledge religious freedom and, in the event of defeat for the Germans, would assume hegemony over Europe. Then it would become not only a threat to the old continent, but also to Western culture and the whole world.[31]

This attitude was based on moral grounds and on the justified perception of Communism as a philosphical doctrine with ambitions of replacing religion and a belief in God by a materialist philosophy. In this form Communism was the most dangerous enemy to the culture of the Western world, possessing moreover a world-wide influence and scope. Naturally this strength was based first on the great might and size of the Soviet Union, but in the Vatican's opinion, even if this Union was destroyed in war, this would not herald the end of Communism. However, by the same reasoning National Socialism was connected exclusively with Hitler and his era in the history of the German state. A defeat in war would have to bring an end to this doctrine, which was based too patently on an absurd notion of the superiority of the Nordic race over others, to be able to survive. It had no philosophical basis and diffused only power and demagoguery, nothing else.

On the basis of such an assessment and seeing that the Germans could destroy, or at least greatly weaken the Soviet Union, Pope Pius XII preferred to show a certain restraint in his condemnation of National Socialism. He knew Germany well, for as Bishop Eugenio Pacelli he had already in 1917 been in Munich as Papal Nuncio to Bavaria and in 1920 had moved to Berlin as Nuncio for the whole of Germany. He had remained there until 1930 and had come to know the country well; he had come to recognise its cultural worth and the deep philosophy of Catholicism there and felt an affection for it. In 1930 – before Hitler came to power – he had been recalled to Rome, given his cardinal's hat and had become the Vatican Secretary of State. It was during his tenure of office, in 1937, that Pius XI has issued his famous anti-Nazi encyclical, *Mit Brennender Sorge*, which

Cardinal Pacelli had even strengthened. It was still binding and Pius XII had not departed from it, but did not repeat it during the war. The Vatican was also restrained by the fact that on territories controlled by or associated with the Reich there were about 150 million Catholics. In some countries they were treated well and there was hope that this state of affairs might continue even in the event of a German victory. Only in Poland were the Germans arresting bishops, while in France, Croatia and Slovakia the Church enjoyed almost complete freedom.[32]

The restrained and reasoned stance of the Vatican, which was justified in the long term, however, did not suit the Poles. The first Soviet occupation lasted twenty-two months and brought the Poles much harm and humiliation, but it ended after the German attack when the whole country fell into the hands of the Nazis. Western and Central Poland had not known Soviet occupation, while Eastern Poland, which had been awaiting the overthrow of NKVD rule, quickly realised that little had changed. The images of Soviet deception, repressions and the great deportations paled rather quickly; the Soviets joined the Allied camp; the Polish Government in London made an agreement with Moscow; over a period a Polish army was formed in the Soviet Union and a small number of Poles joined the Soviet ideological camp. Meanwhile throughout Poland the reign of German terror increased to an incredible level, the concentration camps bulged, round-ups and public executions increased, the mass murder of Jews began.

In this situation the Poles expected that the powerful, clear, authoritative voice of the Vatican would speak out in their defence. This voice did not ring out in the form, extent and with the power that the Poles expected.

Yet Catholicism in Poland was not left to its own devices, the centuries-old ties which bound it to Rome weakened the force of the occupation. The Church's role in the nation's struggle for survival and for its soul was very great and was evident in almost every area of national life. Despite losses and setbacks, the network of parishes covered the whole country and in its ministry brought comfort, faith and hope. Despite personal risk, priests used their pulpits for maintaining national spirit and encouraged resistance, the bishoprics were a visible sign of the existence of an organisation, although not governmental, and the resistance movement was full of clergy in all sorts of positions. A great role in the rescue of Jews, particularly children, was played by the monasteries, and Cardinal Adam

Sapieha, whom even the Germans decided not to touch in his archiepiscopal seat at Cracow, was a symbol of the nation's resistance and pride. Such an attitude had to bring victims and there were very many of them. Thousands of priests died in prisons and camps, thousands of churches were confiscated, closed or destroyed, priceless collections of religious art, holy vessels and liturgical garments disappeared forever, many monasteries were destroyed, many of the Church's possessions were ruined, but the Catholic Church emerged from the war victorious, spiritually strengthened, inwardly toughened by its losses, surrounded by universal respect and ready for the new difficult days ahead. The same must be said for the Uniate and Evangelical Churches, both of which came through the war victoriously.

7 The Collapse of France; The Polish Government in London

THE GERMAN ATTACK ON THE WEST

After his victory over Poland, his rear secure by his pact with Stalin, Hitler was immediately able to turn his gaze to the West. He was so certain of his ally, who was supporting him with great quantities of raw materials, that he left in Poland only as many divisions as the occupation required, concentrating all his forces on the Western front. The triumphant *Blitzkrieg* against the Polish army had so increased his confidence that as early as 9 October 1939 he issued a directive for an autumn attack on France, but the bad weather and his generals' persuasiveness forced him to postpone it.[1] This allowed him peacefully to build up his forces and deploy every necessary unit in the West.

At the beginning of May 1940 the German forces ready for battle consisted of 114 infantry divisions, ten armoured divisions, six motorised divisions (two of them SS), one cavalry division and one airborne division, with 2700 tanks and 3800 aircraft.

This was a powerful force, but in numbers it did not exceed those of the Western Allies who, thanks to Polish resistance, had gained seven valuable months and had been able to mobilise peacefully and carry out a great many improvements. In addition to the units manning the Maginot Line, France possessed 77 infantry divisions, three armoured divisions, three divisions of light tanks, five cavalry divisions, three Spahi brigades, 3000 tanks and 1450 aircraft of which 540 were fighters, but inferior to German ones. The British Expeditionary Force under Lord Gort (1886–1946) consisted of nine infantry divisions, three infantry brigades, three divisions without artillery, 200 tanks, 400 armoured cars and 474 aircarft (ten fighter squadrons). The modest Polish forces were also of value and since Hitler had decided to violate Belgian and Dutch neutrality, he was faced with a further thirty-six divisions there.[2]

German superiority, and it was a crushing one, was expressed in a new offensive doctrine of war, in the courage to implement it and in the practical application of the concept of total war. This meant the continuation of the same brutal methods which had been used in Poland, and Hitler, who was hoping for a quick victory and was benefiting from his recent experiences, had no qualms.

At dawn on 10 May 1940 German aircarft appeared over the cities of Belgium and Holland and dropped bombs, German paratroops captured the airfield at Rotterdam, a 'fifth column' surfaced in Luxemburg and tanks crossed the frontiers of the two small democracies and penetrated onto French soil in what was apparently the least suitable place, namely in the wooded and almost impassable Ardennes.

The Germans encountered resistance everywhere, but after five days, despite the French sending their Seventh Army to help, Holland capitulated. The German threat of more aerial attacks on open towns proved decisive. In Belgium, thanks to the element of surprise, German tanks crossed the undamaged bridges, fanning out then over the flat terrain. The French and the British sent their forces to the rescue, but the German attack was not halted.[3]

However, the most unexpected attack came through the Ardennes. General Heinz Guderian's panzer divisions broke through narrow tracks, the forests and the precipices and, heading for Sedan, crossed the Moselle. The Maginot Line, which was further to the south, played no role whatsoever and the road towards the English Channel stood wide open.[4]

The German attack, which within such a short space of time had achieved more than even Hitler himself had expected, shook the Western democracies. On the first day of the attack, before the outcome was apparent, the conciliatory British Prime Minister Chamberlain, who believed in treaties, resigned to be replaced by the dynamic Winston Churchill (1874–1965), a believer in battle and resistance, who formed a coalition government. Five days later he received a telephone call from Paris from the French Premier, with the short message: 'We have lost the battle'. Churchill boarded an aircraft and the following day was conferring in the French capital with Paul Reynaud, and was opposing any Allied withdrawal from Belgium. The French Premier decided on a firm step: he replaced General Gamelin by the 72-year-old General Weygand as

Commander-in-Chief and appointed the 85-year-old Marshall
Philippe Pétain (1856–1951) as deputy Prime Minister.[5]

Changes of command could no longer save the situation and within
several days north-east France together with Belgium was cut off
from the rest of the country. The whole British Expeditionary Force
was there together with a great many French divisions. General
Guderian moved further north and ocupied the ports of Boulogne
and Calais, only Dunkirk remained in Allied hands. If this port were
also taken, the British army would find itself caught in a trap.

There then occurred an event which to this day remains a mystery
and which historians interpret in different ways. On 24 May Hitler
appeared at Von Rundstedt's headquarters and, on discovering that
the General had halted his forces to regroup, ordered the advance to
be halted for three days. It is possible that political considerations
prompted this decision, for he did not want a war with Great Britain,
was afraid of her and hoped that after defeating France he would be
able to encourage her to make peace. Under these circumstances
sparing the British Expeditionary Force would be understandable.[6]

Irrespective of the motives for Hitler's decision, the three days
grace allowed the British to organise an improvised evacuation. On
27 May there began at Dunkirk the process of loading which
continued until 4 June. On the beaches of southern England around
Dover about 190 000 British and 140 000 French troops now found
themselves, exhausted, ragged, but safe. All their equipment was
lost.[7]

In this first phase of fighting in the West, which can be called the
battle of Flanders, the Polish forces took no part. They were further
south and only when, on 5 June, the Germans struck the French
defensive line strung out along the rivers Somme and Aisne, did their
short battle begin.

The agreement between Generals Sikorski and Gamelin had
stipulated that the Polish units would form their own corps and would
operate as a unit, but events changed this. The Germans broke the
French defences and it turned out the French commanders had not
allocated any reserves. In this situation any unit, however poorly
trained, was thrown into the battle.[8]

POLISH UNITS IN ACTION

Two Polish divisions were in a state of readiness: the 1st Grenadiers
and the 2nd Infantry Fusiliers. The 10th Armoured Cavalry Brigade

was partially available; moreover among the French regiments there were eight Polish infantry companies and two anti-tank batteries; finally the untrained 3rd Division could be of some help as well as two battalions from Coëtquidan. Altogether this amounted to 40 000 men determined to fight for any position.[9]

The 1st Grenadier Division was deployed to the south-west of Nancy within the French Twentieth Corps, whose task was the defence of the Maginot Line near the river Saare. Even before the German thrust in the south the Corps commander deprived the division of its artillery, then of its anti-tank units and then its engineer battalion, considerably weakening its combat effectiveness. The division's involvement in hard defensive fighting began on 14 June, at the very same time that the Germans were entering undefended Paris, and lasted only one week.

The two-day battle at Lagarde on 17 and 18 June was a great military success, but unfortunately of no further use, since the neighbouring French divisions' withdrawal forced the division to surrender the terrain it was defending. During this battle, on 17 June, the new French Premier, Marshal Pétain, approached the Germans with the proposal for a ceasefire and it was clear that the fighting was coming to the end. On 19 June a radio bulletin from General Sikorski was picked up stating that Poland would continue to fight as an ally of Great Britain, and ordered his men to make a speedy breakthrough to the south, to the ports there, or to cross the Swiss frontier.[10]

The 2nd Fusilier Infantry Division found itself in June in the vicinity of Belfort, not far from the Swiss frontier, and joined the Fifteenth Corps. The Germans were expected to attack from the north, but they unexpectedly appeared from the west heading for the Swiss frontier, so the division was given the order to attack in the direction of Besançon. It had to deploy at speed, for the Germans were attempting an encirclement and so the division headed for Pontarlier. The approach of German motorised armoured forces forced it to halt and prepare defensive positions on the hills of Clos-du-Doubs. The battle lasted two days; the Germans were unable to break through the Polish defences, but the men were very tired and ammunition and food were running low; meanwhile Franco-German discussions on a ceasefire were taking place and so the commanding General gave the order to cross the Swiss frontier. This took place during the night of the 19/20 June.[11]

The 10th Armoured Cavalry Brigade was not yet ready and so a unit of 102 officers and 607 other ranks was formed and went to the front under the command of the Seventh Corps. The unit fought from 13 to 16 June in the area of Champaubert and Montbart and that night, realising the futility of continuing the battle, destroyed its equipment and filtered south in small groups.[12]

Of the Polish air force only the I/145 Warsaw squadron took part in the fighting as a complete unit and also six small formations of the 'Montpellier Flight'. A further six such formations operated with various French squadrons, as did five units called 'chimneys' which defended factories and airfields, all over the country. At the moment of the German attack the Warsaw squadron was in the Lyons area, it was then moved to an airfield at Mions and on 6 June was incorporated into the French 42nd fighter group to defend a sector of the Seine between Vernon and Menton. Between 8 and 10 June the squadron was involved in combat with German fighters and bombers over Rouen and Dreux, shooting down eleven aircraft. After a few days at Semaise undergoing training on *Blochs*, the squadron was taken by road on 13 June to Châteauroux, where it was to defend the airfield. During combat operations on 19 June in which the squadron shot down a plane, the Commander-in-Chief's broadcast ordering immediate evacuation was picked up. The airmen proceeded to the port of La Rochelle and the following day sailed for Great Britain.[13]

The 'Montpellier Flight's' formations fought in various places within assorted French units. The results in aerial combat were excellent: twenty-five enemy planes were shot down, for a loss of only three pilots. After the cease-fire, the formations in Southern France, mainly from Perpignan, flew off to North Africa, and a certain number of airmen made their way straight to Great Britain by way of Gibraltar. The other six formations, scattered all over France, shot down five aircraft. The 'chimneys' also did a fine job, notching up eleven victories. Overall the Polish fighters in France shot down fifty German aircraft and almost certainly damaged a further five or six, losing eleven pilots in the air. A further fifteen airmen were killed on the ground.[14]

While the desperate defensive battles were being fought in France, the *Podhalańska* Brigade was fighting in Norway in the Franco-British expeditionary corps. It belonged to that group of Allied forces whose task was the capture of Narvik, inside the Arctic Circle, and the destruction of the port and the railway line.

The Brigade was allotted two tasks: to capture the little town of Ankers, opposite Narvik on the other side of the fjord, and also the little town of Beisfiord. Both tasks were accomplished on 27 and 28

May. On the evening of 29 May the Germans abandoned Narvik and a Norwegian infantry battalion went in. However, several days later the evacuation began and between 3 and 8 June the Brigade left Norway in the company of Allied units. The Norwegian King and Government also left for Great Britain. At the field cemetery near the town of Meiri two Polish officers and ninety-five other ranks were left behind. Also on 5 June the submarine *Orzeł* found its resting place in Norwegian waters with six officers and forty-nine seamen. The Brigade travelled by convoy to the Scottish port at Greenock whence on 13 June it left for France aboard a number of ships in the hope that it might still manage to join in some of the desperate fighting. The following day it landed in Brest only to seek a way almost immediately of returning to Great Britain. About 3000 men, some of them from the *Podhalańska* Brigade, were evacuated from Brest on British ships.[15]

THE SIKORSKI–CHURCHILL MEETING

During these hectic and tragic days General Sikorski left Angers, where the Polish government had been moved, and made his way to his field headquarters near Nancy, wishing to be as close as possible to Polish soldiers in action. He then moved from place to place and was difficult to find, thus causing a great many complications, since he was also Prime Minister. He believed in the greatness of the French, never even contemplating the idea of defeat and so was unable to plan the withdrawal of Polish forces and their evacuation. Moreover, this was completely impossible, for they were operating in isolation, belonged to different operational units and it was difficult to withdraw them during the battle, especially when the Polish soldiers wanted to fight and not run away.

However, when on 17 June Marshal Pétain approached the Germans for a ceasefire, General Sikorski was at Libourne (the current seat of the Polish President and Government), met the French Premier, issued a declaration of Polish determination to continue the fight and demanded help in rescuing Polish units. When he realised that France was definitely going to capitulate and was incapable of any further action, he turned his gaze towards Great Britain and flew to London the following day. Churchill himself facilitated this by sending an aircraft to Libourne. On 19 June Churchill called a conference with the Polish ambassador, Edward

Raczyński, present. The British Prime Minsiter emphasised that Great Britain would continue the war and that she would immediately accept the Polish President and Government and would also help to rescue Polish soldiers from France. Sikorski had talks with the Admiralty, the necessary orders were issued and the BBC transmitted the Commander-in-Chief's orders dealing with the evacuation from sinking France.[16]

EVACUATION TO GREAT BRITAIN

The following day General Sikorski, back again in Libourne, issued a series of orders for the evacuation and during the night returned to England in the company of General Sosnkowski. Urgent political and military problems awaited him there, for after the French phase, there now began co-operation with the British. On the same day, 21 June, the Polish President, Władysław Raczkiewicz, arrived in London to be met at the station by the King, George VI.

The evacuation of the Polish troops began on 19 June from the port of La Rochelle in Western France and two days later from Bordeaux, Bayonne and St Jean de Luz, close to the Spanish frontier. The Polish liner *Batory* came into Bayonne and the *Sobieski* to St Jean de Luz. They took off over 4000 soliders and 500 civilians and set sail for Great Britain. Up to 25 June British passenger and merchant vessels carried out an emergency evacuation under the protection of naval vessels which kept the German aircraft at bay. Ports in north-west France – Brest, St Malo and St Nazaire – were also used. Meanwhile Polish airmen, some of whom had also been in North Africa, were being evacuated from the small Mediterranean ports of Vendres and Sète. In addition to the *Batory* and *Sobieski*, some small Polish vessels also took part. The number of rescued Polish soldiers is not certain and varies between 16 000 and 23 000, of whom a very large number, about 5000, were officers. The official figure released by the deputy minister of military affairs at a meeting of the National Council in London on 30 August 1940, was 19 457.[17]

This comes out at a little less than 20 per cent of the total. This was not a bad result given the chaos of the time, the lack of transport and the dispersion of Polish units, with the additional factor that a significant number of the men mobilised in France from the émigrés living there preferred to return home.

THE SITUATION IN OCCUPIED POLAND

In Poland the news of the fall of France came like a thunderbolt. The two countries had for centuries been linked by strong political and cultural ties, the Napoleonic era had sown a romantic seed and in the darkest years of the partitions Polish patriots had been able to seek refuge and operate freely on French soil. The First World War had consolidated faith in French arms and the Maginot Line was a symbol of French might. Suddenly this idealised, heroic France fell; worse, she surrendered almost without a fight.

At the last moment, just before leaving French soil on 18 June 1940, General Sosnkowski sent a radio signal to Warsaw via Bucharest in which he terminated the artificial temporary command structure, named General Rowecki (who had meantime been promoted) deputy to the Commander-in-Chief of the ZWZ for the whole of Poland and gave him very wide authority for independent action in case of the disruption of communications with the Government. In such an eventuality he was to act in agreement with the political parties. The signal also said that the fight would continue alongside Great Britain and that there should be a reduction of underground activity and that armed actions should cease and the whole effort should now become long-term.[18]

These very understandable orders considerably altered resistance plans, for between 29 May and 2 June, just before the German victory in the West, a very important conference had taken place in Belgrade, which was to set up a quite different arrangement for resistance work in Poland. The conference was attended by representatives of the Polish military authorities in France, representatives of the military resistance from both zones of occupation, German and Soviet, as well as the communications base commanders in Budapest and Bucharest.[19] The situation on the Western Front was disastrous and the conference began at exactly the moment when the dramatic evacuation of the shattered British divisions was taking place at Dunkirk. The participants knew about it, yet the discussions were optimistic and a long war was not foreseen. Many future matters were agreed and decisions taken to improve the efficiency of the bases and the transfer to Poland of instructions and money. There was also discussion of how to galvanise and expand the activities of the underground army in both zones of occupation.[20]

All these plans and hopes collapsed together with France and the reality of the situation was brought home by General Sosnkowski's signal of 18 June; everyone now had to prepare for a long, very hard war of incalculable consequences. It was also to be anticipated that contact with the authorities in the west would be lost, resulting in complete independent action, both political and military, and so on 28 June the Political Advisory Committee became the Chief Political Committee. It was completely independent of the ZWZ command and this had happened with the full approval of General Rowecki. However, this seemed to be an inadequate solution and so on 3 July, on the initiative of the General, the representatives of the three parties brought into being a collective Government Delegacy, consisting of four people: the representatives of the PPS, SL and SN plus General Rowecki. At the same time a radio signal which had been sent from London by General Sosnkowski on 30 June arrived in Warsaw via Bucharest. It contained General Sikorski's decision to set up the ZWZ Headquarters in Poland with General Rowecki in command. The signal also stated that in the case of a breakdown in communications, the bases would be under the complete command of the General and once again exhorted everyone to caution, to long-term work, and to oppose any attempts to come to terms with the occupiers and to maintain faith in eventual victory.[21] This decision placed Stefan Rowecki in one of the leading positions in the Polish nation's fight for survival.

The rout of their opponents in the West enormously increased the Germans' self-confidence, which in its Nazi form appeared above all in increased terrorisation. On 14 June 1940 at exactly the same time that Wehrmacht units were entering Paris, the first transport of Polish political prisoners arrived at Auschwitz and historians have accepted this date as the beginning of the greatest death camp in the history of the world. From the prison in Tarnów were brought 728 young men, mainly caught escaping over the Hungarian and Slovak borders on their way to the Polish army in France, a number of priests, a number of schoolteachers and several dozen Jews.[22] Deportations continued in the lands incorporated into the Reich whence Poles were expelled to the *General Gouvernement*. The already inhuman laws for the Jews were stiffened. A site was also prepared for the creation of a great ghetto in Warsaw, which became fact in November 1940.[23]

Hitler's success in France, particularly in such a short time, did not at all please Stalin, who had hoped for long positional battles on the model of the First World War and blood-letting on both sides. Since, however, that had not happened, he made the most of the situation.

First, after the aggressive war with Finland in which territory to the North of Leningrad had been captured, predatory Soviet hands reached for the Baltic states. Under the pretext that they were not fulfilling the agreements of the autumn of 1939 that the Soviet Union annexed them into its empire between 17 and 23 June and in July held 'elections', which naturally expressed the spontaneous will of the Lithuanians, Latvians and Estonians accepting the Soviet political system and expressing joy that they had been accepted into the brotherly union. Depriving them of their freedom was not enough, these small nations had also to be humiliated by falsified elections. On 27 June, continuing its plunder, Russia detached Bessarabia from Romania. On 1 August 1940 Molotov reported on these matters quite openly at a session of the Supreme Soviet of the USSR.[24] Recalling the attitude of the Western Allies, who had wanted to help Finland and had subsequently intervened in Norway, Stalin preferred to accomplish these annexations while the drama in the West reached its zenith.

In the Eastern Polish territories, which already formally belonged to the Soviet Union, the process of Sovietisation and the weakening of Polish elements was continuing. Towards the end of June and in July further deportations took place involving 240 000 people. Through these lands great supplies of raw materials continued to flow to Germany. Internally Stalin might well chew bitterly on the unexpected Germany success, but ostensibly he was still the most faithful of Allies. Moreover he realised that his German friend, after his victory in France and with so many divisions under arms, could change his political orientation and turn against him.

Poland had not experienced such a difficult time since the dark days of the September campaign. All her hopes pinned on France were in ruins, the partially rebuilt Polish army there had disintegrated and the occupying powers had increased terror to unheard-of heights. Russia continued to plunder new lands and had sent hundreds of thousands of Poles to Siberia, while German propaganda stated that the end of war had come, since it only remained for Great Britain to capitulate. Yet there was no question of surrender, the fight had to continue but how?

GREAT BRITAIN FIGHTS ON

The instructions which had reached General Rowecki from London spread round Poland in the form of secret orders and gave some hope of further struggle and of an eventual, albeit very distant, success, although they did not make it clear how this was to be achieved. France, in whom everyone had believed, had fallen and there remained only Great Britain which was little known in Poland. Her great fleet was no guarantee of a land victory, and it was feared that a realistic assessment of the situation would have to force her to a compromise. The Munich conference and the pliability of the British Prime Minister of the day were remembered. Then it had been Czechoslovakia which had paid for the compromise, now it would be the end not only of Poland, but of almost the whole of Europe.

And then, when hope seemed ever more illusory, on 14 July, the anniversary of the storming of the Bastille and a great French holiday, rang out a voice full of resolution and faith in victory, the voice not of a Frenchman, but of the British Prime Minister, Winston Churchill:

> We shall fight on the beaches, we shall fight on the landing grounds, we shall fight in the fields and in the streets, we shall fight in the hills; we shall never surrender!

8 The Rebuilding of the Polish Army in Great Britain; The Polish Air Force

DIFFICULTIES OF GENERAL SIKORSKI IN LONDON

The fall of France put General Sikorski in a very difficult position, since his political opponents, particularly from the *Sanacja* camp, accused him of having wasted the Polish army and tried to remove him from power. An additional pretext for their attack was a memorandum submitted by the General to the British Foreign Secretary, Lord Halifax. The memorandum suggested that Hitler could only be defeated on the dissolution of his alliance with Stalin and that, in such an eventuality, there would arise an opportunity to form a Polish army on Soviet soil. Although this was indeed what happened not long afterwards, in July 1940 the General's enemies considered him almost a traitor. President Raczkiewicz relieved him of the premiership, but such was the Army's influence that the crisis lasted barely twenty-four hours.[1]

However, relations with the British authorities and the local population were most encouraging and much better than they had been with the French. From their first moments ashore the Polish stragglers felt that they had landed in a country which was not afraid of the approaching threat and was perfectly calm and confident of eventual victory. Everywhere they found smiling, friendly faces and efficient organisation, which was in sharp contrast to the French muddle.

The first ships carrying Polish stragglers appeared in British ports on 24 June, and, on arrival, they were formed into convoys and sent to hastily-erected camps in Scotland. A Polish camp command was set up as early as 5 July with its headquarters at Eastend, near Lanark.

In addition to the British–Polish pact of 25 August 1939 there were two further agreements, the first of which, that of 18 November 1939, covered the Polish navy and the second, of 11 June 1940, the air force. The situation, however, required further clarification. Therefore, on 5 August a British–Polish military agreement was concluded, covering the formation of the Polish armed forces, this time on British soil, and their structure and regulations which conformed to local laws and customs.

REBUILDING OF THE ARMY

At this time the strength of all Polish armed forces – army, navy and air force – on British territory was 26 282 men of whom more than 7000 were officers. Furthermore the 4432 strong Carpathian Brigade had moved from Syria to Palestine and was thus also on territory under British control. These numbers were not great and the problem of finding new recruits had to be tackled. France was now completely out of the running; more than 23 000 men were still in Romania and Hungary, but because of German and Soviet pressure, their evacuation was becoming more difficult, while the Baltic states, now occupied by Russia, no longer counted. The supply of manpower from Poland had now become very much more difficult, and only the western hemisphere remained. As early as July General Sikorski had sent an officer to Ottawa as head of a recruiting mission. Presently the United States and South America, principally Argentina, were to be the target for a voluntary recruiting drive.

These were long-term exercises, meanwhile something had to be done with what was currently available in Great Britain. The Poles' British hosts were conspicuously helpful in this, for it was an extremely difficult time, with a threat of invasion, and every soldier was vital. The Polish units were entrusted with the defence of an area of the Scottish East Coast about 100km long from the Firth of Forth to Montrose with Perth more or less in the middle. Two brigades of almost completely motorised fusiliers were hastily formed, with armour, artillery, engineers, signals and other supporting arms. Because of the great surplus of officers, five further skeleton brigades were formed, with a complete command structure, but a nominal number of men. In addition to this, four squadrons of armoured trains were formed, each with three trains, manned almost exclusively by officers (forty-seven officers and five other ranks on each train). There still remained a significant surplus of officers of active-service age and so the British assigned 264 captains, lieutenants and second lieutenants to their own units in West Africa. In early spring the First Polish Corps began to be formed, the 2nd Fusilier Brigade was called the 10th Armoured Cavalry Brigade and General Maczek was appointed to command it. General Marian Kukiel, who had been in charge of the Polish camps, was appointed to command the First Polish Corps.[2]

FURTHER DEVELOPMENT OF THE AIR FORCE

When the Polish authorities arrived in Great Britain, the Polish Air Force there still had no units of its own. All its equipment had been lost in France and its personnel was still getting out by various routes, while within the British Isles it was a period of organisation. So the first Polish pilots to take part in air operations over Great Britain served in British squadrons. At first there were about forty of them and later their number rose to eighty-one. The first Polish fighter squadron to be formed was 302 Poznań squadron at Leconfield on 13 July and based on personnel from I/145th squadron evacuated from France. On 27 July it received its Hurricane aircraft and on 14 August became operational. It was commanded by a Scot with his Polish counterpart. The next squadron to form was 303 'Tadeusz Kościuszko' on 2 August at Northolt, near London. In 1940 further fighter squadrons were fomed: 306, 307 (night fighters) and 308 as well as 300 and 301 bomber squadrons and finally 309 reconnaissance squadron, but none of them was able to contribute to the decisive battles of that year.[3]

The Polish squadrons were under direct British command in all matters of organisation, active duty, training, supply and resupply, manpower levels and discipline, but a Polish Air Forces Inspectorate was created to act as liaison with the British Air Ministry. It co-operated in the administration of Polish personnel and had the right to inspect Polish squadrons. It was formed in October under the command of General Stanisław Ujejski (b. 1891).

Two Polish destroyers had taken part in the evacuation of British forces from Dunkirk, the *Błyskawica* and the *Burza*, the latter being seriously damaged by two bombs. After the refit she returned to active duty in August and together with the *Błyskawica*, the first Polish cruiser, the *Garland* (handed over by the British in May 1940), and the single submarine, *Wilk*, formed a small Polish navy under British command.

In London General Sikorski was simultaneously rebuilding the army high command. Within a few weeks a skeleton staff for the Commander-in-Chief was set up in the *Rubens* hotel close to Buckingham Palace. Since the ZWZ Headquarters had been moved to Poland an independent Sixth Bureau was set up under General Sosnkowski within the staff to liaise with the occupied country.

THE 'BATTLE OF BRITAIN'

On 17 July 1940 Hitler issued secret directive no. 16 dealing with the attack on the British Isles which was given the code-name *Sea Lion*. This apparently simple plan could only succeed if the German Air Force gained superiority in the air, which Grand Admiral Erich Raeder laid down as an essential condition for beginning the whole operation.[4]

Marshal Hermann Göring was quite confident of this, since in the West he had at his disposal great forces numbering 3000 aircraft. This figure consisted of 1400 medium-range bombers (*Dorniers, Junkers* and *Heinkels*), 300 dive-bombers (*Stukas*), over 800 single-seat fighters (*Messerschmidt 109s*) and about 300 two-seater (*Messerschmidt 110s*). Of these about 2500 were ready for action, 656 of them *Messerschmidt 109s*.

Against this formidable force Great Britain could muster fifty-seven fighting squadrons with barely 531 *Spitfires* and *Hurricanes* ready for immediate use. The Germans also had an advantage in numbers of pilots who, moreover, were for the most part veterans of the fighting in the Spanish Civil War, in Poland and in France. On the other hand British industry led Germany, producing monthly 500 fighters which were better than the *Messerschmidt 109s*, of which the Germans could produce only 140 in a month.

The whole of Fighter Command was headed by 60-year-old Air Chief Marshal Sir Hugh Dowding, who would not have had much chance in the battle with the great German odds had he not possessed a great advantage, which was shrouded in the utmost secrecy. This advantage was the ability to be able to read the German's most secret radio signals. This was only possible through the achievements of

Polish cryptologists, who before the war had broken the secret of *Enigma*, the German coding machine, and had passed on their results to the French and the British. The latter made full use of them and built a secret cryptological centre at Bletchley Park midway between Oxford and Cambridge with 10 000 people working there, and throughout the whole war they read German messages encoded on *Enigma*. The Germans had complete confidence in their system and during the Battle of Britain Göring sent all his orders by radio. Marshal Dowding belonged to a small group of people who knew the secret; he knew the German orders and knew his enemy's intentions. Göring's aim was to engage all the British fighters in one great battle and destroy them, thus opening the road to the British Isles. Dowding never let that happen, he husbanded his forces for the decisive moment, surprised the Germans and won the final victory. He had a great many enemies, who attacked him for his apparently incomprehensible decisions, since they did not know the secret of *Enigma*. As a result of their pressure Dowding was retired shortly after such an important victory. He kept the secret and died before the breaking of *Enigma* was revealed.

In the Battle of Britain, which has been described many times, about 1500 RAF pilots took part, 151 of them Polish. This was the largest contingent of foreign pilots, for New Zealand contributed 101, Canada ninety-four, Czechoslovakia eighty-seven, Belgium twenty-nine, and France fourteen.[5] In British squadrons there were eighty-one Poles and the other seventy comprised the crews of 302 and 303 squadrons. 302 squadron was in action on 15 August and six days later shot down its first *Junkers*; 303 squadron became an active unit on 30 August in the most irregular fashion when, during a training flight and without orders, Lieutenant Ludwik Paszkiewicz shot down a *Dornier*.[6]

The Battle's climax was reached on 15 September when Göring launched 328 bombers and 769 fighters against Southern England. Marshal Dowding, forewarned by Bletchley Park of this decisive German attack, sent up twenty-three squadrons. More than 300 *Spitfires* and *Hurricanes* engaged the Germans, scattered them, forcing them to drop their bombs blindly, and then chased them off. The same fate befell the second wave of German aircraft at the hands of twenty-nine British squadrons.[7]

Because of considerations of propaganda, both sides during the war published false figures, minimising their own losses and exaggerating those of their enemy. Therefore, there were subsequently many difficulties in calculating real figures which are now hard to assess. From 10 July to the end of October RAF pilots shot down 1733 German aircraft of all types (propaganda figures were 2698) and damaged a further 643. This figure includes the 203 aircraft shot down by Poles: 302 squadron – sixteen, 303 squadron – 110, Poles serving in British squadrons – seventy-seven. British losses amounted to 914 *Spitfires* and *Hurricanes* (the Germans claimed 3058) as well as 450 damaged. 481 pilots were killed, 422 were wounded, some of them never returned to active duty. The number of dead includes thirty-three Poles. 302 squadron lost seven, 303 – six, the RAF squadrons thirteen and seven died of wounds.[8]

NEGOTIATIONS WITH THE CZECHS

During the hectic time, just after the Battle of Britain, Polish–Czech political discussions began, on the initiative of General Sikorski's government. The Czechs were traditionally pro-Russian and well-disposed towards the notion of Pan-Slavism, but the Nazi threat was so great that a favourable climate had been created. After an exchange of letters between General Sikorski and Edward Beneš, who was head of the émigré Czech government (not yet recognised by the British), a joint declaration was issued on 11 November 1940 anticipating a union between the two states at the end of the war. This was still only the first step and did not specify the exact nature of the union, since the Czechs were in favour of a loose confederation, while the Poles preferred a federation.[9]

SPECIAL OPERATIONS EXECUTIVE – SOE

Meanwhile, as this important battle was taking place over their islands, the British, who after the fall of France found themselves almost alone, were looking for ways of increasing secret resistance in the occupied countries of Europe. Churchill himself was extremely active in this, since he wanted to turn as speedily as possible to the offensive against the victorious Germans. The idea was formed of setting up a secret diversionary organisation which would send equipment and trained people from the British Isles to France, Belgium, Holland, Norway, Denmark and even to distant Poland and Czechoslovakia. The underground organisations already in existence there would receive support, weapons and explosives and they would be sent instructors and trained saboteurs. On 22 July 1940 Churchill's War Cabinet accepted these previously-prepared plans and the organisation called *Special Operations Executive* – SOE – came into being. It eventually had 10 000 men and 3200 women, with a high proportion of officers or agents of similar rank, and contained many European sections: Albanian, Austrian, Belgian, Czechoslovak, Danish, Dutch, French, General de Gaulle Free French, German, Greek, Hungarian, Iberian, Italian, Norwegian, Polish, Yugoslav. SOE sections also operated in the Far East (Borneo, Burma, Malaya).

France was the closest, so the SOE command's gaze turned first in that direction and thus the French section was the first to be formed, but it was followed closely in summer 1940 by distant Poland's section. Almost from the beginning its head was Captain (later Colonel) Harold Perkins, who remained in this post until the end of the war. He had a small textile factory in Bielsko in Poland, spoke Polish and knew Polish customs. The section immediately established contact with the Sixth Bureau of the Polish Staff and only in this way did it have knowledge of Polish affairs and contact with Poland. In contrast to the other sections of SOE who sent out their own people to the various occupied countries and who continued to be subordinated to their superiors in London, the Poles enjoyed the privilege of exclusivity. They recruited their own emissaries, couriers and parachutists who were sent to Poland; each of them swore the oath of loyalty in force in the underground army and immediately on finding himself on Polish soil became its soldier. The English historian, H. T. Willets, has formulated this succinctly and clearly:

> The responsibilities of the Polish section of SOE consisted of helping the Polish Sixth Bureau in preparing and developing communications with Poland and in operational training, of obtaining equipment and arranging the flow of equipment and personnel. Much of this work consisted in liaison between the Poles and interested British authorities.[10]

Immediately after the formation of the Polish section of the SOE, the Sixth Bureau began a discreet and secret search for volunteers for special duty in Poland to be reached by parachute. First they went through various tests, and after acceptance were sent on courses which were to prepare them for their difficult tasks. Only after their completion were the candidates sent to a camp in Scotland for physical training and instruction and then all that remained were the training jumps at the great parachute centre at Ringway near Manchester. Thus prepared the candidates finally went on a briefing course to acquaint them with various details of life in occupied Poland. At the end of this course all that remained was holding station and a moonlit night suitable for flying and the jump onto Polish soil. However in 1940 all these preparations were still in an experimental and trial phase.[11]

LIAISON WITH POLAND

The victory of the Battle of Britain, which for the first time arrested Hitler's triumphant progress, made a great impression in Poland and raised morale. The underground press transmitted the news round the country that Polish airmen had taken part in the victory and had covered themselves with glory. The image of defeated France began to fade and its place was taken by the sharp outlines of the British Isles. The Poles realised that Churchill's words were not idle ones and that Poland had an ally who could be counted upon; hope and belief in victory returned.

The fall of France and the transfer of the Government and General Staff to Great Britain created a completely new situation for communications with Poland. It also affected radio communications, as well as courier routes, and everything had to be rebuilt.

Radio station *Regina*, which had been set up in France was lost during the evacuation, only the codes and the crystals had been saved, so now a new one had to be built in London. It was set up towards the end of July 1940, given the code name *Marta* and began to call up the stations on the communication bases. Contact was established and on 10 August the first message was sent to Bucharest and two days later communication with Budapest was set up. Finally, on 18 September, for the first time since the Poles had appeared in the West, including their time in France, a direct link was made with Warsaw.[12]

The whole movement of couriers and emmissaries between Poland and the West became very much more complicated. Before the fall of France it had been possible to reach the bases in Budapest and Bucharest normally using a diplomatic passport, and only the crossing of the Polish frontier into either German or Soviet occupied territory had caused a serious problem. Now this route was closed and an additional difficulty had been created by the entry of Italy into the war. On 10 June Mussolini, recognising that Hitler was winning and that it was time to share the booty, attacked France. The hitherto easy arrangements using Mediterranean routes were no longer feasible and quite new routes and methods of reaching the neutral countries bordering Poland had to be sought.

The French interlude needs also to be summed up in figures. Eighteen emissaries were sent from Paris to the German-occupied zone of Poland and ten arrived in France from Warsaw. During the same period five were sent to the Soviet zone and four arrived in return. The simple figures show how very much greater were the difficulties involved in crossing the frontiers of Eastern Poland in the hands of the Soviet Union.[13]

The British were also working on new routes. In the Near East they had the army of General Archibald Wavell and were providing it with supplies, moreover they had already activated a number of SOE outposts and had to remain in constant touch with them. At first these routes from Great Britain to the area of the Suez Canal were mainly by sea, around South Africa, or by air over the Dark Continent. The Polish section of SOE carried out its liaison role and thus the first Polish emissaries leaving London were able to use these routes. The journey was long, exhausting and in its final phase very dangerous, although also very exotic. An emissary who left London on 7 November and reached Warsaw on 18 December had travelled by various means of transport through Portugal, Gambia, Sierra Leone, Nigeria, the Belgian Congo, Sudan, Egypt, Palestine, Cyprus, Turkey, Yugoslavia and Hungary.[14]

Such a state of affairs could not continue for long, the country's needs were growing every day, thus communications had to be improved at all costs. They would rely on the bases which were now to receive all possible attention, particularly since current arrangements were very seriously endangered.

After the loss of Bessarabia to the Soviet Union, Romania was faced with new territorial losses: Hungary demanded the return of Transylvania and Bulgaria wanted Dobruja. On 30 August 1940 arbitration in Vienna by Germany and Italy recommended that Romania accept these demands. The Romanian King, Charles II, abdicated in favour of his son, Michael, a military coup took place and power was assumed by General Ion Antonescu, while on 7 October the Germans invaded the dismembered country on a trivial

pretext. Their main aim was to secure the oilfields at Ploesti. Under
pressure from the Nazis, Romania joined the 'Pact of Three' which
had been concluded on 27 September in Berlin by Germany, Italy
and Japan. Consequently Romania, which was friendly towards
Poland, broke off diplomatic relations on 5 November. The closing of
the embassy forced the rapid concealment of the functions of the
communications base *Bolek* there and its move to Istambul where it
strengthened station *Bey* there. A secret station remained behind in
Bucharest and was given the code-name *Bolek II*.[15]

The Polish–Hungarian friendship of centuries survived the harsh
test of the Nazi menace, but even in Hungary the Polish embassy was
eventaully closed, since in the second half of November Hungary also
joined the 'Pact of Three'. This was, however, a decision more formal
than practical and the embassy retained some ability to operate as did
the communications base, *Romek*. It continued to co-operate successfully with occupied Poland.

The fate of base no. II in Bucharest was shared by base no. III in
Kowno, but because of the Russians and not the Germans. In
mid-June 1940 Red divisions invaded Lithuania, the whole country
was occupied and the base had to be moved in great haste to
Stockholm. There it received the code-name *Anna* and soon became
very active and efficient. It was difficult to reach it from Poland, but
use was made of contacts with friendly Swedes, who were able to
travel freely between Stockholm and Berlin carrying secret mail. This
route was later discovered by the Gestapo, arrests ensued and the
route had to be discontinued, although base *Anna* still played its part,
since there were easy air connections between it and London.[16]

The three main bases were inadequate and a further network of
additional stations needed to be set up to carry out the difficult work.
The first such station was set up in Cairo in August 1940 with the
agreement of the British authorities; it was given the code-name *Alek*
(or A) and was of key importance for emissaries travelling through
Africa. This was a secure, but very long route and there was a need,
therefore, to set up a way of getting to England by a direct western
route through Germany, Switzerland, France and Portugal.

It was easiest to set up a contact point in a neutral country which
still had a Polish legation, and so the first such point on the western
route appeared in Bern and was given the code-name *S*. A number of
border crossings were arranged and if a courier, travelling through
Germany, managed to reach them and arrived on Swiss territory, he

could then fly to neutral Portugal and thence to London, or cross into unoccupied France.[17]

It was much harder to organise something on German territory, but an additional point was eventually set up in Berlin based on the embassy of Manchukuo and from there the route led towards the Swiss frontier. Sometimes, with good documents, it was possible to go by train from Berlin to Paris, where after a time a station, code-named *Janka*, was eventually set up. Another route to France led through Alsace where a number of good border crossings were organised. On arrival in unoccupied France the courier headed for Marseilles, where another station, code-named *F*, was set up and where there were chances of a sea voyage to Lisbon and to station *P* there. A station (*H*) was also set up in Madrid in conjunction with the Polish legation and from time to time it was possible to fly there from Paris and then fly on to Lisbon. A further such point was Athens and station *Grzegorz*, as well as Rome where a number of semi-legal sections of the Poland embassy had remained and where it was always possible to count on Italian leniency and lack of strict control. From Rome it was possible to fly to Switzerland.[18]

This state of affairs continued until the first months of 1941. After the night of 14/15 February when the first parachutists were dropped into Poland, all couriers used only this route.[19] Naturally, however, the overland routes still remained for use by couriers travelling from Poland to the West. They were also necessary if London sent out emissaries whose age prevented them from jumping.

NEW POLITICAL SITUATION

For Hitler enemy number one was Great Britain and only defeating her or forcing her to conclude peace guaranteed a German victory. He therefore issued orders for an invasion of the British Isles and his air force attempted to clear the skies above them, yet deep within him the decision was forming that he had to destroy Russia. He thought about this ceaselessly; his words on 31 July 1940 to the Army High Commanders in Berlin are proof of this:

> The decision to destroy Russia must become a part of this struggle ... The sooner Russia is crushed, the better. The attack will be successful only when the Russian state has been smashed to its

foundations with a single blow ... If we begin in May 1941, we shall have five months to complete the task.[20]

The Germans lost the great air battle, the German Chancellor's earlier peace proposals of 19 July had been rejected by Great Britain, so new plans for the continuation of the war became more pressing. The attack on Russia continued to be closest to Hitler's heart, but his advisers also suggested other possibilities. Grand Admiral Raeder, together with Göring, urged him to attack Gibraltar via Spain and to undertake a joint attack with Italy in the direction of Suez, Palestine, Syria and Turkey.[21] The Chancellor was favourably disposed to these suggestions and was considering them at the end of 1940, but the Gibralter idea fell through when in October 1940, the Spanish dictator, General Francisco Franco, refused to involve his country in the war.[22] Hitler then observed the situation in the Balkans, where traditionally there was a battle between Russian and Western influences.

The secret protocol attached to the Ribbentrop–Molotov pact clearly stated that the Germans had no political interests in south-eastern Europe, but in practice things were different. After invading Romania, Hitler busied himself with Bulgaria and Yugoslavia, while his Italian ally took on Greece. When Greece refused to have bases on her territory, Mussolini, without consultation with Hitler, began a war with her towards the end of October. This, of course, led to a change in the balance of power in that area. Meanwhile at the other end of Europe German divisions appeared in Finland. This was also contrary to the German–Soviet pact. After the predatory Soviet attacks occupying the Baltic states and depriving Romania of Bessarabia and norther Bukowina, the Germans were now widening their sphere of influence. It was clear that neither side trusted the other, that they both expected conflict and were trying to gain the most favourable positions.

Various possibilities were explored: the Germans suggested to Stalin the division of the British empire and tried to encourage the Russians to expand to the South in the direction of the Indian Ocean. Hitler went so far as to propose that Russia join the 'Pact of Three', which united Germany, Italy and Japan. Stalin considered these propositions and put forward his own plans and conditions. Among others they embraced the withdrawal of German divisions from Finland and the speedy assurance of full rights for Russia in the Dardanelles. These conditions were almost provocative and naturally

Hitler was unable to accept. He gave no reply to his Eastern ally and on 18 December 1940 issued secret war directive no. 21 dealing with the attack on the Soviet Union, which was given the code-name *Barbarossa*. With their own hands the two aggressors were destroying the political state of affairs which could have brought them control over the whole world.

However, before it came to open conflict, Great Britain remained alone face to face with the might of Germany. Initial British hopes for help from the United States had been vain, since on the other side of the Atlantic there was a conviction that France and England could deal with Hitler on their own. However in May 1940, seeing what was happening, President Roosevelt turned to Congress for credits to expand the armed forces and on 22 June won $5000 million. Within less than a month the Congress voted a further $5000 million. In August an American military mission came to London to establish for itself just what were the chances of defending the island against an invasion by Hitler, and when it produced a favourable opinion, the United States gave Great Britain fifty old destroyers in exchange for the right to use bases in the Caribbean, Bermuda and Newfoundland. In November Roosevelt was elected for a third term; he was in continual contact with Churchill and was working on a formula which would allow him to provide Great Britain with assistance without compromising his own neutrality. Since in June 1940 Congress had adopted a resolution permitting war materials to be delivered to other countries if the security of the United States was endangered, the President ordered that convoys carrying such goods to Great Britain would be protected by the Navy off the coast of the United States. Continuing this line of argument, Roosevelt ensured that Congress approved the Lend-Lease Act, on 11 March 1941. This empowered the President of the United States to 'sell, exchange, lease or loan' any means of defence to another country, whose security the President deemed essential for the defence of the States.[23]

From the first days of the German–Soviet alliance Great Britain had not ceased trying to get the Soviet Union to change its orientation. Fighting still continued in France when on 30 May Stafford Cripps, a member of the Labour Party and one of Britain's most distinguished politicians, arrived in Moscow to assume the post of ambassador. Slowly and with great patience he began to develop the difficult relations with the Soviet leaders. They were extremely careful, for they knew that every meeting with the British ambassador was being observed by German diplomats and reported back to Berlin; nevertheless an exchange of views did begin. These talks were very cold, but their temperature rose somewhat when 150 or so German divisions suddenly found themselves with nothing to do on the continent of Europe.

NORTH AFRICA AND THE BALKANS

During his most recent conference with Molotov, on 12 November, von Ribbentrop had been conducting affairs as if Great Britain were already on her knees. Meanwhile, on 9 December, General Wavell began an unexpected offensive in North Africa. So the British, who had apparently concentrated every effort to prevent an invasion at home, still possessed enough reserves to be able to prepare and arm in Egypt an army capable of offensive action. This army numbered only 30 000 men, but had modern equipment and within a few weeks had destroyed a great Italian army numbering over 200 000 men commanded by Marshal Rudolfo Graziani. Starting from Sidi Barrani in Egypt, Wavell, after a twenty-four-hour siege, captured Tobruk and reached Benghazi in Cyrenaica covering almost 800 kms and taking about 150 000 prisoners and huge quantities of equipment.[24]

The Carpathian Brigade which after the fall of France had moved from Syria to Palestine, did not take part in this victorious advance. This was because of a misunderstanding, which has only now been cleared up. Poland was not formally at war with Italy and General Sikorski's initial decisions envisaged only defensive action should there be any confrontation with Italian forces. The British were aware of this position and honoured it, so it was for this reason that the Brigade had been allocated defensive positions around Alexandria. New instructions from General Sikorski dispelled any misunderstanding and the Brigade commander's plan to motorise the unit was accepted and from mid-January 1941 began to be put into effect. Reorganisation envisaged the creation of three independent battalions, a heavy machine-gun battalion, an artillery regiment, a reconnaissance regiment of Carpathian *uhlans*, two anti-tank companies, signals and engineer detachments as well as support units: transport, supply, medical, field court-martial, a company of military police, an anti-gas section and others. The total strength was 348 officers and 5326 other ranks.[25]

The British victory in North Africa greatly raised the temperature of Stafford Cripps' discussions at the Kremlin and forced the Germans to speed up the implementation of the plans they had already made some time before. Five days after the British capture of Benghazi, on 12 February, General Erwin Rommel landed in Tripoli, appointed by Hitler as commander of the 'Afrika Corps', to be followed by his armour. On 31 March a German offensive began, supported only slightly by the Italians, which brought lightening results. Within about a fortnight all the British gains were lost and Rommel stood on the Egyptian frontier. Only the small force locked in Tobruk fought on. Indeed a British squadron did win a decisive victory at Cape Matapan in the Mediterranean on 28 March, as the result of which the Italian Navy hardly ever left port up to the end of the war, but the balance of power in that area again became unfavourable for Great Britain.[26]

Further German penetration of the Balkans embraced Bulgaria and forced her to join the 'Pact of Three'. On 1 March 1941, causing an immediate arrival of German divisions. Yugoslavia was the next to come under pressure and on 25 March she signed a document expressing agreement to join this 'pact', but two days later a coup took place there, the regent Paul left the country and King Peter, still a minor, called together a new government. This forced the Germans to change their plans, defer their attack on Russia and attack Yugoslavia and Greece on 6 April. The same day an almost 60 000-strong British Expeditionary Corps, which was to help the brave Greeks in their final repulse of the Italian invasion, began to land. The Carpathian Brigade was meant to join the British corps, it had been rearmed and prepared for mountain warfare, and had even partially embarked, but at the last moment it was recalled and sent back to Alexandria. This decision had been brought about by the rapid advance of Rommel's offensive.[27]

Hitler, furious at the need for unnecessary fighting and the delay to his Soviet plans, ordered the fighting in the Balkans to be without mercy. Belgrade was bombed, armour was committed and on 18 April Yugoslavia capitulated. The country was swiftly dismembered, independence was proclaimed for Croatia; Slovenia, together with Lubljana, was annexed by Italy, Banat by Hungary and Macedonia by Bulgaria. The Polish communications station in Belgrade, *Sława*, had to be dismantled. Greece capitulated on 23 April and the British evacuated their corps partly to Egypt and partly to Crete, which was captured by the Germans at the end of May, after a great airborne operation. The occupation of Greece caused the rapid elimination of the Polish communications station, *Grzegorz*, in Athens.[28]

Meanwhile General Sikorski, wishing at all costs to increase the modest Polish forces in Great Britain, left on 1 April 1941 for the United States and Canada for direct negotiations with President Roosevelt and the Canadian Prime Minister to ensure the right to recruit volunteers. The meeting with the President was also to raise the question of aid for Poland within the framework of *Lend-Lease*. After receiving encouraging promises and making many contacts with the Polish community which was to provide the volunteers, the General returned to London on 12 May.

The Germans, having conquered the Balkans and thrown back the British in North Africa, and moreover, with their own divisions in Finland, found themselves in a most convenient position and nothing now stood in the way of their attack on Russia. That part of Poland which was under their occupation was packed with divisions and no intelligence network was need to see this. Nevertheless warnings were going to Stalin from many sides. President Roosevelt warned him, Churchill warned him several times, General Rowecki sent urgent intelligence reports from Warsaw detailing the deployment of the German divisions and thier strength, the Soviet intelligence network in Western Europe, called the *Rote Kapelle* (*Red Orchestra*), was sending the most up-to-date information by radio. Above all, however, warnings were sent from Switzerland by Sándor Radó, a Soviet agent who had settled there before the war and who had set up an intelligence group benefiting from the co-operation of a mysterious German, called Rudolf Roessler. The German concealed himself under the pseudonym *Lucy* and by means still unknown managed to extract from Germany priceless information straight from the main centres of power in a remarkably short time. All this met with Stalin's indifference. He did not believe these urgent messages and took the warnings for Western provocation.[29] He continued to send the Germans vast loads of raw materials, oil and wheat as if unable to see that he was helping a system which was bound to turn against his own country.

9 The German Attack on USSR and the Uneasy Polish Alliance with Russia

GERMAN ATTACK ON USSR

In the early morning of 22 June 1941 the German attack on territory in the hands of the Soviet Union began. On a front more than 3000 km wide, stretching from the Baltic to the Black Sea, struck three army groups – North, Centre and South – with a strength of 135 divisions, seventeen of them panzer, with more than 3500 tanks supported by more than 4500 aircraft. The additional Finnish front, about 700km wide, contained twenty divisions supported by 600 aircraft. The reserve consisted of twenty-four divisions, two of which were armoured. Altogether this came to about 5.5 million men equipped with modern weapons and already to a large extent hardened by fighting in Poland, Norway, France and the Balkans. Within a few days later, the Germans were joined by Italian, Romanian, Slovak, Finnish and Hungarian divisions. Amongst the German units and usually in the *Waffen SS* were detachments of Belgian, French, Dutch, Norwegian and Spanish volunteers. There were even also around 800 Swiss.[1]

The Soviet army surpassed the Germans and their allies in numbers of men and also amounts of equipment, with approximately 7000 tanks and 5000 aircraft in the West, but the Great Purge of 1937–8 had deprived the army of a great many commanders, its morale was poor, its training bad and its equipment, much of it old, was in the process of being replaced. All this, however, was overshadowed by the complete psychological unpreparedness for the German attack. Stalin did not believe it would come and this conviction had taken root not only in his closest circle and the senior commanders, but had also permeated down to the ordinary soldiers. Within about a fortnight the front had collapsed in several places, the Baltic states had been occupied, Minsk had been captured and armoured columns had reached the gates of Kiev. The front had moved several hundred kilometres further east, around 300 000 prisoners had been taken, more than 2500 Russian tanks had been destroyed or captured and about 3000 aircraft had been shot down or destroyed on the ground.[2]

The defeat at the front was not, however, the most painful blow for the Soviet Union. Within about ten days, wherever the Germans appeared, the Soviet political system collapsed immediately before the simultaneous and spontaneous outburst of sentiments of the local population. Along the whole front, from the Baltic states as far as the Black Sea the Germans were greeted as liberators, despite the fact that they were invaders and enemies.

The outbreak of the Russo–German war was greeted in London with a feeling of great relief. At last the secret hopes, supported by the efforts of British diplomacy, had been realised, at last the German dictator had made a mistake, which had to influence the course of the war. At 9 p.m. that same evening Churchill made a radio broadcast:

> Now I have to declare the decision of His Majesty's Government – and I feel sure it is a decision in which the great Dominions will, in due course, concur – for we must speak out now at once, without a day's delay. I have to make a declaration, but can you doubt what our policy will be? We had but one aim and one single, irrevocable purpose. We are resolved to destroy Hitler and every vestige of the Nazi regime. From this nothing will turn us – nothing. We will never parley, we will never negotiate with Hitler or any of his gang. We shall fight him by land, we shall fight him by sea, we shall fight him in the air, until with God's help we have rid the earth of his shadow and liberated its peoples from his yoke. Any man or state who fights on against Nazidom will have our aid. Any man or state who marches with Hitler is our foe ... That is our policy and that is our declaration. It follows, therefore, that we shall give whatever help we can to Russia and the Russian people.[3]

Churchill was an experienced politician and parliamentarian; he well knew the importance of words, particularly if they contained promises, he weighed them many times before speaking and he knew that haste is usually fatal and yet, within barely a dozen hours after the German attack, he had promised Russia all possible aid with no political conditions. The moment was exceptional and Hitler's attack on Russia was a gift from heaven for Great Britain, yet it is difficult not to believe that the British Prime Minister was hasty and committed a serious blunder for which a high price would have to be paid in the future.

War between Poland's two enemies created, as always, a new and promising situation for Polish affairs and General Sikorski was not slow to react. He realised that in Poland itself the German attack had caused great excitement, that the Poles were impatiently awaiting a comment from London outlining the Government's new position and on the evening of 23 June he made a radio broadcast:

What we have been anticipating has occurred. Though sooner than we had expected. The Nazi–Bolshevik combination which was at the source of the terrible disaster that brought about the fate of Poland has been shattered. Since dawn of June 22 the former accomplices are at strife.

Such a sequel is very favourable to Poland. It changes and reverses the former situation. Behold, Germany, the foremost foe of the Polish Nation, has torn asunder an alliance which has so long been the source of our greatest misfortunes ... At this moment we are entitled to assume that in these circumstances Russia will cancel the Pact of 1939. That should logically bring us back to the position governed by the Treaty concluded in Riga on March 18th 1921 between Russia and Poland recognised on March 15th 1923 by the conference of Ambassadors and on April 5th by the United States of North America ... Will it not be natural, even on the part of Soviet Russia, to return to the traditions of September 1918 when the Supreme Soviet Council solemnly declared null all previous dictates concerning the partitions of Poland rather than actively to partake in Her fourth partition.

For the love of their country, their freedom and honour, thousands of Polish men and women, including 300 000 war prisoners, are still suffering in Russian prisons. Should it not be deemed right and honest to restore to these people their liberty?[4]

Politically speaking this statement was correct, for General Sikorski, who clearly had to say that a Polish–Soviet agreement ought to be reached, had made it conditional on a return to the decisions of the

Treaty of Riga and thus to the pre-1939 situation. He moreover raised the issue of the political prisoners and prisoners of war and also mentioned the misery of the hundreds of thousands of people deported into the depths of Russia.

POLISH–SOVIET PACT AND POLES APART

The conditions proposed by the Polish premier became the basis for the start of Polish–Soviet negotiations, with the British as intermediaries, On 5 and 11 July two conferences took place at the Foreign Office, with the Polish side represented by General Sikorski and the Foreign Minister August Zaleski, the Soviets by Ambassador Ivan Maisky and the British by the deputy Foreign Secretary Alexander Cadogan (Eden was also present at the second meeting). A fundamental difficulty immediately emerged, for the Soviet side, while agreeing to an independent Polish state and to its right to its own political system, saw it within ethnographical boundaries and thus without those eastern Polish territories seized by the Soviet Union. Other points dealing with political prisoners and prisoners of war, as well as the Polish army in the USSR and its control, although equally important, were not of such fundamental significance.

At the first session Ambassador Maisky summarised the discussion in a number of points which he was to transmit to his superiors:

1. Provided the Soviet Government denounce the two treaties with Germany of August and September 1939, the discussion of frontiers is not material.
2. Return of normal relations between the two Governments and the appointment of a Polish Ambassador in Moscow.
3. Poland would then be prepared to collaborate in the common fight against Germany.
4. A special Polish Army would be formed as a unit on Soviet territory or to be transported elsewhere if that were desired. The exact status of the Polish Army would be assimilated into that of the Polish Forces in the United Kingdom.
5. Polish military and political prisoners to be liberated.[5]

The formulation of the first point did not satisfy the Polish side, which therefore handed in a memorandum to the Foreign Office dealing with the Polish eastern territories occupied by Russia. The final point also raised some far-reaching reservations, for Maisky had stated that only 20 000 Polish prisoners of war were in the Soviet Union, when in fact the real figure was some ten times higher.

At the second conference, during which General Sikorski made it plain that the Polish position on the pre-war Soviet–Polish frontier must be clearly stated, Maisky proposed four points which could be agreed upon reasonably quickly:

1. that the Treaties of 1939 were dead;
2. that diplomatic relations should be restored;
3. that the Polish army should be recreated;
4. that both Governments should agree to fight against Germany.[6]

General Sikorski emphasised that these points ignored the question of political prisoners and compensation for the state and private property seized by the Soviets, but both sides agreed to such an agenda for the preliminary discussions. Anthony Eden became the intermediary as events developed, since direct Polish–Soviet talks were not renewed.

A secret protocol was also to be added to the open agreement and the question of its content arose. The Polish side was insisting on reparations while the Soviets, quite without justification, were trying to turn this into a two-sided problem, so Eden proposed that this issue be included in the secret protocol. Agreement on every sentence caused great problems.

Churchill himself became involved in the negotiations and in a letter to Sikorski on 15 July emphasised that a Polish–Soviet agreement was of great importance to the common cause. In his reply to the British Prime Minister General Sikorski stated that such an agreement depended solely on the decisions of the Soviet government, which ought to recognise the pre-September 1939 frontiers of the Polish state and release Polish subjects held in prisons and camps.

Unfortunately the Russian position continued to differ from Polish demands and on 17 July Ambassador Maisky presented Moscow's reaction. It ignored the idea of returning to the *status quo* existing before September 1939, it raised the issue of the frontiers for discussion, it insisted on Soviet approval of the commander of the Polish forces in the Soviet Union and made the release of Polish prisoners of war subject to the resumption first of diplomatic relations. The Poles stuck to their demands, especially the recognition of the pre-war *status quo*, but since they could not achieve this, they suggested a formula whereby the Soviet government would annul treaties made with the Germans dealing with territorial changes in Poland. This idea was not accepted by the Soviet side which suggested the following wording: 'The treaties dealing with the division of Poland are no longer valid'. The point about the release of Polish citizens from camps and exile as well as prisoners-of-war camps was also the subject of disagreement, since the Poles insisted that it be in the open protocol, while the Russians wanted to include it in the secret one.[7]

These negotiations were in progress at a time when the German forces were advancing rapidly into the Soviet empire, the Red Army was retreating in panic, and a possibility of a swift German victory was appearing. This was doubtless the only time at which it would have been possible for Poland to conclude a satisfactory agreement with the Soviet Union, for Stalin's position would harden immediately were he to hold up the Germans, while his defeat would negate the value of any Soviet promises. It was on this score that there was a fundamental disagreement between General Sikorski and three members of his cabinet: Marjan Seyda (National Party), August Zaleski and General Kazimierz Sosnkowski. They maintained that as Russia was in a desperate position and needed Western aid, it would thus be possible to secure from her an agreement on a return to Poland's pre-war borders and on the release of all prisoners in Soviet hands.

On 21 July there was a discussion at the Council of Ministers, which was interrupted for General Sikorski to confer with Anthony Eden to obtain his support for the Polish wording. When this was settled, the government unanimously accepted the text with its amendments. Unfortunately the Soviet government did not accept this final wording and on 25 July there took place another meeting of the Polish government at which General Sikorski stated that 'there is and can be no hope of obtaining either today or tomorrow Soviet agreement for a change to a wording more favourable to us ... Moreover, the text which they do accept is no different, from the legal and political point of view, from the one which the Council of Ministers has accepted'. The General also added that, in the event of the rejection of this agreement, British support would be lost.

By a majority the government accepted the General's position and supported signing the agreement, three of its members, as already mentioned – Seyda, Zaleski and Sosnkowski – voted against and during a break in the deliberations resigned. The decision of the Polish government did not mean the end of the negotiations, which moved to Moscow where the British Ambassador, Stafford Cripps, tried to negotiate with Molotov a change in the Russian position closer to the Polish point of view. On 28 July Eden notified General Sikorski of some concessions on Stalin's part and the following day the General dispatched a letter to the President of the Polish Republic informing him of these advantageous changes and requesting authority to sign the pact on the following day. Despite the intervention of the British Ambassador to the Polish Government, President Raczkiewicz refused the request and the General took it upon himself to take this important decision. The Agreement was signed on 30 July 1941 at the Foreign Office, in the presence of Sikorski, Churchill, Eden and Maisky.

The Agreement

The Government of the Republic of Poland and the Government of the Union of Soviet Socialist Republics have concluded the present Agreement and decided as follows:

1. The Government of the Union of Soviet Socialist Republics recognises that the Soviet–German treaties of 1939 relative to territorial changes in Poland have lost their validity. The Government of the Republic of Poland declares that Poland is not bound by any Agreement with any third State directed against the USSR.

2. Diplomatic relations will be restored between the two Governments upon the signature of this Agreement and an exchange of ambassadors will follow immediately.

3. The two Governments mutually undertake to render one another aid and support of all kinds in the present war against Hitlerite Germany

4. The Government of the Union of Soviet Socialist Republics expresses its consent to the formation on the territory of the Union of Soviet Socialist Republics of a Polish Army under a commander appointed by the Government of the Republic of Poland, in agreement with the Government of the Union of Soviet Socialist Republics. The Polish Army on the territory of the Union of Soviet Socialist Republics will be subordinated in operational matters to the Supreme Command of the USSR on which there will be a representative of the Polish Army. All details as to command, organisation and employment of this force will be settled in a subsequent Agreement.

5. This Agreement will come into force immediately upon its

signature and without ratification. The present Agreement is drawn up in two copies, each of them in the Russian and Polish languages. Both texts have equal force.

Secret protocol

1. Various claims both of public and private nature will be dealt with in the course of further negotiations between the two governments.
2. This protocol enters into force simultaneously with the Agreement of 30th July 1941.

Protocol

1. As soon as diplomatic relations are re-established the Government of the Union of Soviet Socialist Republics will grant amnesty to all Polish citizens who are at present deprived of their freedom on the territory of the USSR either as prisoners of war or on other adequate grounds.
2. The present Protocol comes into force simultaneously with the Agreement of July 30 1941.

Władysław Sikorski   I. Maisky[8]

On the same day there was an exchange of notes between Eden and Sikorski. The British document stated that the British Government did not recognise any territorial changes in Poland after August 1939 and that the Government had not entered into any undertaking with the USSR which would harm relations between the Soviet Union and Poland. The Polish note confirmed receipt of the British note and once again repeated Poland's position as to the inviolability of her borders. However, during a debate in the House of Commons on the very same day, Eden, when asked specifically about this point, replied clearly that the British note 'does not involved any guarantee of frontiers by His Majesty's Government'. This declaration was consistent with the decisions of the Polish–British pact of 25 August 1939. On 31 July the American Under-Secretary of State made a formal declaration that 'the Polish–Soviet Agreement conformed to the policy of the government of the United States not to recognise any territorial changes achieved by conquest'.[9]

The signing of the Polish–Soviet pact under such conditions and with such fundamental disagreements caused a very damaging crisis. On 25 July, during the negotiations, Sikorski relieved General Sosnkowski of his position of Commander of the ZWZ. In fact it was really removing him from overall control of military activity in Poland, since General Rowecki had been ZWZ Commander since June 1940. General Sikorski assumed these responsibilities himself and subordinated the Sixth Bureau directly to the Chief of Staff. Further difficulties were apparent in the attitude of the President of the Polish Republic, who was contemplating resignation and only accepted the resignations of the three ministers on 22 August, and also in the departure from the three-party coalition of the National Party. The Government of National Unity depended on this coalition.[10]

OPINION OF OCCUPIED POLAND

Despite the concentration in Great Britain of a great many major departments, titles and ranks, the real of Polish opinion could come only from Poland itself. The question of a Government Delegacy had now been settled and on 3 December 1940 Cyryl Ratajski (1875–1942), a former mayor of Poznań and member of the Labour Party (SP), was appointed to the post. Using the code name *Wartski*, he assumed chairmanship of the 'Chief Political Council', which readopted its former name 'Political Advisory Committee'.[11]

On 4 July, just one day before the first conference between Sikorski and Maisky, there was a meeting of the 'Political Advisory Committee' in Warsaw, under the chairman of the Government Delegate and at which underground representatives of the country approved the policies of the Government towards the Russo-German war and the new political situation. The exact position of this body was that Russia should:

1. immediately recognise the independence and sovereignty of the Polish state;
2. reintroduce Polish diplomatic and consular activities on the territory of the Soviet Union;
3. release Polish prisoners of war and other prisoners from confinement, camps and exile;
4. provide assistance for the civilian population forcibly deported from Poland and pay full reparations for all material losses sustained.[12]

The unanimity of the views of the Committee and the Government Delegate with those of General Sikorski suggested that the final agreement would also be acceptable in Poland, as long as its decisions matched the agreed points. Hopes for this were even higher, since General Sikorski was also in touch with General Rowecki and had explained the reasons for his decision to him. Indeed that is what happened. The eventual wording of the Polish–Soviet pact did produce differing reactions in Poland, caused above all by the long-standing mistrust of Russia, but eventually on 18 August the Government Delegate was able to cable London as follows:

> I submit a unanimous declaration of the Committee on the subject of the Polish–Russian agreement.
> The Committee sees the agreement as a positive step to the eventual regularisation of relations between Poland and Russia although having reservations about the clause dealing with the eastern and northern frontiers. I shall submit later the declarations of the various political parties.
> I might add for myself that it is widely held here that the Polish–Soviet agreement should not become an object of personal or party dispute.
>
> Wartski[13]

This was a document of great importance for General Sikorski, since it helped him to implement the agreement with the Soviets.

THE 'ATLANTIC CHARTER'

At that time there occurred a political event not only of potentially far-reaching consequences for the immediate future but also capable of raising the spirits of all those who had agreed to the Polish–Soviet pact with a heavy heart, seeing its faults, but cherishing the hope that the Western powers would not permit Poland to be wronged. On 14 August 1941 Churchill and Roosevelt met on the deck of the British battleship *Prince of Wales* off Newfoundland and signed a declaration, which has gone down in history as the *Atlantic Charter*. Both leaders emphasised in it the principles which their countries would follow and by which all other parties involved in the war should abide. The Charter declared that conquest of foreign territory should be renounced, that the right of every country to sovereignty and a choice of appropriate government should be recognised, that force should be renounced in international relations and that after the war all countries should co-operate with one another on an equal footing.[14] Both Western leaders hoped that Stalin would also sign the Charter, but it never got further than the assent of the Soviet ambassador in London. The dictator had far-reaching plans of territorial conquest and even at such a difficult moment was not prepared to support any declarations which were inconvenient for him.

POLISH–SOVIET MILITARY AGREEMENT AND THE POLISH ARMY IN USSR

The first important matter resulting from the Polish–Soviet pact was the appointment of an ambassador. General Sikorski hesitated before eventually appointing a close confident, Professor Stanisław Kot, but before he left for Russia, Józef Retinger preceded him as *chargé d'affaires*. Ambassador Kot arrived only on 4 September. Both these appointments were very unfortunate. Retinger, almost certainly a British political agent, immediately incurred the suspicion that he might be more concerned with interests other than those of Poland. Kot, a member of the Peasant Party, beside his difficult character and tendency to intrigue, came from the south of Poland which during the partition had belonged to Austria; he knew neither Russia nor Russians and furthermore had no diplomatic experience. Moreover, the problems with which he was soon to be faced were of the utmost importance for Poland and called for great and diverse qualities.

It was clear that one of the generals in Soviet hands would have to be appointed to command the Polish army in the USSR and General Sikorski's choice fell on General Władysław Anders, who had spent the last year or so in the Lubyanka prison in Moscow. This appointment entrusted the fate of the Polish units forming there to a man of great energy, who enjoyed the confidence of his soldiers and who had an excellent knowledge of the country in which he would now have to operate under difficult circumstances.

General Zygmunt Bohusz-Szyszko, who, like General Anders, knew Russia and Russians very well, was appointed head of the Military Mission. He was entrusted with the negotiations leading to the Polish–Soviet military agreement which he signed on 14 August.

MILITARY AGREEMENT

The first three paragraphs said that the agreement derived from the political agreement of 30 July, that the Polish army would be organised on the territory of the USSR, that this army would form part of the Polish forces, that the soldiers would take an oath of allegiance to the Republic of Poland and that operationally it would be subordinated to the High Command of the USSR. The Commander of this army would be appointed by the Polish Commander-in-Chief, but that he had to be approved by the Government of the USSR.

Paragraphs 4 and 5 said that this army would consist of land forces only and that servicemen who had previously served in the Polish Air Force and Navy would be sent to Great Britain for the Polish units already in existence there.

In further paragraphs details concerning the place of formation of the Polish army, its supplied, various other expenses, hospitals and courts marital were determined. The most important point referred to sending Polish units to the front where they were to operate in groups not smaller than divisions.[15]

The agreement, which was modelled on the texts of similar earlier agreements with France and Great Britain and did not depart from them, was a good basis on which to begin raising Polish units. The work could only begin after the Soviet authorities had announced an 'amnesty' for all Polish subjects, both military and civilian, who were deprived of their freedom on Soviet soil. This took place two days before the agreement was signed in the form of a decree of the Praesidium of the Supreme Soviet.

At the best of times the Soviet state machine was not efficient, but now, in wartime, it functioned even less efficiently and so the 'amnesty' instructions began only slowly to reach the camps, places of exile and prisoners-of-war camps throughout the whole vast area of the USSR and were carried out in a variety of ways. In some places people were released almost at once, in others matters dragged on for months and in some parts of the country the instructions were not carried out at all. Nevertheless, hundreds of thousands of Polish citizens were released and set off in search of the Polish army. There were soldiers ready for active service, although exhausted by work and hunger; there were old people hoping that they might be accepted; there were children who had lost their parents and, ragged and hungry, lied about their age just to get a chance to put on a Polish uniform; there were women, sometimes alone, sometimes with small children, and whole families coming from distant exile. Their journeys lasted weeks and involved camping out on stations and in hungry cities, waiting days on end for trains which were running erratically and infrequently in the war-torn country. Many died from typhus, dysentery, starvation and extreme exhaustion. Those who reached their goal, were welcomed with friendly arms, a bowl of soup and accommodation under canvas. A large proportion of this huge mass of people never reached the army but was directed by the Soviet authorities to 'settlement' in Central Asia where everyone had to work very hard and hunger raged. The Polish embassy secured from the authorities the right to organise a network of twenty delegates who hastened to help these unfortunate people[16]

The Soviet authorities endorsed the appointment of General Anders as commander of the Polish forces; he was immediately released from prison and on 11 August received official notification of his appointment from General Sikorski as well as promotion to Major-General. His headquarters were established at Buzuluk on the Samara river to the east of Kuybyshev, the General arrived there on 18 August and immediately got down to work. Within a few days he had had five conferences with the Soviet authorities in order to settle a great many important details, such as daily organisation and supply of weapons, hospitals, etc. The towns of Totsk, 40km to the south-east of Buzuluk, and Tatishchevo, to the north-east of Saratov, were designed as assembly areas for the larger units.[17]

The basic problem was the number of potential soldiers, for on this depended the size of the hastily-formed army. Cursory calculations suggested that there ought to be in the Soviet Union about 1 250 000 Polish subjects who had been taken from Polish eastern territories in three great waves of deportations. This figure included about 180 000 prisoners of war who had been captured in September 1939 as well as 150 000 men of military age who had been called up into the Red Army. Naturally the Soviet side did not corroborate these figures, insisting on a figure of 20 000 prisoners of war and an unspecified number of civilians in Siberia and the Urals. Nevertheless, it was agreed that at first plans should be made to raise two infantry divisions and an additional regiment. All senior appointments were filled by officers who had recently been released from Soviet prisons and camps.[18]

It was then that a problem arose which caused consternation. The number of officers arriving was very much smaller than anticipated.

According to the calculations of those who had already arrived, there ought to have been around 11 000 and yet there were barely several hundred. There was no cause yet for alarm, but General Anders did raise the matter with the Soviet authorities and received a reply, which in these early weeks appeared quite reasonable: there was a war on, transport had been disrupted and probably within a few weeks or months everyone would turn up.

Raising the Polish unit turned out be exceptionally difficult and took place in conditions far removed from those the Poles had encountered in France, and Great Britain. There they had been dealing with allies with whom Poland had no conflict of interest, while here in Russia, although an agreement had been reached in the interests of defeating the common enemy, not for a moment were mutual relations free of suspicion – so integral a part, moreover, of the Russian character. Yet the Poles approached this co-operation with goodwill, although their experience in the USSR would have justified a different attitude. The problem was forcefully expressed by General Anders in a report to General Sikorski on 14 August: 'It appears that only we, and indeed above all we, who experienced the purgatory and ill-treatment of Soviet prisons, labour camps and exile in often dreadful conditions, could oppose on moral grounds any attempts at agreement with Russia. And yet all of us without exception are coping with the task and our personal misfortunes, since the more fact that we are able to fight for Poland with a weapon in our hands clearly shows us the path towards a great goal'.[19]

That was the attitude of the Poles: both countries were threatened by the same enemy, Russia was in mortal danger and yet at each step Soviet unwillingness honestly to implement the signed agreement could be felt. Only in the first few weeks were there visible any signs of some spirit of co-operation, but already at the beginning of September things looked different. Volunteers were arriving – often with their families, who had to be fed – but the Russians were not even providing enough rations for the actual units. Autumn was approaching and the soliders were living in tents, they had no boots and were wearing what remained of the rags in which they had left the camps, the 'amnesty' was not being honestly implemented and weapons were promised for only one division. There was yet another matter which bothered General Anders. There was apparently a small group of officers who, in the spring of 1940, had been separated by the Russians from the other prisoners of war and were now held somewhere near Moscow in supposedly excellent conditions for reasons known only to the Russians.[20]

Reports on all this went to London and General Sikorski decided to go to Moscow to discuss these matters personally with Stalin, and on the way to visit the Near East. The Staff of the Polish Army in the East was already in Egypt and the Carpathian Brigade was taking part in the defence of the fort at Tobruk.

From 16 October all Soviet government offices had moved from endangered Moscow to Kuybyshev and so General Sikorski, after inspecting the Carpathian Birgade and dealing with a great many matters in Cairo, headed in that direction and landed on the local airfield on 30 November. The Soviet authorities took care to greet the General suitably and there was a guard of honour and a band, but his stay in Kuybyshev was confined to courtesy visits, one of which was to Mikhail Kalinin, the head of the Soviet state.

Just before the General's flight to Moscow to meet Stalin himself, yet another problem arose, complicating the already difficult situation. On 1 December the Soviet government issued a note stating that all inhabitants of Poland's eastern territories occupied by the Soviets who had been resident there on 1 November 1939 had acquired Soviet citizenship and now only Poles and not Ukrainians, Byelorussians and Jews would be recognised as Polish subjects.[21]

GENERAL SIKORSKI AND GENERAL ANDERS MEET STALIN

The meeting in the Kremlin took place late in the evening of 3 December 1941. On the Polish side were Sikorski, Anders and Kot, while on the Soviet side were Stalin and Molotov with his secretary as interpreter, and in the last phase General A. Panfilov, the deputy Chief of Staff of the Red Army. The talks were very difficult, for the German attack on Moscow had been halted and Stalin had recovered his self-confidence, while the Soviet side had to be told that the political agreement of 30 July and the military one of 14 August were not being observed. For Sikorski, supported by General Anders, there were three basic problems to be discussed and insisted upon: (i) despite the 'amnesty', Polish subjects continued to be held in camps and places of exile; (ii) the several thousand Polish officers captured in 1939 could still not be found; (iii) the forming Polish army was poorly and inadequately equipped and thus it would be late coming into active service. With goodwill it would be possible to raise seven divisions and have a strong Polish corps, operating as a unit alongside the Red Army.[22]

Stalin's answers were somewhat evasive: he said that the slowness in releasing Poles was the resulting of problems of war, and the lack of officers he explained by their flight to Manchuria. It was the discussion on the forming army which was the most difficult. The Soviet dictator did not want to agree to the formation of a large Polish corps, he justified the lack of the supplies by conditions of war, he assured them that Polish soldiers were receiving the same supplies as the Red Army. He flew into a rage when General Anders said that his 44 000 sets of rations had been reduced to 30 000. Stalin was particularly incensed by a suggestion from General Sikorski that perhaps it might be better to continue forming the Polish units in Iran where they would be properly supplied by the British. 'I am an old and experienced man and I know that if you go to Persia, then you won't return here. I see that England has much work to do and needs soldiers.' The Polish side continued to argue that that was not the case and eventually they agreed on a new location for siting and organising the Polish army. Within a short time and despite the winter, they were to move to the Uzbek and Kirghiz republics and the headquarters were to be located at Yangi Yul, near Tashkent. The choice of this location was justified by its nearness to Iran and the easy transport of supplies promised by Great Britain.[23]

The following day there was a banquet at which General Sikorski raised the issue of the Byelorussians, Ukrainians and Jews who had been Polish subjects before the seizure of Poland's eastern territories by Russia and who should now have the right to join the Polish army. The discussion moved on to the question of frontiers and the General made it very clear that Poland's pre-war frontiers were not negotiable. Stalin dismissed the subject with platitudes and tried simultaneously to ensure that there arose a difference of opinion about the nations resident in Poland's eastern territories. Later the same day, in another building, Stalin and Sikorski signed a joint declaration expressing their intention to fight the Germans to a victorious conclusions; it contained fine words about democracy and respect for international law, but said nothing new about Polish–Soviet relations.[24]

The results of General Sikorski's meetings with Stalin were positive. It was agreed that six Polish divisions would be formed, that 20 000 men, mainly specialists, would be evacuated to the Near East and that the Polish army would move east to the Caspian Sea. Furthermore, the Russians promised to allocate 100 million roubles in the form of a loan for the civilian population, they agreed to having embassy representatives wherever there were large concentrations of Poles and they undertook to release them from work battalions.[25] Naturally everything depended on how these promises were carried out.

General Sikorski returned to Kuybyshev and, having a train at his disposal for several days, visited Buzułuk, Tatishchevo and Totsk, meeting the soldiers. For everyone these were moments of great emotion. Visiting the 6th Infantry Division in Totsk the General told the soldiers: 'God sees into my heart. He sees and knows that my intentions are honourable and honest. My sole aim is a free, just and great Poland. I am leading you towards that Poland and, God willing, will do so.'[26]

On 15 December the General left Russia and, via the Near East, returned to England leaving behind over 40 000 Polish soldiers organised in Russia. Winter was at its height when preparations were begun to move the Polish army to its new quarters.

USA ENTERS THE WAR

Living conditions and opportunities for military training were very poor, but the soldiers' morale was high and even more so since the mighty United States were now in the Allied camp. On 7 December the surprise Japanese attack on Pearl Harbour had taken place and the following day President Roosevelt had declared war on Japan. On 11 December, Hitler, Japan's ally, committed a new blunder and declared that his country was now in a state of war with the powerful North American democracy.

10 The Polish Underground State

THE WHOLE OF POLAND UNDER GERMAN OCCUPATION

The German attack on the Soviet Union and a quick occupation of the whole of Poland by the Nazis made fundamental changes in the country. The area of the *General Gouvernement* was enlarged by the three south-east Polish districts: Lwów, Stanisławów and Tarnopol, with $45\,554$km^2 and a population of $4\,574\,776$. Wołyń and Polesie were incorporated into *Reichskommissariat Ukraine*, districts Wilno and Nowogródek into *Reichskommissariat Ostland*, with the decision to give Wilno to Lithuania and to incorporate the district of Białystok into East Prussia.[1]

The new boundaries were guarded very closely, but the fact that the whole of Poland remained under the same system made underground activity much easier. It covered the whole country and penetrated into all aspects of national life. This activity was liveliest in the *General Gouvernement*; very limited in the territories incorporated into the Reich, because of mass deportations of Poles and tight police control, and downright tragic in the territories annexed by Soviet Union. Apart from the massive deportations into Russia, the occupation authorities had destroyed the local communities with the assistance of the ethnic minorities and Polish communists. The great waves of arrests considerably weakened the underground work in the Białystok area and in the independent District Wilno. In the Lwów area things became so bad, that the commander, after several arrests, was forced to become an NKVD agent and had to be liquidated by the underground. General Rowecki at once made capital out of the short-lived favourable situation, which arose after quick German advance, and reorganised the underground network.

German rule in the whole of Poland was fundamentally different from the same rule in Western Europe. There, although Hitler pursued the idea of hegemony in Europe and the division of the world into spheres of influence, he had no desire to annex territory, except for Alsace and Lorraine. He did not wish to destroy the culture of the nations who lived there.

In all these countries – in France, Belgium, Denmark, Holland, Norway – all secondary schools, unversities, theatres, art galleries and radio stations remained open and cultural life was almost normal. The conquerors were wary of brutality and of hurting the pride of the native population; acts of terror were isolated. In Denmark university students ostentatiously wore small woollen caps in RAF colours; in Holland, in seaside pubs, people listened to the BBC and hummed military songs almost openly.[2]

Things were very different in the East, especially in Poland. There the Germans were looking only for *Lebensraum* and for hands to work, at the lowest social level. Therefore the occupation was one massive attack on the Polish leading classes and on all aspects of cultural and national identity.

On 31 October the Governor, Hans Frank, met in Łódź the Reich's Minister of Propaganda, Joseph Goebbels, and discussed with him the cultural future of the *General Gouvernement*. Goebbels advised him to oppose all Polish attempts to promote Polish culture, to confiscate all radio sets, to close theatres, to liquidate the press. Frank agreed and added to this list some ideas of his own. On the same day that they held this conference, Frank's instructions had been published in which he gave permission for only preparatory and technical schools to be opened. On 4 November he went to Berlin and reported to Hitler, who accepted his activities in the *General Gouvernement*. The dictator especially praised his decision to destroy the Royal Castle in Warsaw, all the more, as the city was never to be rebuilt. He also accepted Frank's possession of the historical castle, Wawel, in Cracow and the removal of works of art from Poland. On 16 December Frank issued new instructions in which he ordered the confiscation of cultural relics and threatened penalties for hiding them. The next instructions concerned the registration of publishers, booksellers, writers, musicians, painters, actors and journalists. All concerts, lectures, serious plays and singing of folk songs were prohibited. Within several months every aspect of Polish cultural life was obstructed and deprived of any chance of further development.[3]

In this situation, when in the West the underground movement was first of all concerned with sabotage, diversion, partisan war and propaganda, in Poland it had to embrace all spheres of national life.

Not only political activity, not only the army, not only propaganda, connected with the war, but also courts, education (on secondary school and university level) the publication of books, protection of cultural relics, theatre and press had to operate as 'underground' activities. Thanks to this, after the war, a very appropriate name for this activity was created: 'The Polish Underground State'.

THE UNDERGROUND STATE

According to the theory of law the definition of a state requires the existence of three elements: territory, population and authority. The first two aroused no doubts, but the problem of authority was different because Poland was under occupation. On the surface the occupiers ruled the country, since they were in a position of power, they had their own courts and police and could enforce obedience, but at every opportunity their orders were sabotaged, since the nation obeyed the Government in the West, represented within the country by the underground authorities. Thanks to this the Underground State was not a myth, but a reality; nevertheless it had to have its own jurisdiction since the execution of the orders of the underground authorities had to rest on a legal basis.

First there had to be certain guidelines, according to which the liquidation of traitors and particularly offensive representatives of the occupying powers could be carried out with a veneer of legality. This point of view was understood in the underground and in the West, and thus the first code of military law was prepared by the Polish Government in France.

UNDERGROUND COURTS

The code envisaged the establishment of courts by the underground commanders in the German and Soviet occupied zones. Death sentences, which required the appropriate Government Delegate's sanction, were meant for persecutors, traitors, spies and *agents provocateurs*.

The first code turned out to be too generalised and therefore the commander of ZWZ prepared his own project and under the name, Special Military Courts, sent it to London on 20 November 1941. Several procedural points were introduced, among them one which stated that the death sentence must be unanimous, General Sikorski approved the new code and it was used in the occupied country, although it received it final form only on 5 January 1944. The cases which most often came before these courts concerned denunciations and working for the enemy police, and, in the second half of the war, plunder committed by partisans who had slipped into banditry.[4]

In the second half of 1942 the Delegacy formed Special Criminal Courts, which were to take the load off the military ones and decide on cases involving civilians.[5]

SECRET EDUCATION

At the very beginning of the occupation, when for a short time the Wehrmacht was the only authority, instructions were issued that all Polish employees were to report to their place of work. This was immediately utilised and all schools, elementary and secondary, were opened. In Cracow, already on 9 September 1939, a Temporary Education Committee, acting openly, was set up, with the Chancellor of the Jagiellonian University at its head.[6]

This situation, however, did not last for long. The German plans of conquest, the destruction of Polish culture and Germanisation had to be commenced at the level of schools and they were the first target. The greatest pressure was employed in the territories incorporated into the Reich, exerted in two directions: establishing new German schools and closing down Polish establishments. The basis for the first moves were the German schools which existed before the war: 500 elementary and fifty seconary schools. All that needed to be done was to enlarge this base, to find a sufficient number of teachers and decide what should happen to Polish children. Should they be sent to the German schools and be subjected to Germanisation, or should some Polish elementary schools be preserved, but at a very low level? This problem was never regulated overall and in the territories incorporated into the Reich it was solved in various ways, but always on the principle that Germanisation must be carried on and that Polish schools must remain at a primitive level.[7]

Things were not quite so bad in the territory of the *General Gouvernement*, since there the German authorities did not attempt the Germanisation of the young generation and the newly-opened German schools were to serve only the children of Nazi civil servants and *Volksdeutschen*. But there also, on Frank's instructions, all secondary schools were closed.

The necessity of continuing education at the secondary level, and in the territories incorporated into the Reich, even at elementary level, was so obvious, that parents, heedless of the prohibition and penalties, at once started to organise secret study-groups. These consisted of a dozen or so pupils who met in private homes. In Silesia, Pomerania and Wielkopolska this was very difficult and not only because of the rigid police control. There was a great lack of teachers. Many had been killed in the September campaign, taken prisoner of war or been deported to the *General Gouvernement*. Nevertheless some secret study-groups at secondary level did start up in many towns and several thousand children benefited from them. The majority were active in Poznań, less so in Pomerania, where they never reached a higher figure than twenty, fewest of all in Silesia, since the the progress of Germanisation there made it necessary to organise study-groups at elementary level.[8]

Similar activity, but on a much larger scale, was initiated in the *General Gouvernement*. It was started at secondary school level with considerable assistance from the Secret Teachers Organisation (*Tajna Organizacja Nauczycielstwa* – TON), which was formed in Warsaw in the autumn of 1939. Within the SZP was a Committee for Public Education (*Komisja Oświecenia Publicznego* – KOP) which aimed at co-ordinating its activities with those of TON. The result was the formation of the Department of Education and Culture within the Government Delegacy in early 1941. All educational matters were brought under its control.[9]

The Germans allowed some Polish elementary schools to open, but no more than 30 per cent of the pre-war number. Nevertheless this was advantageous, since it provided opportunities for giving lessons to older children at a higher level. This began in country areas, where many educated people had taken shelter. Among them were qualified teachers and they offered their services free of change. The same applied to technical schools, legally opened, where the teachers lectured at a higher level than they were allowed to do. The German authorities also accepted agricultural colleges and there it was also possible to organise lectures on the secondary level. Thanks to all this it was possible to organise almost 2000 secret secondary schools in the *General Gouvernement*, based on the study-groups system, and about 65 000 children made use of them.[10]

Of course, the Germans were aware that Poles were fighting Germanisation and cultural degradation and that they were organising underground educational courses, but in their opinion this was not such a bad crime as, for example, underground propaganda, and quite incomparable to armed fighting or industrial sabotage. Therefore the German police, especially during the latter part of the war, spent less time and energy in tracking down underground classes, but in this region the Poles also sustained losses. The clandestine school network was badly hit by new waves of arrests and had to be set up again. For example, in the middle of 1942 the Gestapo arrested 367 teachers, the majority of whom were sent to Auschwitz and in most cases died there.[11]

There was no question of universities being open. The Cracow and Lublin attempts ended with the arrests of the professors, in Warsaw; after the proclamation by the governor, Ludwig Fischer, nobody even tried it. The only concession in this field was the Germans' agreement to last-year students of the Institute of Technology and of the Medical Faculty taking their final examinations. Scientific and Cultural Societies were all also closed down.[12]

But this was not all. Despite the war, which was absorbing so much of the energy and men of the German state, the conquerors had planned to replace the Polish universities by German ones. In Poznań, Arthur Greiser even achieved this, but lack of students caused the university finally to become a research institute working for the war economy. Governor Frank did not want to lag behind Greiser and also planned to establish a German university in Cracow, although the *General Gouvernement* had a different character from Wielkopolska, incorporated into the Reich. Nevertheless war conditions made it too difficult and the plan was abandoned, the final decision being taken by Hitler himself. In Warsaw the Germans had no such plans, but showed their contempt for Polish learning by using the University as a police barracks.[13]

In the mid-1940s Warsaw University began to operate secretly. It was the largest in the underground and in 1944 had 2176 students. In addition, the Institute of Technology operated in the capital as did the Central Agricultural College, the Central School of Commerce and the Open University. At the end of 1940, the Secret University of the Western Lands was established in Warsaw, comprising teachers and students deported from Poznań. These institutions depended to some extent on the technical and agricultural schools and the hospitals, which were operating openly. Altogether about 9000 students passed through the secret institutions of higher education in Warsaw.[14]

In Cracow, where the German *General Gouvernement* authorities were situated, conspiracy was much more difficult than in Warsaw. Also the arrest of the professors from the Jagellonian University in November 1939 and their deportation to Sachsenhausen concentration camp, from which not all of them returned, hampered the first steps towards clandestine lectures. More or less at the same time secret lectures were started at the Stefan Batory University in Wilno and the Jan Kazimierz University in Lwów. Together with the Jagellonian University they comprised about 1000 students.[15]

Since the decision of the 'final solution' concerning Jews had been taken in January 1942 and was impossible to put into practice at once, their life in the ghettos had some semblance of normal life. The Jewish Councils got permission from the Germans to open schools, but they had to support them themselves. In the Warsaw ghetto this action was started in Spring 1941 and in the middle of the next year there were there twenty elementary and technical schools, embracing about 7000 students. The official language was partly Polish, partly Yiddish. Despite the very difficult conditions, some secret teaching at secondary school and university level was also started, chiefly in the range of medicine and chemistry. There lectures were given only in Polish and TON offered limited assistance, since this organisation had some contacts with the ghetto. Legal Jewish schools existed also in the Łódź ghetto, which came into being before the ghetto in Warsaw. In the summer of 1941 there were thirty-six elementary schools there, several special (such as religious and those for deaf and dumb children) and two secondary schools. Altogether they comprised about 15 000 students. A similar situation existed in other ghettos, as in Białystok, Częstochowa, Będzin, Lublin, Lwów and others.[16]

In the *General Gouvernement*, which was enlarged to the south-east after the German offensive in the East, there was also a Ukrainian educational system. The Germans sympathised with this and gave support so the number of schools rose to five times higher than it had been before the war. At the end of the 1943 the number reached 4214, comprising over 600 000 children and over 9000 teachers. Furthermore the Ukrainians had 200 agricultural and 120 technical as well as twelve secondary schools. Formally they had no university, but there were some institutes and several courses at university level which educated doctors of medicine, agronomists, chemists and veterinary surgeons, needed by the German administration. Against the intentions of the occupying power many Poles profited from these facilities. The Byelorussians also had a free hand in organising their educational system; they had their own Inspectorate in Białystok, and young Poles, behind the Germans' backs, used these schools as well.[17]

THE THEATRE

The problem of the theatre in occupied Poland was different from the problem of schooling and the Germans tried to solve it in another way. First they intended to open their own theatres as soon as possible, because this was important for propaganda and in the territories incorporated into the Reich helped quicker Germanisation. Before German theatres were opened in various towns, travelling theatres came around: in Silesia a theatre from Bytom; in Pomerania from Gdańsk. In December 1939 a permanent German theatre was opened in Bydgoszcz, in January 1940 in Łódź; in March 1941 in Poznań.[18]

The *General Gouvernement* was to be the territory where the Poles had the right to exist, but the Germans had to have their own theatres there, not for Germanisation, but to emphasise the superiority of German culture over Polish. Therefore Poles had no right to visit the German theatres. The first German play was staged by a German company on 31 October 1939 in Cracow, at the Słowacki Theatre. Hans Frank wanted to have a representative theatre of his own, so it was opened in Cracow, in September 1940 as *Staatstheater des Generalgouvernements*. One month later the *Theater der Stadt Warschau* was opened on the premises of the *Teatr Polski*.

In contrast to the secondary schools and universities, the Germans did not order all Polish theatres to close, since they saw in them an instrument to be used for propaganda and depravity. Therefore, while forbidding the staging of operas, serious plays and peculiarly Polish spectacles, they permitted the opening of cabarets and small theatres showing cheap entertainment and pornography.[19] Ths was connected with a long-term plan, since they ordered a registration of Polish actors, which unfortunately brought them 1356 names. A certain percentage of these agreed to act on the small stages sponsored by the occupants, several accepted the invitation to act in a few propaganda films. One of these, *Heimkehr* (Homecoming) was a lampoon on the Polish nation.[20]

The theatre, essential for the normal, cultural development of the nation, was also active in the underground. By private initiative theatrical groups, often composed of amateurs, began to form in Warsaw, Cracow, Lwów, Poznań and many other towns. At first they confined themselves to reading plays to a dozen or so spectators and then became more ambitious, producing plays in small private homes, cellars and small halls. They performed Polish and foreign classics in costume and with scenery to fair-sized audiences. Reading and poetry evenings also took place. In the autumn of 1939, the National Theatrical Institute (PIST) was re-established in Warsaw, and in 1941 the secret Theatrical Council was formed there. Its task was to oversee PIST and prepare plans for the rebuilding of theatres and theatrical use after the war. The Department of Education and Culture of the Government Delegacy exercised overall control and provided financial assistance.[21]

During the whole war the achievements of these underground activities were considerable. Twenty dramatic and poetic theatres were organised, comprising two professional, eight partly amateur and ten children's theatrical groups. Furthermore, first of all in Warsaw, there were twenty-one puppet theatres, five poetry groups and three schools of drama. Some dramatic competitions were organised.[22]

The German method of deception towards Jews, to lull their suspicions in the face of total destruction, brought about apparent paradox where the theatre was concerned. The authorities raised no difficulty and in the Warsaw ghetto there were several theatres operating openly. The first was *Eldorado* which opened in December 1940 and gave performances in Yiddish, the next *Femina* where operettas and musical comedies were performed in Polish. In July 1941 the most ambitious *Teatr Kameralny* was opened with many first-class Jewish actors; in November of the same year *Nowy Azazel*, with performances in Yiddish. There was also a cabaret, *Na pięterku*. In July 1942, when the liquidation of the ghetto began, all these theatres ceased to exist.[23]

There was a similar situation in the ghetto of Łódź, where concerts of classical music and revues were organised in the *Dom Kultury*. Jewish theatres were also open in the ghettos of Lwów and Wilno before they were stopped by the mass extermination.[24]

Things were different where the cinema was concerned. The

Germans used films as an instrument of propaganda and the underground did not start to give secret performances of its own, but ordered a boycott of German films, especially those that were anti-Polish and connected with the war, which were shown in 200 cinemas in the *General Gouvernement*. Unfortunately the results of this boycott were poor, although the underground press carried constant propaganda, slogans were written on walls and fences, and tear-gas was thrown into the cinemas. According to the German figures, in 1941 9 million Poles watched films in the *General Gouvernement*, but, of course, these statistics included the same people several times over.[25]

It was a different story under the Soviet occupation. There the occupants did much to maintain the fiction that cultural life was free and therefore all the theatres remained open. The majority of the actors, producers and scene-painters who had not been arrested, returned to their profession and the repertoire was not specially slanted against the Polish classics. Of course, nobody had a free hand and the choice of famous Polish plays, such as *Wesele* by Stanisław Wyspiański or *Dziady* by Adam Mickiewicz was out of the question. In Wilno, during the short Lithuanian occupation, cultural life was reasonably free, in Kowno Polish refugees were able to stage two of Wyspiański's very patriotic plays. In Lwów the Board of People's Commissars decided upon the opening of five state theatres: two Ukrainian (opera and drama), two Polish (drama and revues) and one Jewish. This decision was realised. There was also one theatre in Białystok.[26]

PROTECTION OF CULTURAL RELICS AND BOOKS

Poland has been the ground for many wars in her history and the country has been plundered and robbed many times, but her cultural relics and works of art were never so systematically destroyed and carried away as during the German occupation. Monuments were blown up and demolished, historical buildings were burned down, cemeteries – where lay those who had fought for freedom – were ploughed up, art galleries and museums were stripped and their collections taken to Germany; thousands of books were burned or sent for pulping. The losses were very heavy. Parallel to the mania of destruction and individual robbery, there was a systematic, almost scientific action of surveying, recording, segregating and finally carrying away thousands of valuable items. On the territories incorporated into the Reich there were teams of specialists originating from *SS-Ahnenerbe*, which was to study the 'Indogerman' heritage. They belonged to the *Einsatzgruppen* which followed closely behind the army. Another similar institution, the *Haupttreuhendestelle Ost*, subordinated to the head of the SS, Heinrich Himmler, was also active there. He wanted to widen its activities in the *General Gouvernement*, but Hans Frank, who was also interested in plunder, managed to stop him.[27]

Another very powerful man, interested in loot, was the commander of the German Air Force, Hermann Göring, a very keen collector of works of art. He sent his own representative to Poland, Frank offered him help and legalised everything by his decree of 16 December 1939. Two collecting points were established, one in Warsaw, another in Cracow and no more than six months had passed before Poland had lost all her valuable relics that were within reach of German hands.

What could not be carried away was destroyed on the spot. In the territories incorporated into the Reich practically every Polish monument was destroyed; in the *General Gouvernement* those which specially annoyed the Germans. In Cracow the monument commemorating the great Polish victory over the Teutonic Knights at Grunwald in 1410, as also those to Polish national heros, such as Tadeusz Kościuszko and Adam Mickiewicz, were blown up. Kościuszko (1746–1818) was a Polish hero, leader of the first Polish uprising against Russia after the second partition of Poland, also a hero of the USA, participant of the War of Independence. Mickiewicz (1798–1855) was the greatest Polish poet, a romantic, and a contemporary of Byron and Shelley. In Warsaw the Germans behaved in a ridiculous way by putting on the monument of the great Polish astronomer, Nicholas Copernicus, a plate describing him as a German.[28]

It was very difficult to withstand this looting by the Germans, but it had to be done and much effort was expended in this respect. At the end of 1939 a special secret committee was formed in Warsaw with responsibility for registering losses and protecting the most valuable works which had been removed from threatened places and hidden. It also carried out conservation work on pictures, sculpture and old prints, and registered the condition of monuments and private libraries. Later on the committee worked on the register of German relics and works of art which would be claimed after the war as compensation for Polish losses.[29]

Thanks to the considerable number of people involved in this action thousands of works of art, valuable manuscripts and documents were protected from German hands. Some of them were destroyed in later military actions, but the majority, especially outside Warsaw, were saved for future generations. Many very valuable items and collections of books were also recovered from Germany after the war and brought back to Poland.[30]

Frank's decree of 26 October 1939, that all printed matter and its distribution needed permission, was only the first step towards stopping all publishing. Later another decree was issued about the registration of all printing presses, publishing firms, bookshops and libraries, and the occupying power began the destruction of all publications dangerous to German political plans. The Chief German Propaganda Office published a list of 1500 Polish writers who were completely banned.[31]

In the territory incorporated into the Reich all Polish printing presses were confiscated; in the *General Gouvernement* some printers managed to remain at their presses and although they were controlled, they did have some possibility of printing illegal papers, books and pamphlets. Further possibilities had to be created by setting up secret presses literally under ground and they were very important, since publishing was essential for resistance work. From time to time the occupying power allowed a new book to be published, but it had to be purely instructive: cookery books, books on planting vegetables and such like. Alongside the necessity of possessing a printing press, it was very difficult to get hold of paper, bring it to the presses and later distribute the printed matter.

Life went on, however, and people wanted new books and reprints of old ones, which had to be produced. In addition to large quantities of school textbooks and military manuals, many books and pamphlets on literature, poetry, plays, science, music, politics and scouting were also printed. Very often underground books had false dust-jackets and title-pages describing quite innocent and fictitous contents. Mostly they were reprints of pre-war books, but there was a secret literary movement and some part of the newly-published texts were new. In this way, in 1940, Czesław Miłosz published his new poem in Warsaw, under the pseudonym *Jan Syruć*, in only forty-six copies. The most famous underground publication was *The Squadron 303* by

Arkady Fiedler, published in 4000 copies. This book about the battle of Britain and Polish participation in it, got the highest price on the black market.

The Home Army possessed its own secret publishing units in Warsaw and Cracow; its books usually carried the mark KOPR. The Government Delegacy, many political groups and military and social organisations also carried out publishing work. 1075 different titles of books and pamphlets were published under the German occupation, testifying to the extent of underground publishing activity. This figure does not include works which appeared during the Warsaw Uprising, since this activity was quite open, but it does, however, include publications from the Warsaw ghetto.[32]

THE UNDERGROUND PRESS

Both the occupying powers had almost immediately closed down all the Polish independent Press and replaced it by papers printed in Polish, but entirely under their control. Under the German administration the papers in Polish were published only in the *General Gouvernement* and there were about fifty of them, mostly in the larger towns. There were among others: the *Nowy Kurjer Warszawski* in Warsaw the *Goniec Krakowski* in Cracow, the *Kurjer Częstochowski* in Częstochowa and the *Gazeta Lwowska* in Lwów, after June 1941.

Under the Soviet administration there were two papers in Polish in Lwów: the *Czerwony Sztandar* and the *Nowe Widnokręgi*. In Wilno, under the short-lived Lithuanian administration, there were two Polish papers: the *Kurjer Wileński* and the pro-Lithuanian *Gazeta Codzienna*, both to a certain extent independent. Later, when Wilno was occupied by the Germans, the *Propaganda Amt* published the *Goniec Codzienny*.[33]

The aim of these papers, staffed unfortunately by Polish collaborators, was to persuade the Poles that they had themselves to blame for their defeat, that their conquerors were magnificent and undefeatable and that they must accept the reality, which nevertheless was better than possession of their own state. This attack on the morale of the nation, low as it was after the defeat of September, had to be withstood and therefore, almost immediately after the beginning of the occupation the first underground papers were published. On 10 October 1939, only several days after the capitulation of Warsaw, the first weekly, *Polska Żyje*, appeared, followed on 5 November by the first edition of the *Biuletyn Informacyjny*, which was the organ of SZP, later ZWZ and then AK.[34]

After these first steps an avalanche of newspapers appeared, published in several towns, but above all in Warsaw and Cracow. It was very difficult to publish and distribute them in the territories incorporated into the Reich; however some, copies published in Łódź in 1941–2 have been preserved: *Drogowskazy, Horyzont, Jutrzenka, Pochodnia, Na Zachodnim Szańcu* and the organ of ZWZ, *Kronika Polska*.[35]

It was even more difficult to achieve anything in this field under the Soviet occupation, since the NKVD, with the help of the ethnic minorities and Polish Communists, managed to infiltrate society completely. Nevertheless some underground newspapers were published in Lwów and Wilno, but if there is anywhere one single copy in existence, it is really a *rara avis*. Everything was destroyed when Soviet Russia returned to Poland in 1944. It is difficult to imagine that there is even a single copy in the archives in Poland, but in the Polish archives in London there is one photocopy of a monthly, *Polska w Walce*, published in Wilno in 1940 by the ZWZ.[36]

The range of subjects and forms of publication of the underground press was enormous. Not only did the official military and political authorities have their own publications, but every organisation, every political party, every secret group tried to justify itself by having its own organ. Ideological, political, military, social, literary, philosophical, scouting and humorous magazines were founded, both in Warsaw and the provinces. The underground press not only provided information about the development of the political and military situation all over the world, thus keeping up morale and the will to survive, but also publicised plans for the future, printed literary and scientific works, helped in the development of political thought and organised competitions. The official underground authorities used the press for publishing decrees, proclamations, orders and death-sentences on traitors.

The real figure for individual magazine titles is unknown, since not all of them survived in the form of a single intact copy. In the Polish archieves in Poland and in London there is a total of 1174 titles. There were probably more – up to about 1400.

It is also very difficult to establish where respective papers were published, since conspiracy demanded that the name of the town should not be printed. Now we know where more than 900 papers were published. Mostly they were run off on Roneo, but 325 of them were printed on normal presses and this was the highest figure in occupied Europe, although conditions in Poland were the most difficult. In this way the French underground managed to print 270 papers and the Dutch only 160. Normally the life of an underground paper was short, sometimes it survived for only one issue, but there were some, which appeared regularly throughout the whole occupation. In this respect Poland was also the best in Europe, since there were seventeen such papers there while in France there were only thirteen and in Holland eight. The number of separate titles corresponded with the growing underground activity. In 1939 there were thirty clandestine newspapers in Poland; in 1940 above 200; in 1941 – 290; in 1942 – 380, in 1943 – 500 and in 1944 – 600. One of the reasons for this growth was the necessity for decentralisation, since the problem of distribution to the provincial towns each year became more and more difficult. The circulation was normally small, but the organ of the Home Army, *Biuletyn Informacyjny*, in 1943, twice printed 47 000 copies. In this respect the West was much superior: the French *Combat* several times reached the number of 300 000 copies and the Dutch *De Waarheid* 100 000, but there the printing presses worked almost in the open.[37]

Statistics on the publishers of the clandestine papers are also important, because they show their influence and help in an objective estimate of their strength in the underground. The Home Army, the Delegacy and all the political and military groups, associated with them, together published 1033 journals, the Communists eighty-two, the Jews (mostly in the Warsaw ghetto), forty-three, the National Armed Forces (NSZ) thirty-three, the Ukrainians four, and unattributed titles nine. Fifteen journals were published in hebrew and Yiddish, fourteen in German (*Operation N*), one in French and one in English (the last two were for prisoners of war in German camps in Poland). A special role was played by the fourteen papers published in German by Operation N, which belonged to AK. It was a kind of diversion in the German army and administration.[38]

DIVERSION AND SABOTAGE

Open fight, arms in hand, was still impossible, so action had to be restricted to sabotage. To increase efficiency, in April 1940, Rowecki formed the Reprisal Organisation (*Związek Odwetu*), as an integral part of the ZWZ. It had its units not only in the *General Gouvernement* and territories incorporated into the Reich, but also deep inside Germany, and possessed its own means of manufacturing explosives.

With the outbreak of the German–Soviet war and the opening-up of large areas in the East, General Rowecki brought into being a special diversionary group under the code-name *Wachlarz* (Fan) at the end of 1941, the two aims of which were to continue diversionary and sabotage work, and to foster a general uprising at the end of the war. *Wachlarz* was intended to operate in five regions from the Baltic to the Black Sea, but in practice its activities were limited to the three central districts. Amongst other officers, thirty-three British-trained parachutists were sent there. German lines of communication were the primary target.[39]

Some good results were achieved by the Intelligence. Before the German attack in the East, it sent valuable information to London on the dispositions of German forces and afterwards reports from behind the front lines. These reports helped Churchill to warn Stalin that Hitler was preparing an attack. This Intelligence also operated deep inside the Reich.

The establishment of a strong underground army, under one command, required the amalgamation of many army groups, which operated in occupied Poland. There were about a hundred, most of which were not directly connected with any political movement and were thus quite easily brought under the unified command of ZWZ. However, because of the lack of a government of national unity in 1939, some of the political parties began to form their own underground military cadres, not only to fight invaders, but also to ensure strength at the end of the war and in the subsequent struggle for power. It was a difficult problem, especially since the politicans suspected that the pre-war ruling group (*Sanacja*) in the ZWZ command had too strong an influence. Therefore in the first years of the war it was impossible to subordinate to the ZWZ command *Narodowa Organizacja Wojskowa* (National Military Organisation) of the National Party and *Bataliony Chłopskie* (Peasant Battalions) of the Peasant Party. The same applied to *Narodowe Siły Zbrojne* – NSZ (National Armed Forces) of the National Radical Camp and to some military units of *Obóz Polski Walczącej* (Fighting Poland Camp) of *Sanacja*. But General Sikorski was not discouraged by the initial lack of success and on 14 February 1942 issued an order changing the ZWZ into the *Armia Krajowa* (Home Army). It did not change the strength of the underground units, but had a psychological effect on all those who were reluctant to accept the command and authority of General Rowecki.[40]

THE DEVELOPMENT OF THE GOVERNMENT DELEGACY

The decision to have politico-military dualism in Polish underground affairs by creating the Government Delegacy did not make things easier. During the war even the most democratic countries, such as Britain and the United States, gave almost absolute power to Churchill and Roosevelt, understanding that the situation demanded it. As General Sikorski was simultaneously Prime Minister and Commander-in-Chief, the helm of Polish afairs was also controlled by one man. But in Poland itself, where the reign of terror ruled and where every step was fraught, everything had to be settled via two channels. The underground could not itself change the situation, so that the chief efforts of General Rowecki and Delegate Ratajski were directed to alleviation of the evils of dualism. In practice, the authority of the ZWZ and Home Army commander prevailed and he was the real leader of the underground struggle.

THE DIRECTORATE OF CIVIL RESISTANCE

During Cyryl Ratajski's time in office, the Delegacy's operative machinery was created. Twenty departments, corresponding to the main pre-war ministries, were set up. Some of them – internal affairs, information, education, finance control, Directorate of Civil Resistance (*Kierownictwo Walki Cywilnej*) and justice – were working for the present, while others such as industry and trade, agriculture, etc., were preparing plans for the post-war period. There were also district representatives. The Delegacy had also its own press, its first publication being the official fortnightly *Rzeczypospolita Polska*. To a certain extent, the Delegacy organised underground cultural life and every three months sent reports to London.[41]

The Directorate of Civil Resistance (KWC) requires greater attention. In April 1941, the Government Delegate, in agreement with the ZWZ commander, set in motion the KWC. Its task was to organise a boycott of the occupying powers' actions, the liquidation of collaborators and to carry out 'minor sabotage'. KWC was based on political and social organisations, from which a General Council of the KWC was formed in Warsaw.[42]

POLITICAL PARTIES

The Delegacy drew its support only from part of the political forces operating in Poland; that is to say from the four parties comprising PKP. Many smaller groups, which had existed before the war or which had grown up during it, and were therefore not admitted to the PKP, assembled together in the Self-Defence (*Społeczna Organisacja Samoobrony* – SOS). Through KWC and SOS they were thus connected with the mainstream of underground work.[43]

A special position in SOS was occupied by two groups of former Piłsudski followers: the afore-mentioned Fighting Poland Camp (OPW) and Convocation of Organisations for Independence (KON). They recognised the Government Delegacy, the Home Army and the existing political arrangement, but they criticised the four main parties for monopolising power, although they themselves had only small support.

In contrast to these, there were other political groupings which continued to oppose the Government Delegacy and the Home Army, although they fully recognised the Polish State and resisted foreign influence. They represented the far right in the form of two organisations: *Szaniec* with a weekly paper under the same name and the military cadres called *Związek Jaszczurczy*, and *Konfederacja Narodu* with the fortnightly *Nowa Polska* and military cadres, *Uderzenie*. When at the beginning of 1942 the National Party had decided to subordinate its military cadres (NOW) to the Home Army, a considerable number of soldiers opposed to it, joined *Związek Jaszczurczy* and in September 1942 created the National Armed Forces (*Narodowe Siły Zbrojne* – NSZ). They were subordinated to the newly-created Provisional National Political Council (*Tymczasowa Narodowa Rada Polityczna*). NSZ fiercely fought against communism, and opposed the open struggle with the Germans, since this automatically aided the Red Army, and its propaganda was directed against the *Armia Krajowa*, recognised as their main rival.[44]

All these parties and groups, irrespective of their individual programmes and sympathies, accepted the full independence of

Poland, and therefore they were part of the Underground State. The fact that they were fighting for influence and that they were thinking about post-war Poland and preparing themselves for the struggle for power, did not disqualify them. Only a few countries, first of all Great Britain and the United States, had real governments of national unity and were able to avoid a fight for power during the war.

A NEW POLISH COMMUNIST PARTY

This general trend towards regaining full independence was broken by only one political group. This was the communist party. After the Ribbentrop–Molotov pact it found itself in a difficult situation, and did not know what to do, but under the Soviet occupation it co-operated with the NKVD, even after discovering that the fact of being a communist did not guarantee a man's safety. Stalin did not tolerate the slightest national or patriotic feelings and accepted only those who were 100 per cent Soviet agents.

After the German attack the communists left East Poland together with the Red Army, some of them found themselves in Kuybyshev and continued their activities there, publishing *Nowe Widnokręgi*. After the Sikorski–Maisky pact they became more active and on the night 28/29 December 1941 two of them, Paweł Finder (1904–1944) and Marceli Nowotko (1893–1942) were dropped by parachute into Poland, to organise the Polish Workers' Party (*Polska Partia Robotnicza* – PPR). It became a reality on 5 January 1942, but despite considerable assistance from the USSR, its influence amongst the Polish population was slight. Nevertheless the party issued a declaration, full of patriotic slogans, in which Poles were incited to immediate military action, although the Germans were still on the outskirts of Moscow.[45]

11 Further War Developments and Polish Participation

THE BATTLE OF THE ATLANTIC

For over two years the United States remained neutral, but they watched carefully the events in Europe and slowly prepared themselves for intervention. After Congress had decided to open large credits for rebuilding the army, President Roosevelt followed up with his decision about protection for the covoys and at that time the United States practically found themselves in military conflict with the German Navy in the Atlantic, although the declaration of war by Hitler was still far away. The Lend-Lease Bill, accepted some time later, was the culmination of these steps and the Atlantic, after the Battle of Britain, became the most important theatre of war for Europe.

During the First World War German submarines had strangled the British Isles to the extent that the civilian population had been on the verge of starvation. Therefore it had to be expected that Hitler, once planning a new war, would have them very high on his list of priorities. But it did not happen. When deciding the speedy rebuilding of the Navy, he gave the order to go ahead with capital ships (Z-Plan Fleet). His achievements were trivial and at the beginning of the war every comparison favoured Great Britain: in battleships the advantage was 7:1, in cruisers 6:1, in destroyers 9:1. The result – very pleasant for the British – was that on the outbreak of war, Admiral Karl Dönitz, the Commander of the German submarine fleet, had only fifty-seven vessels, of which forty-five were ready for action. According to his calculations he needed 300 boats for his task.[1]

In September 1939 the British merchant navy, at that time the largest in the world, possessed almost 18 million tonnes, but the lines of communication of the colossal Empire were very widespread, and so she assigned only 8.5 million tons directly for war purposes, although even that represented a powerful force. The substantial French fleet of almost 3 million tonnes in the first phase of the war, was occupied by its own imperial sea routes and after the defeat no longer counted, but there were the merchant fleets of less powerful allies: Norway, Belgium and Holland, which to a certain extent had managed to keep out of German hands. The same applied to the small Polish fleet, which at the beginning of the war had forty-two vessels of 140 000 tonnes. Fortunately the majority fo them were at that time outside the Baltic Sea. The merchant fleet of the United States amounted to 12 million tonnes of which 6 million were designated for the war on the Pacific and Atlantic.[2]

The German intelligence was aware of these figures and of the capacity of the British and American shipyards, and although the final figures were too optimistic, it gave Admiral Dönitz the basis for his calculations. In his opinion the level of Allied tonnage sunk monthly should be kept at 700 000 tons in order to gain the upper hand and win.[3]

On 3 September 1939 the German submarine, U-30, sank the passenger liner, *Athenia*, and this was the beginning of the Battle of the Atlantic, one of the most important of the Second World War. Until recently only the figures of losses of both sides were known, thanks to conventional intelligence. The Allied losses were considerable and in the first four months of the war the Germans sank 755 392 tonnes on the Atlantic and later about 200 000 tonnes per month. Suddenly, in February 1942, the figure leaped to 440 000 tonnes and in June even to 652 000, near to Admiral Dönitz's target. For several months this state of affairs remained unchanged until suddenly, in December 1942, the Allied losses fell to 300 000 tons.[4]

THE ENIGMA SECRET

To-day it is possible to write about it quite openly, since the most guarded secret of the Second World War has already been disclosed. The problem was connected with the pre-war success of the Polish cryptanalysts, when the secret of *Enigma* was broken. The German Admiralty was the first to introduce *Enigma* to the service, it had complicated it considerably and the British had great difficulties in breaking the barrier of the German sea codes. And that time the Allied losses at sea were enormous.[5]

The cryptanalysts carried on their stubborn, secret struggle and both sides were successful, since the Germans had also managed to break the British codes, but finally Bletchley Park was triumphant. In December 1942 there was a breakthrough; later the British cryptanalysts overcame other difficulties and in May 1943 the Germans were able to sink only 200 000 tonnes, but lost forty-three submarines. This was the turning-point of the Battle of the Atlantic. The German losses in U-boats were going up. During the first quarter of 1943 they lost forty, during the second, seventy-three; during the third, seventy-one, and during the last, fifty-three U-boats. In May 1944 the German Admiralty issued an order to withdraw the U-boats from the North Atlantic. The battle was over and this was mainly the result of the excellent job done by Bletchley Park and the initial success of Polish cryptanalysts.[6]

POLISH TECHNICAL INVENTIONS

Besides breaking the *Enigma* secret, Poles in England had other successes of a similar kind, which helped the Allies in their final victory. Rudolf Gundlach designed a reversible periscope which allowed observation of the foreground and the background. The British used it as widely as possible and equipped the following tanks with it: Crusader (two periscopes), Churchill (four periscopes), Valentine (four periscopes) and Cromwell (five periscopes). Because of Anglo-American co-operation this periscope was sent to the United States and then, under the Lend-Lease Bill, found its way in mass transports to Russia and was used in Soviet tanks: T-34 (three periscopes) and JS-1 (five periscopes).[7]

The next achievement of this kind was a 'transceiver' radio set constructed by Tadeusz Heftman. It was used by intelligence agents and underground soldiers in the occupied countries and with a range of 1000km, weighed only 4.5kg and measured $27 \times 20 \times 7$cm.

Another successful inventor was Józef Kosacki who in 1941 constructed a mine-detector. After many tests the British accepted it and started mass production under the name *Mine Detector Polish Type, no. 1*. It was used on a considerable scale in 1942 in North Africa as well as at the invasion of the European continent in 1944. In addition, an anti-aircraft gun, designed by Jan Podsędkowski, was accepted for mass production, since it was a quarter the price of any other. 50,000 of them were produced and supplied to the British Navy and Army.[8]

THE POLISH NAVY IN THE WEST

Polish warships took part in the operations at sea, mostly on the Atlantic, where on several occasions more than 100 ships were engaged, protecting over 700 vessels. The small Polish fleet, which after the collapse of France had possessed only three destroyers and one submarine, was strengthened by others. They were: the destroyers *Piorun*, commissioned on 5 November 1940, *Krakowiak* and *Kujawiak* on 30 May 1941, *Ślązak* on 14 April 1942 and *Orkan* on 11 November 1942. They were joined by three submarines: *Sokół*, commissioned on 19 January 1941, *Jastrząb* on 4 November 1941 and *Dzik* on 11 October 1942.

The submarines were active first of all in the Mediterranean, where two of them, *Dzik* and *Sokół* got the name 'the terrible twins', because they sank altogether thirty-eight ships of about 60 000 tonnes. The destroyers operated mostly in the Atlantic, protecting convoys. *Piorun* took part in the chase of the battleship *Bismarck* and *Ślązak* in the very difficult raid on Dieppe, during the night of 18/19 August 1942.

There were also three Polish liners, *Piłsudski*, *Batory* and *Sobieski*, which were engaged in carrying troops on many occasions: to Norway, from France to Great Britain, from Australia and New Zealand to Europe and North Africa. Unfortunately *Piłsudski* was sunk by the Germans as early as 26 November, 1939.[9]

THE LEND-LEASE BILL AND AMERICAN HELP TO USSR

The Battle of the Atlantic was inseparably connected with the Lend-Lease Bill passed by the Congress of the United States, since supplies had to be carried across the Atlantic Ocean to Europe. It was a great burden on the American economy, but Congress had decided that from every point of view it was cheaper to help those who were still fighting Hitler, than in the end to remain alone face-to-face with him.

American output had to be stepped up enormously immediately after the beginning of the Russo–German war, because President Roosevelt at once promised Stalin help. On 1 October 1941 an agreement was signed whereby the Soviet Union received 14 795 aeroplanes, 7056 tanks, 385 883 cars, 4 478 000 tonnes of food and so on. This was help on a colossal scale, but Soviet propaganda has done everything possible to minimise it and after the war Russia never paid for the goods received. Soviet history also minimised this help as far as possible.[10]

FLIGHTS AND PARACHUTE DROPS TO POLAND

After the first experimental drop of parachutists to Poland, in February 1941, there was a long pause until November. Many problems had to be solved in connection with these very difficult operations. First, General Sikorski wanted to use Polish pilots in flights to Poland and he approached the British authorities about it. They agreed and in the autumn of 1941 three Polish bomber crews reported to 138 Squadron at Newmarket, and two months later, another two arrived. They consisted of volunteers who had already completed the normal contingent of bombing sorties and received extra training in very low flights and astronomical and visual navigation, since Poland was too far for radar signals.

After the slow, heavy Whitley had been abandoned, four-engined Halifaxes were brought into use. These were bombers, also slow, flying at only 300km per hour, with a normal range of 2500km, a load capacity of 1900kg and a crew of seven. Since the distance from London to Warsaw over Denmark is almost 1600km, they had to be adapted by being given extra fuel tanks. The range was increased to 3500km, but at the expense of its maximum load, which fell to 1100kg.

Getting five Polish crews into the special squadron was a step forward, but General Sikorski could not stop at that. He continued to press the British authorities for an independent Polish flight for liaison with Poland and at the same time looked around for better equipment. He had in mind American Liberators, with a range of almost 5000km, a speed of 480km per hour and high load capacity. Both these problems were to be settled in the future, but for the present the flights were possible under very limited conditions. They had to be at night and when there was a full moon, so flights were possible only in winter, the later autumn and early spring. Taking into account the moon's phases, this meant at most forty operational nights over the year.[11]

The second important problem was to secure proper equipment in a sufficient quantity for the underground army in Poland. After the fall of France Britain was the only source of supplies for the Polish forces. It would be a simple problem if the British had had plenty of equipment to spare, but this was not the case. The British war preparations were complete only in a few narrowly defined sectors and industry was only just going over to rapid and large-scale military production. The Polish section of SOE did its best to meet both Polish requirements, but its goodwill was not enough. Therefore General Sikorski turned to the United States and raised this question with President Roosevelt. The underground army needed automatic weapons, all kind of equipment for sabotage and irregular warfare, cameras for intelligence purposes, printing machinery, duplicators, typewriters for underground propaganda and so on. At first the British protested and raised objections to direct contacts between the Polish General Staff and the Americans, but finally a mutually satisfactory solution was reached.

The third problem was connected with the receiving end of the drops in occupied Poland, quick and efficient radio liaison and sufficient protection for these operations.

For the dropping-zone it was necessary to find an open space, as remote as possible from main roads and difficult of access for German motorised transport. It might be a large forest-clearing or an open field, ploughed or otherwise, from a quarter to half a kilometre. From the pilot's point of view it should ideally be a few kilometres from a lake or river-bend to locate the small but vital piece of ground. The reception station consisted of two parts, one on a small hill with a radio set and red guiding light, the second at the actual dropping-zone, responsible for displaying a set of lights in arrow-formation to indicate the direction of the wind, taking charge of the parachutists and collecting the containers and packages.

The BBC was involved in these operations allowing its transmitters to be used by the Polish Radio in London. The idea was not new, for the BBC had been used for various secret activities during the war.

Almost every Polish programme contained musical interludes and certain tunes were selected, earmarked 'reserved' and the underground army in Poland was given the details in strictest secrecy. The tunes were then divided into groups and communicated to the various dropping-zones. When the appropriate tune was played at the end of the Polish Radio transmission, the reception committee would know that the planes were to be expected that very evening, about midnight. These operations had the code-name *Jodoform*.

In the first, experimental period, which lasted until the end of April 1942, only nine drops were carried out, consisting of forty-eight parachutists (forty-one soldiers and seven political couriers), 2 tonnes of supplies, $1 660 850 in banknotes and gold, £1775 and 885 000 German marks. For technical reasons the drops reached no further than the Warsaw region.[12]

FURTHER BUILD-UP OF THE POLISH AIR FORCE

After the Battle of Britain, in which Polish pilots distinguished themselves so much, the tendency to expand the Polish Air Force was increased and in this respect the British backed the Polish authorities. There were, however, difficulties, the main one being lack of manpower. This was common to all Polish formations in the West. The strength of the Polish Air Force after the evacuation from France was only 8384 officers and men and by the end of 1940 was 700 soldiers less. This was the result not only of losses sustained in battle but also by transfers to other services. This decline continued although 290 Polish pilots had come from Palestine, where they had arrived by various routes from occupied Poland.[13]

The authorities tried to improve things in several ways, but with poor results. Several hundred volunteers arrived from the United States, as well as from South America, but the standard of education of the latter was low and they were used only in non-combatant service. Only at the end of 1941 did the situation improve rapidly, since as the result of the military agreement with Soviet Russia almost 2000 airmen arrived in Great Britain.

Despite these difficulties the rebuilding of the Polish Air Force went on and the British were helpful. Departing from their own rigid regulations, they pretended not to see that the Polish ground staff was not up to strength, in fact was never more than 80 per cent of the required number. Lack of personnel was the reason for still greater dependence on the British authorities than had been anticipated in the agreement. There were no Polish operational commands – liaison and all services were entirely in British hands.[14]

This expansion resulted in the building up of more Polish squadrons: three of fighters – 315, 316 and 317, and two of bombers – 304 and 305. From April 1941 the first Polish fighter Wing, No. 1, was in operation; from August, the second, No. 2. Altogether, at the beginning of 1942 the Polish Air Force in Great Britain consisted of nine fighter and four bomber squadrons, possessing 144 fighters, seventy-two bombers and twelve reconnaissance planes. There were also some schools and workshops.[15]

After its defeat in the Battle of Britain, the German Air Force abandoned attacks on the islands, reducing them to raids on the Midlands and Merseyside, and the situation was slowly changing. The British started aggressive sorties and each day they became stronger. Bomber formations were appearing above military and industrial targets in Northern France, in Belgium and later in Germany.

Polish squadrons took part in these raids and achieved some successes. All of them underwent training in night flights. The fighter squadrons received new planes, *Beaufighters*, equipped with radar. In 1941 they shot down or destroyed on the ground 198 German planes, with a further fifty-two probably destroyed and fifty-seven damaged. this was 27 per cent of the total achieved by all the fighter squadrons stationed in Great Britain.

At the end of 1940 all four Polish bomber squadrons received *Wellingtons 1*, sixteen for each squadron. These were heavy two-engined bombers with a crew of six.

In 1940 and 1941 Polish bombers took part in many raids and attacked railway lines, factories and airfields in Northern France, Belgium and Germany, flying over Cologne, Mannheim, Düsseldorf, Essen and Berlin. *Wellingtons* were slow, their speed being no more than 290km per hour, their ceiling no more than 6000m, and the German night-fighters and anti-aircraft guns were good, so losses were heavy. Up to the end of 1941, 145 Polish airmen were killed, five posted as missing sixty-seven became prisoners of war and thirty-eight lost their lives during training. Forty-nine aircraft were lost.[16]

THE CARPATHIAN BRIGADE IN THE DESERT

General Rommel's victorious offensive in North Africa changed the balance of force in that region. German tanks were now at the gates of Egypt and would probably have advanced further if not for the fortress of Tobruk which was still in British hands. It was defended by the 9th Australian Infantry Division with a Bengal Regiment of Motorised Cavalry and British artillery and the 32nd Brigade of Tanks. The line of fortifications with a radius of 15km stretched for about 50km and reached the sea at both extremities.

At this time the Polish Carpathian Brigade was in the fortified camp of Mersa-Matruh, guarding the entrance to the Nile Delta and from there, in the middle of August, General Kopański (promoted on 3 May 1940) was summoned by the new British commander. This was General Claude Auchinleck, who in June had taken over from General Wavell. From him General Kopański learned that General Sikorski had agreed to the brigade's being transferred to Tobruk to relieve the Australian division. After hasty preparations the brigade was conveyed to the fortress by sea and without loss, during the nights of 18–28 August. At that time it numbered 288 officers and 4777 other ranks.

The brigade, while a comparatively small unit, was at the same time an élite formation with rare qualifications. Outside purely officer formations one did not find military detachments containing such a high percentage of soldiers with secondary or even higher education. They were either volunteers from various parts of the world, eager to fight, or experienced soldiers who had gone through the September Campaign. Recent rearming and reorganisation had made of the brigade a modern unit, capable of fighting against even the best-equipped enemy. It was also an exceptionally close-knit unit, in which there ran a thread of understanding and friendship among the commander, officers and men that guaranteed unforced discipline and precision in carrying out orders. At that time the Brigade was the only land-formation of the Polish Armed Forces fighting the enemy and this in special circumstances, far from their own people, with comrades-in-arms with whom they had first to become acquainted. This created a symbolic situation, which increased still further the responsibility resting on the shoulders of the 5000 Polish soldiers.

After initially remaining in reserve and relieving the Australian units, the brigade took over a western sector of about 20km. Its numbers however were too small to undertake the task, so a Czechoslovak battalion and an Australian battalion, still remaining in the fortress, were put under its orders. The defence of this sector was difficult, for a German division, beside three Italian divisions, besieging Tobruk, had broken through the first line of fortifications. The breach through which there was always a threat of a new enemy attack, was made opposite the hill of Medauar, so ceaseless alert and constant activity had to be maintained to stress a state of permanent readiness. Artillery fire, patrols, clearing minefields, laying mines oneself, these were the basic elements of the fighting. Respite came into the usual two-hour armistice just before nightfall, when rations could be distributed, the wounded evacuated, ammunition brought up and repairs made to the defensive positions.[17]

During the taking-over of the positions formerly held by the Australians and while in contact with the soldiers of the Australian battalion, which remained in the fortress and came under General Kopański's command, very close Polish–Australian relations were forged. Relations with the British soldiers were also good. During the middle of November General Sikorski made an inspection of the Brigade which again raised the spirits of the Polish detachments. Their fighting qualities brought them to the fore among all the formations in Tobruk. In the breach – the most exposed position of the whole defence – the Brigade units held out for a full ten weeks, when even the exceptionally bellicose Australians had held out for barely thirty days.[18]

During the never-ceasing defensive fighting the garrison of the fortress was at the same time making preparations for offensive action, for General Scobie, the commander, had been informed by General Auchinleck, that an attack by the Eighth Army on General Rommel's position was being planned. In fact, on 18 November operation *Crusader* was launched with the objective of throwing the Germans back to the west, seizing their strongholds and relieving Tobruk. There were some initial successes and on 21 November the garrison of the fortress made a sortie, in which units of the Carpathian Brigade took part. Fighting went on at a distance of barely 15km from the defenders' positions and later a corridor was established connecting the attackers and the besieged, but a German counter-attack upset all the plans. A crisis in the battle occurred; General Alan Cunningham, leading the offensive, was replaced by General Neil Ritchie and chaos reigned for a short time at the headquarters of the Eighth Army. It was only in the second phase of the battle, which lasted from the beginning of December to 5 January 1942, that victory was achieved. The Carpathian Brigade took part in it. On 10 December they took the hill of Madauar, which in effect meant the end of the siege, and they took part in the battle of Gazala, which was of great significance in the second phase of the now victorious offensive. After carrying out various other duties, lasting until March 1942, the Brigade was withdrawn to Egypt, whence it was to go to Palestine and be reorganised there into a division.[19]

12 The Polish Army in Russia and its Evacuation

DIFFICULT POLISH – SOVIET COOPERATION

At the beginning of 1942 Polish–Soviet relations were at their most paradoxical. The two countries had signed a treaty supported by a military agreement and should have embarked on a period of mutual co-operation and goodwill. However the relatively honest fulfilment by Russia of her obligations was inversely proportional to the situation at the front. While the Germans were pressing towards Moscow and it seemed that they might capture it, Stalin made vague gestures indicating that he was acting in good faith and real progress was possible, yet when Soviet defences strengthened, thousands of problems immediately presented themselves.

The transfer of the Polish army to a new base east of the Caspian Sea took place between 15 and 25 January 1942 with temperatures reaching 50° below zero and with a high mortality rate caused by typhoid. It immediately became apparent that a bad climate had been exchanged for one even worse and that poor living conditions were replaced by plain squalor. During the winter months the temperature in the mountains reached 30° below zero, whilst strong winds constantly blew in the valleys and persistent rain transformed the ground into an impassable quagmire. In spring the area was a breeding-ground for millions of malaria-carrying mosquitoes while in the summer the scorching sun burnt all the vegetation and made the rivers run dry. The troops lived in tents or in mud huts; their food, which lacked any fresh vegetables, amounted at the most to only two-thirds of the ration stipulated in the regulations. Thousands fell ill with typhoid, malaria and stomach complaints, but the field hospitals lacked medicines. Training presented extraordinary problems quite apart from the shortage of equipment, because distances between detachments could be up to 900km, which, bearing in mind the one-track railway, was an absurd situation.[1]

Despite the great difficulties caused by the terrain and the lack of even the most basic supplies, the Polish leadership made every effort to fulfil its basic goal which consisted of gathering into the units as many ex-soldiers and volunteers as possible. This was primarily in order to form a large and powerful force and secondly to save the lives of those who came from the northern areas of Russia where they would otherwise undoubtedly have perished.

There were difficulties from the very beginning since the Soviet authorities protested against the acceptance into the ranks of those Polish citizens who belonged to national minorities, such as Ukrainians, Byelorussians and Jews, assuming them to be Soviet citizens. The Soviet authorities also sabotaged the recruitment of Poles who had already been inducted into the Red Army and work battalions, although they had previously agreed to the formation of enlistment committees. Despite the opposition of the authorities and the transportation difficulties, the rush of Poles into the ranks was such that by the middle of March the Polish Army had 70 000 soldiers as well as a number of familes who camped alongside the detachments. For all these people only 40 000 individual rations were provided and on 6 March, a notice was received that even this quantity would be further reduced to 26 000.[2]

This situation spurred General Anders into immediate action. Having been born in a country ruled over by Russia, he knew Russia and the Russian mentality well; he understood the way the Soviet system worked. He was able to deal with many minor difficulties and problems on his own. He turned a blind eye to the eavesdropping organisation and various excesses of the NKVD, he attributed many of the elementary shortages to the wartime conditions but he could not permit the mass starvation of his men. It was true that the first English transports had arrived bringing uniforms, underwear and a certain amount of food, but these had been put into storage as an 'iron reserve'.

A second problem which goaded the General into decisive action was the constant and increasingly worrying absence of thousands of officers who after the September campaign had found themselves in prisoner-of-war camps at Kozielsk, Ostaszkow and Starobielsk. Exhaustive searches were made for them and each newly-arrived Polish officer was questioned as to their whereabouts.

Apart from these two matters there were many more which required intervention. The Poles were being pressured into sending one division to the front. The division was barely ready for such a task and many of its soldiers had not recovered enough strength for combat; other divisions had hardly any weapons. General Anders decided to send two telegrams: one to Stalin asking for a meeting and a second to General Sikorski informing him of this move and giving him reasons for it.[3]

General Sikorski answered immediately and it is in his telegram dated 10 March that the word 'evacuation' appeared for the first time, referring not only to airmen and sailors, but to all soldiers in excess of 30 000 in number, who could not remain in Russia because of the lack of food. This was a crucial statement, because the Polish Premier together with the whole Government adhered resolutely to the policy that a Polish Army should be formed in Russia, that it should remain there, go to the front and be the first to cross on to Polish soil. This was a maximalist view which demanded from Russia a change in her politics, far-reaching goodwill, as well as an earlier settlement to the problem of Poland's eastern borders. Nevertheless such a view was justified and the Polish government could not adopt any other.[4]

Unfortunately the reality was somewhat different. The Soviet Union halted the German advance outside Moscow, the most favourable moment for negotiations had passed and the diplomatic exchange of views between Great Britain, the United States, Russia and Poland began to take on aspects which were largely unfavourable to the question of Poland's eastern boundaries.

Stalin sent a positive reply to General Anders' telegram and on 18 March received him and his Chief of Staff, Colonel Okulicki, with Molotov also present. The discussion was cordial but the Polish side was unable to achieve its most important goals. Admittedly, the Soviet dictator revoked his decision to limit rations for the Polish troops to 26 000 but firmly refused to consider any more than 44 000. The question of the missing officers he dismissed in general terms, returning once again to the explanation that they had escaped. On the other hand he agreed with unexpected ease to the evacuation to Persia of all those troops – and many families as well – who could not be assured sufficient rations. This decision was highly significant because it signalled the adoption by the Soviet leader of an entirely new strategy in relation to the Polish question.[5]

THE FIRST EVACUATION

The initial evacuation, carried out with the energetic assistance of the Soviet authorities which merely emphasised Stalin's intentions, commenced almost immediately. The first ship sailed from Krasnovodsk for Pahlevi in Iran as early as 24 March and further transports arriving at the port departed daily thereafter. By 3 April the entire operation had been completed. The evacuated military personnel consisted mainly of airmen and sailors who had been waiting for several months to leave the country; in addition there were the nuclei of the three divisions which were yet to be formed – surplus personnel, armoured units, engineers, sappers and army administrative staff. Naturally all were without any weapons. In all, the evacuees numbered 33 000 soldiers to which it had been possible to add over 10 000 civilians, including more than 3000 children. At first the British were reluctant to accept the civilian evacuees fearing that excessive pressure would be placed upon the available food resources, but when they saw the first destitute and pathetic figures, in particular the young, their attitude immediately changed. The authorities' attentive and professional care was indispensable since the evacuation had concentrated on the weakest who – almost without exception – were ill and many close to death. Nevertheless the British Army observers remained optimistic because they could see the discipline and high moral of the newly-arrived troops.[6]

After the evacuation the Polish Army in Russia numbered somewhat in excess of 40 000 including over 1000 women volunteers and nurses and 1000 cadets of both sexes. It was anticipated that there would be an influx of fresh volunteers and a certain number of conscripts but these calculations turned out to be partly erroneous. All units suffered from a poor state of health although only the strongest had remained, but the level of equipment, particularly with regard to weapons, was even worse. It had been intended that three divisions would be prepared for action at the front, but in all there were only 8651 rifles, 108 machine-guns, a number of machine-pistols and twenty-eight artillery pieces. Given this situation only the first division could be armed and more or less prepared for battle.[7]

DIFFERENCES OF OPINION IN THE POLISH CAMP

General Anders no longer had any doubt that it would be quite impossible to form fully-effective Polish military units on Russian soil which would at the same time be independent of the Soviet authorities and so he informed General Sikorski, suggesting that a total evacuation should take place. However, the situation was perceived differently in London where political talks and negotiations were carried on ceaselessly and hope had not been lost that the agreement with Russia would still be carried out. In this light the opinion prevailed that the withdrawal of the Polish army from Soviet soil would only cause further problems. Admittedly General Sikorski's visit to the United States in March 1942 did not prove a great success but neither was it a defeat, and it created the impression that pressure on Moscow would emerge from that quarter so far as the question of Poland's eastern borders was concerned. A new German offensive was expected at any moment which might again place Russia in a critical situation and weaken Stalin's recalcitrance. It is true that there were also other factors which made Polish–Soviet co-operation more difficult. The Russians firmly opposed any plans for union between Poland and Czechoslovakia which might have altered the balance of power in Central Europe, but General Sikorski considered that the less vital problems could somehow be sorted out. He had just achieved an important success because, thanks to Polish intercessions and pressure, the British–Soviet Pact of 26 May 1942 did not contain any negative provisions about Poland's Eastern borders and his optimism rose appreciably. The continued presence of the Polish army on Russian soil was a trump card in his political fight.[8]

A serious difference of opinion now arose between the generals which was reflected in an exchange of telegrams. They were both right but saw the problem from different points of view and in different dimensions. It would have been better if history had confirmed the reality and correctness of General Sikorski's views but unfortunately the reverse occurred. The German spring offensive even had some success but it failed to break the Soviet resistance. Stalin's policies *vis á vis* Poland changed not one bit and consequently he followed through his plans, whilst the Western Allies were primarily interested in stabilising the Eastern front and preventing a victory for Germany. Deeply embedded in the consciousness was the fear that the two warring leaders could again come to an understanding. The threat of a separate Russo-German peace played an important role in the Western Allies decision-making.

Independently of the Polish–Soviet talks, the British themselves were interested in the evacuation of the Polish Army to the Middle East, as they needed more troops. Towards the end of the May and the beginning of June General Rommel began his new offensive in

North Africa, in which he secured a spectacular victory. On 21 June he captured Tobruk and within a few days had reached the gates of Egypt. Her fall threatened the loss of the Suez Canal and could signal the end of British hegemony in the Mediterranean region. Such a development would be unwelcome to the USSR as it could encourage Turkey to declare for the Axis which in turn would increase the already substantial threat to the Caucasus, the oil-wells and the Dardanelles. Foreseeing such a development an Anglo-Soviet Commission was set up in 1942 (without the knowledge of the Polish Government) which discussed the problem of the evacuation of the Polish Army to the Middle East.[9]

No doubt this was not the only motive of the British who knew that they would not risk their alliance with the USSR over the Polish–Soviet dispute about frontiers, but the risk of losing the Polish divisions in Russia could become a reality. The first major Soviet success on the front could harden Stalin's attitude and could lead him to change his plans. Instead of agreeing to the evacuation he could order the disbandment of the Polish formations and deport the soldiers and their families to labour camps.

Towards the end of June the question hung in the balance. The Polish Government feared that an evacuation would lead to a worsening of the plight of those Poles who might remain in the USSR, whilst General Anders pressed for the evacuation, fearing a change in the Soviet attitude, and the British, seeing things in the same way, negotiated with the Russians. The pressure they brought to bear gave results. On 2 July the Polish Government was informed by the Foreign Office that Stalin had come down in favour of Churchill's opinion and had given his agreement to the evacuation of the Polish divisions to the Middle East. They were trained, but without equipment. The Polish Government gave its consent on one condition. A recruiting centre would remain on Soviet soil and the evacuation would encompass families and above all the children. A few days passed in further councils and negotiations and on 26 July General Anders received from the Soviet authorities the following message:

> From Moscow, No. 2651/1224. Deliver at once. Urgent. Government matter. Jangi Jul. The Commander of the Polish Army in USSR, General W. A. Anders. The Government of USSR has accepted the efforts of the Commander of the Polish Army in the USSR, General Anders, to evacuate Polish units from USSR to

the Near East and has no intention of making any difficulties in the immediate realisation of this evacuation.

The Plenipotentiary of the Council of the People's Commissars of the USSR for the affairs of the Polish Army in USSR, Major of state security, Zhukov.[10]

THE SECOND EVACUATION

The decisions were taken, and General Anders began preparations for the evacuation. From the Soviet side it was the NKVD which dealt with these matters. It was efficient and therefore already on 31 July the first conference took place in Tashkent where a number of problems were settled; the most important being the agreement that the families – some 25 000 people – could also leave. Together with the soldiers this gave a total of about 70 000 evacuees. A further important point was the agreement that families of soldiers who were Polish citizens but not of Polish nationality could also be evacuated. This mainly affected Jews for whom General Anders made special efforts. An important point which could create difficulties in shifting all the personnel encompassed by the evacuation from the USSR to Persia was that the evacuation was to take place between 5 and 15 August, within a very short period of time.[11] On 1 August an organisational order of the Polish Army Staff was issued. Nine days later the first rail transport left for Krasnovodsk there to transfer on to ships.

Up to the last moment the greatest difficulty proved to be the question of the national minorities, as the Soviets did not want to let them go, whilst the Poles tried to make it easy for them to leave. The Soviets even began to spread rumours that as anti-Semites the Poles did not want to take Jews. It was necessary to correct these rumours continuously. On the whole, however, the transports left regularly and the figure of 70 000, including 4000 Jews, was nearly reached. The last ship left Krasnovodsk on 31 August.[12]

The embarkation base at Krasnovodsk was commanded by Lt-Colonel Zygmunt Berling. He belonged to a small group of officers whom the Soviets had separated from the prisoners of war in the spring of 1940 and had been kept isolated somewhere. Berling joined General Anders' Army but there were many difficulties. In accordance with the orders he was to join the last echelon of Staff to be evacuated; he did not carry out this order, but instead hid himself so as not to go. This was nearly a symbolic step which was to herald a new phase in Polish–Soviet relations.[13]

General Bohusz-Szyszko still remained in the USSR where he was to tidy up and settle all outstanding matters and secure evacuation for all those who, because of illness or searching for their families, had not left on the last transport.

POLISH COMMUNISTS IN THE USSR

Stalin's agreement that the Polish Army be evacuated from the USSR was a logical consequence in the changing political situation which in relation to Polish–Soviet affairs underwent a number of phases. The first began in 1939, when Poland was divided between Germany and Soviet Russia and Stalin did not want any Poland at all. This rebounded on Soviet attitude even to the Polish communists who found themselves in labour camps and prisons, some being liquidated. Only those who did not show any national aspirations and accepted Soviet internationalism were tolerated. To these belonged Wanda Wasilewska (1905–64) who, although a socialist, became the most servile exponent of Soviet ideology. She was elected to the Supreme Council of the USSR, Stalin took note of her and summoned her for talks in March 1940.[14] He had already taken his decisions concerning Poland, but the war was in progress, its outcome was by no means certain and he wanted to know what were Polish attitudes and views.

Not many months passed before it became obvious that it was not so easy to foresee the future. The French front was broken within a few weeks and suddenly Hitler found himself alone on the European Continent with a powerful army which did not have a worthy opponent. The German–Soviet agreement was still in force, but Stalin felt uneasy and decided on the first, though small, revisions of his politics. Since the signing of the Ribbentrop–Molotov pact British diplomats had tried by every means to establish friendly relations with the USSR only to be met by a wall of indifference. Was it not time to change this now? An opportunity had arisen with the arrival in Moscow of the new British ambassador, Stafford Cripps. Stalin's wish was decisive, so the wall of ice which surrounded the British diplomat began to thaw. Tentative talks and exchanges of opinions began. Great Britain was the only country which at that time could put up any defence against Hitler and Stalin appreciated this and secretly counted on this despite being Germany's ally.

In considering the position of Great Britain it was difficult to avoid coming across the Polish problem, since her Government was in London and she had an alliance with the British Empire. Was the decision for the complete erasure of Polish affairs from future plans and forecasts correct? Or could that card be used successfully in a new situation in which Great Britain would be very much needed? Stalin gave his orders and the NKVD removed a few dozen Polish officers from Griazowiec camp and in September 1940 took them to Moscow. None of them had any idea what had happened to the thousands of their fellow officers who had also been transported though to an unknown destination. The chosen were now taken to Malachovka not far from the capital and were located in a comfortable house which later received the expressive name 'villa of happiness'. Daily duties related to political lectures and discussions. Military matters were also mooted. Among the chosen was Lt-Colonel Zygmunt Berling. It looked as if a plan for a Polish army under Soviet command was being considered, but no decisions as yet were disclosed.[15]

At the same time there were small groups of Polish communists in Lwów, Białystok and Minsk who were allowed to be active culturally and to publish a number of periodicals. In Lwów the *Czerwony Sztandar* began appearing towards the end of 1939; later, in 1941, there appeared the ideological *Nowe Widnokręgi*, with which Wada Wasilewska was associated. *Sztandar Wolności* began to appear in Minsk in the autumn of 1940. However as yet this was not a political action with a clear organisational structure.[16]

Before anything had changed, the German attack in the east was launched and immediately a new situation arose. Within a few weeks the Soviet Union found itself in a desperate situation and aid from the West became essential for survival. In a moment Great Britain had become the most beloved and the most respected ally. Her willingness to co-operate would be bound to draw in the United States after her. Taking advantage of this situation became the most important aim of Soviet policy.

Immediately the Polish problem took on a clearer shape. The British Government, aiming at harmonious co-operation among all the forces fighting Hitler, initiated mediation between Poland and the USSR. Within a few weeks they had led to the Polish–Soviet Pact which resulted in the resumption of diplomatic relations and the decision to form a Polish army on Russian territory but subordinated to the Polish Government in London.

The Polish communists who were attempting to be active in Lwów, Białystok and Minsk and who after the German attack quickly retreated eastwards together with the Red Army, were as yet unaware of this pact. The Lwów group found itself in Moscow, later in Saratov and Ufa where it began radio broadcasts in Polish. The Białystok and Minsk groups found themselves in Homel.[17] There, in Homel, the initiative was taken to form a Polish battalion which would fight within the framework of the Red Army. The initiators of this plan worked out a proclamation to the Polish nation and published it on 3 July 1941. It contained surprising aspects: 'We are forming an armed volunteer unit allied with the Red Army – an army of liberation. These will be the only units truly fighting for the liberation of the Polish nation ... Organise resistance units! Co-operate with the Red Army! Let partisan warfare begin in all corners of Poland with a red flame!'[18]

Lt-Colonel Berling was even quicker off the mark. On the day of the German attack, 22 June, he sent a declaration signed by thirteen inhabitants of the 'villa of happiness' to the Commissar of Security, Mierkulov. It ended with the following words:

> As members of one of the nations under the tyranny of the fascist aggressor we see only one path to liberating the nation and that is through co-operation with the Union of the Soviet Socialist Republics, within whose framework our fatherland will be able to develop fully. We wish to be disciplined soldiers of the army of liberation, to carry out our bounden duty towards our own nation and the workers of the whole world.[19]

Neither of these pronouncements played any role at that time, as Stalin put them on one side wanting to keep up appearances of honest co-operation with the Polish Government in London. Ambassadors were exchanged, the army began to be organised, the Poles in Homel, Saratow and Ufa were silenced and the officers from the 'villa of happiness' were instructed to report to General Anders. Stalin also thought that Wanda Wasilewska should make a statement as it was generally known that she belonged to Stalin's trusted group. On 11 August she issued an appeal to the Polish nation in which she stressed the courage of the British, the heroism of the Red Army and expressed her happiness that a Polish army was being created in Russia.[20]

This was the zenith of Polish–Soviet co-operation caused by victories of Hitler, whose armies were on the outskirts of Moscow. The fate of the Soviet empire hung in the balance. Every tonne of Anglo-Saxon aid was of the utmost necessity. Unfortunately this period lasted only a few months. Towards the end of October the German attack on Moscow was repulsed and in the following month the Siberian divisions, hurriedly brought over from the Far East, counter-attacked and the front was stabilised.

Stalin still honoured the Polish–Soviet agreement but various difficulties began, which led to General Sikorski going to Moscow. On the surface many things were settled in the direct talks but complications began to mount. The formation of the army progressed only slowly, the 'amnesty' was not fully carried out, recruitment centres were plagued by continual difficulties whilst the initially silenced Polish communists began to organise themselves. In the second half of 1941 in Moscow the Polish radio station, *Tadeusz Kościuszko*, was set up and transferred to Ufa. It became the mouthpiece of the Polish communist doctrine, controlled by the Soviet authorities. A similar mouthpiece was the Polish section of the Ukrainian radio station, *Taras Shevchenko*, in Saratow. At first their broadcasts were conciliatory or neutral in tone but month by month they became increasingly hostile towards the Polish Government in London and the Polish Army on Soviet territory.[21] However as long as that army remained on Soviet soil not even the most vociferous Polish communists, who pursued total subordination to Moscow's directives, gained freedom of action. Wanda Wasilewska had an altogether special role: after the German attack and with the rank of colonel of the Red Army, she become the political commissar of the South-Western Front and later propagandist of the Central Political Office.[22]

A NEW PHASE IN POLISH–SOVIET RELATIONS

Certain steps, however, were taken and they were an indication that the situation would undergo changes. In Kuybyshev, on 5 May, the first issue of the renewed *Nowe Widnokręgi* was published. Its editor was Wanda Wasilewska who travelled up from the front every so often. The publication of this fortnightly with an ideologicalprogaganda character was the first external step on the path of creating a Polish political communist centre within the framework of Soviet reality.[23]

A new phase in Polish–Soviet relations began with the departure from Krasnovodsk of the last ship carrying Polish soldiers and families, and the decision by Lt-Colonel Berling to remain on Soviet soil. Formally the agreement was in force and the embassy in Kuybyshev was active. In the latter there occurred a change when, because of illness, Ambassador Kot was replaced by Tadeusz Romer. All the embassy outposts were still active. The most important of them were the ones bringing aid to Polish citizens dispersed throughout the vast country. They began their work in mid-February 1942 and, despite difficulties had in a short time organised 800 welfare centres among which were seventeen schools, 176 nutritional points for children, eighty-three playgrounds, eight old people's homes, forty-seven workshops, forty-one medical centres and many others. At first funds were very meagre but appeals for help were effective and from the USA, the British Empire, many neutral states, the International Red Cross and Jewish organisations presents in the form of clothes, food and medicines began to pour in.[24]

Unfortunately the activities of the outposts were shortlived – only a few months. The first arrests among the workers of these outposts took place when the decision concerning the Polish army and whether it was to be evacuated to Iran hung in the balance. The employees of the outposts were accused of spying and also that, contrary to the Soviet note of 1 December 1941, they were giving aid and care to those Polish citizens whom the Soviets regarded as Soviet citizens. Over 100 employees were arrested. The intervention of the Polish Government led to a few dozen being released, but over eighty were ordered to leave the USSR. Some were sent to labour camps. Not all of them survived and returned to Poland after the war. Although formally the Polish embassy was still active, nearly a million Polish citizens in the USSR found themselves once again without any protection and dependent on the goodwill of local authorities.[25]

General Sikorski, seeing that Poles on Russian territory were walking on quicksand and that the situation of those remaining there would again become desperate, sought help from the Western Allies. During August and September the Polish Premier held a number of talks with Churchill, Eden, Ernest Bevin and President Roosevelt's special representative in the USSR, Averell Harriman.[26] Above all he was concerned with the continuing protection for the civilian population. Unfortunately he did not succeed in obtaining any definite commitments and with this state of affairs the decision was taken for General Sikorski's third journey to the USA.

It took place at the beginning of December 1942 and led to three meetings with Roosevelt, during which the General raised the problem of the future strategy of the war, declaring himself for an invasion of the European Continent from the Balkans so as to reach Central Europe as quickly as possible, making contact with the resistance movements in Yugoslavia, Czechoslovakia and Poland. This was tied in with the problem of the post-war settlement of East–Central Europe and the federation of the countries there. However, neither Roosevelt nor his Under-Secretary of State, Sumner Wells, wanted to engage themselves in these discussions. In their opinion this should be raised with the British who were responsible for central Europe. General Sikorski's appeal to Roosevelt for support for Poland in her difficulties with the USSR was also unsuccessful.[27]

Not long after General Sikorski's return to London, on 16 January 1943, the Polish Government received a Soviet note which contained the information that all Polish citizens, even ethnic Poles, who lived in eastern Poland annexed by the Soviets in September 1939 were regarded as Soviet citizens. This meant that further protection of Polish citizens in the USSR was impossible, that diplomatic relations would have only a formal character, but above all that the Soviets had definitely concluded that the Polish eastern territories were their property.[28]

In Polish political circles in London and among those Poles who knew the contents of the note, there was uproar. The opponents of the Sikorski–Maisky pact immediately began a new attack on the Polish Premier and even managed to mobilise for this purpose a part of the army, including General Anders. Apart from the accusations which were partly justifiable, they were concerned with removing Sikorski and replacing him with persons who had from the first days of his premiership put obstacles in his way. It was argued that the Polish Government should resign in protest and that such a step would make a deep impression on the Western Allies.[29]

Fortunately General Sikorski did not give in to these pressures, dismissed ill-timed advice and prevented a crisis which would have changed nothing. His policies did not produce the expected results, they did not lead to a renunciation by the Soviets of the lands seized from Poland or even to a clear-cut declaration on the matter from

Great Britain and the United States. Neither were the aims connected with the Polish Army in the USSR realised nor was he able to save all the Polish citizens deported into the depths of Russia, but was this at all possible? Though only partial achievement of the Polish–Soviet pact was realised, it did make the West aware of the problem and altogether some 115 000 soldiers and civilians with General Anders were evacuated from Russia. This accounted for some 10 per cent of all those deported. It was not much but would even this have been possible if in July 1941 the opponents of the pact had been successful and no agreement have been signed with the USSR? Further events showed it would probably not.

13 The Plight of the Polish Jews

FURTHER FATE OF JEWS ON POLISH SOIL

After the German attack on the east and the occupation of the whole of Poland, about 2 500 000 Jews were within reach of German hands. They were all in danger, but, except for sporadic cases, mass murders had not yet started, although the Jews had to move into ghettos, which in the territory incorporated into the Reich were set up in the spring and in the *General Gouvernement* in the autumn of 1940. They were ordered to wear armbands with yellow stars; they were dismissed from work in public institutions; all their real estate and some of their movable possessions were confiscated, they were forced to do hard labour and deprived of the freedom of movement. But at the same time they were allowed to have a kind of self-government and in the ghettos they had their own Councils (*Judenrats*) and police. In this way the Germans secured the co-operation of the Jews, who, after so many centuries of experience, hoped that if they offered no resistance they would survive in spite of everything. This was above all the opinion of the older generation.

GHETTOS AND PLACES OF EXTERMINATION AND DECISION OF 'THE FINAL SOLUTION'

The largest ghetto was the one in Warsaw with 450 000 inhabitants; next the ghetto in Łódź with 160 000 people. Others were set up in many smaller towns, and after June 1941 also in Lwów, Wilno and several towns in east Poland.[1]

In the spring of 1941, before the attack on Soviet Russia, the German authorities issued a secret instruction about the liquidation of political commissars and Jews. The special units of SS and police, called *Einzatzgruppen*, who moved just behind the front, were to do

163

the job. By the end of 1941 about half a million Jews had been shot, mostly in the forests, but Himmler, dissatisfied with the slowness and openness of the action, gave orders that places of instant extermination were to be set up. The first one was established in December 1941 at Chełmno, in Pomerania; the second in March of the next year in Bełżec, near Lublin; the third in April in Sobibòr and the fourth in Treblinka near Małkinia, between Warsaw and Białystok.[2] Himmler's decision got official backing from the State Security Office (*Reichssicherheitshauptamt* – RSHA) because in January 1942 the German authorities had decided that the 'Final Solution' was to be put into operation, comprising all Jews already in German hands and those who would be taken in the future.[3]

At first the Jews were simply mown down by machine-guns or killed by the exhaust fumes from motor cars carried through pipes to wooden, leak-proof huts built on lorries, and the bodies were burned in the open. This was simple, but not efficient and later, gas was used and the bodies were burned in crematoria. About 1 800 000 Jews were killed in these extermination places. They had been brought there not only from Poland, but from many other countries of Europe. Besides these four places Himmler decided that in both the concentration camps on Polish soil – Auschwitz and Majdanek – the mass killing of Jews was to begin. In the summer of 1943 four big gas chambers and crematoria were built in the Auschwitz sub-camp, Birkenau, and about 3 million Jews from all over Europe were killed there. A further 200 000 were killed at Majdanek.[4]

The annihilation of Jews deeply affected Poles under German occupation. Several centuries of common co-existence had created very strong ties, uniting both nations, but on the other hand there was also strong animosity, worsened by extremist political groups as well as by mutual intolerance. The great majority of Jews held to their own way of life and did not want to be assimilated, which irritated the Poles. Nevertheless over the centuries a *modus vivendi* had been established – until the Germans came on the scene. They made Draconian rules, threatening the death penalty for any help given to Jews, and these threats were carried out. If one Jew was hidden in a block of flats all the male inhabitants were executed; for hiding one Jewish child a whole Polish family was murdered.[5] No wonder that many people were frightened and did not want to risk their own lives. This immoral situation released some people's worst instincts, of which the Germans made good use. There were many cases of blackmail and denunciation to the German police, the dregs of society made profit out of human tragedy.

ASSISTANCE FROM THE POLISH COMMUNITY

The Polish community was not impassive to the fate of their hunted and humiliated fellow-countrymen. As usual the first assistance was given by ordinary people, without any special organisation. Many Polish families in towns and villages offered shelter, sometimes for money, sometimes out of pure human kindness. There were cases of a dozen or more Jews being hidden in one place. This created severe problems, since not only food but also medical help had to be procured and even the most primitive hygiene to be assured. To save one Jew at least ten people had to co-operate and in the utmost secrecy, since blackmailers and cowards were everywhere ready to inform the German authorities.

At first the German regulations relating to Jews were not of great concern to Poles and the Underground movement since everyone was affected by the hardships of the occupation: the arrests, deportations and resettlements. But when the first news about the German atrocities in the ghettos resounded in Poland, the underground press raised its voice. The first to do so were the periodicals of the secret army (ZWZ/AK) and the Polish Socialist Party, bringing regular reports on events in the ghettos and German behaviour. They warned the Polish community not to co-operate with the Germans in appropriating Jewish property. At the beginning of August 1942 the clandestine Catholic organisation, Front for Reborn Poland, issued 5000 copies of a special leaflet called *Protest*. Its author was the well-known writer, Zofia Kossak. 'Whoever remains silent in the face of murder becomes an accomplice of the murderer, whoever does not condemn, condones.' On 17 September 1942 the Directorate of Civil Resistance (KWC) issued a statement concerning the German extermination campaign in Poland, which ended with the words: 'Unable to stop these actions, the Directorate of Civil Resistance protests on behalf of the entire Polish community at the crimes being committed against Jews. All Polish political and social groupings join in this protest'. Many underground papers, from the right to Communists, published this statement, except for the extreme right.[6]

The alarm thus raised increased the assistance so far given to Jews. Besides individuals, among whom the most active were intellectuals, such as writers, scientists, artists and their like, as well as many peasant families, an important part was played by institutions. Some of them, such as the Polish Red Cross, hospitals, orphanages and hostels, already engaged in welfare work, were better able to help with comparatively less risk. A special chapter in this assistance was written by the Catholic and Protestant clergy, as well as the monastic orders and convents. Although themselves under constant German harassment, frequently searched and resettled, they rescued thousands of Jewish women and children.[7]

The problem of aid was so big and the economical resources requested so great, that spontaneous social reaction was not enough. It was therefore tackled by the Government Delegacy in Warsaw and there, on 27 September 1942 a Provisional Committee was set up. Its aim was to get Jews out of the Warsaw ghetto, to provide them with papers and money as well as shelter. The Committee had branches in other towns, first of all in Cracow, where Jews could also get help.[8]

THE COUNCIL FOR AID TO JEWS

Preparations were made for setting up a permanent organisation and on 4 December 1942 the Provisional Committee was disbanded and a Council for Aid to Jews, attached to the Government Delegacy, was set up. The Council adopted the cryptonym *Żegota* in order to avoid using the word 'Jews', for this was dangerous in occupied Poland. It consisted of the representatives of the democratic political parties and two men from the Warsaw ghetto. The Council carried on the work of the Provisional Committee, but on a much larger scale, receiving money from the Polish Government in London, via the Government Delegacy. At first these payments amounted to 150 000 zlotys per month, reaching the figure of 2 million in 1944. In Warsaw alone, where 20 000 Jews were hidden among Poles, 4000 of them received assistance. Also some foreign Jewish organisations sent considerable sums of money which reached the Jewish underground via the Government Delegacy, to assist 7000 people. Similar work was carried on in Cracow.[9]

The Polish Government in London received reports on the situation of Jews in Poland and was well-informed. Very important information concerning the concentration camp at Auschwitz was constantly received thanks to the underground movement there, initiated in the autumn of 1940, only a couple of months after that horrible place had been set up. The movement was organised by a Polish officer, Witold Pilecki, who, with the consent of his underground superiors, deliberately allowed himself to be picked up by the Germans in a round-up in Warsaw in order to be sent to Auschwitz. He arrived there on 22 September 1940 under the false name of

Tomasz Serafiński, and under extremely difficult conditions started to build up the secret network of a military organisation. It was in November 1940 that his first report reached Warsaw and was at once used by General Rowecki in his secret despatches to London. They were sent via Sweden and received by the Polish authorities in Great Britain in March 1941. In this report there was nothing about Jews in Auschwitz, since the camp was at that time almost purely Polish, but the situation was to change in the near future. On 26 March 1942 the first Jewish transport arrived at the camp, sent by Adolf Eichman from RSHA and in May mass gassing began. Then Pilecki's reports sent to Warsaw started to bring the details of these transports giving the numbers of people murdered and specifying the countries from which they had been brought. The underground organisation in Auschwitz expanded, got in touch with other national groups and thus increased its efficiency.[10]

INTERVENTIONS OF THE POLISH GOVERNMENT

One of the most important documents received in London on 1 September 1942 was a report prepared by the Jewish department of the Home Army in Warsaw. Entitled 'The 1942 Anti-Jewish Action', it contained comprehensive documentation of the events which were taking place in occupied Poland and detailed evidence of the partial destruction of the Warsaw ghetto. Unfortunately the facts and figures contained in it were treated as unbelievable, they were so far beyond Western imagination. Nevertheless many meetings, discussions and talks took place in London, during which the Polish Government tried to awaken the interest of Western politicians and intellectuals.

The next important step was the arrival in London, in November 1942, of a Home Army special emissary, Jan Kozielewski, using the name of Jan Karski. He had been in Warsaw during the extermination of the greater part of the population of the Warsaw ghetto and the transports to Treblinka and was thus an eye-witness to the Nazi crimes. He had also met some representatives of the Jewish resistance movement and represented them abroad. Karski met Churchill, Eden, the leader of the Labour Party, Arthur Greenwood, and many other politicians and intellectuals. Shortly afterwards he went to the United States and was received by President Roosevelt. He also met Szmul Zygelbojm who represented the *Bund* on the Polish National Council in London.[11]

The information received from Karski enabled the Polish Government to publish a note, on 10 December 1942, which was directed to
the Allied nations. Part of it read:

> Most recent reports present a horrifying picture of the position to
> which the Jews in Poland have been reduced. It is not possible to
> estimate the exact number of Jews who have been exterminated in
> Poland ... but all the reports agree that the total number killed
> runs into many hundreds of thousands ... Of 3 100 000 Jews in
> Poland before the outbreak of war, over a third have perished
> during the last three years.

Two days later General Sikorski, who was at that time staying in
Washington, raised this problem with the Secretary of State, Sumner
Wells, and supplied him with details about the extermination of Jews
in Poland. As a result, on 17 December 1942, the Governments of
twelve countries, including the United States, Great Britain and
Soviet Russia, issued a joint declaration, announced simultaneously
in London, Washington and Moscow. It said:

> We condemn in the strongest possible terms this bestial policy of
> cold-blooded extermination. We declare that such events can only
> strengthen the resolve of all freedom-loving peoples to overthrow
> the barbarous Hitlerite tyranny. We reaffirm our solemn resolu-
> tion to ensure that those responsible for these crimes shall not
> escape retribution, and to press on with the necessary practical
> measures to this end.[12]

WARSAW GHETTO

Indeed, the older Jewish generation was opposed to active resistance
in the hope of survival, but the younger ones thought differently. The
Jewish resistance movement in Warsaw began in 1940. In the first
place the active political force was the *Bund* which collaborated with
the Polish Socialist Party, as well as the Jewish Zionistic organisations
from both the left and the right who stood for the creation of a Jewish
state in Palestine. The Communist organisations, such as *Spartakus,
Hammer and Sickle* also played an important part, joined later on by
the Polish Workers Party (PPR) and others. The Jewish underground

published several papers and strove to set up a joint organisation which materialised in March 1942 as the Anti-Fascist Bloc.[13]

In July 1942 the Germans began their great extermination operation and all hopes for survival were finally shattered. Day after day the Jewish police had to bring several thousand people to the place, called by the Germans *Umschlagplatz*, whence the trains went to Treblinka. The Jewish policemen carried out this horrible task to save their own lives for the time being. In this tragic atmosphere of terror, murder and man-hunts the chairman of the Jewish Council, Adam Czerniakow, seeing himself unable to help, committed suicide on 24 July. It was a symbolic death, for Czerniakow, who had given himself entirely to his people, represented the policy of concession and co-operation.

THE JEWISH FIGHTING ORGANISATION

Four days later the younger generation of Zionists and Socialists formed the first Fighting Organisation taking the decision to defend themselves. Assistance could only come from the Polish underground, so several people, both men and women, were sent outside the ghetto to establish liaison with the Home Army. General Rowecki was entirely in favour and promised help, although this was very difficult to carry into effect. His motives were first of all humane, but also self-defensive: after the Jews the Germans might start to exterminate Poles. But the Jewish leaders were not so pessimistic, they did not expect the final liquidation of the ghettos and that time asked only that their appeal should be sent out into the whole world and to the Allies fighting the Germans. This request was fulfilled.[14]

However, the action of extermination was intensified. Day after day about 10 000 people were sent to their deaths and the determination to fight grew stronger among the young underground activists. Unity was called for and by the end of October 1942 almost all the democratic and progressive Jewish organisations had joined together in a Jewish National Committee. The *Bund* alone stayed outside, but promised co-operation. The Committee published a proclamation in which it agreed to subordinate all its actions to the Government Delegate and the Home Army Commander. On 2 December 1942 the next step was taken and the Jewish Fighting Organisation (*Żydowska Organizacja Bojowa* – ŻOB) was set up. This undertook to train fighters, obtain technical devices such as weapons, ammunition and explosives in order to take an active stand against further deportations to death. The organisation was led by a very young man, Mordechaj Anielewicz (1920–43) and contacted the Home Army. General Rowecki immediately sent a positive written reply, recognising ŻOB as a paramilitary organisation and promising assistance in the form of instruction and arms. After years of submission and hope for survival the day was approaching on which the Jews were determined to offer armed opposition to the Germans. On 4 December 1942 the ŻOB published an appeal to the inhabitants of the Warsaw ghetto:

> There can be no doubt that Nazism has set itself the goal of exterminating all Jews. Its tactics consist of fraud and hypocrisy. Sinking the knife into the throat of a victim it tosses a card to the next victim, before driving him to the slaughter ... Let us face the truth with courage and boldness ... Jews, Citizens of the Warsaw Ghetto, be vigilant. Do not trust any talk, any moves of the SS gangsters ... Let us drop all illusions ... Prepare to defend your own life ...
> Long live freedom![15]

FIGHTING IN THE WARSAW AND OTHER GHETTOS

Similar views were expressed in the ghettos of Będzin, Białystok and Częstochowa and preparations made to fight. But not in the large ghetto in Łódź. There the chairman of the Jewish Council, Mordechaj Rumkowski, did not follow Adam Czerniakow's example, but co-operated with the Germans to the end. His police assisted in the deportations to the death camps, dangling hopes of survival before the people remaining. In this way he obstructed any spontaneous resistance and made impossible every initiative to set up an organisation which would stand up to the Germans.[16]

After General Rowecki had endorsed ŻOB as a paramilitary organisation the Home Army sent into the ghetto ten pistols and a small amount of ammunition. Of course, this was very little, but at that time, the end of 1942 and beginning of 1943, the Home Army supplies were very limited and the parachute drops from the West quite insufficient. It should also be said that not every Home Army soldier believed that the Jews would really fight. Nevertheless joint

1. Józef Piłsudski

2. Ignacy Mościcki

3. Edward Śmigły-Rydz

4. Felicjan Sławoj-
   Składkowski

5. Stefan Starzyński

6. Michał Karaszewicz-
   Tokarzewski

7. Władysław Raczkiewicz

8. Władysław Sikorski

9. Kazimierz Sosnkowski

10. Ignacy Paderewski

11. Adam Sapieha

12. Stefan Rowecki

13. Cyryl Ratajski

14. Władysław Anders

15. Jan Piekałkiewicz

16. Jan Stanisław
    Jankowski

17. Stanisław Mikołajczyk

18. Tadeusz Bór-
    Komorowski

19. Stanisław Kopański

20. Kazimierz Pużak

21. Stanisław Maczek

22. Leopold Okulicki

23. Tomasz Arciszewski

24. Stefan Korboński

25. Polish officers accept the German capitulation at Wilhelmshaven

26. Jan Grudziński, commander of submarine *Orzeł*, killed in action 5.6.1940

27. Eugeniusz Horbaczewski, commander of Squadron 315, killed in action 18.8.1944

28. Maciej Kalenkiewicz, killed in action, 21.8.1944

29. 'Ponury', killed in action, 5.6.1944

30. Witold Pilecki, murdered in Poland in 1948

31. Copy of Enigma built by the Poles in France, in 1940

32. Wanda Wasilewska

33. Zygmunt Berling

34. Władysław Gomułka

35. Bolesław Bierut

36. Edward Osóbka-
    Morawski

37. Michał Rola-Żymierski

38. Stalin, Churchill and Roosevelt in Teheran

39. Pius XII

40. Adolf Hitler

41. Harry Truman

military action by the Home Army and ŻOB inside and outside the ghetto was planned and in January 1943 the representatives of both sides met. It was decided that the only practical chance of giving the ghetto effective aid would be to make an opening in the walls from outside, thus providing an opportunity of escape for a large number of people. A special unit of the Home Army was assigned for this action.[17]

On 9 January 1943, the head of the SS, Heinrich Himmler, unexpectedly visited the Warsaw ghetto. The number of inhabitants was at that time about 70 000 and should only have been 35 000, so he immediately gave orders for further deportations. German police units entered the ghetto on 18 January, 1943, but for the first time they met with armed resistance. Some shots were fired by the Jews, and although the Germans killed several hundred people and deported about 6000, they were taken by surprise and the action was halted.

This first success by ŻOB had a decisive effect on further help from the Home Army. The Jewish fighters were supplied with 100 pistols with ammunition, 500 grenades and some explosives with fuses and detonators. Some people from the ghetto were sent to the 'Aryan' districts of Warsaw to buy more arms and cement for the underground bunkers.[18]

On 19 April 1943 the Germans started the final assault on the ghetto under the command of the SS and police General, Jürgen Stroop. He had at his disposal 850 *Waffen SS* soldiers with tanks and artillery, supported by German police, Ukrainian and Latvian collaborators plus some units of Polish police, altogether about 2000 men. The Germans did not want to risk losses, so they used artillery to demolish buildings from a distance and set them on fire. The Jews resisted, throwing grenades and bottles of petrol, they destroyed one tank and killed several Germans. Two flags, Polish and Jewish, were hoisted on to a high building. The Home Army fulfilled its promise and on the first day of the fighting an armed unit attacked the ghetto wall, but without success, as the Germans were too strong. The next day a Communist People's Guard patrol destroyed a German machine-gun. Later on, Home Army units attacked the walls of the ghetto three times and one of them even fought inside the Jewish district beside the fighters from ŻOB.[19]

All the time the fighting in the ghetto was in progress, London was kept informed by the Government Delegate and the Home Army command by radio signals. A despatch issued by the fighting Jews was delivered to the representatives of the Jewish minority in the Polish National Council in London.[20] Unfortunately the Polish Government, except for fruitless interventions, was completely helpless, quite unable to give any assistance. The best proof of this awful situation was a despatch sent from Tel Aviv by the Committee to Save Jews in Occupied Europe to the Jewish National Committee in the fighting ghetto: 'All the war we have been seeking ways and means of getting in touch with you and bringing you help. Unfortunately we meet with unsurmountable indifference ...' The world remained completely unmoved while the Germans were destroying the ghetto and slaughtering the inhabitants.[21]

The Jews fighting in the ghetto had no chance of victory nor of saving their lives; they were fighting only for their honour and to die with dignity. The longest resistance was offered by the underground bunkers and the Germans subdued these by burning the houses above them and throwing grenades through the ventilation outlets. Only a few dozen of the fighters were saved with the help of the Home Army and the People's Guard, crossing through the sewers over to the 'Aryan' side of the city. On 8 May the Commander of ŻOB, Mordechaj Anielewicz, and dozens of his closest associates, surrounded by the Germans in their bunker, committed collective suicide. Some sporadic fighting went on up to 16 May, when the last defenders were killed and the Synagogue was blown up.[22]

As well as those who escaped through the sewers, some dozens saved themselves by hiding in the ruins, deep underground. The Germans took 56 065 people, killing 7000 on the spot and sending the rest to death camps. 6000 Jews were killed in the fighting, shooting a dozen or so Germans and wounding over a hundred. The whole district was turned into one colossal cemetery of ruins. On 13 May, just before the end of the fighting, Szmul Zygelbojm, a member of the National Council in London, committed suicide, in protest against the complete indifference of the world.[23]

The fighting in the Warsaw ghetto was not the only attempt by the Jews at resistance against the Germans. The younger generation, encouraged by the Warsaw example, of which they learnt through underground channels, started to fight in other ghettos at the decisive moment. In June 1943 fighting broke out in Lwów, where the Jewish Military Organisation was active; in the same month the Germans had to break the resistance in Częstochowa. On 3 August the ghetto in Będzin started a defensive fight, on 16 August the same happened in Białystok. There the fighting was so heavy that the Germans had to use artillery, a tank and the air force. The resistance was directed by the Jewish Organisation of Self-Defence. There were also uprisings in two places of mass extermination: in Treblinka on 12 August and in Sobibór on 14 October. Some prisoners managed to escape.[24]

There was no fighting in the ghetto of Łódź, the second largest ghetto after Warsaw. This was the result of German perfidy in its most depraved form, and Jewish co-operation carried out to the limit. Mordechaj Rumkowski was so powerful, thanks to the Germans, that he lost touch with reality. At first he was allowed to set up schools, a cultural centre, a bank issuing its own money, a sports council, a post office, a prison, a health service, etc. This wide-spread self-government gave some semblance to the idea that there was a real chance of surviving the war and Rumkowski got the backing of the Jewish community, first of all from rich people who still had some of their possessions.[25]

Later, when the Germans cut down the food rations and started mass deportations, Rumkowski did not change his attitude. He was still of the opinion that his collaboration with the Germans would allow him to save at least those people who worked for industry. Together with the Jewish police he carried out the task of bringing the contingents of people to the death-trains and helped the oppressors to camouflage their crimes. His achievement was that the ghetto at Łódź existed for over a year longer than that at Warsaw. It contained 70 000 inhabitants when in the summer of 1944 Himmler gave the order to liquidate it. Almost all, including Rumkowski, perished in the gas chambers of Auschwitz, deported there with their belongings and the hope that it was only 'resettlement'. From the large ghetto of Łódź only 877 persons survived the war.[26]

Besides the liquidation of the ghettos – and there were several dozens of them on Polish soil – the Germans also murdered Jews in the labour camps. As in the ghettos all these camps worked for German industry, the war situation was desperate, yet still the murder madness appeared to be stronger than cold logic. Nevertheless the extermination action did have some gaps; Jews did remain in some places, some ghettos were rebuilt and some new labour camps created. One of them in Częstochowa lasted till January 1945 and was freed by the Red Army.[27]

Apart from the help offered by the Polish population, the Jews helped themselves by escaping to the forests and living there with the support of the local villages or by organising partisan units. Some of them joined the partisans of the Home Army near Cracow and

Kielce, some of the partisans of the People's Guard and some similar Soviet units to the east of the River Bug. The Council for Aid to Jews was active right up to the end of the German occupation, helping people in need, and the Directorate of Civil Resistance traced and punished informers and blackmailers.[28]

Nobody knows the exact numbers of Jews who survived the war in Poland, under the German occupation. It fluctuates from 60 000 to 100 000 people. In 1946 there were 240 000 Jews in Poland and when we remember that 157 000 had returned from the Soviet Union, the number of survivers is probably 83 000.

A different problem is the exact number of Jews who lived in Poland before the war and who survived the war elsewhere. It is estimated that about 700 000 escaped to the Soviet Union and only a few of these were captured by the Germans. As stated 157 000 of them returned to Poland after the war. About 110 000 Polish Jews spent the war in other countries, such as Sweden, Italy and Romania. Taking all these figures into consideration and remembering that before the war 3 113 000 Jews lived in Poland, it should be accepted that fewer than 900 000 survived the war.[29]

14 The Polish Army in the Middle East and Crisis in London

THE WAR IN NORTH AFRICA AND THE ALLIED LANDINGS THERE

Thanks to the breaking of the Japanese coding machine, popularly called by the Americans *Purple*, Admiral Chester Nimitz obtained a resounding victory over the Japanese fleet at Midway on 4–6 June 1942. This gaining of superiority in the Pacific allowed the Americans to continue with their previously-taken decision of regarding the European theatre of war as the most important. Their influence noticeably increased in the decision-making of the Western Allies and further planning of the war against Germany was dependent on them.

The possibility of a landing in Europe had been mooted but it was too early for such an undertaking and the Americans favoured the British suggestion of an invasion of North Africa. This was justified on a number of counts. The war had been waged there for nearly three years, the British had gathered a substantial force there, opposed by the German Afrika Corps. The Italians too had a large army there. The control of North Africa was an ideal starting-point for an invasion of the European Continent. Thus in July 1942 the decision was taken to plan the operation, which was given the code name *Torch*.[1]

Erwin Rommel tried to turn back the fortunes of war and in June 1942 he launched a new offensive in which he captured Tobruk and again reached the gates of Egypt, where however he was halted. On the last day of August the Germans attacked again and again were held. The balance of forces tipped in favour of the British. Despite his victory General Auchinleck was transferred to India and his place as Commander-in-Chief of the Middle East was taken over by General Harold Alexander. He had previously commanded the Eighth Army whose command was now taken over by General Bernard Montgomery. There were no Polish units in the Eighth Army as the forces evacuated from the USSR and the Carpathian Brigade were undergoing a reorganisation in Iraq.[2]

Knowing that Churchill expected from him a total victory and the destruction of the enemy, Montgomery was in no hurry to launch his counter-offensive. He gathered his strength and only on 23 October 1942 did he attack the German positions at El Alamein. After ten days of fighting, the German retreat began, through Cyrenaica and Tripolitania. However Field Marshal Rommel's army was not destroyed and was to play an important role in the further battles. Among other factors Montgomery's victory was so quick because he received copies of the Germans most secret orders, sent by radio, thanks to the cracking of the Enigma secret.

Montgomery's offensive was sychronised with the landings of the Western Allies in Morocco and Algieria which took place on 8 November. The American General Dwight D. Eisenhower (1890–1969) was in overall command of the operation.[3]

THE CONFERENCE IN CASABLANCA AND 'UNCONDITIONAL SURRENDER'

Not long after the successful landings Roosevelt and Churchill met in Casablanca, on 14–24 January 1943, to discuss future strategy with their military commanders and political advisers. It was decided that after establishing total control in North Africa, the invasion of Sicily and then the Italian peninsula should be undertaken. It was expected that victory there would come quickly, that Mussolini would fall and in that way the 'Berlin–Rome Axis' would be broken. At that time the British and Americans had not decided on any future plans on how to take advantage of the expected victory in the Mediterranean basin. However the first difference of opinion arose between Roosevelt and Churchill, as the latter attached a basic importance to an attack on the continent through the Balkans.[4]

An event occurred at the end of the conference with was to play an important role in the further prosecution of the war and in future political decisions. During the press conference, Roosevelt, without prior consultation with Churchill, declared that the only logical conclusion to the war must be the unconditional surrender of Germany, Italy and Japan. This was one of the most important psychological blunders made by the West *vis-à-vis* the enemy. It had no influence on the fanatical Japanese; the Italians were already going down the path to capitulation, but in Germany Goebbels' propaganda took advantage of it immediately. At the time that Roosevelt was publicly declaring his intent, Hitler was in an exceptionally difficult situation. Not only had the victory in Russia not materialised, but the first serious defeat, at Stalingrad, was imminent; in Africa, on the one hand Rommel was defeated, on the other the Allied landings had taken place; German cities were under a hail of bombs changing them into ruins; in the Far East the Japanese retreat had begun. Despite its ostensible monolithic structure the Third Reich had powerful internal opponents, who held important positions in the army and the state administration. It was a large network of a political–military conspiracy called by the Nazi security authorities, *Die Schwarze Kapelle* (The Black Orchestra). This maintained secret contact with the Western Allies and was preparing to take power if Hitler were removed. The leading politician of this conspiracy was the ex-mayor of Leipzig, Carl Goerdeler. The army was represented by the ex-Chief of General Staff, the most senior officer, General Ludwig Beck, Field Marshal Erwin von Witzleben, General Friedrich Olbricht and many others, but above all by the Chief of Military Intelligence (*Abwehr*), Admiral Wilhelm Canaris.[5] It was a long time since the conspiracy was in such a favourable position and that the *Führer's* authority was at such a low point and his life threatened by many assassination attempts, when Roosevelt's speech saved the situation. The slogan 'total war' was at once used by Goebbels, a fight to the last man as Germany had only unconditional surrender to wait for and with it a terrible retribution by the victors.[6]

Roosevelt's move was all the more telling, because his special envoy, Allen Dulles, was at that time in the Swiss capital, Bern, with the task of maintaining secret contacts with the emissaries of *Die Schwarze Kapelle*. Less than a month after the Cassablanca Conference, in February 1943, Dulles met Canaris' envoy, Prince Maximilian Hohenlohe-Langenburg, and outlined his point of view on post-war Europe. The Germans, though defeated, should not be partitioned and should maintain their position in Central Europe even with Austria within her frontiers. It was necessary to weaken aggressive Prussian militarism. In Dulles' view the greatest danger to

Europe and the world was the Soviet Union with her destructive communism. For this reason Poland should not only regain her eastern provinces, but even expand them to block off the USSR from Europe by a '*cordon sanitaire*',[7]

Unfortunately further events showed that Roosevelt saw the future of Europe differently. He did not possess enough elasticity to take advantage of the existence of *Die Schwarze Kapelle* and to draw the German nation to the side of the West. At the same time he made all possible concessions to Stalin, not envisaging the consequences of such action, which were visible on the horizon. Great Britain also did not manage to take advantage of this trump card because she did not trust *Die Schwarze Kapelle* and demanded the removal or assassination of Hitler before becoming involved.[8]

The far-sighted moves of Soviet policy stood in stark contrast to this unbending policy of the Western statesmen which lacked political vision. On the last day of January 1943 the German sixth Army surrendered at Stalingrad, 100 000 prisoners were taken, among them thousands of officers and many generals. Only a few weeks passed before the 'Free Germans Committee' began its activity in Moscow with General Walter von Seydlitz and General Aleksander Edler von Daniels at its head. Radio broadcasts began immediately with speeches containing the slogan: 'we are not fighting the German nation but the Nazis'.[9] Until then only Soviet propagandists had broadcast to the Germans, now German voices were heard and not insignificant ones: those of generals enjoying until then the respect of the nation and the supreme state authorities. Cracks began to appear on the hitherto smooth façade of German resistance.

THE POLISH ARMY IN THE MIDDLE EAST

Whilst these events were occurring, the Polish units in the Near East were being reorganised. The nucleus of these modest forces was the Carpathian Brigade which had returned from Tobruk to Palestine and there it was to be reorganised into a division. This whole picture was changed when the first transports from the USSR began to arrive. Together with the civilians there were over 100 000 Poles in the Near East. Besides military reorganisation and the creation of new formations, it was necessary to think about schools, hospitals, books, newspapers, theatres and other amenities needed in the ordinary life of such a human mass.[10]

The British authorities were most interested in the creation of well-trained and well-armed combat formations. Simultaneously, out of humanitarian considerations, they partially alleviated the civilian problem by sending the women and children to India and Central Africa. This had the consequence of enabling them to concentrate efforts on purely military matters. Initially it was planned to create the Second Corps out of the Carpathian Brigade which was being transformed into a division, and the 4th Infantry Division with an HQ which had been transferred to Palestine from Cairo. However the evacuation from Russia changed this plan. General Sikorski, who was in constant touch with the British authorities as they were to equip the Polish forces, issued an order on 12 September 1942. The names 'HQ Middle East' and 'Polish Armed Forces in the USSR' were abolished and a new one was brought in: 'The Polish Army in the East'. In accordance with General Auchinleck's decision the organisation of this army was to take place in Iraq, 140 miles north east of Baghdad, between Khanagin and Quizil Ribat. In the autumn of 1942 the organising was begun. Army HQ was established at Quizil Ribat. Its formations were four divisions: 3rd, 5th, 6th and 7th. The whole lot numbered 5709 officers and about 62 000 men, the average age – especially of the officers – being high. General Anders was appointed the commander of the new army and was subordinated to the new British command 'Persia–Iraq'.[11]

Though the new army was an important addition to the strength of the Polish military effort outside Poland, these were still small forces, totally dependent on the allies as far as equipment was concerned. For this reason they did not change one iota Poland's desperate political situation.

NEW POLISH CRISIS IN LONDON

Unfortunately this situation which needed the greatest degree of unity in the Polish camp found it politically divided. With great external difficulties, General Sikorski had also to sacrifice much time, energy and nerves in fighting off attacks carried out by his own entourage. Despite the daily observance of Western attitudes whereby the army should not be used for political in-fighting and propaganda, Sikorski's opponents who had fought against him since 1939 began to search for allies within the Army to undermine the position of the Premier and Commander-in-Chief.

The new army in the Near East soon became an arena for sharp political propaganda, fortunately only among officers, whose main accusation against Sikorski's government was the abandonment of thousands of Poles in the USSR at Stalin's mercy. It repeated also the old accusations such as that of having lost the Polish Army in France, the inability to stand up against Soviet wishes, the lack of a political concept as regarded Germany and many others. It was suggestive that in these attacks there appeared a new aspect. Up to that time Poland was proud of not having produced a Quisling, but now there came accusations from the Army in the Near East that the government's refusal to allow a degree of collaboration with the German occupiers had resulted in horrendous biological and material losses. General Anders also joined in the sharp criticism of the government and especially of Sikorski, demanding that he resign.[12]

The difficult atmosphere was fuelled by the Western press which choked with praise of the Soviet Union, attacking Poland for not meekly submitting to Stalin. In Britain the conservative *Times* excelled in this whilst in the USA there were a number of such leading papers. The famous publicist, Walter Lippman, had enormous influence. In 1943 he published his book, *US Foreign Policy*. In it he blankly stated that it would be an enormous mistake if the USA after the war were to aim at the re-creation of the smaller states between Germany and Russia. This should not be promised as it was impossible to carry out. The Soviets would never allow Great Britain and the USA with the help of the governments in exile to rebuild the state of Eastern Europe as anti-Soviet outposts of the Western coalition.[13]

THE SITUATION IN OCCUPIED POLAND

With the situation becoming increasingly grave, with storms approaching from all sides and with no support in the West General Sikorski, led by experience and instinct, turned as always to occupied Poland. He did this after the fall of France, during the Polish–Soviet negotiations and the signing of the pact, so it was natural and understandable that his secret correspondence with Warsaw was animated.

Independently of the difficult international situation important events were occuring in Poland which had to be settled. First of all the Government Delegate was changed. Cyryl Ratajski, who was old, ailing, not suitable for secret work and under attack from the left-wing parties, was dismissed on 5 August 1942. In his place General Sikorski appointed Professor Jan Piekałkiewicz of the Peasant Party. He began his duties on 17. September.[14] The new Delegate showed more energy than his predecessor and did not automatically agree to General Rowecki's domination of the underground movement. Paragraph 1 of the statute made it clear that the 'Government Delegate was the highest representative of the government in occupied Poland. His authority extended over the whole of the territory of the Republic'. This was merely a confirmation of the existing state of affairs, in accordance with democratic rights. However General Rowecki did not want to agree to this as he rightly feared difficulties, dualism of authority and conspiratorial complications. During the settlement of co-operation between the civil and military authorities there occurred a new change of the Government Delegate. On 19 February 1943 Professor Piekałkiewicz was arrested and murdered by the Gestapo. His function was taken over by Jan Stanisław Jankowski of the Labour Party. His relations with General Rowecki were to be very good.

A second important problem was to unite all the underground military organisation into the Home Army. This was a military and a political problem, as it concerned the cadres formed by the two large parties, namely the National Military Organisation (NOW) of the National Movement and the Peasant Battalions (BCH) of the Peasant Party. In addition there were the National Armed Forces (NSZ) of the National Radical Camp. It was still a long way to the end of the war, a change for the better was possible and a united stand by all Poles or at least by their majority was essential. This led to General Sikorski's order of 15 August 1942: 'all military organisations and the Auxiliary Military Service which existed on Polish territory whose aim is to co-operate in the struggle against the enemy, I subordinate to the Commander of the Home Army'.

This order, which was synchronised with the developments of the political situation, played its role, as the National Party finally made its decision and on 4 November subordinated its military units to the Home Army. Unfortunately negotiations with the Peasant Party were more protracted and at that moment the Peasant Battalions remained independent. The situation was even worse as far as the National Armed Forces were concerned. There were too many fundamental political differences between them and the Home Army to be straightened out even when mortally endangered.[15]

A third important problem was the necessity to take up a position against the new enormous German crime which was the expulsion action in the Zamość and Lublin regions. Heinrich Himmler, the head of the SS, intended to create extensive German colonisation of these territories. On 12 November 1942 he issued an order as a result of which over 100 000 Poles were expelled and in their place tens of thousands of Germans were brought in. A number of those expelled ended up in the Auschwitz gas chambers and their children left in the camp only to be also murdered later. The commander of the Home Army, having come to an understanding with the Government Delegate, ordered a 'self-defence' action. This was decided in spite of the principle, so far abided by, not to provoke German retaliation on Polish territory. The 'self-defence' action manifested itself through attacks on German colonists, the burning of their homes, the slaughter of cattle and attacks on communication lines. The Germans were taken by surprise by this action, they wavered and in February 1943 halted further expulsions.[16]

However it was the fourth problem, which presented the greatest difficulties and dangers and which, because of the political situation, was of special note. The problem concerned the growing activities of the communists organised within the Polish Workers' Party (PPR) which had begun its activities at the beginning of 1942. Initially their influence was minimal especially as there was co-operation between the Polish and Soviet Governments and in Russia, General Anders' army was being organised. The situation changed with the evacuation of that army to Persia. The PPR, though it had barely 4000 members and its military arm, the People's Guard, only 3000, began to be aggressive and spread propaganda which could influence the unenlightened part of the social masses. After the fall of France the resistance leaders took on a waiting role calculated to be prudent and prepare for the moment when a general uprising could be declared in the deciding phase of the war. This did not bother the Polish communists as long as the Hitler–Stalin pact was in existence. After the German invasion of the USSR and the successes of the German army, the communists, instructed by Moscow, began to demand an increase in diversionary, sabotage and partisan activity to hit at the German rear. They rejected the argument that it was too early for such large-scale action and did not care about the enormous losses caused by German retaliatory action. Their propaganda landed on fertile ground among the lower ranks of the Home Army and led to ferment. They also took advantage of the success of the armed action taken by the Home Army in the Zamość region.

During the last weeks of 1942 the PPR, although still weak, decided to make contact with the Government Delegacy to discuss the possibility of co-operation, for they understood that on their own they could not display any great activity. Talks between the representatives of the Delegacy and the HQ of the Home Army with the respresentatives of the PPR (one of these was Władysław Gomułka) took place on 18, 22 and 25 February 1943. The communists at the very beginning were informed of the conditions necessary for an agreement. These were (i) recognition of the Government in London and its political and military organs in occupied Poland; (ii) the PPR must formally give an undertaking that it is neither an organ of Comintern nor an agency of a foreign government; (iii) that it confirms that it will fight uncompromisingly for the freedom of Poland against all invaders and that it recognises the inviolability of the Polish frontiers of 1939. The representatives of the PPR also put forward conditions for an agreement; (i) a new government should be called into being in occupied Poland and the London government be recognised as the representation abroad; (ii) the People's Guard be recognised as independent and equal to the Home Army, and (iii) the question of the eastern frontiers must be left open. The difference of opinion was so great that agreement proved impossible.[17]

General Sikorski, informed by Warsaw, understood the serious threat which the PPR posed to the Polish question, because Russia was aiming to create a situation in which those Poles who served her would themselves prepare for the political control of the country. Despite this Sikorski still hoped to scotch the danger at its source. He was in contact with Churchill and Roosevelt, especially with Churchill, and retained his optimistic view that the Western democracies would be able to influence the USSR in the deciding phase of the war to recognise Poland's eastern frontier. And this was not all: he counted on Russian support for the Polish stipulation concerning the Western territories where he expected to gain East Prussia, Gdańsk and Silesia near Opole. In this spirit General Sikorski sent a long telegram to General Rowecki on 28 November 1942, in which among other things he included directives as to how the Home Army was to react when the Soviet armies found themselves on Polish territory. It would be madness to fight them, they were to be treated as allies, and at the same time they were to be shown Polish strength through the mobilisation of the Home Army divisions, the fight against Germans and finally by revealing its units. In this way Polish sovereignty would be manifested on Polish territory taken by the Soviets from the Germans.[18]

In his reply of 12 January 1943 General Rowecki confirmed that he had received the directives concerning the Soviet entry into Poland and gave assurances that he would try to carry them out. Simultaneously he laid down certain conditions which would have to be fulfilled if the directives were to be carried out successfully. Above all he expected airborne landings, not only in central Poland but also in the east, and not only Polish but also Anglo-American. 'These landings, mainly in the eastern areas of Poland would be a clear sign of Anglo-Saxon co-operation with us and would restrain possible Soviet attacks of disloyalty towards us.' This one sentence was clear enough proof that General Rowecki had no knowledge of British and US plans for the future prosecution of the war and that he was ignorant of the views of the Western leaders. Much of the blame for this lies with General Sikorski who did not take the evasive answers of Churchill and especially Roosevelt as rejections and deluded himself that the Anglo-Saxon nations would help Poland in her dispute with the USSR over the eastern territories. He partially infected General Rowecki with this optimism. After all, airborne landings by Anglo-American forces in eastern Poland would in practice mean war with the USSR. At the time that General Rowecki was writing his telegram, preparations were being made for the conference in Casablanca at which there was to be a clear difference of opinion between British and American strategy. Though no final decisions were taken, it was clear that the USA would not sanction a landing in the Balkans and a northward thrust into Central Europe as they wanted to avoid any misunderstandings with the Soviet Union. Churchill pressed for an invasion of the Balkans but he did not think in terms of any clashes with the USSR in defence of the states of Central Europe.

Independently of the increasingly unproductive negotiations with the Poles, the Soviet government did not forget its further interests. Stalin wanted not only eastern Poland but also the Baltic States and tried to sound out British and American opinion on these matters. The British complained that the Poles had too great territorial ambitions. Though in principle against giving the Baltic States to the USSR, Roosevelt declared that 'he had no intention of bargaining with Poland or any other small states when the peace of the world was at stake'.[19] Such statements only convinced Stalin that he could go ahead with his aggressive plans as the 'Atlantic Charter' was already cracking up.

THE DISCOVERY OF THE KATYŃ GRAVES

In this very difficult period when the Western Allies were increasingly agreeing to all concessions to the USSR and with growing embarrassment at having Poland in its camp, Berlin radio on 13 April 1943 announced some astounding news. In the region of Smoleńsk in the vicinity of a small village called Katyń the Germans had discovered mass graves of Polish officers. They were clearly prisoners of war from Kozielsk camp from which they were transported in spring 1940. The total number was calculated at 10 000 and the murders had been committed by the Bolsheviks by firing a pistol shot into the back of the head.[20]

The news was so unexpected that in Polish London the information was not at first treated seriously and was interpreted as another German propaganda trick. The information was treated very differently by the officers and soldiers of the Polish Army in the East, most of whom had come out of Russia and who, during the organisation of the army in the USSR, had searched in vain for thousands of their missing colleagues. On 15 April General Anders sent a telegram to the Minister of National Defence in London expressing the feelings among his subordinates and reminding the minister of his efforts to find the missing prisoners. He suggested that the Government should demand an official Soviet explanation. That same day Radio Moscow made a statement in which it said that the crime had been committed by the Germans in 1941 when they occupied the Smoleńsk area and took thousands of Polish prisoners of war employed in building works. Two days later the VI Bureau of the Polish General Staff in London received a telegram from General Rowecki, sent from Warsaw on 14 April, confirming the German communiqué on the basis of information from a number of Poles who had been sent to Katyń by the Germans.[21]

The Polish Government was faced with a difficult problem which had several aspects to it. It was clear that the Germans had begun a vociferous propaganda campaign on the discovery of the graves for political purposes, wanting to spread dissension in the Allied camp. It was important not to be swept into the German nets, yet at the same time it was hard to forget the attitude of the Russians towards Poland. The emotional side of this question was so strong in the minds of Poles that the Polish Government could not ignore it.

On 16 April the Minister of Polish National Defence issued a communiqué which, after making a précis of the whole problem of the Polish prisoners of war missing in Russia, finished in this way:

> We have become accustomed to the lies of German propaganda and we understand the purpose behind its latest revelations. In view however of abundant and detailed German information concerning the discovery of the bodies of many thousands of Polish officers near Smoleńsk, and the categorical statement that they were murdered by the Soviet authorities in the spring of 1940, the necessity has arisen that the mass graves discovered should be investigated and the facts alleged verified by a competent international body, such as the International Red Cross. The Polish Government has therefore approached this institution with a view to their sending a delegation to the place where the massacre of the Polish prisoners of war is said to have taken place.[22]

The following day the Polish Government issued a declaration containing two points: (i) confirmation that it had asked the International Red Cross in Geneva to send a delegation to Katyń to secure the facts. In this point the government underlined its attitude towards the Germans saying that it 'rejects them the right to use the crime for which it blames others – as an argument in defence of their own crimes', (ii) establishment of the text of the note to the Soviet Government which was delivered on 20 April in which it asked for an explanation as to the fate of the missing Polish prisoners of war, as the Soviet Government had more knowledge on this matter than it had so far divulged.[23]

The Germans also turned to the International Red Cross but not through political channels. They employed their own Red Cross which sent an appropriate telegram to Geneva on 16 April. There the request was considered positively and there was a tendency to agree to the sending of its own experts, but on one condition. This was that all the interested parties had to turn to Geneva. It would be expected that Russia would take advantage of this occasion to show its innocence. However things turned out differently. The Soviet radio, press and TASS news agency began a vicious attack on the Government of General Sikorski, stating that the Polish appeal to the International Red Cross showed how strong were the pro-German elements in the Polish Government.[24]

The Katyń massacre caused great disquiet among the British and American leaders. Though the murder was dreadful, it did not act on them emotionally as it did on the Poles, their most important aim being the winning of the war against Germany and Japan. They understood perfectly the aim of German propaganda; they were afraid of dissensions and difficulties in the Allied camp; they feared a separate German–Soviet peace – and that possibility was always on the cards. At that time the 'Free Germans Committee' was established in Moscow, which was proof that the Soviets wanted to find a common language with the German nation. This fact greatly disturbed President Roosevelt. He was already planning the future of the world in which he saw the USA as the leading power after the eclipse of the British Empire. The natural partner of the USA was to be the victorious Soviet Union and the maintenance of good relations with it was of paramount importance. The international outcry of the Poles was especially undesirable for him as it could change the attitude of American society towards Russia. True, few people at that time believed the German propaganda, but the free and sensation-seeking American press began to write that there was little difference between Hitler and Stalin. For the Poles this was a welcome side-effect of the discovery of the Katyń graves but the Western leaders had no intention of allowing a lasting crack in their co-operation with the USSR.[25]

The pressure on General Sikorski began immediately. Churchill had a meeting with him and tried to prevent him from magnifying the affair and making a request to the International Red Cross. This time however the Polish Premier was adamant. The anger of the Poles was rising fast especially with new information from Katyń sent by institutions and trustworthy people. First of these was the international medical commission giving the opinion of the members of the Polish Red Cross who had gone to Katyń with the secret approbation of the Polish underground authorities, as well as the statements of Allied POWs taken to the scene of the crime by the Germans. All the evidence pointed to the crime having been committed by the Soviets in spring 1940. There were letters, notes and bits of Soviet newspapers, all from the period February and March 1940. These coincided with the statements of witnesses. The experts confirmed these views on the basis of the condition of the corpses. Above all one unanswered basic question remained: as the Soviet radio had stated that the corpses found in the graves were those of Polish prisoners of war who had been employed on building works in the Smoleńsk area in 1941 and had been captured by the Germans, why had this explanation not been put forward to the Polish authorities when the Polish army was being organised in the USSR when, during a ten-month period these prisoners were being sought?[26]

RUSSIA BREAKS OFF DIPLOMATIC RELATIONS WITH POLAND

Stalin, when agreeing to the evacuation of General Anders' army from Russia, had already decided on his plan for Poland. He now took advantage of this pretext and broke off diplomatic relations with the Polish Government. On the night of 24–25 April Molotov read out the Soviet note to the Polish Ambassador, Tadeusz Romer.

> On behalf of the Government of the Union of Soviet Socialist Republics, I have the honour to notify the Polish Government of the following:
> The Soviet Government consider the recent behaviour of the Polish Government with regard to the USSR as entirely abnormal and violating all regulations and standards of relations between two Allied States. The slanderous campaign hostile to the Soviet Union launched by the German Fascists in connection with the murder of the Polish officers, which they themselves committed in the Smoleńsk area on territory occupied by German troops, was at once taken up by the Polish Government and is being fanned in every way by the Polish official press.
> Far from offering a rebuff to the vile Fascist slander of the USSR, the Polish Government did not even find it necessary to address to the Soviet Government any enquiry or request for an explanation on this subject.
> Having committed a monstrous crime against Polish officers, the Hitlerite authorities are now staging a farcical investigation, and for this they have made use of certain Polish pro-Fascist elements whom they themselves selected in occupied Poland where everything is under Hitler's heel, and where no honest Pole can openly have his say.
> For the 'investigation', both the Polish Government and the Hitlerite Government invited the International Red Cross, which is compelled, in conditions of a terroristic régime, with its gallows and mass extermination of the peaceful population, to take part in this investigation farce staged by Hitler. Clearly such an 'investigation', conducted behind the back of the Soviet Government,

cannot evoke the confidence of people possessing any degree of honesty.

The fact that the hostile campaign against the Soviet Union commenced simultaneously in the German and Polish press, and was conducted along the same lines, leaves no doubt as to the existence of contact and accord in carrying out this hostile campaign between the enemy of the Allies – Hitler – and the Polish Government.

While the peoples of the Soviet Union, bleeding profusely in a hard struggle against Hitlerite Germany, are straining every effort for the defeat of the common enemy of the Russian and Polish peoples, and of all freedom-loving democratic countries, the Polish Government, to please Hitler's tyranny, has dealt a treacherous blow to the Soviet Union.

The Soviet Government is aware that this hostile campaign against the Soviet Union is being undertaken by the Polish Government in order to exert pressure upon the Soviet Government by making use of the slanderous Hitlerite fake for the purpose of wresting from it territorial concessions at the expense of the interests of the Soviet Ukraine, Soviet Byelorussia and Soviet Lithuania.

All these circumstances compel the Soviet Government to recognise that the present Government of Poland, having slid on the path of accord with Hitler's Government, has actually discontinued allied relations with the USSR, and has adopted a hostile attitude towards the Soviet Union.

On the strength of the above, the Soviet Government has decided to sever relations with the Polish Government.[27]

Ambassador Romer refused to accept the note stating that it contained lies and slanders. Three days later, on 28 April, the Polish Government made public the following statement:

The Polish Government affirm that their policy, aiming at a friendly understanding between Poland and Soviet Union on the basis of the integrity and full sovereignty of the Polish Republic, was and continues to be fully supported by the Polish Nation.

Conscious of their responsibility towards their own nation and towards the Allies, whose unity and solidarity the Polish Government consider to be the corner-stone of future victory, they were the first to approach the Soviet Government with a proposal for a common understanding, in spite of the many tragic events which had taken place from the moment of the entry of the Soviet Armies on the territory of the Republic, i.e. September 17th, 1939.

Having regulated their relations with Soviet Russia by the agreement of July 30th, 1941, and by the understanding of December 4th, 1941, the Polish Government have scrupulously discharged their obligations.

Acting in close union with their Government, the Polish people, making the extreme sacrifice, fight implacably in Poland and outside the frontiers of their country against the German invaders. No traitor Quisling has sprung from Polish ranks. All collaboration with the Germans has been scorned. In the light of facts known throughout the world the Polish Government and Polish Nation have no need to defend themselves from any suggestion of contact or understanding with Hitler.

In a public statement of April 17th, 1943, the Polish Government categorically denied to Germany the right to abuse the tragedy of Polish Officers for her own perfidious schemes. They unhesitatingly denounce Nazi propaganda designed to create mistrust between Allies. About the same time a note was sent to the Soviet Ambassador accredited to the Polish Government asking once again for information which would help to elucidate the fate of the missing officers.

The Polish Government and people look to the future. They appeal in the name of the solidarity of the United Nations and the elementary humanity for the release from the USSR of the thousands of the families of Polish Armed Forces engaged in the fight or preparing in Great Britain and in the Middle East to take part in their fight – tens of thousands of Polish orphans and children for the education of whom they would take full responsibility and who now, in view of German mass slaughter, are particularly precious to the Polish people. The Polish Army, in waging the war against Germany, will also require for reinforcement all fighting Polish males who are now on Soviet soil, and the Polish Government appeal for their release. They reserve the right to plead the cause of all these persons to the world. In conclusion, the Polish Government asks for the continuation of relief welfare for the mass of Polish citizens who will remain in the USSR.

In defending the integrity of the Polish Republic, which accepted the war with the Third Reich, the Polish Government

never claimed and do not claim, in accordance with their statement of February 25th, 1943, any Soviet territories.

It is and will be the duty of every Polish Government to defend
the rights of Poland and the Polish citizens. The principles for
which the United Nations are fighting and also the making of all
efforts for strengthening their solidarity in this struggle against the
common enemy, remain the unchanging basis of the policy of the
Polish Government.[28]

Not expecting such a far-reaching Moscow reaction, the Western
leaders attempted immediate intervention. On the same day that
Molotov handed the Polish Ambassador the note, Churchill sent a
telegram to Stalin. Roosevelt did likewise twenty-four hours later but
neither produced any results. On 4 May Anthony Eden made a
statement in the House of Commons in which he expressed his regret
that the Poles and Russians had not taken a more conciliatory line of
action. At the same time he stressed that the disharmony among the
Allies would not weaken their determination in seeking a complete
victory over Germany. That same day Stalin granted the *New York
Times* a press interview. In it he stated that he expected a 'strong and
independent Poland' after the war. His words could be interpreted in
many ways, but they were at total variance to Molotov's declaration
in 1939 about the 'ugly offspring of the Versailles treaty'. On 5 May
Ambassador Romer left the USSR; the British Government took
over the protection of the remaining Polish citizens, later handing
over to the Australian Government.

In 1951 the US Congress called into being a special Committee
whose task was to examine the Katyń crime and collect all possible
facts and evidence. On 2 July 1952 the Committee published its
report: *Interim Report of the US Congressional Select Committee, July
2nd, 1952*. In its conclusion the following sentence was included:

The Committee declares unanimously that the first phase of the
investigation proves definitely and irrefutably that the Soviet
NKVD (*Narodny Kommissariat Vnutrennich Dyel*) carried out the
massacre of the officers of the Polish Army in the forest of Katyń,
near Smoleńk, in Russia, not later than the spring of 1940.

15 Polish Communists in USSR

Relations with the Polish Government were broken off, Western aid kept flowing in large quantities, the Soviet contribution to the victory over Germany was big though this did not guarantee that Great Britain and USA would agree to all Soviet demands. Stalin was thus very careful and played his political game with great precision. One of the main problems was the future of the Polish state. It seemed that Stalin already had control over it and yet he took care over each step he took. He did not take much notice of the extremists in Homel or from the 'villa of happiness', who, immediately after the German attack began to call for the formation of Polish army units on Soviet territory. General Anders' army left Russia in August 1942. It was obvious that another Polish army – totally dependent on the Soviets – would be created. Yet Stalin did not allow the formation of this army whilst Polish–Soviet diplomatic relations remained intact. He broke them himself, but still waited for the reaction of his Western partners. He only took his next step after having received Churchill's and Roosevelt's telegrams which apart from attempting to persuade him and complaining about their own difficulties did not hold any forms of pressure. Even then he was careful. The Polish Ambassador left Soviet territory on the 5 May 1943 and only then was the question of a new Polish army raised publicly. On 8 May the Soviet press and the new Polish paper, *Wolna Polska*, published a communiqué in which the Soviet Government gave its agreement to the formation of a Polish infantry division named after Tadeusz Kościuszko. [2]

STALIN AND POLISH COMMUNISTS IN THE USSR

Before a complete public change in Soviet policy towards Poland took place, secret talks were held aiming at creating a new Polish political representation composed of communists and totally dependent on Moscow. On 1 March 1943 the Organisational Committee of the Union of Polish Patriots under the chairmanship of Wanda Wasilewska was set up in the Russian capital. This date should be accepted as the beginning of the new political phase. On 8 March this committee published the first issue of the weeky, *Wolna Polska*, which became the organ of the Union. The editorial outlined its programme which became the basis for a future declaration of ideological principles. On 16 April an article appeared in *Wolna Polska* entitled 'Poland's Place in Europe'. Without leaving any room for doubt it stated that Poland's eastern territories should go to the USSR because the Ukrainian, Byelorussian and Lithuanian populations must have the right to join the Soviet republics. Already at this stage this meant an agreement to shift Poland westwards because the article mentioned Polish rights to the Baltic and the lands of the Oder river.[3]

Only towards the end of April, after diplomatic relations with the Polish Government had been broken, did Stalin receive Wanda Wasilewska's letter about a new Polish army. In it she wrote that

the creation of a Polish military formation is possible through the mobilisation of Poles of Soviet citizenship from Poland as well as from the western provinces of USSR and the transferring of Poles from labour battalions. I am of the opinion that it will be necessary for the delegation of a number of Red Army commanders – Poles and Russians – in order to aid the Polish formation.

Almost immediately after this letter the leaders of the union of Polish Patriots met General Zhukov, the Red Army's representative on Polish problems. They decided to form the Tadeusz Kościuszko Infantry Division with Colonel Berling as its commander and a Polish communist, Włodzimierz Sokorski, as his deputy for political matters. On 8 May a communiqué to this effect was published and some days later the first organising group arrived at Sielce on the Oka river.[4]

A NEW POLISH ARMY ON SOVIET SOIL

As the result of the mass deportations of Polish citizens from the plundered eastern territories of the Republic, over 800 000 persons found themselves in 1940 in the depths of Russia. Afterwards, prior to the German attack, a new wave of deportations brought the figure to over a million. Many died from emaciation and starvation, over 100 000 left Russia with General Anders, but the remaining hundreds of thousands formed a potential pool for the newly-created army. These people had every reason to be angry and to have no trust in Russia or its authorities, they remembered September 1939 when Hitler and Stalin together divided Poland. Many of them cursed the USSR because the local authorities had prevented them from leaving their areas of inprisonment to reach General Anders' army, which for them was the real Polish army. These feelings strengthened when in January 1943 a decree of the Supreme Council of the USSR took away their Polish citizenship and the instruction to return Polish passports were issued. [5]

With such sentiments, volunteering to join the division which was regarded as a half-overt unit of the Red Army should have met with difficulties, yet this was not so. The greater majority of deported Poles vegetated in the most appalling conditions, they failed to reach General Anders' units and suddenly rumours reached them of the formation of a new Polish army in the USSR. There was no belief in the honesty of the Soviet authorities, yet what could be worse than the present situation? Tens of thousands decided to go to Sielce. Their families stayed behind but volunteers hoped that finally they would bring their wives, children and parents to the Poland they dreamed about.[6]

The majority of volunteers were deportees. Another group, numbering some 100 000, had not been deported but had been forcibly mobilised into the Red Army and after the German attack transferred to labour battalions as an 'unsure element'. Then there were those who after the 'amnesty' of 1941 had not managed to reach General Anders' army. There was a small group who having been mobilised into the Red Army were not transferred to the labour battalions and were now permitted to transfer to the Polish division. A certain number of volunteers were Poles living in the USSR, many of them descendants of Polish patriots deported to Siberia after the uprisings against Russia in the nineteenth century, who had either served in the Red Army or were mobilised during the war. These had some front-line combat experience and were officers, or NCOs; few spoke Polish, but had excellent training in their specialisation.[7]

The division was to be formed on the lines of a Red Army guards division. It was to have three infantry regiments, one regiment of light artillery and other independent units. As it was planned to expand the Polish Armed Forces in the USSR, a tank regiment, an anti-aircraft artillery battery, a howitzer battery, a flight of fighters and a women's battalion to be included. The strength of the divison was to be 1095 officers, 3258 NCOs and 7093 soldiers -- in total 11 446 men; however, the large flow of volunteers meant that by July it already numbered 14 380. A reserve infantry regiment was formed. As planned, Colonel Zygmunt Berling was appointed commander of the division.[8]

With the mass of volunteers there were few problems where soldiers were concerned; there was, however, a problem with officers. The transports of volunteers came to Sielce, but among them there were practically no officers apart from a small number of reservists who during the deportation had not admitted their rank. Those who could, had left Russia with General Anders; those murdered at Katyń and in other places could not rise from their graves. As for the inhabitants of the 'villa of happiness', there were barely a dozen or so. In this situation the Peoples Commissariat of Defence had to direct many ethnic Russian officers to the division. They had nothing to do with Poland and, of course, did not speak Polish. Thus the officer cadre was composed of three groups. The largest group was composed of those of Polish descent, inhabitants of the USSR; the second of Russians acting as Poles and the third and smallest was comprised of Berling's colleagues, reserve officers, newly-promoted NCOs and the graduates of the quickly-formed military schools. There was a shortage of NCOs also. This was solved by training chosen candidates in the regimental NCOs schools.[9]

In accordance with Soviet methods this mixed group of many thousands of soldiers had to go through an intensive course of political training and indoctrination. The right people for this could only be supplied by the Union of Polish Patriots as the education officers had to be exclusively Polish because of the necessity for perfect communication with the soldiers. Moreover they had to be communists and thus they took over all the leading posts, accounting for 40 per cent of all the personnel. The remaining 60 per cent was filled up by Poles of left-wing views or non-party people who had undergone the necessary training. The political enlightenment training was very intensive in the division, if one considers that in August 1943 168 officers worked in this department. The majority of them in fact did not have officer ranks but were given them or were confirmed as 'acting education officers'.[10]

Political education was so important that it was put on a par with, and sometimes even above, military training in the formative months of the division's existence. For this purpose the Organisation Committee of the Union of Polish Patriots wrote a provisional instruction booklet which in its most important section contained the following point: 'only in alliance with the USSR will the German invader be smashed and Poland liberated'.[11]

The decision to create Polish military units in the USSR – totally subordinated to the Soviet authorities and their tool, the Union of Polish Patriots – had to have a series of logical consequences. Against the background of the mobilised and fighting millions of Soviet citizens, the Polish Army in the USSR was a drop in the ocean; at most it could have only a symbolic and propagandistic character, but above all a political one. Stalin had already created his concept for the future post-war Poland. For its realisation he needed people who would agree to co-operate with his country, on his terms. These people should be in the vanguard of the Soviet armies entering Poland so that they could immediately begin the task of building the new political reality. This role was to be filled by the Polish Army whose first division was now being formed. It was a combat formation, but in practice it had to fulfil the role of a political instrument and thus the indoctrination of its soldiers was very important.[12]

The organisers of the division were aware that the masses of volunteers were anti-Soviet Russia, rightly holding her responsible for nearly all the misfortunes that had befallen the Polish deportees and their homeland. It was necessary at all costs to weaken these feelings and that is why the organisers tried to create the impression that the division was totally Polish and that it was totally independent. The white and red flag fluttered over the divisional HQ; uniforms and distinctions resembled those worn before the war, the pre-war salute was maintained and on the square caps were the eagles, without the crown, but Polish. Even a Polish priest, who was kidnapped by Soviet partisans in Poland and taken to Sielce, was available. The Polish national anthem was sung.[13]

These first impressions had some influence on new arrivals but this did not last long. Volunteers had seen something of life despite their youth; they had made up their minds about the USSR and it was very difficult to convert them. However they had come freely, decided to serve and fight, so their distrust could be overcome and their hearts reached by political work in the right direction. This could only be one: the necessity of the common struggle against Germany, forgetting of the wrongs done to them by the Soviets and the clear statement that the authorities admitted their sins and would not repeat them.

However neither the Soviet leaders nor the Polish communists were capable of presenting the case in this way. The former, living for many years in a system of the utmost deceit, neither wanted to, nor could, admit to any faults; the latter, consumed by blind hatred for the pre-war Polish state and for everything which did not accord with their narrow-minded communist doctrines, were unable to shake this off. Political lectures and discussions began with criticism of pre-war Poland and praise of the Soviet Union and its achievements.[14] Such lectures could be given in Central Africa or Japan, to people who had not the slightest knowledge about the topic. Here however the listeners were Poles, who not only loved their country but above all knew it very well. The vast majority of them came from eastern Poland which was the poorest region, in which the young State had not yet completed the task of establishing law and order and where the authorities overstepped their bounds. However against the backdrop of the horrendous, unparalleled poverty of the USSR, and the complete lawlessness, lies and police terror reaching the limits of human endurance, the attempt to explain that Poland had been bad and the USSR a paradise was doomed to failure. Yet this was the line taken by the education officers, who in reality were political officers, known in the Red Army as *politruks*.

UNION OF POLISH PATRIOTS

Whilst the first cadres of the division were being formed, the communists close to the Organisation Committee of the Union of Polish Patriots were aiming at giving the Union a formal structure. On 9–10 June 1943 a meeting was held in Moscow attended by sixty-six delegates from various regions of the USSR. Its main task was to pass the 'Ideological Declaration of the Union' which, though it put the defeat of the Germany enemy as the main task, also painted a picture of a post-war Poland. It was in agreement with the thesis put forward in the article of 'Poland's Place in Europe', published in *Wolna Polska* on 16 April. Liberated Poland had to have just borders in the east taking into account the rights of the Byelorussians and Ukrainians 'to their own national unification', which meant agreeing to the Soviet plunder of Poland's eastern territories. In the west there must be a return to the old Polish lands on the Oder and Baltic. The agricultural structure would be reformed, the peasants would receive free land, and the nation would see 'Poland liberated from the rule of landowners, cartel barons, usurous bankers and speculators'. However the most important point of the declaration, confirming what was to happen in the near future was the statement that 'the only wise policy today, as before 1939, is an alliance with the USSR'. An executive council of the Union of Polish Patriots was elected and Wanda Wasilewska became its chairman.[15]

THE FIRST POLISH CORPS

When the division exceeded its organisational structure a reserve regiment was formed, but there were so many volunteers that the possibility of forming a Polish corps began to appear. This was in accordance with Stalin's plans, so on 10 August a decree of the state Committee of Defence of the USSR was issued permitting the formation of such a corps. Berling was appointed its commander, being promoted General and retaining command of the 1st Division. General Karol Świerczewski, a Pole, but an officer of the Red Army who had participated in the Spanish Civil War, took over deputy command for combat matters. Besides 1st Infantry Division there were foreseen 1st Artillery Brigade, 2nd Infantry Division, Armoured Brigade, fighter regiment, a battalion of parachutists, one reserve infantry regiment and various independent units. Later, at the beginning of 1944, the formation of the 3rd Infantry Division was begun. This was primarily formed from Poles mainly from Silesia, Pomerania and Wielkopolska who had been forcibly conscripted by the Germans into the Wehrmacht and who had been taken prisoner by the Red Army. By early spring, 1944, the Corps numbered 43 508 including 4 564 officers.[16]

Towards the end of August 1943 large tactical exercises of the 1st Division took place to check whether the intensive training of the past three months had given the expected results. Immediately after the exercises, new officers and NCOs, who had completed very short courses, received promotion justified by the necessities of war. The exercise had also been an opportunity to assess the work of the political officers. In this respect the results of their indoctrination were meagre, as many of the soldiers continued to believe that the Polish Government in London represented the real interests of the nation, and that an understanding with them should be sought and that the continuous criticism should cease.

It was decided that the Division would almost immediately be sent to the front to Vyazma where it would undergo its best combat training. Besides the infantry a tank regiment, which had existed for a few months, would also go. Within a few days, at the turn of August–September, the division and the tanks arrived at their new destination. There they were subordinated to the commander of the Western Front.[17]

THE BATTLE OF LENINO

This was the period, following the decisive victory at Kurs, in which the Red Army was rolling westwards. The division which formed part of the Thirty-third Army, marched through newly-captured Smoleńsk to the area of Lenino, east of the Orsha. There it received its first combat task which was to force the marshy river Miereja and to destroy a number of German battalions. Prior to the attack, on 9 October, Order No. 580 was issued by General Berling. It would be difficult to find a more convincing proof of the character of the Polish Army in Russia and the tasks that lay in front of it:

> As we are fighting, spilling our blood and marking our route to the Motherland with graves, then our voice in the Motherland must not and will not be belittled... We will create a provisional authority and ensure its freedom to act. We will guard against all attempts at the return of fascism in any guise to Poland. We will guard our alliance with the Soviet Union with whom we wish to preserve allied loyalty and sincere friendship.[18]

The division counted barely a dozen or so thousand and already there was talk of taking power.

On 12 and 13 October the division undertook its planned attack in co-operation with the neighbouring Soviet divisions. The river Miereja and its marshes was crossed, the infantry broke into the German lines to a depth of a few kilometres but the resistance of the enemy proved too strong. The defence was not broken, the neighbouring Soviet divisions had remained at their positions, German counter-attack began and the danger of encirclement became a possibility. A quick withdrawal from the most exposed positions allowed for a partial rescue but many men of the 1st Infantry Regiment were taken prisoner. For a time there was chaos. The command lost their heads, whilst the young, inexperienced soldiers, at the front for the first time, not knowing how to hide and overwhelmed by the artillery and exploding bombs, died in a hopeless fight. During the night of 13–14 October the division was withdrawn and replaced by the 164th Soviet Division. The losses were enormous: 502 dead, 1776 wounded and 663 missing, thus either dead or taken prisoner by the Germans.[19]

The participation of the Polish Army, subordinated to Russia, was undoubtedly necessary in the war being waged, but mainly to attain its political aims. For this reason the Battle of Lenino was given massive propaganda treatment, yet the Polish communists themselves understood that it had been commanded disastrously and that the losses were too high. The officers and soldiers had fought bravely but if they were to continue to fight in this way there would be precious few people left to undertake the planned political actions which were to open the way to Soviet control of Poland. Above all this applied to the most faithful who in the main were political officers. In the 1st Infantry Regiment, which suffered the most, of the thirty-three political officers, twenty-five had been killed or wounded. In other units losses were also high. That is why after its withdrawal to the Smoleńsk area, and after it was brought up to strength, it did not return to the front, but began a new period of training. In January 1944 the division was joined by the main forces of the Corps which until then had remained and trained in Sielce. These forces were: the Corps HQ, the 2nd and 3rd Infantry Divisions, an Artillery Brigade, an Armoured Brigade, an Air Force fighter regiment, a parachute batallion and a number of independent units. A lot of time was to elapse before the Polish Army in the USSR was once again in the first line of the front.[20]

16 Underground Fight in Poland; Arrest of General Rowecki; Death of General Sikorski

The break in diplomatic relations between Russia and the Polish Government disrupted the political line along which General Sikorski had been moving for a year and a half. This would have been less harmful if it had been accompanied by a reduction in the popularity of the Soviet Union in the West, as occurred in the United States for a short time after the revelation of Katyń. Unfortunately this did not happen. Russia had so many concealed and open friends in the United States and in Britain and her propaganda was so adroit and so unscrupulous, that the short-lived reduction in her fortunes was rapidly replaced by new and great successes. The victory at Stalingrad was claimed to be the turning-point of the war, while the Western press expatiated on the heroism of the Soviet soldiers and the great sacrifices of Soviet society. At the same time they attacked the Poles and the Polish Government for disrupting the unity of the allied camp. Their stubbornness over the eastern frontiers was depicted as nonsense because, after all, Poland was not entitled to them. The situation became somewhat paradoxical, because although the Polish Government neither wanted nor intended misunderstanding among the Allies, these were the only hope for Polish affairs. A glimmer of hope appeared in May 1943 after the decision taken in Washington to postpone the invasion of Europe until 1944, when Stalin withdrew his ambassadors from the USA and Britain, but this was a gesture without consequences. At the same time, on 22 May, under Western pressure, the Soviet dictator abolished the Comintern, an act which was understood to be a conciliatory gesture.[1] The Comintern (abbreviation of the words Communism and International) had been called into being by Lenin in 1919 and also known as the Third International, was an organisation intended to foster world revolution and had its agents all over the world.

POLAND'S DIFFICULT SITUATION

The situation of Poland was poor, worse than before the fall of France; nowhere was there any hope of assistance, no-one offered effective friendship, but it was impossible to cease fighting and relinquish the struggle because the war continued undecided and much could still change. General Sikorski still did not lose hope that there could be a change in circumstances which would result in a renewed agreement with Russia or some other possibility. He continued to regard Germany as Poland's greatest enemy, because it was attempting to exterminate the nation,[2] but he could not completely reject the possibility of another sudden change in the political arrangement of the world. The Allies did not inform him of secret discussions conducted with the Germans in several neutral capitals, but he needed at least to consider them, because Polish diplomats had also carried out similar negotiations. After the entry of the United States into the war, and especially after the Battle of Stalingrad, when the fate of Germany was becoming apparent, some of her forced satellites were searching for an escape route from her camp and opened secret contacts. Such links were made with Polish diplomats in Lisbon, where they negotiated in an extremely discreet manner with the Rumanians and Hungarians. This was not all. Halina Szymańska, the wife of the last Polish Military Attaché in Berlin, worked in the Polish Consulate in Switzerland, and was the link between Admiral Canaris and his Black Orchestra and the British Intelligence. She undertook this role with the knowledge of the Polish authorities and General Sikorski certainly knew about it.[3] A successful attempt on Hitler's life could be made at any time, and in that event an entirely new situation could arise suddenly. Hitler's Third Reich was a lethal danger for Poland, but if Hitler died and power fell into the hands of members of the Black Orchestra, there would be opportunities for great changes. General Sikorski's hopes for a rapid and favourable change in fortune were therefore not groundless, although there was one major drawback. The Polish Government had not devised any policy on Germany beyond the complete rejection of any collaboration. This was laudable and pertinent from a moral point of view, but it could not support any further consideration which would have been essential in the event of major developments within Germany before the end of the war. The people in the Black Orchestra were, after all, Germans and their attitude to Poland, to her western frontiers and to many other matters would be difficult to accept and would require prior consideration.

BUILDING UP THE UNDERGROUND ARMY

These were, however, only political speculations, necessary to bear in mind, but which could not strengthen the very poor position of Poland. One way in which it could be improved was by augmenting underground cadres within Poland, which could play a major role in the decisive phase of the war. Fortunately General Sikorski possessed a man of outstanding qualities in Warsaw: General Rowecki. During the more than three years of his underground activity the General had gained a lot of experience. He was respected both by his subordinates and by the politicians and, although rather over-optimistic, became a real leader of the nation.

It is difficult to determine what forces are available to a conspiracy at a given time, but calculations based on platoons of fifty men each indicate that the Home Army numbered about 200 000 soldiers in the first half of 1943, and that this number was increasing. The shifting of the front to the east permitted the establishment of further underground districts. In fact the forces of the Home Army were much larger, because use was made of the help of thousands of people who were not formally enrolled, but who provided places for meetings, searched for information and fulfilled many other tasks.[4]

SCOUTING

A valuable contribution to the work and struggle of the Home Army was also made by the scouting movement which took the underground code-name *Szare Szeregi* (Grey Ranks). It was divided into male and female sections and through the central command was linked with the Home Army. The main purpose of the scouts was and is to train youth and this task was fulfilled during the occupation, although under war conditions other major functions became of first importance.

The male section worked in three groups: the youngest (13–16 years of age) prepared for the general uprising in auxiliary functions; the older (16–18) engaged in propaganda (slogans on the walls, etc.) and the oldest were involved in the armed struggle. The womens' section, strongest in central Poland, was prepared for auxiliary service, but also, together with the boys, supported acts of sabotage and diversionary action.[5]

PARTICIPATION OF WOMEN

The role of women in underground work and in the resistance against the occupants was great and for this reason the commander of the Home Army, towards the end of 1941, established the Women's Military Service. It was an auxiliary service: the law stated that the recruitment of women must be voluntary; the commander of the AK specified their functions, but in practice they were everywhere, even among the partisans. Without their contribution underground Poland could not have existed.

There were many soldiers, but their armament was very poor. Their weapons came from four sources: (i) those buried in September 1939; (ii) manufactured by the underground; (iii) captured or bought from the enemy; and (iv) dropped from the West.

ARMAMENT AND DROPS FROM THE WEST

Burying weapons was a widespread practice during the September campaign, but mostly took place on the sites of the last big battles. They were not always correctly conserved; it was sometimes impossible to discover where they had been buried; some were discovered and destroyed by the Germans, but many were secretly recovered, cleaned and made safe. These actions had been carried out during 1940 in Warsaw and the Districts of Kielce, Cracow, Katowice and Lublin together with the Area of Lwów. Results were significant: 566 heavy machine-guns and 472 785 rounds of ammunition; 1097 light machine-guns and 175 365 rounds of ammunition; 31 391 rifles and 2 848 250 rounds of ammunition, as well as over 6000 pistols one and a half million rounds of ammunition and even twenty-eight anti-tank guns. Unfortunately the new, conspiratorial overhaul of these weapons was often badly done, eventually involving some destruction, and the same applied to the ammunition. In addition, the distribution of the weapons did not cover the needs of the renewed struggle. When this arose, only part of the September equipment was fit for use.[6]

The domestic production of weapons started as early as the beginning of 1940, when the chances of open conflict were minimal. The initiators were engineers in Warsaw, who wanted to be involved in the struggle in this way. The commander of the ZWZ accepted this offer very willingly, because weapons were in short supply and the mood before the German attack on France was very belligerent. A start was made with grenades, explosive materials, fuses and railway mines which were needed for the Reprisal Organisation (*Związek Odwetu*). Initially the simpler products were manufactured in workshops controlled by the Germans and working openly. Later, when work was started on flame-throwers and machine-pistols copied from the Sten guns dropped by air from England, it became necessary for the underground to establish its own secret workshops. For the manufacture of various complicated parts use was made of great industrial plants, even on the territory of the Reich. This was possible thanks to the infiltration of a secret network into German industry. It was also necessary to obtain secret grounds for testing and proving weapons.[7]

Apart from the dual necessity of concealment and of maintaining strict security, the greatest difficulty in the production of the weapons arose from the lack of raw materials and prefabricated parts. Special steels, explosives and non-ferrous metals were all necessary. These were purchased where possible, stolen from factories and railway transports or even captured by force. Their possession produced further problems, because it was necessary to transport them to secret pools, and thousands of kilos were involved.[8]

The manufacture of hand grenades was relatively simple and they were produced in thousands. Making machine-pistols was another matter, however, as they required rifle barrels and many other parts which were difficult to produce. For this reason, the copying of Sten guns and the Polish *Błyskawica* (Lightning), modelled on them, only started in the second half of the 1943 and the results were modest: in the whole of Poland only 1000 specimens from eleven secret factories.[9]

The capture of enemy weapons only started on a significant scale with the opening of the partisan campaign, that is, towards the end of 1942. An advantage of this method of capturing weapons was the ease of remedying deficiencies in ammunition, because it came from the same source and fitted the captured weapons. This problem is also connected to some extent with the purchase of weapons from the Germans and their satellites. During the earliest period of the war this was very difficult, but when the Nazis fell upon harder days and their armies started to include forcibly-recruited soldiers of other nationalities, the trade in arms increased to such an extent that the Home Army even established standard prices for individual types of weapons. Mostly pistols were purchased and in small quantities, but there were cases of larger transactions involving heavy machine-guns. There were occasional transports of Italian divisions through Poland, destined for the eastern front, from whom it was much easier to purchase weapons. The Hungarians, whose divisions were often found on Polish soil, were the most willing to take part in these transactions, since they tended to sympathise with the Poles. There were even negotiations with them for the purchase of artillery and anti-tank guns. These took place in Stanisławów and in the Kampinos Forest during the Warsaw Uprising, but led to nothing. It is impossible to establish figures for the purchase of arms throughout Poland.[10]

The fourth source of weapons for the underground soldiers was the supply by parachute from the West. The greatest hopes were placed on this source, but they were not fulfilled. After an initial trial period a second phase was opened, under the code name *Intonation*. This lasted from 1 August 1942 to the end of April 1943 and was characterised by the end to experiment in technique and the establishment of drops as a regular occurrence.

At the turn of the year 1942–3 the struggle within Poland was conducted mainly through sabotage and diversion. Consequently, after several trials, an outfit was evolved comprising equipment for 'mining and diversionary' purposes (known as 'MD'). This was intended to serve for the accomplishment of one major act of sabotage and several minor ones, and also for the armed protection of those carrying them out. Each outfit was divided among six containers. Equipment in load MD: 265kg explosives, ten Stens plus 3000 rounds of ammunition, twenty-seven revolvers (045) plus 775 rounds of ammunition, twenty Mills bombs; eight anti-tank grenades; fifteen anti-tank detonators and thirteen railway charges.[11]

Preparations were also being made in Poland for a general uprising in the decisive phase of the war. For this purpose another outfit, 'fighting area' (known as 'OW') was developed. It would enable ten platoons or about 500 soldiers of the Home Army to go into overt action. These outfits were to be stored until the time came for a country-wide insurrection. Equipment in Load OW: two Brens plus 2520 rounds of ammunition; eighteen Stens plus 9400 rounds of ammunition; twenty-seven revolvers (045) plus 575 rounds of ammunition; forty Mills bombs; seventy-six anti-tank grenades, twenty-seven anti-tank detonators and 118kg explosives.[12]

These two outfits did not meet the great needs of the underground army, so signals equipment, medical supplies, uniforms, chocolate, cigarettes were also dropped. During the *Intonation* period forty-two drops were made which involved 119 parachutists (including nine political couriers and one Hungarian), 49.5 tonnes of equipment, over 13 million dollars in banknotes and gold, and 5 million German marks. The losses were six aircraft, four parachutists and over 8 tonnes of equipment. These results were not only far from the needs and demands of occupied Poland, but also from the promises made to the Polish staff by the British. One hundred flights were promised, while barely forty-two were made, and the dark cloud of political difficulties was already rising over the entire problem. The Poles were requesting supplies not only for the current fight, but also to equip the uprising and this was something the British did not want at all. They had already decided that Poland would be in the sphere of influence of the Soviet Union, with whom they wanted no conflict, so they were not willing to help the Poles prepare an uprising, which could also be anti-Soviet.[13]

DIVERSION AND PARTISANS

The intensification of the resistance created the necessity for a new organisation, the Directorate of Diversion (code name *Kedyw*). This originated in the autumn of 1942, when several briefings took place, and verbal instructions were issued, but its organisational form was established by two orders issued in the early spring of 1943. The functions of *Kedyw* were acts of sabotage and diversion, forming the cadres of partisan groups, retalliatory actions against the Germans, liquidating Polish traitors after condemnation by underground courts and the self-defence of society in the broadest sense of the word. *Kedyw* naturally absorbed the Reprisal Organisation (*Związek*

Odwetu) which ceased to exist. Also everything that remained from *Wachlarz* was absorbed.[14]

The military actions of *Kedyw* mainly involved attacks on communications, both railways and telephones, on an increasing scale each month. Self-defence included the liberation of prisoners, the liquidation of Gestapo agents and German officials, the destruction of documents in German offices, and the suppression of banditry. The terror of the occupants had to be met with an equivalent response.[15]

Another task of *Kedyw* was to establish cadres for partisan groups, but before this was done there were already armed groups in the country which arose spontaneously. The Home Army partisan groups were a logical extension of the continuous struggle.

The first large partisan action in the Zamość area, which showed that positive results were possible, led to the formation of a cell within the *Kedyw* to deal with these matters. Partisan groups started to rise in various areas, initially in close contact with the *Kedyw* and later independently. These undertook various military actions. Apart from armed diversion these units protected secret radio stations and centres for the reception of parachute drops. In addition they fought bandits and continued the policy of 'self-defence'. Their armaments were most diverse, originally obtained from weapons buried in 1939, and in the east from Soviet arms abandoned in 1941. Later, when more intensive action began, weapons captured from Germans were used. In central and southern Poland the partisan units used weapons dropped from the West, among them the most popular machine-guns, Stens, anti-tank guns, Piats and radio stations. Uniforms were very varied, from ordinary civilian clothes with a pre-war field or forage cap with an eagle and red-and-white band, to re-tailored German uniforms with Polish insignia, and full Polish uniforms, even with helmets, mainly German ones. Food, winter quarters and laundry facilities were given generously by the local population. Without this help the partisans could not have survived long in the forests. The population carried out local reconnaissance and over and beyond this, they gave their sons as soldiers. The situation with medical care was generally bad, because many units lacked their own doctors. They made do with their nurses and in the case of major accidents sought local help. The Home Army partisan units, apart from their chief functions, fulfilled one other major role: they were a visible mandated sign of the existence of an underground authority which administered immediate justice, protected the local inhabitants, liquidated criminals and bandits, while the leaders of partisan units (who were generally very young men) acted as arbitrators in local disputes and even conducted weddings.[16]

The necessity for 'self-defence', before it came to an open fight with the occupants, brought about the organisation of the first partisan units near Wilno and Nowogródek. This happened in the spring of 1943, when it was necessary to fight bands of robbers, seek revenge on the Germans for outrages and murders and also to defend the Polish population against Soviet partisans. These were supported by drops from the east and attacked Polish villages to weaken Polish elements in order to facilitate the Sovietisation of these lands. Commanders of the Polish units were officers in hiding locally and parachutists, trained in Great Britain and sent from Warsaw. One of them was Lieutenant Colonel Maciej Kalenkiewicz (*Kotwicz*) who parachuted into Poland on the night of 27–28 December 1941, one of the first to do so, in the third parachute operation to Poland. He was an outstanding representative of the younger generation of the Polish Army and was one of the initiators of the parachute drops. A characteristic feature of the Polish partisan warfare in the north eastern borderlands was its unity. In other places units of the Peasant Battalions, the National Armed Forces and the Peoples' Guard (later the Peoples' Army) operated, but apart from the Soviets, there were only the units of the Home Army.[17]

Similarly, the need to protect the Polish population led to the undertaking of partisan warfare in Volhynia and around Lwów. There, despite the German terror, the greatest threat to the rural Polish population came from the Ukrainians who could operate almost openly, since they benefited from German assistance. Politically they relied on the Germans expecting to receive their independence from them and Ukrainian military formations arose on the German side. Among others there were the SS Galizien Division. Ukrainian police co-operated with the *Gestapo*. The attacks of the Ukrainian units were directed against Polish villages, which were burned and the inhabitants murdered in a horrific manner. Their aim was the same as that of the Soviet partisans in the area of Wilno: the elimination of the local Polish element. The Ukrainians' arms were good, because the Germans helped them during the first phase, and in the second, after their political hopes had been dashed, entire Ukranian battalions went to the forests with complete equipment.

The Polish defence depended on the concentration of the population in the larger villages, on the construction of defence positions and on manning these positions with members of the Home Army.[18]

Exceptionally strong and effective partisan units of the Home Army also arose in the region of Radom-Kielce and in the Świętokrzyskie mountains where one of the most renowned of the Polish partisans, the parachutist Major Jan Piwnik (*Ponury*) started his service in the spring of 1943. He was later transferred to Nowogródek where he was killed in a battle with the Germans on 15 June 1944. Around Radom and Kielce the partisans could concentrate their attentions almost exclusively on the Germans, on their transport, sentries and patrols which collected levies of food. Further units arose in Polesie, in the Bisłystok, Lublin and Cracow areas, in Sub-Carpathia and even in Central Poland, near Łódź and Warsaw and later also in Pomerania.[19]

Beside the partisans of the Home Army there also stood the units of the Peasant Battalions, the National Armed Forces, the Peoples' Army and Soviet groups. The last came from soldiers who had concealed themselves during the frantic retreat of 1941, or who had escaped from German captivity as well as parachutists dropped from the East. There were also a few purely Jewish units composed of young people who had managed to evade confinement in the ghetto or had escaped from German control. In the spring of 1944 the effective absorption of the Peasants' Battalions units into the Home Army took place so this problem ceased to be troublesome.

The first units of the National Armed Forces arose towards the end of 1942 near Lublin, but their strength only became considerable in 1944. Units of the Peoples' Guard (Army) started to appear significantly later, in 1944 and mainly in the second half of that year. Soviet units, organised by parachutists, appeared in the early autumn of 1941, when the Germans were on the road to Moscow with every prospect of success. Later, in 1942, they were already fairly strong on the eastern borders and this strength increased. In central, southern and western Poland they did not appear until 1944.[20]

The growth of partisan and diversionary actions independent of the plans for a general uprising, as well as numerous political problems, compelled the HQ of the Home Army to form a special centre. This was called the Directorate of Clandestine Resistance (*Kierownictwo Walki Konspiracyjnej* – KWK) and was headed by the Commander of the Home Army with his Chief of Staff as his deputy. The most important aim of this new centre was to gather together all matters concerned with the current struggle. The main instrument of operation was *Kedyw* together with the Bureau of Information and Propaganda. Contact with the Government Delegacy was maintained by a representative of the Directorate of Civil Resistance. This is when the well-known symbol of Fighting Poland (*Polska Walcząca*) appeared in the form of an anchor, incorporating the letter PW, by order of General Rowecki to indicate areas where diversionary actions had taken place.[21]

The existence of the KWK alongside the KWC immediately gave rise to confusion, since both did similar work. After a few months the Government Delegacy and the Commander of the Home Army decided to unite them in one body. This was the Directorate of Underground Resistance (KWP), still with the Commander of the Home Army and his Chief of Staff at the head. The Delegacy was represented by the Director of Civilian Resistance.[22]

LIAISON AND INTELLIGENCE

The current struggle could not overshadow Polish affairs entirely for these were partly determined within Poland, partly in London and also in other territories controlled by the Western Allies. Maintaining continuous contact between General Sikorski and Warsaw required a most efficient system of radio signals, the standard of which rose with each succeeding month thanks to the rapidity of technical development. Equipment was dropped from Great Britain while in Warsaw discussions went on as to how the weak radio stations within Poland could communicate among themselves if a general uprising became necessary. A project emerged for building a large radio centre sufficiently powerful to receive without difficulty weak and distant signals and transmit them to where they were required. Since a centre of this type would occupy an area of approximately $1km^2$, it was impossible to built it in occupied country. So Warsaw suggested that the project should be undertaken in Great Britain. After some early doubts the project was accepted and in June 1943 work was commenced on a station near London. It played a great role during the later fights in Poland.[23]

The use of radio stations which sent messages to London became much more difficult with time, as the Germans became expert in discovering them. They organised a location system and special units which used tracker vans and sometimes even aircraft. They were so efficient that it was necessary to reduce transmission time in Warsaw to as little as ten minutes daily and later to move the transmitting stations to the provinces where they sometimes worked under the protection of partisan units. This made their work much harder, as the messages were composed and enciphered in Warsaw and needed to be sent to the radio stations by messengers. These used various means of transport, even bicycles.[24]

Early successes in the Intelligence field by the underground army, which were acknowledged gratefully by their British Allies,[25] encouraged the expansion of this branch of military activity. The Intelligence of the Home Army specialised above all in obtaining information about German war industry, their transport and the results of Allied bombing missions. Despite very widespread police control access to German territory was relatively easy, because hundreds of thousands of Poles worked there, mostly transported by force. Some worked on the land, but many were sent to industrial plants and were involved directly with German production. Those who went to Germany after Intelligence training obtained much important information which was sent by courier to Warsaw. Two expert sections operated there: the Bureau of Economic Studies and the Economic Council which co-operated with and complemented each other in working on the material obtained for them, analysing and preparing synthetic reports. These were sent to London in the form of radio dispatches at least once a month. Very urgent information, composed solely of facts, was sent more frequently, sometimes even daily. The Home Army Intelligence also operated in the east, in the hinterland of the front and the information obtained there was also sent to London. The British were mostly interested in the results of German industrial production, as they knew that work was being conducted on secret weapons, which could turn out to be highly effective.[26]

This was a problem of special interest to the Intelligence of the Home Army and it obtained a signal success in the first months of 1943. Lack of workers led the Germans to bring nearly 2 million foreigners into their country. They were employed everywhere, even near the most closely-guarded sites of secret experiments. In this way Polish workers found themselves in a multinational camp on the Island of Usedom, close to Peenemünde, where the Germans were conducting experiments with flying bombs (V–1) and rockets (V–2) about which nothing concrete was then known in Britain. Aliens were not admitted to the sites themselves, but the Poles, some of whom had received Intelligence training, had seen flying objects leaving vapour trails behind them, and they put out this information over the Intelligence network of the Home Army. An alarm signal was sent by radio to London and through the VIth Bureau of the General Staff it reached the British Intelligence Service. This possessed a special cell for scientific Intelligence which devoted itself exclusively to secret German experiments. Immediately there started a feverish exchange of dispatches between London and Warsaw, since the British demanded further details. These arrived from Poland in April 1943 in a report brought by courier, which included a sketch of the Island of Usedom with the area of Peenemünde indicated in thick pencil lines, a description of the flying bombs and their method of launching and of the German security measures. The report was immediately sent to the British authorities and was one of the most important elements in the mosaic of reports from different sources.[27]

The information received from the Poles permitted the British Intelligence to define precisely the function of Peenemünde and the significance of the experiments conducted there which concerned the V–1. Information from other sources led to the reconstruction of the experiments conducted with rockets (V–2) which were significantly more dangerous because they flew in the stratosphere and there was no defence against them. The completeness of the picture of the work and experiments conducted there led later to an air attack by British bombers on the eastern part of Peenemünde, where the V–2 experiments were carried out. The night raid of 17 and 18 August 1943 resulted in great destruction, killing hundreds of expert technical personnel. The British lost forty aircraft. After this great onslaught the Germans transferred the experiments with V–2 to Polish soil, at the junction of the Vistula and San rivers, near the villege of Blizna. At that time this location was beyond the range of Allied bombers.[28]

GENERAL ROWECKI'S ARREST

All these elements which constituted the strength of the Home Army reached a high level of efficiency mainly thanks to General Rowecki who also worked harmoniously with the underground political parties and with the Government Delegate. The position of the General was very strong, in fact, it was crucial: on him to a great extent depended the future actions of occupied Poland and his authority could be conclusive in decisive moments when difficult and even unpopular decisions might be necessary.

Naturally, the Gestapo made every effort to get hold of him. They had his photograph and numerous agents were circulating in Warsaw and trying to hit upon the trail of the General. Among the people working within the Gestapo network unfortunately, was, a Polish officer. This was Ludwik Kalkstein of the Home Army Intelligence who had been arrested in 1942, broke down under interrogation and went over to the Germans. He organised a group of a few individuals who began slowly to encircle the man who was so essential to the country in an increasingly complicated political and military situation. On the day of 30 June 1943 the renegades revealed the address at which the General was to be found and within a few minutes the Gestapo surrounded the house and took the Commander of the Home Army. He was taken at once to Gestapo headquarters and before the underground could recover and attempt to rescue him, this man, so important to both Poles and Germans, was taken by plane to Berlin.[29]

DEATH OF GENERAL SIKORSKI

The situation in London was very tense, the Polish political problems continually increasing and the presence of General Sikorski in the capital of Great Britain essential, but the development of the war dictated an early journey to the Near East. On 12 May 1943 the German army in Tunisia finally capitulated and the whole of North Africa was in allied hands. An attack on Italy was now close and with it the use of the Polish Army in the East. The Second Corps was to be formed from it and General Sikorski was meant to go to Iraq to carry out an inspection and to take several important decisions. He was informed that the mood in these Polish units was not good, the government was subject to incessant criticism and that he must take care because an attempt on his life could not be ruled out.[30]

The General flew from Britain on 25 May 1943 and two days later met General Anders in Cairo. From 1–17 June there was an inspection of the troops in Kirkuk which went well. The morale of the soldiers was excellent, their physical condition was improving daily and their training was going well. Agreement was reached on the reorganisation of the army and the establishment of the Corps with General Anders in command. From political discussions it emerged that General Sikorski was still counting on a change of Russian policy under Western pressure and on the rescue of further thousands of

Poles who were still there. After further discussions in Cairo, on 3 July, the Polish leader flew from Egypt to Gibraltar.[31]

In the late evening of 4 July the aircraft carrying General Sikorski and those accompanying him, took off from that airfield intending to make a night-flight to Britain. Within a few minutes the aircraft had fallen into the sea and sunk to the bottom. General Sikorski, his daughter Zofia, the Chief of Staff, General Tadousz Klimecki, the Chief of the operations section of the Staff, Colonel Andrzej Marecki, the liaison officer between the Polish and British premiers, British MP, Colonel Victor Cazalet, and several others, all died in this catastrophe. Only the pilot, a Czech, T. Prchal was rescued, very severely injured.[32]

The body of General Sikorski was recovered within a few hours and was conveyed in the Polish destroyer *Orkan* to Great Britain. On 16 July he was buried in the Polish airmen's cemetery in Newark, in the county of Nottingham. After the immediate bewilderment at the unexpected tragic accident, voices started to be raised enquiring into the causes and responsibility for the catastrophe. As usual, the owners of these voices disagreed among themselves, ranging from those who became reconciled to the fact that it was only an accident, to the most extreme accusations of sabotage and murder. They were directed at the Germans, Soviets, British, and even against those Poles who were political opponents of General Sikorski. As the German radio was apparently the first to give the news of the crash, the finger was pointed at Berlin as the perpetrator with the added opinion that after the discovery of the graves at Katyń this was a further attempt by German propaganda to exacerbate misunderstandings among the Allies. Others blamed the Soviets saying that they had liquidated Sikorski to deprive the Poles of a leader of exceptional ability and to increase their chances of success in the Polish case. Those who blamed Britain argued that Churchill, surrendering entirely to the pressures of Stalin, chose to remove Sikorski because he had personal obligations towards him. The accusations directed by Poles towards other Poles were the least important and absolutely without foundation. They were connected with the gloomy atmosphere which the attempt to co-operate with the Russians had produced in Polish circles and the consequences which arose from it.

Several select commissions studied the causes of the catastrophe: the British Air Ministry, the Polish Ministry of Internal Affairs, the Polish Inspectorate of the Air Force and finally the Polish Council of

Ministers. None of these was able to establish why the accident had occurred and none concluded that it was sabotage. It was generally agreed that the most likely cause of the crash was a blockage in the rudder. The fact that the pilot escaped alive from the crash could not be held against him as an indication that he was a tool in the hands of saboteurs, because his escape was miraculous. He was a very experienced pilot and had frequently carried important passengers, among them General Sikorski.[33]

QUEBEC CONFERENCE

Less than two months elapsed between the arrest of General Rowecki and the death of General Sikorski, when in the middle of August, at Quebec, in Canada, the next meeting of Churchill and Roosevelt took place. It had been foreseen that the main subject of the conference would be the war in the Far East, but it also concerned Europe. Churchill arrived strongly determined to obtain a common decision to attack the old continent from the south, through Greece and Yugoslavia in order to reach the centre of Europe as quickly as possible. Unfortunately the Americans appeared at the conference with the definite opinion that the attack on Europe must take place in the West, in Northern France, and Roosevelt did not intend to make any concessions. He had set a great war-machine in motion and already had a vision of the post-war world. He saw the decline of the British Empire, and his country occupying the leading place in the world. In his plans he foresaw co-operation with Soviet Russia and he did not want any conflicts with her. This point of view prevailed and Churchill had to accept the American proposal to divide Europe into spheres of influence. It was cut into half along a line which was approximately the same as that later known as the 'Iron Curtain'. It had already been foreseen that the Russians would obtain the whole of central and eastern Europe and that they would be the first to enter Berlin.[34]

Stalin was not at Quebec, but even if he had been, he could not have obtained a better outcome. Polish hopes, represented in their plans and aspirations by both Generals, one already in the grave and the other in the hands of his cruel enemies, dissolved into ruins.

17 Difficulties with Communists; 'Tempest'; Teheran

GENERAL SIKORSKI'S SUCCESSORS

The sudden loss of General Sikorski caused great confusion in Polish London, since the General had held two offices, and the struggle began at once to fill them. The question of who should be appointed Commander-in-Chief seemed easier, because General Sosnkowski was the most senior officer of the Polish Armed Forces. He had led the Piłsudski camp, he had intervened several times in political crises and he had been put forward as an opponent to General Sikorski, so his nomination was virtually automatic and he received it from the President of the Polish Republic on 8 July. Because the previous Chief-of-Staff, General Tadeusz Klimecki, had died in the Gibraltar disaster, the new Commander-in-Chief appointed General Stanisław Kopański to that position on 2 August.

The candidacy for Premier was a more difficult problem but here, too, although gossip and intrigue tried to present matters differently, a fairly obvious successor to Sikorski was Stanisław Mikołajczyk, till then Vice-Premier; he was Chairman of the Peasant Party whose numbers and dynamism placed it among the foremost movements that were active in the country. President Raczkiewicz recognised this state of affairs and entrusted Mikołajczyk with the task of creating a new government, which was accomplished on 14 July.[1]

General Sosnkowski was opposed to the Sikorski-Maisky pact and for that reason withdrew from the government and was deprived of his function of chief of military works in Poland. He did not trust Russia and did not believe her, neither did he believe the Western Allies and in both cases he was right, but this did not relieve him of his duty to remain politically active. He was the second most

217

important person in the State, he took part in cabinet meetings and the enormous responsibility for the fate of the nation weighed heavily on him. It was a very difficult situation but for that very reason it was necessary to possess some political plan, adapted to circumstances within which it would be possible to function. A negative attitude and lack of faith did not constitute a basis for action.

The new Premier was born in the Rhineland, into a peasant family which moved to the Poznań area where Mikołajczyk became a local activist for his movement. He was not predestined to become a great statesman, but when fate demanded, however, that he should match himself against the most distinguished leaders of the great nations of the day – against Churchill, Roosevelt and Stalin – he displayed toughness and a sense of the dignity of the position he occupied. He was never a puppet in Churchill's control.[2] He did not, of course, know Russia and he did not understand the Russian mentality; he sought compromise: life had taught him to be level-headed and he conducted his politics in the way he considered possible at that time. He wanted what was best and fought for his country.

From his first days as Commander-in-Chief, General Sosnkowski displayed open dislike and even contempt for the new Premier; he avoided him and wrote him letters instead of seeking opportunities to talk. Mikołajczyk could see this and retaliated in a similar manner, and a completely impossible situation arose: the Premier and the Commander-in-Chief, the two leading representatives of a nation at war, avoided each other and could not agree upon some united line of conduct.[3]

There was a need for action, however, and Mikołajczyk presented himself and the Government with those tasks that were the most urgent. The necessity to regularise relations with the Soviet Union in some way headed the list because the Red Army was advancing and in a few months time could be in the territories of eastern Poland. The Governments of Great Britain and the United States tried to bring about a Polish–Soviet dialogue and in Moscow on 11 August they presented a demand for the renewal of diplomatic relations, but Stalin rejected it. In July he had won a victory over the Germans in a decisive battle near Kursk and he felt himself to be stronger than ever.[4] The Polish Premier was not discouraged by the Soviet stance and continued to seek a platform for political action. He had reservations as regards the attitude of the Western Allies to the Polish cause, but at the same time his clear-thinking mind was telling him that without them Poland would be completely lost.

A NEW COMMANDER OF THE HOME ARMY

In Poland the arrest of General Rowecki was a great blow, and was still fresh when, only a few days later, came the news of the death of the Premier and the Commander-in-Chief. It might well have been feared that there would be enormous problems in filling such an important position as that of Commander of the Home Army, but the underground politicians and officers of the HQ of the Home Army were agreed that General Tadeusz Komorowski, who had been General Rowecki's deputy until then, should take over. This opinion was relayed to London and on 17 July General Sosnkowski announced the necessary nomination by radio cable.[5] General Komorowski, who took the pseudonym *Bór*, had a splendid war record from the Polish–Bolshevik war in 1920, had taken part in the September campaign in 1939, and in conspiracy had expanded the Cracow District between 1939 and 1941. In August 1941 he had become deputy to General Rowecki. He had not been to the Staff College and had no experience in solving difficult military and political problems, but he did not shirk responsibility and was an easy man with whom to work.[6]

Several urgent problems faced the new Commander of the Home Army. Above all, agreement had to be reached with London as quickly as possible about the plans concerning Poland's position if the Red Army was to cross into Polish territory. It was already the second half of 1943, the Germans were retreating in the East and the Soviets could cross into Poland within a few months. In the Wilno and Nowogródek areas, in Volhynia and Polesie strong partisan units of the Home Army were already in action. They often came into contact with even stronger units of Soviet partisans, and the outcomes of these encounters varied. In these areas the Russians behaved as though they were the rightful owners; they issued requisition orders; they introduced formal conscription in Polesie, together with a medical examination, but at the same time they sought contact with Polish units and proposed joint action more than once. This state of affairs at least demanded the temporary regularisation of mutual relations and General *Bór* issued orders for the two Districts of Wilno and Nowogródek. These permitted co-operation with Soviet units only if they were to honour Polish sovereign rights in those territories, refrain from acting against Polish citizens and unite in fighting the Germans.[7]

A particularly complicated situation arose in Volhynia where the Polish population was greatly threatened by the Ukrainians, who raided Polish villages and cruelly murdered the inhabitants. This forced the Home Army's partisan units to organise self-defence. The Germans encouraged this fratricidal struggle since they profited from it politically, and did not always intervene.[8]

The Polish Government in London understood the need to take decisions on these matters and also consulted the Allies, since any plans concerning Poland were closely linked with the supply of arms from the West and the recognition of the Home Army as an integral part of the Allied Armed Forces. Unfortunately this problem looked very serious because a memo on the subject submitted some few months earlier by Colonel Leon Mitkiewicz, representative of the Commander-in-Chief to the Combined Chiefs of Staff in Washington had met with no success. He was at once told that Polish matters came under the sole jurisdiction of Great Britain, and when he demanded that some sort of stance be taken, the answer was delayed until the Quebec Conference. There it was decided that Poland came under Soviet Russia's sphere of influence and after a delay of over a month, Colonel Mitkiewicz received a letter dated 23 September 1943 stating that Poland would receive equipment only for sabotage and diversion. The Chairman of the Combined chiefs of Staff, Admiral William Leahy, personally informed the Colonel of the political decisions that precluded either the inclusion of the Home Army in Allied operations on its provision with arms in order to prepare an uprising. In a diplomatic manner the Admiral explained that the Poles ought to come to an understanding with the Russians over these issues.[9]

Colonel Mitkiewicz kept London informed about all this and in the first half of October he flew to England to make a full report to General Sosnkowski. This confirmed the information that had reached London from the Quebec Conference and from fragmentary statements from several well-informed Englishmen. In the light of the decisions taken by the West, the Polish position was perfectly clear. Added to this was information from Poland which concerned the situation there and which moreover contained schemes relating to an uprising, the participation of the Polish Air Force, help from the Allies and many other details proving that Warsaw did not yet know of the West's decisions and was still expecting help from there.[10]

It was a tense situation, decisions had to be made and it so happened that London and Warsaw took the initiative literally at the same time. On 28 October General *Bór* sent an urgent telegram to London, demanding that immediate instructions be sent as to how to proceed and what orders to give, since 'the military attitude in Poland as regards the encroaching Russians must not be indecisive, but must be consistent, resolute, politically expedient and historically pure'. A day earlier, in London, the Government passed an essential order which was at the same time an order from the Commander-in-Chief, and which was sent to the Commander of the Home Army and the Government Delegacy on 1 November. General Sosnkowski greatly influenced its formulation and for that reason it contained three possibilities, *A*, *B* and *C*, with no indication as to which was the most accurate pointer to likely action.[11]

In the first, *A*, it was anticipated that an uprising in Poland would be supported by the Western Allies, who would not only send supplies, but would also cross into Polish territory and help the Poles to negotiate with Soviet Russia in order to guarantee the country's security and to co-ordinate action against the Germans. The whole of Poland would, of course, find itself in Polish and Allied hands.

In the second, *B*, if it turned out that the Allies did not agree to version *A*, but if Polish–Soviet diplomatic relations already existed, the Polish Government would take control of the whole Polish territory. Representatives of Great Britain and the United States would appear in Poland at the same time, the reconstruction of the Polish Armed Forces would begin and co-operation with the commanders of the Soviet Armies would start. If Polish–Soviet diplomatic relations did not exist or if the Soviet authorities did not honour Polish sovereignty, and arrests and repression were to begin, the Polish Government would make formal protest to the United Nations, the political and military authorities in Poland would remain in the conspiracy and open activity would be restricted to self-defence.

In the third, *C*, if another German–Soviet understanding were to occur, at Poland's expense, the country's political and military authorities would have to enter even greater conspiracy, limiting themselves to self-defence alone and conserving their strength for the arrival of the Allied Armies.[12]

This order aroused consternation in Warsaw, in the HQ of the Home Army, and in the Government Delegacy. The Red Army was already at the gates of the country, and any week now would probably be in the eastern territories of Poland, and in London they were considering variations on a situation that would have no bearing on reality. When several sentences that might be accepted as guidelines in a real situation were taken from the order that was sent, they read as follows:

- to intensify diversionary action, but in a conspicious manner;
- to continue to remain in the conspiracy and to wait for further orders;
- if repressions were to occur, to limit action to self-defence.

At the same time the Government in London was to protest against the violation of Polish sovereignty and to refuse to co-operate with the Soviets.[13]

The political and military underground leadership could not accept this point of view; it could not agree to its activities being limited to a few demonstrative acts, when the country was being passed from the hands of one occupier to those of another. The Home Army's passivity would bring out the communists, who would claim to speak for all Poles. There had to be an intensive struggle with the retreating Germans and the commanders of fighting units and the civil administration would have to come out into the open, to demonstrate that the Poles were masters in their own land. This would, of course, lay the commanders and representatives of the civil authorities open to arrest by the Soviets, but there was no help for it. At least the world would learn of the real intentions of the Kremlin, which would have to act openly.[14]

'TEMPEST'

On the basis of this understanding the Commander of the Home Army, after discussing the matter with the Government Delegacy and with the Home Political Representative Body, on 20 November gave an order, which was partly based on the Government's order of 27 October and established a manner of procedure if the Red Army were to cross into Polish territory. The whole operation was given the cryptonym 'Tempest'; it did not cancel the plans for a general uprising and it was to depend upon the local mobilisation of larger Home Army units and on attacking the retreating Germans, as well as on powerful diversion, mainly on communication lines. Tactical co-operation with the Red Army was possible and if it were to take place, the commanders and representatives of the administration would come out into the open. The order to begin action was to be given later.[15]

On the question of the military and civil leaders coming out into the open, this important document was not in agreement with the Order of 27 October. The Government accepted the very important change that had been introduced and the Commander-in-Chief also expressed his agreement, although he was of a different opinion.[16]

Two further questions faced the Home Army and the Government Delegacy: the complete merger of all military organisations and the establishment of relations with the Polish Workers' Party. The first problem had already been largely dealt with by General Rowecki who, at the end of 1942, had managed to subordinate the National Military Organisation. The problem of the Peasant Battalions and the National Armed Forces (NSZ) however, had yet to be solved. On 30 May 1943 General Rowecki managed to issue Order No. 90, calling for the incorporation of the Peasant Battalions into the Home Army on 1 July, after reaching agreement with the leaders of the Peasant Party, but it was not carried out while he was still at liberty. The process of subordination lasted a long time and General *Bór* had many problems with it. Difficulties arose over the positions which were to fall on the commanders of merged units of the Home Army, but they were solved within the scope of possibility, and in spring 1944 the ultimate outcome was reached, which brought the Home Army about 50 000 soliders.[17]

The question of the National Armed Forces was considerably more difficult, for their political leadership demanded extensive autonomy and the retention of their own forms of organisation. General *Bór* did not want to agree to this, although General Sikorski's order dated 15 August 1942 permitted the retention of organisational separateness alongside general subjection to the Home Army leadership. The General's pressure created a reaction in the Command of the NSZ, which sent a liaison officer to London. He reported to General Sosnkowski and obtained approval for the conditions he presented. Ultimately this section of the NSZ, which derived from the National Military Organisation, was incorporated in the Home Army in March 1944, while that part which derived from the *Jaszczurczy* Union remained independent.[18]

DIFFICULTIES WITH COMMUNISTS

The problem of establishing relations between the Government Delegacy, the Red Army and the communist underground was similar to relations between Poland and Soviet Russia. In both cases these relations were broken in 1943 and in both cases it would have been good for the Polish cause if they could have been re-established. Unfortunately it would have been possible only on conditions laid down by the Soviets and communists. Stalin and Molotov stressed many times that the establishment of diplomatic relations with the Polish Government depended upon the Poles themselves, who ought to agree to the Curzon Line and make changes in their own Government; the Polish Workers' Party agreed to co-operate on condition that a new Polish government would be formed in Poland (with their participation of course) that the People's Guard would remain independent and that the question of Poland's eastern borders would remain open till such time as it could be decided between Poland and Russia alone.[19]

As each month passed Russia, victorious in the East, became stronger and, in this way, diminished any chance of some sort of compromise. Talks between the Government Delegacy and leaders of the Home Army, and the Polish Workers' Party, begun in the spring of 1943, ended in fiasco and the communists, urged on by the Soviet victories, moved onto the political offensive. On Russian territory they pondered 'the plan to create democratic representation of the Polish nation', in the form of a Polish National Committee; on Polish soil, preparations were under way to create a Polish National Council. These two initiatives were not co-ordinated because a secret radio link between Warsaw and Moscow was broken between November 1943 and January 1944. Moreover, a feeling of competition existed between the two groups of Polish communists and a difference between their views of the system of government in post-war Poland emerged. While the Polish Workers' Party saw itself in the role of the political grouping governing the country within a fictitious framework of parliamentarianism, the people around General Berling expected a government with a strong hand, reliant upon the army and completely avoiding any political parties.[20]

These differences did not play a larger role at that particular stage; it was to be expected that Stalin's powerful hand would settle them at the appropriate time and in the interim Soviet propaganda created an anti-Polish atmosphere where it could, above all attack the Polish Government in London. In Detroit, at a meeting of Americans of Polish origin, poorly informed on European political matters, a resolution was passed, stating that 'the present Polish Government is the prisoner of reaction'.[21] In their cunning propaganda the Soviets avoided the issue of frontiers, assigning greater importance to the alleged reactionary nature of the Polish Government and the great social injustice that prevailed in Poland before the war.

General *Bór*, together with the entire HQ, understood the danger of a division in society caused by Soviet and communist propaganda and informed London of this, demanding from the Government of the Republic appropriate legal acts relating to the reconstruction of the social system. It was not possible, however, to deal with these matters offhand and in the meantime, the activities of the communists were increasing each day and were gaining recognition for them among groups which felt they were socially underprivileged and which easily accepted the loud propaganda. Similarly, the problem of the current battle and the so-called inactivity of the Home Army, constantly harped on by the Polish Workers' Party, gave Soviet propaganda a strong weapon, and conflicts in the London camp facilitated this propaganda. Some units of the NSZ, which attacked the partisans of the People's Guard, did the Polish cause an ill service.[22] The unification of all political and military forces in occupied Poland did not have any prospect of success.

TEHERAN

Between 18 and 30 October 1943 a conference of the Ministers for Foreign Affairs of the three powers (Anthony Eden, Cordell Hull and Vyacheslav Molotov) took place in Moscow, which discussed and dealt with many subjects, but in the case of the Polish problem achieved nothing. The efforts of the British and, to a certain extent, the Americans, aimed at finding a compromise between the Polish and the Soviet standpoints, failed to produce any results.

One of the tasks of the conference was also to prepare the ground for the first meeting of the Big Three; Churchill, Roosevelt and Stalin. Despite the Soviet victories, however, it would have been difficult to suggest a meeting on Soviet territory, so after testing the opinions of the Western leaders, Teheran, the capital of Persia, was proposed. The Soviet border was not far, Soviet soldiers moved freely throughout the country and the conference was to take place in the Soviet Embassy. This was wired off, surrounded by mines and a guard of uniformed and civil members of the NKVD. It later transpired that these were everywhere, even in the living quarters of the British delegation.[23] It was decided that the meetings would take place from 28 November to 1 December.

From the outset of the conference a joint front emerged, created by Roosevelt and Stalin, who were striving for their own aims and pushed Churchill to one side. Roosevelt who, although he had been crippled for many years as a result of polio, had carried off a series of victories thanks to his personal charm, was relying on it even now, and the Soviet dictator he did not know seemed an ideal subject on which to try out this power. Stalin, cold, controlled, unusually skilful and subtle in all the negotiations, relied less on charming the American President and more on the technique of action, which had never failed him before. On the first day of the conference even, under the pretext that German agents led by *SS-Brigadeführer* Otto Skorzeny were preparing an attempt on his life, he talked Roosevelt into moving into a villa in the grounds of the Soviet Embassy. In this way, he not only secured the President's gratitude for 'saving his life', but he also gained easy access to him. Roosevelt was prepared to make concessions in favour of Soviet Russia.

In their first personal discussion he told Stalin directly that he would agree to any of his plans concerning Poland but he would not be answerable to them in public until he was elected President of the United States for the fourth time. There were 6 or 7 million Americans of Polish origin among the electorate and he did not intend to lose their votes.[24]

Three days of the conference were devoted to matters concerning the further conduct of the war. Left to himself, Churchill tried to fight over the Italian front and for a decision to make a landing in the Balkans, but Stalin, strongly supported by Roosevelt, was emphatically opposed to this. He fought over all plans for military operations in the eastern part of the Mediterranean, arguing that the whole Allied effort must be directed towards an attack on northern France, which ought to take place no later than May of the following year, and which should be supported by an additional landing in southern France. Churchill's resistance had no effect; it was decided that the Balkans should be abandoned and that the offensive in Italy could not cross the gothic Line (from Pisa to Rimini).[25]

With some other smaller issues, one day was devoted to political matters and to the post-war administration of the world, which concerned the fate of many countries, and to the organisation of the United Nations. And yet, apart from the Big Three and their advisors, no-one else was invited to the conference, not even de

Gaulle, although France, despite the disaster of 1940, still possessed a colonial empire, and was one of the world powers. The president of Great China, Chiang Kai Shek, was not present either.

Premier Mikołajczyk made fruitless efforts to obtain the right to participate in these discussions, which were of such importance to Poland, and when he received a refusal he tried to have an earlier meeting with Churchill and Roosevelt. When that too did not work out, he prepared a memorandum which was handed to both the governments of the great democracies. It was a comprehensive document and contained a series of arguments which justified the Polish position; it mainly concerned post-war Polish frontiers, however, expressed under three points:

1. Poland, who entered the war in 1939 in defence of her territory, has never given up the fight and has not produced any Quisling, is fully entitled to expect that she will emerge from this war without reduction of her territory.
2. The Polish Eastern lands which are the object of Soviet claims extended to half of the territory of the Polish republic. They contain important centres of Polish national life. They are closely knitted with Poland by ties of tradition, civilisation and culture. The Polish population which has resided there for centuries forms a relative majority of the population of these lands. On the other hand the lower density of their population and their possibilities of economic development furnish Poland with a socially sound means of solving the problem of the over-population of her Western and Southern provinces.
3. The Polish Government could not see their way to enter a discussion on the subject of territorial concessions above all for the reason that such a discussion in the absence of effective guarantees of Poland's independence and security on the part of Great Britain and the United States would be sure to lead further and further to ever new demands.

   The attribution to Poland of Eastern Prussia, Danzig, Opole Silesia and the straightening and shortening of the Polish western frontier are in any case directed by the need to provide for the stability of future peace, the disarmament of Germany and the security of Poland and the other countries of Central Europe. The transfer to Poland of these territories cannot therefore be treated fairly as an object of compensation for the cession to the USSR of Polish eastern lands which for reasons adduced above do by no means represent to the USSR a value comparable to that which they have for Poland.

The attempt made to prejudge the fate of Polish Eastern territories by means of a popular vote organised under Soviet occupation by the occupying authorities is without any value either political or legal.

It would be equally impossible to obtain a genuine expression of the will of the population inhabiting these territories in view of the ruthless methods applied there today, those which have been applied in the past by consecutive occupants.[26]

Further on in the memorandum details were given of an Order dated 27 October, sent by the Polish government to Poland; it stated that within a very short period the Soviet armies would cross the frontiers of Poland which might result in a very difficult situation for the citizens of Poland; and it ended with an appeal:

> In this situation the Polish Government address a pressing appeal to Mr Churchill to intervene with Marshal Stalin with the view to restoring Polish–Soviet relations, safeguarding the interests of the Polish State and the life and property of its citizens after the Soviet troops have entered Poland.[27]

The memo clearly reveals that Mikołajczyk's Government, wishing to enter into relations with the Soviets, did not intend to agree to territorial concessions in the East, and at the same time expected to make territorial acquisitions in the west and north.

The Polish problem was discussed at the conference on 28 November and 1 December, twice by Churchill and Roosevelt in private conversations with Stalin, and at the last, joint meeting. Where it concerned the eastern lands, Mikołajczyk's memorandum was entirely pushed to one side and the decision was taken that Poland should be moved to the west. Her eastern border was to coincide more or less with Ribbentrop–Molotov line, the border in the west was to be based on the Oder and the Neisse; in the north Poland was to gain wide access to the Baltic Sea, with Gdańsk and Szczecin. The change in the Polish borders did not exhaust the subject; the country was to have 'friendly relations' with Russia, which in plain language meant complete dependence upon her eastern neighbour. Other countries were also subjects for peremptory decisions, without their knowledge or agreement. Apart from Poland, Stalin was promised Romania,

Bulgaria, Hungary, the Baltic States, part of Austria and Yugoslavia, half of East Prussia and the Japanese Kuril Islands. In return, the Soviet dictator promised that he would join the war against Japan, but only after the defeat of Hitler.[28]

THE RED ARMY ON POLISH SOIL

The political and military decisions taken in Teheran sealed Poland's fate conclusively, since hopes for an invasion of the Balkans and a rapid march into Central Europe, either from there or from Italy, were dashed. There could no longer be any doubt that during the next few weeks the Red Army would enter Polish territory without Polish–Russian political agreement, and that the western democracies were not going to become involved. The Polish Government was still trying to save the situation, a series of talks were held with British statesmen, but this did not alter the situation at all.

On the night of 3–4 January 1944 the Red Army crossed the eastern border of Poland.[29]

18 Second Polish Corps in Italy; Other Polish Formations

CAPITULATION OF ITALY

Churchill's hopes concerning the Italian campaign, shaken in Quebec and eventually expanded in Teheran had been based on practicable foundations and might have materialised if support had been forthcoming from his partners in the Big Three. After the victory in North Africa the Allies landed on Sicily in July, captured her within a month and began preparations for a landing on the Italian Peninsula. The disasters suffered by Mussolini led to his fall; he was arrested on 25 July 1943 and placed in isolation on the Gran Sasso mountain. Marshal Petro Badoglio took control and began secret negotiations with the Allies, while outwardly continuing to work with the Germans.

On 3 September the Allies landed in Calabria, in the very south of the Italian Peninsular, and on that same day Italy surrendered; this was announced on 8 September. The Germans, however, had foreseen such a sequence of events and had already brought over twenty divisions into Italian territory earlier and the battles turned out to be considerably tougher than had been expected. Field Marshal Erwin Rommel was in command in Northern Italy, while Air Field Marshal Albert Kesselring, who turned out to be an excellent strategist, was more to the south. He at once occupied Rome and the neighbouring airports; he organised resistance everywhere the Allies went and began to hinder their progress inland. He was out off from east to west by two defence lines: to the south of Rome by the Gustav Line, which followed the rivers Garigliano, Rapido and Sangro, as well as by the Gothic Line, to the north of Rome, which led from Pisa to Rimini. The Germans exploited these lines to the full. The Americans achieved a further landing near Salerno, but they met with very strong resistance.[1]

The entire Allied army in Italy was under the command of the British General, Harold Alexander, soon to be made a Field Marshal, who headed the 15th Army Group, consisting of the American Fifth Army under General Mark Clark and the British Eighth Army, under General Montgomery, and later General Oliver Leese. The Americans landed in the west, from the Tyrrhenian Sea, the British in the east, from the Adriatic, and their first landing took place on 9 September, when a parachute division captured Taranto.[2]

The attack on the Italian Peninsula came too late. The rains began, hampering the advance of the heavy machines; the Germans put up fierce resistance and it was clear that the Allies would not achieve their targets, in particular the capture of Rome, before winter. Alexander, however, was optimistic and was sure that when spring came and he received the support of more divisions and air power, he would manage to reach Vienna within a few months and stand on the banks of the Danube. He had a champion for these plans in Churchill, since the presence of the Allied armies in Vienna in the spring of 1944 would provide an opportunity for reaching advantageous political solutions. Roosevelt's war plans, however, were different; Stalin seconded him in them and the Teheran decisions shattered the hopes of Churchill and Alexander. Not only did the British Commander receive no support, but the Americans, when they heard of his Vienna plans during a press conference, deprived him of seven divisions and part of the air force, redeploying them in a completely unnecessary landing in southern France ('Operation Anvil').[3]

Such was the situation with the larger part of the Allied forces having to remain in Great Britain because preparations were already under way for the invasion of northern France, when the day approached for the arrival of the Second Polish Corps on Italian soil. It had already been fully organised and consisted of two divisions, a brigade of tanks, an artillery group, a reconnaissance regiment, and a battalion of sappers and communications personnel. In all, there were over 50 000 soliders, including 3099 officers and 559 volunteers from the Women's Auxiliary Service.

Since the Corps was to fight in Italy it had to undergo mountain training, and so the divisions and other units carried out exercises in the mountains of Syria and later began the march to Palestine. The commanding staff stopped near Gaza and a town of tents and barracks was erected all around.

During this stay in Palestine, General Anders was faced with a problem that he had not foreseen. Out of an overall 4000 soldiers of

Jewish origin, more than 3000 (Begin, later to become the Premier of Israel, among them) deserted and went over to the underground Jewish organisations fighting for the independence of Palestine. Many of them were well-trained and their loss created gaps in the units prepared for combat, but the commander of the Corps forbade any searches and arrests, and not one deserter was found. The British authorities, who were carrying out the function of mandatary in Palestine, had many problems with them later because almost all joined terrorist groups.[4]

Before the Second Polish Corps was sent to Italy, the problem of its reorganisation emerged, since the British and American authorities attached great and justifiable importance to building up reserves, which were supposed to amount to 20 per cent of normal strength and which the Polish units were almost entirely lacking. Moreover, the Polish Air Force Inspectorate in Great Britain demanded about 4000 soldiers because it was constantly suffering from deficiencies. These matters had to be settled and so General Sosnkowski set off for the South at the beginning of November. In Algiers, on 6 November, he conferred with General Eisenhower, the Commander-in-Chief of the whole Mediterranean area; a few days later he met General Alexander and came to the conclusion that reorganisation was vital. General Anders was very much against it, arguing that a lot of time would be lost and the Corps ought to be at the Front as soon as possible, and at greatest possible strength, in order to give the lie to Soviet propaganda, which was saying that it had left Russia in order to avoid confrontation with the Germans. Henry Maitland Wilson, to whom the Corps was directly answerable, supported him; the plans for reorganisation were abandoned and 900 category D soldiers (ground staff), 500 volunteers and 500 cadets were sent to the Polish Air Force.[5]

SECOND POLISH CORPS ON ITALIAN PENINSULA

In the middle of December the process began to transport the Second Corps to Italy, and was carried out by the British fleet with several Polish ships: the troop-carriers *Batory* and *Pułaski*, and the destroyers *Krakowiak* and *Ślązak*. On 15 December part of 3rd Division (Carpathian) (8600 men) was embarked and taken to Taranto in six days. After that first group more went to the ports of Bari, Brindisi and Naples. The whole operation lasted until the middle of April 1944; it went perfectly and there were no losses.[6]

After a brief period of concentration, units of the Corps began to move into the territory of operations. 3rd Division which had arrived in Italy first, relieved the British unit on the river Sangro, on a front 45km wide, as early as 2 February. The 5th (*Kresowa*/Frontier) was not able to do this until 8 March and it relieved the French Moroccan Division on another stretch, 14km wide. The Second Corps found itself, roughly speaking, at the point where the American Fifth Army met the British Eighth which General Leese was commanding by then. His task was to keep the front intact, to hold the line in the mountains there and to secure communications between the two armies. It was an appalling time of year for any operations; snow lay in drifts, the mountain roads were almost impassable to traffic and combat activity was limited to ambushing patrols. Attention was concentrated on training, clearing the roads and strengthening defences. The Corps was relieved in the middle of April.[7]

The first steps of the Polish soldiers on Italian soil, involving so many historical reflections, immediately met with political problems, like those that had also dogged General Henryk Dąbrowski when, 150 years before, he had trodden the same route at the head of the Polish Legions fighting under Napoleon. After his arrival, General Anders came across the field newspaper, the *Eighth Army News*, and immediately discovered that it expressed the same tone which was characteristic at that time of the vast majority of the Allied press. The paper printed false anti-Polish information and represented the Soviet point of view. This matter was raised at the first meeting with the Commander of the Eighth Army, General Leese, because there was no doubt that Polish soldiers would read the English army press and that its tone would infuriate them. The British Commander took note of this but his first reaction was typically Western and, in his mind, just, since the iron rule in those democracies had long been that the army is the tool of the politics carried out by Government and Parliament. Under no circumstances could even the most high-ranking military leader express political judgements. So it was that General Anders received a telegram a few days later, in which was the sentence: 'As your commander I must remind you of your position and point out that it is undesirable that the Commander of the Corps should publicly express, especially at this time, any views on political events now taking place'. However, when the Polish divisions found themselves under fire and when the British General was convinced of the value of those soldiers, who had come through the Soviet camps and had lost their homes and lands, and when he had become properly acquainted with the tragic web of events and political decisions, no trace of the initial difficulties remained.[8]

PREPARATIONS FOR LANDINGS IN NORTHERN FRANCE

Preparations for the invasion of the continent from the British Isles began as early as 1942, when no decision had as yet been taken to direct the attack on Northern France. Later, when it had been finally decided, huge transports of troops and war material arrived day after day from the United States and preparations were intensified. Of course, the Germans were also getting the French coast ready for defence and constructed the 'Atlantic Wall' with hundreds of thousands of mines and many kilometres of barbed wire, thousands of bunkers and barrages of tanks and guns.[9]

An exceptionally complicated problem was that of concealing the preparations from the eyes of German Intelligence agents. The first step was to cut the islands off from the outside world and to put a stop to all unnecessary radio communication. Strict orders were issued, against which Allied and neutral Embassies and Legations protested; these also applied to emigré Governments and National Committees, which sent information and orders from Britain every day to underground movements in German-occupied countries. Only the Poles continued to retain this privilege, although at first they had to surrender all the codes.[10]

The Polish Armed Forces were also to take part in the invasion of the continent as that was of prime importance from the political point of view. Unfortunately the great recruitment campaign, which had taken place mainly in the United States and Canada, virtually came to nothing (772 volunteers); South America also provided very little (908 volunteers); France was cut off, so there were only very modest numbers in the British Isles. At the end of 1942 and beginning of 1943 the Air Force presented the healthiest picture since it possessed 1640 officers and 8100 other ranks, but it too was suffering from deficiencies and insufficient reserves. The Navy had 200 officers and 2200 other ranks and was managing, while the First Polish Corps, which was to possess an armoured division, an independent brigade of fusiliers and many additional services, was far from being viable. And yet there was an Independent Parachute Brigade, which was also crying out for soldiers, while there were only 5250 officers and 23 500 other ranks in the British Isles at that time, not all of whom were suited to active service. The above figures already included over 8000 men from the Near East.[11]

1ST ARMOURED DIVISION

From the first months of the reconstruction of the army on British soil, General Sikorski had been thinking of an armoured motor corps, prepared for modern warfare, but a lack of human reserves frustrated these plans. Preliminary organisation permitted the creation of two brigades of fusiliers, motorised and with tanks, and with a relatively full complement of men, whereas a further five brigades were strictly cadre in character, reduced to officers and almost no other ranks. The same applied to the armoured trains. Admittedly the 2nd Brigade of Fusiliers was called the 10th Brigade of Armoured Cavalry with General Maczek as Commander, and was known overall as the First Corps, but that calculation was making considerable allowance for growth. It could be like that during a period of wartime inactivity, when only the Navy and the airmen from the Polish formations were fighting in the British Isles, but there had to be a change in the light of the preparations for an attack on Northern France.

Whoever could be of use was brought from the Near East; over 1000 people were brought in from different countries, some of which were within German reach; several hundred came from the USA, but all these barely sufficed for one division and a parachute brigade, and this was where the whole problem lay. The British demanded Polish participation in the landing but at the same time their pragmatic thinking shrank from arming incomplete units. Churchill's opinion won the day, however, and the decision was taken that a full armoured division of the new type would be prepared for the invasion of the continent. Its formation went slowly, every soldier fit for service was seized, equipment was fought for, but eventually in spring 1944 the 1st Armoured Division, under the command of General Maczek, was more or less ready. It numbered 885 officers and 15 210 other ranks, including reservists, and possessed 381 tanks of the Sherman and Cromwell types, 473 cannons and 4050 motor vehicles. Formally, everything was in order; however, the division never possessed full numbers, let along any extra personnel, and the value of the battalion of fusiliers, bearing in mind the age and therefore the relative physical fitness of the soldiers, was not the best. Once the decision had been taken that the division would be formed, however, the British authorities turned a blind eye to this: the best quality arms and all other supplies were provided, training was arranged, and the inspection committee did not interfere or ask questions about details. The division was to take part in the second stage of the invasion, immediately after the seizure of the small tracts of French territory, and so it was not sent to Aldershot, in the South of England, until 1 July, where it was to wait its turn impatiently.[12]

1ST INDEPENDENT PARACHUTE BRIGADE

Parallel to that of the armoured division a problem was arising over a parachute brigade, whose history went back to the French period. There was not enough time to form it there and the idea was revived on British soil. After much preparation and training General Sikorski went to Scotland to carry out an inspection and on 9 October 1941 issued an Order that an Independent Parachute Brigade should be formed.[13] The main part of the Brigade was created quite quickly but there were problems in developing it further, similar to those with the armoured division and other Polish units: there were not enough men and the British held back from supplying arms. The Brigade needed 2500 soldiers but had fewer than 2000 and in May 1944 one of the battalions was dissolved.[14]

From the very beginning of its existence, General Sikorski foresaw that the parachute unit would be used in Poland, just as soon as the crucial moment came for a general uprising there, and it was therefore at his disposal only. Political and military events, however, did not proceed as had been expected; the Allied armies' progress in Italy was held up, the invasion of Northern France was postponed until the middle of 1944 and the Red Army was already on Polish territory. It was obvious that the decisive events would take place in Poland at a time when the Western armies were still too far away to be able to help, even if favourable political decisions were taken. Besides, the transportation to Poland of the Brigade, even if it amounted to only 1500 soldiers with light equipment and ammunition for one day of fighting, would have required 265 specially-adapted Liberators with a reduced crew. Nobody had such a fleet at his disposal; the whole SOE employed a maximum of twenty-four

Liberators for all its sections. Transporting the Brigade into Poland was technically impossible and a dilemma arose: whether to keep it for the Polish Army's own use with the possibility that it would not take part in the war at all, or to give it to the British for the second thrust of the invasion of the continent.

General Sosnkowski was in constant contact with the Government over these matters and the prevailing opinion was that it was necessary to agree to the British proposals, to hand the Brigade over for the invasion of the continent and not to impose any conditions concerning losses, since the British leadership would not want to agree to any. In May 1944 a motion on this was passed by the Council of Ministers and at the beginning of June General Sosnkowski informed the British Government in writing that the Brigade was at their disposal. The process of rapidly adjusting the deficiency in arms supplies began.[15]

POLISH AIR FORCE

The Polish Air Forces also suffered from a lack of men and because they were constantly in action and suffered losses, this was a particularly serious situation. For this reason, while at the beginning of 1942 they had possessed eight fighter squadrons, one fighting-reconnaissance and four bomber squadrons, they increased by barely one fighting-reconnaissance squadron. This came into existence on British soil in March 1943 with the purpose of supporting the artillery of the Eighth Army in Italy, of which the Second Polish Corps formed a part. Similarly, at the beginning of 1943, the 301 Bomber Squadron had to be reorganised because of a lack of crew. It was necessary quickly to create a special duties flight, consisting of seven crews, whose purpose would be to fly with the parachute drops into occupied countries, mainly Poland, so the squadron was reformed and the rest of its crew directed to 300 Squadron. The flight became no. 1586 and was attached to RAF 138 Squadron. What little the Polish Air Force possessed was maintained, though with difficulty, mainly thanks to the arrival of 1500 soldiers from Russia and 500 volunteers from USA, as well as to the forbearance of the British Government which, normally very pedantic, turned a blind eye to the deficiencies in manpower. This mainly concerned the ground services.[16]

After the exceptionally intensive year 1940, in which the Battle of

Britain took place, and after the considerably quieter year 1941, the next twelve months were fairly dull in the West, because after attacking Russia the Germans concentrated the greater part of their military forces there. So the Polish fighters shot down only ninety planes in 1942. The Polish Wing of 302, 306 and 308 Squadrons, together with 303 and 317 Squadrons, took part in the raid on Dieppe on 19 August 1942, training for future duties in supporting the invasion of the continent. The year 1943 was considerably more intensive, for then the great bombing raids increased, aimed at destroying German industry both within the Reich and in Western-occupied countries. The huge armadas, especially of American Liberators and Flying Fortresses, attacking by day, but from great heights, were accompanied by the same number of fighters which screened them. The Polish fighter squadrons particularly excelled on these trips; they employed a new tactic, – hiding the bombers from above and from below – and, furthermore, they helped to save crews that had been shot down. A special Polish fighter group also took part in battles in North Africa, fighting in a British squadron and carrying off many successes. In all, in 1943, Polish fighter pilots achieved 113 victories, with sixty-six damaged planes to their credit and forty-two probably shot down.[17]

1942 saw the climax of the Polish bomber squadrons' war action, but also their heaviest losses. The British were already prepared for large expeditions; their war industry was working at full strength and so, on 30 May, they succeeded for the first time in sending 1000 machines over Cologne. Two days later 1000 bombers set out again. Polish bombers took part in both these night raids, 104 in each. It was a huge effort and cadets had to be brought out of training in order to make up the necessary number of crew and machines. The Poles also flew over many other German towns: Bremen, Emden, Essen and Hamburg. They attacked targets in France; they flew over Milan and Turin in Italy, and over the Baltic port of Rostock. In 1942 the Polish bomber squadrons carried out a total of 2450 air missions, and dropped 2764 tonnes of bombs and 528 tonnes of mines. 291 pilots were lost, sixteen died and ninety-one were captured. A further thirty-nine died during training and because of accidents; eighty-nine planes were lost.[18]

In 1943 tremendous emphasis was put on the Battle for the Atlantic and for that reason the Polish bomber squadrons flew most often over German ports, Hamburg in particular. French ports used by the Germans were also mined: Brest, Lorient and St Nazaire, as well as the Dutch coast. The lack of crew and the reorganisation of the Air Force limited its achievements; only 1306 air missions were carried out, and 784 tonnes of bombs and as many mines were dropped. Losses amounted to 112 dead, one missing and nineteen captured, as well as twenty-eight planes destroyed.[19]

A change took place in 1943 in the upper ranks of the Polish Air Force in Great Britain; General Stanisław Ujejski left and on 1 September the Inspectorate was taken over by Colonel (General from 1 March 1944) Mateusz Iżycki (1899–1952).

In the first half of 1943, in anticipation of the landing in France, the British initiated a joint air formation which they called the Tactical Air Force. They set up field posts, to which Polish fighter squadrons were also assigned, and organised two wings, No. 1 and No. 2. It was anticipated that after the successful landing in Northern France and after suitable terrain had been captured, these posts would be transported there. This caused great excitement among the Poles, for they saw a chance to move their bases closer to Poland and eventually to return there themselves. In the autumn of 1943, 302, 308 and 317 Squadrons, belonging to No. 1 Wing, were provided with Spitfire IXs and in March 1944, 306 and 315 Squadrons belonging to No. 2 Wing, received Mustang III planes. Of the bombers, only 305 Squadron was transferred to join air operations, as 300 Squadron remained in heavy bombing duties and 304 Squadron in coastal flying. 301 Squadron, as mentioned above, had been reformed when Flight No. 1586 came into existence for special operations.[20]

Polish crews also took part in air transport, which had played an important role in the last war. Its function above all lay in participating in battles by transporting air armies, dropping supplies to them, evacuating the wounded and equipment, and also transporting important personages. The largest Polish transport unit was organised in the Near East; at first it operated from the Gold Coast and then was transferred to Cairo and flew over Cairo, the Sudan, Arabia, Palestine and (from 1943) India, Ceylon, Algeria and South Africa. There was also a Polish unit in 45 Transport Group, which flew the route Canada–Great Britain–Near East, and another in 229 Transport Group, which flew in India and Burma. Apart from this, 26 Polish pilots belonged individually to four British squadrons. Within the entire air transport in the West, Poles made 23 202 flights, delivered 12 635 aeroplanes, carried 25 187 people and 1769 tonnes of cargo.[21]

The mainstay of the Air Forces was the training, which prepared air and ground personnel, accepted minors and trained candidates for officers, and in the second half of the war even more advanced training was carried out. Polish pilots were also trained in Canada and in all, both there and in the British Isles, 4434 Poles were trained during the war.

A Polish balloon squadron also existed, consisting of five officers and above 150 other ranks, created from pre-war Polish personnel who had worked on the barrage balloons which defended Glasgow, then other targets in Scotland and, from the end of June 1944, London, from attack by V-1s.[22]

POLISH NAVY

In 1943 and at the beginning of 1944, before the decisive attack in the West, the small Polish war fleet was active in various waters, though not as a squadron, because each ship was individually allocated to British groups. The battle for the Atlantic was raging at that time and, as cover for the convoys, the Polish destroyers *Burza* and *Garland* especially distinguished themselves. After this extremely gruelling service in the cold North Atlantic, they were later transferred to warmer waters where, in October 1943, they took part in the capture of the port of Angra in the Azores. *Garland* was sent even further south and, while operating in those waters, crossed the Equator for the first time in February 1944.[23]

Other destroyers, *Błyskawica* and *Piorun*, operating from British bases, were fighting the German Navy in Norwegian waters, just like *Krakowiak* and *Ślązak*, which were moved to the Mediterranean in June 1943 and took part in the attack on Sicily in July. In November the *Krakowiak* found itself in great difficulties during the invasion of the Dodecanese. In that same year the Polish fleet received the first cruiser in its history, the *Dragon*, but it did not go into service until 1944, as it had to undergo major repairs.[24] Two Polish submarines, *Dzik* and *Sokół*, were also active in the Mediterranean and were very successful there. Both took part in the attack on Sicily and on the Italian Peninsula; *Sokół* distinguished itself near Navarino, *Dzik* near Bastia. The results were impressive: *Dzik* sank 50 000 tons, *Sokół* 25 000. In spring 1944 *Sokół* returned to Great Britain as it had to undergo a major overhaul. It remained there until September 1944 and did not take part in the invasion of Northern France. *Dzik* followed shortly after and anchored in Plymouth.

2ND DIVISION IN SWITZERLAND

Apart from the Polish formations which had already taken part in combat or prepared for it, however, a large number still remained in a neutral country as a result of the fall of France. This was 2nd Fusilier Division, amounting to over 13 000 soldiers, who were interned in Switzerland.

Though occupied with the reconstruction of the Polish Armed Forces after the French disaster, General Sikorski did not forget this division, and knew that it had maintained its organisational framework; he considered it his rearguard. It could be used if Polish hopes were fulfilled, above all if the Germans were defeated by the Western Allies and if the Polish Army found itself on the European continent, marching towards Poland. He therefore issued an Order that the division must retain all the features of a military unit, that it was to carry out training in secret, that it ought to organise a secret military college and that no-one was to escape. At the same time, training had to be expanded, university studies made possible and educational work carried out. The Division's Commander, General Bronisław Prugar–Ketling, was in secret contact with London; he received orders from there and sent back reports, and also carried out certain interrogation tasks. For these activities he possessed two pseudonyms: *'Radlicz'* and *'Mars'*.[26]

The Swiss fell in with the Polish plan and turned a blind eye to the military activity, which contravened the rules of internment, for they too had an interest in all this. The country was threatened by Hitler, who had been near to deciding to take it by force several times. The little democracy had decided to defend itself; all tunnels and viaducts were mined, 400 000 soldiers were mobilised in 1940 and in the event of attack the plan was to abandon the lowland provinces and defend the 'alpine redoubt'. The Polish Division was included in the defence plan and would immediately be armed if circumstances demanded it. The Swiss authorities therefore agreed to the retention of the established units and, because the interned soldiers had to work, small camps were set up and whole companies were directed to building roads and bridges, and to other such work. This was the so-called 'Wahlen Plan', which was so advantageous to Switzerland because the Polish soldiers constructed 277km of new roads, repaired almost 200km of old ones, erected sixty-three bridges, built over 10km of new canals by regulating the rivers, and carried out a lot of work in the forests and mines.[27]

ALL THE POLISH FORCES IN THE WEST

The war did not end in 1944 but decisive events took place, and at that time the Polish Armed Forces abroad, at the disposal of the authorities in London, were as follows:

First line

2 Corps	50 000
1 Armoured Division	16 000
1 Independent Parachute Brigade	2 500
Air Force	10 000
Navy	2 500
	81 000

Second line (units in the rear, mostly unsuitable for combat)

Great Britain	11 000
Near East	17 000
Staff, Women's Auxiliary Service, etc.	5 000
	33 000

Total   114 000[28]

In relation to the millions in the armies of the Western nations and Soviet Russia, all supported by their own, powerful industry, these were insignificant forces which, even when combined to create one entire body, could barely form one corps on land. Their value to Poland was above all symbolic; it proved that the Poles were determined to fight to the last and that they would remain in the Allied camp regardless of any harmful political decisions. These considerations required that these forces be used carefully, for they had no reserves and might lose their value after the first heavy losses. It would have been best if they could have been constantly in action but in relatively small units, no larger than divisions, as this would have drawn attention to them and achieved a propaganda purpose. That purpose was more or less achieved, mainly thanks to the Air Force, Navy and Carpathian Brigade, and in the last phase of the war thanks to 1st Armoured Division, 1st Independent Parachute Brigade and the Second Polish Corps, which was the most powerful force and therefore made its mark the most strongly in battles on land.[29]

19 New Developments in Poland; Monte Cassino; Falaise; 'Tempest'

POLISH NATIONAL COUNCIL AND ITS MANIFESTO

Three days before the Red Army entered Polish territory, on the night of 31 December, 1943–1 January 1944, Polish communists created the Polish National Council (*Krajowa Rada Narodowa* – KRN) in Warsaw. It was based on a very narrow political platform, for apart from the Polish Workers Party the signatories of the manifesto were virtually fictitious organisations of little more than a dozen or so members each. The Council was led by Bolesław Bierut (1892–1956), a long-standing member of Comintern and a confidant of Stalin, who found himself in occupied Poland in 1943 and in July entered the Central Committee of the PPR. As from November 1943, after the Gestapo had arrested Paweł Finder, the secretary of the Committee was Władysław Gomułka (1905–83) a pre-war ideological communist by conviction, who represented a line somewhat independent from that of Moscow.[1]

The Council's manifesto denied the Polish Government in London the right to represent the Polish nation, and announced that a provisional government would soon be created in Poland. The manifesto made no mention of socialism, but gave warning of the impending nationalisation of industry and a total agricultural reform, that would result in breaking-up larger landed estates. The eastern frontiers would be drawn on an ethnographic basis in total and friendly understanding with Russia. The Western frontier would reach the Oder and the Baltic. The People's Army (AL) was created, its nucleus being the already-existing People's Guard, under the leadership of General Michał Żymierski (*Rolav*, 1890–), a one-time officer in Piłsudski's Legions.[2]

The creation of the KRN with hardly any political backing other than the PPR, would have been without political significance, were it not for the fact that it was synchronised almost to the day with the Red Army's entry into Poland's eastern territories. There was no longer the slightest doubt but that the liberation of Poland from German occupation would come from the East. No-one had forgotten 17 September 1939, nor the mass deportations from the eastern borderlands, but the German occupation had been so cruel that people were prone to think kindly about their potential liberators from the Germans. The second factor connected with the communist declaration was the promise of broad social reforms contained in the manifesto. General *Bór* had already put forward such a motion, but London had other problems on hand and, more importantly, was divorced from the real situation in Poland and therefore did not react, whereas the underground party organised in the Polish Political Representation (KRP) was unable to reach a consensus. The problem was now an urgent one, for no doubts were entertained as to the communists' success.

COUNCIL OF NATIONAL UNITY AND ITS DECLARATION

On 9 January 1944, a Government Delegate's decree appeared appointing the Council of National Unity (*Rada Jedności Narodowej* – RJN), which was synonymous with the abolition of the Polish Political Representation. The underground parliament thus created consisted of seventeen members: three representatives each from the four major parties (PPS, SL, SN and SP), one each from the lesser parties and representatives of the ecclesiastical hierarchy and the co-operative movement. Kazimierz Pużak, a socialist, was named chairman and the bulk of the work fell on the Council's Chief Committee, which possessed full powers and could meet more often, as this was easier in the underground.[3]

Formally the RJN came into being in January, but it began to function properly only in March. On 15 March it issued a declaration bearing the operative title *What the Polish Nation is fighting for*. The document represented the views held at that time by politicians in German-occupied Poland concerning governmental, economic, social and political affairs. It likewise voiced their views on the problem of Poland's post-war frontiers.

The declaration consisted of three basic parts. The first expressed the Polish point of view of the conditions on which a permanent peace could be established in Europe, with which the problem of Poland's frontiers was closely connected. After formulating the opinion that the Germans should be deprived once and for all of the chance to start a new war of conquest, the declaration emphasised the need to call an international organisation to regulate the coexistence of nations: it should possess authority and power, and the weaker nations would also participate in its decisions. An important peace factor was the formation in Central Europe of federative unions that would not allow any single state to attain hegemony. On the question of frontiers the declaration stated that Poland must retain her pre-war frontiers in the east, based on the 1921 Treaty of Riga. To the west and north the frontiers would expand to take in all of Eastern Prussia, part of Pomerania, the lands between the Noteć and the Warta, and Opole-Silesia. This part of the declaration also included a formula expressing the intention of maintaining good relations within the USSR on condition that Poland's frontiers were recognised, and that there should be no interference in Poland's internal affairs.[4]

The second part of the declaration defined the political regime that should be set up in post-war Poland, viewed as a parliamentary democracy with a strong executive. The new constitution would guarantee universal freedom of religion, political convictions, freedom of word, print, public assembly and association. National minorities would enjoy the same rights.[5]

The third point was the most important. It concerned social and economic reforms. It was planned that in the new Poland there would be common ownership of property both in the country and in the towns, so that the widest possible social stratum could benefit from the country's natural assets. This would call for nationalisation by the state or collectivisation of key industries, large financial institutions and public utilities. The larger landed estates (over 50 hectares) would be split up, and self-sufficient one-family peasant farming units would be set up. All forests would be nationalised. Social policy would enable working people to rise in society and to have some control, through the unions, on the economic life and in taking part in decisions that concerned them. Schooling would also be expanded so that all layers of society might benefit from it, particularly the peasants and workers. Extra school education would be developed. The declaration ended on the optimistic view that the united Polish nation, rooted in its milennial tradition of freedom and Christian culture, would come into a bright future.[6]

The declaration, which in the second and third parts contained very many judicious formulations, appeared however several years too late, as the communists, supported by the military and propaganda power of Moscow, had already gained a certain position within Polish society, which had long since been awaiting the announcement of plans concerning post-war Poland. On the other hand the first part of the declaration concerning the frontiers and hopes for a federal union of states in that part of Europe, was a maximalist programme, totally unrealistic in the fifth year of the war, and proving that in a country under German occupation even seasoned politicians were indulging in unfounded delusions.

After the call of the Council for National Unity, the Government Delegate proceeded along the line of strengthening the powers of the underground and by virtue of the degree of the President of the Polish Republic dated 26 April 1944, created the National Council of Ministers consisting of three members with the delegate as deputy premier. This took place on 3 May 1944.[7]

THE BEGINNING OF 'TEMPEST' AND PREMIER MIKOŁAJCZYK'S POLITICAL ACTION

At the same time as the two rival Councils were coming into being and beginning to function, there were already red divisions on Polish territory, and the moment came when the Home Army was to launch the execution of *Tempest*. Before things came to such a pass there was a further exchange of opinion, and a final attempt was made to harmonise the Polish and Soviet positions regarding the territories in the East. As soon as Soviet soldiers had appeared on these territories, the Polish government decided to make a public declaration and try to co-ordinate it with the British. Under pressure from the latter the paragraph concerning Polish sovereignty was altered and instead of the words 'over the whole of the liberated lands' the phrase 'above the liberated lands' was used. The declaration appeared on 6 January and elicited an instant Soviet reaction in the form of a statement published on 11 January. It ultimately prejudged the issue of the Polish lands in the east, as a referendum had taken place there in 1939, the upshot of which was that they would belong to Soviet Byelorussia and Ukraine. Poland on the other hand would return to her age-old territories in the west. The Polish Government instantly responded and on 14 January issued a statement in which it did not assess the case on its merits. Instead it emphasised the importance of opening up diplomatic relations, as they would make it possible to regulate points of dispute, and the importance of Great Britain and the United States participation in discussions. Two days later a new Soviet declaration stated that as the Polish Government had not touched on the question of an eastern frontier along the Curzon Line, this amounted to a rejection on their part. Negotiations were out of the question when it was conducting an anti-Soviet campaign in connection with Katyń.[8]

The British government, in agreement with the resolutions of Teheran, applied pressure on the Polish government to accept the Curzon Line as a basis for negotiations together with the suggestions that Poland's frontiers would be extended in the West. Churchill took the matter up in public and, on 22 February, in the House of Commons, he delivered a speech in which he stated that he considered the Soviet demands and the shifting of Poland to the west justified. The Russians in fact went further still in their attacks and even insisted on changes in the Polish government, even though they had no relations with this government. The Polish authorities did not yield to the pressure and made no concessions, and the country thought likewise. This found expression in the resolution of the Council for National Unity dated 20 January, which rejected Soviet claims to the eastern territories. Lacking the strength to oppose Russia, it still had to carry on the fight with Germany and stand on the ground of Polish moral rights to a share in the common victory.[9]

General *Bór's* orders concerning operation *Tempest* envisaged that local Home Army leaders would themselves decide when to mobilise the larger units and start the fight with the retreating Germans. This is what in effect took place in Volhynia, on whose territory the Red Army had first appeared, and where by mid-January the district commander of the Home Army had ordered a concentration on the wooded terrain between Kowel and Włodzimierz.[10]

The division that was given the name 27th Volhynian, in a short time numbered some 6000 soldiers. Their equipment consisted of armaments that had been buried in September 1939, Soviet weapons left behind in 1941 and arms captured from the Germans. Once only, against the British injunctions based on political assumptions, two planes from Italy flew over the terrain occupied by the division and dropped supplies of pistols, ammunition, anti-artillery guns, radio transmitters and uniforms.[11]

In February, after fighting with the Germans and the Ukrainians, came the first encounter of the division patrol with a Soviet detachment. This led to co-operation, and several joint operations were carried out. On 26 March the division leader met the commander of the Soviet army, General Sergeyev, and at this meeting conditions were established for joint fighting. In the operational area the division had to subordinate itself totally to the Soviet leadership, in return for which it would receive full equipment and absolute freedom to liaise with the army chiefs in Warsaw and in London, to whom they were still answerable. The Home Army commander confirmed the wisdom of this agreement, emphasising the importance of tactical co-operation with the Red Army, which could bring advantageous political consequences.[12]

It is in the context of this co-operation that the basic differences of views between General Sosnkowski and Mikołajczyk appear most sharply. The first had a pessimistic view of the situation, saw no possibility of action, limited himself to accepting *faits accomplis* and voicing negative opinions, and therefore when he received a despatch on this subject from General *Bór*, he signalled back to Warsaw:

> I doubt if the promises of the Soviet command will be kept, or whether the additional conditions of your instruction will be accepted, even if they are I do not believe in the final success of this experiment, and the division's subordination to you and to myself will in all likelihood be completely illusory... I anticipate that in due course an attempt will be made to incorporate the division to Berling's army, or some repressions will be enforced.

His prognosis, so easy to formulate, was correct and proved itself true, but what was the alternative? To renounce the fight with the Germans and watch passively as the Russians took over Polish territory without Polish participation?[13]

Premier Mikołajczyk, who was also operating in extremely difficult conditions and could see what was going on, nevertheless sought positive solutions, and endeavoured to convince his Western allies that Polish–Soviet co-operation was possible, and therefore cabled to the Government Delegate:

On April 6th, 1944, the Polish Government fully accepted the just dispositions that were issued by the Commander of the Home Army in agreement with the Commander of the Volhynian sector, in response to the Soviet proposals. We immediately negotiated this politically in notes to the British and American Governments, at the same time proposing that the chance be seized to activate their policy and demand that Allied missions be sent out. Regardless of what the Soviets will do tomorrow, the proposals once made by them, even if altered or not fulfilled, will be and will remain an important political argument. At this moment the increase of military activity in the Wilno region and the meet up and ensuing co-operation of Home Army detachments in Volhynia in the fight against the Germans are an incredibly important political argument, as they reveal the falsehood of the accusation of co-operation with the Germans, prove their loyalty to the state authorities and destroy the theory held in Moscow that the Poles intend armed resistance against the invading Soviet army.[14]

The chances of a change in policy of the Western Allies were slender, but it was important to aim in that direction, and every opportunity must be put to good use. This was apparent to the Polish Government and therefore in February 1944 it put forward the project of sending Allied Military Missions to Poland, where they could apprise themselves of the true state of affairs and see how much it had in common with Soviet propaganda. At the same time Poland realised the necessity for carrying on the fight with the Germans. To cease the fight on home ground would provoke the fury of the entire nation, which loathed the occupants and wanted to fight. No one could make a better present for the Russians and the communists; it would prove the best way of filling the ranks of the People's Army and the hitherto proud name of the Home Army would become a symbol of passivity and capitulation. Both Allied Governments rejected the proposal of sending Military Missions to Poland. There were therefore no Western observers at hand, and the fate of the 27th Volhynian division partially confirmed the forecasts of the pessimists. After their joint seizure of Kowel the division was left to its own devices, surrounded by Germans. With enormous effort it succeeded in pulling through, but it suffered severe losses. Ultimately the main nucleus of the division crossed over to the West bank of the Bug and hid in the forests, and one concentration passed through the Soviet front and was there incorporated into General Berling's army.[15]

The Home Army detachments' first encounter with the Red Army brought no clear answer to several rankling questions, and most important it had not ultimately clarified the Soviet stance. Co-operation functioned smoothly enough on the battlefield, but this did not result in relations being established between the two governments, and only subsequent events could reveal what were the Kremlin's long-term intentions.

POLISH COMMUNIST ARMY IN USSR

After the battle of Lenino and the transfer of the entire First Corps to the region of Smoleńsk, it remained there until March 1944, and went through the process of reorganisation, completing establishment and further training. At this time the Red Army moved far to the West, retrieved the Ukraine on the west bank of the Dnepr from the Germans and found itself on the south-east territories of Poland, in Volhynia and Podole. Despite massive deportations in the period of the first Soviet rule in 1939–41, there was still a numerous Polish population in those parts. Recruiting could significantly strengthen the ranks of the Corps; which is why the Union of Polish Patriots proposed to the Soviet authorities that the Polish units be deployed to the army cadres. On 16 March the relevant decree was issued by the Presidium of the Supreme Soviet of the USSR. Earlier still, on 10 March, General Berling, who anticipated that the Soviet authorities would agree to his expanding the forces under his command, gave the order to transfer the Corps to the region of Zhitomir and Berdichev, which took place in March and in April. The town of Sumy in the Ukraine, situated over 300km east of Kiev, was chosen for the formation of new units.[16]

The first Polish Army consisted of three elements: the army in action, the Formation Staff and the Polish Partisan Staff. The Formation Staff was situated initially in Sumy, but was transferred to Zhitomir in July under the leadership of General Świerczewski. The 4th Infantry Division, the first cavalry brigade, field and anti-aircraft artillery, the 2nd Air Regiment of night fighters and auxiliary detachments were all organised, and, at a later stage, the 1st Armoured Corps, two infantry divisions and officers' schools were also formed.[17] The Polish Partisan Staff was intended to assist the partisan detachments on the territory of German-occupied Poland. It provided training for radio-telegraphists, coding, communications, reconnaissance and many other specialities necessary in partisan warfare. It began its activity in April 1944, based near Rovno, and was in charge of larger communist partisan detachments. The Polish Partisan Staff was also responsible for landing partisan parachutist groups onto Polish territory for reconnaissance and sabotage purposes.[18]

The most important element of the First Army was its fighting force, which consisted of the 1st, 2nd and 3rd Infantry Divisions together with reinforcement units. Towards the end of April it was transferred to the region of Kiverce in Volhynia, and became the second echelon of the Byelorussian Front, commanded by General Konstanty Rokossovsky (1896–1968) who, during the Stalinist purges in the 1930s had been put in a camp, from which he came out at the beginning of the war. Towards the end of April, 1944, he was appointed marshal. The army had the task of organising the defence of the east bank of the Styr, near Łuck. When the left-wing grouping of the Front launched the offensive on 18 July, units of the First Army took part and on 20 July they crossed the Bug.[19] From the Soviet point of view this signified that First Polish Army units had moved to the easternmost point of Polish soil whereas in actual fact these units were on the territory of central Poland.

MONTE CASSINO

The progress of the Allies in Italy was considerably slower than strategic considerations would have called for. Independently of German resistance several tactical errors were committed, in particular the landing near Anzio on 22 January, to the south of Rome, instead of in the neighbourhood of Leghorn, north of the Goths Line. The Anzio landing nearly ended in catastrophe and was of little benefit to the Allies' formations, which on the way to Rome had to force the Gustav Line. Across its path soared Monte Cassino, a mountainous massif that was exceptionally difficult to capture, and on one of whose summits stood the old historic monastery of the Benedictines dating back to the seventh century. The massif controlled the road and the Naples–Rome railway line, and had therefore been soundly fortified by the Germans, and manned with the crack 1st Division of parachutists.[20]

The first attempt to break through the Gustav Line was carried out in the period of 22 January–10 February, with the participation of the

American Fifth Army, the 3rd division of the Algerian Army from the French Corps and Britain's Eighth Army. Disastrous atmospheric conditions and German resistance made success impossible, although the French divisions and the Second American Corps came close to the monastery. Before a fresh attempt was launched, on 15 February the Allies carried out a highly controversial air attack on the monastery, which they had reduced to ruins. There were no monks around, as the Germans had deported them to Rome, but the magnificent library and the great number of priceless works of art were destroyed. The New Zealand Corps made two attempts, lasting from 15 February to 24 March, neither of which achieved any result.[21]

After three failures and severe losses the Allied Command in Italy decided that the final attempt to break through the Gustav Line and open the road to Rome, which necessitated the capture of Monte Cassino, would be undertaken by the British Eighth Army. During briefing on 24 March its commander, General Leese, informed general Anders of this decision and asked him if, as leader of the Polish Corps he would undertake to capture the massif, which had so far resisted all attacks. He was admittedly subordinate to British command but as he represented the Polish formation he had the right to refuse. Unfortunately he had only a few minutes in which to form his decision.[22]

The Commander of the Corps was faced by a very difficult problem on which he had to make an immediate decision, with only his chief of staff at his side.

It was a great moment for me. The difficulty of the task assigned to the Corps was obvious. The stubbornness of the German defence at Cassino and on Monastery Hill was already a byword, for although the Monastery had been bombed, and the town of Cassino was a heap of ruins, the Germans still held firm and blocked the road to Rome. I realised that the cost in lives must be heavy, but I realised too the importance of the capture of Monte Cassino to the Allied cause, and most of all to that of Poland, for it would answer once and for all the Soviet lie that the Poles did not want to fight the Germans. Victory would give new courage to the resistance movement in Poland and would cover Polish arms with glory. After a short moment's reflection I answered that I would undertake the task.[23]

The General's decision was in keeping with the basic principle for deploying Poland's Armed Forces outside Poland. They could not play a major role, their participation would have no impact on the final outcome of the war, but if there was ever a time when the Poles needed a resounding success, it was now.[24]

General Anders realised that his two divisions, Carpathian and *Kresowa*, consisted of only two brigades each, and that numbers were low in the ranks. Heavy losses could deprive the Corps of the possibility of further participation in military action. It was therefore necessary to strive to prepare the plan of attack as carefully as possible. The Corps' Commander carried out his reconnaissance from the air and received many particulars and explanations from the Allied Command who had previously stormed the as yet impregnable mountain massif. It measured between 4 and 6km in width and some 8km in length, and its highest peak, Mount Cairo, had an altitude of 1669m. The launching-points for the attack were on the eastern slopes of the massif. In order to occupy them it was necessary to cross the valley of the Rapido, 5km in width, which was possible only by night. The Germans had replenished their forces with two additional battalions, and all important defence-points were covered by artillery and machine-gun fire.[25]

The attack on the Gustav Line was meant to be carried out by international forces grouped in such a way that the Second American Corps was situated by the coastline of the Tyrrhenian Sea. Next to it, further to the north-east, was the French Corps, further still the Canadian Corps in contact with the Thirteenth British Corps, which had the Polish Corps on its right wing. On its right wing was the Tenth British Corps. This lay-out shows that the main onus of fighting would fall on the British Eighth Army, hence also on the Polish Corps.[26]

After gathering all necessary information, General Anders prepared a plan of attack for his Corps: this involved assailing not the monastery hill but the two neighbouring hills, Hill 593 and San Angelo. Simultaneous attack would reduce the Germans' potential for shooting and would disperse their reserve forces. If both hills were captured the monastery would be isolated and would prove an easier prey. Lots were drawn, and it was thereby established that the 3rd Carpathian division would attack Hill 593 and Massa Albanetta, where it would form a base for attacking the monastery, which was their ultimate target. The task of the 5th *Kresowa* division was to gain control of Hill San Angelo and guard the crest of Monte Castellone, so as to cover the attack on the monastery hill from the north and the west. Numbers in both divisions were so low that all forces had to be used, without leaving any reserves behind. The difficult terrain limited the use of tanks to such an extent that only two of their squadrons, one for each division, could be brought into battle. 11 May was fixed as the day for the attack, so on the previous night the battalions made ready for attack had to come across and lie in ambush on the slopes of the massif at Monte Cassino.[27]

At 11p.m. the artillery of the Allies opened fire along the whole line of the front on which that night the attack was to be launched, and for forty minutes tried to destroy the enemy's artillery position. Later fire was concentrated on the infantry positions and at 1a.m. the two Polish divisions sallied forth to the attack. They moved forward under constant fire from German artillery and machine-guns, whose defence barriers, put to the test for months, were highly effective. In spite of losses the battalions of the 1st Brigade of Carpathian gunners succeeded in gaining control of Hill 393, to move forward towards the Throttle in the direction of Massa Albanetta and unite in the battle for Hill 569, which was almost uniformly rock. At the same time the 5th Wilno Infantry Brigade, fighting heavily, reached as far as the crest of the Spectre and tried to proceed further, but enemy resistance was too strong. Fighting went on throughout the night until the afternoon of the following day without the hope of bringing in reinforcements, as all roads and paths leading to the front were covered by German fire. Despite the huge fire-power the Allied artillery did not succeed in reducing the German cannons to silence. In the evening of 12 May the commander of the Corps issued the order to withdraw to departure-points. Considerable losses and a state of exhaustion made it impossible to use the same battalions in a renewed attempt to gain control of the enemy's positions. The withdrawal only ended on 13 May.[28]

Although the attack had not been a success, General Leese was pleased with the result, as it had tied up the German forces in the massif of Monte Cassino, drawn artillery fire away from neighbouring sections and enabled other detachments of the Allies to achieve their aims. General Anders was planning a fresh attack, but reconnaissance reported that the German division had received reinforcements, so General Leese gave orders to wait until the Thirteenth British Corps had proceeded further up the valley of the river Liri, threatening the German lines and tying up part of the enemy's reserves and artillery fire.[29]

On 17 May, at 7 a.m., fresh battalions of both Polish divisions sallied forth to a fresh attack with the mission of attaining the same targets at which their predecessors had been aiming. The attack was launched by day, so the march had to be executed as swiftly as possible, regardless of mines and other obstacles, so as to break through the German defence fire as quickly as possible. Hill 593, Throttle and Spectre were again taken, as well as part of the Hill of San Angelo, but it proved impossible to gain any more ground. Exhausted, the soldiers huddled into the rocks. An attempt was made to evacuate the wounded, to provide ammunition, water and food supplies. A point of crisis had been reached, as the enemy must likewise be exhausted. Victory depended on the ultimate effort of one of the sides. The lack of reserves made it necessary to introduce battalions into the fighting: they had lost much blood on 12 May, and their numbers were very low. The commander of the Corps resorted to the commandoes, the crew operating the anti-tank ammunition, even drivers and mechanics. On 18 May a renewed attack was made on the battle ground of the Carpathian division, and it transpired that even the crack German formations had given it up as a bad job. Most of them had withdrawn in the night, leaving behind only a feeble defence that was soon broken through, and at 10.20 a.m. a patrol of the 12th Regiment of Uhlans hoisted the Polish standard on the ruins of the monastery.[30]

The losses of the Second Polish Corps were considerable: the Carpathian Division lost 1571 soldiers, of whom over 20 per cent were killed; the *Kresowa* more still – 2174 men, of whom 22 per cent were lost in battle. Seventy-two officers were killed, including one brigade commander and two battalion leaders, and there were 209 wounded. It was however a considerable military and propaganda success. The news soon went round the world and reached Poland, where it had many an echo. This was voiced in a dispatch sent by the Council for National Unity to London, with the request that it be passed on to General Anders:

> In the name of the Polish Underground and the whole of Polish society we wish to express to the General our sincere words of admiration and approval for the commanders and soldiers of the Second Corps for their heroic deeds and their magnificent achievement in Italy.
>
> You have given the world fresh proof that the Polish Nation is unremittingly fighting for independence and for a glorious future for its state.[31]

The road to Rome was open and on 4 June detachments of the American Fifth Army were marching along it. The Germans offered no defence, they considered Rome to be an open city.

V–2

After transferring their V–2 experiments onto Polish soil, the Germans soon built an experimental centre there in the forests surrounding the village of Blizna, in the junction of the Vistula and the San, and began exploding rockets into the stratosphere and observing the places where they landed.

The rocket-heads contained only sand, but on landing they exploded because of the fuel combustion of liquid oxygen and alcohol. Towards the end of 1943 the Home Army local reconnaissance observed the first launchings and explosions, and reported accordingly to Warsaw, whence an urgent cable was sent to London. The response was immediate: the matter was highly important and had to be thoroughly investigated. The Home Army intelligence extended its activities. In Blizna an attempt was made to reach as closely as possible to the place of the launchings; parts of the mysterious exploding objects were sought near Częstochowa and in the north, as far as the Bug. The Germans did likewise, so that a formal race went on between their motorised patrols and the ground reconnaissance of the Home Army.[32]

In London British scientific intelligence treated these further German rocket experiments very seriously. There was no protection from them, as they flew at an altitude of 90km. Their dimensions and the power of their explosive charge were still unknown quantities. A debate was moreover going on at British Intelligence HQ between two factions. One, headed by the young scientist Reginald Jones, viewed the threat of the German rocket very seriously. The other, led by Lord Cherwell, the eminent physicist and Churchill's scientific adviser, minimised the alarmist reports and maintained that the rockets were a myth, as the Germans could not possess liquid fuel that would drive the rockets into the stratosphere.[33] The ideal solution would be to get hold of a whole rocket or at least of its major parts, and subject them to scientific analysis.[34]

Such then was the aim of the Home Army intelligence which worked out several plans to steal their secret from the Germans. They toyed with the possibility of a partisan attack on the polygon in

Blizna, or of gaining control of a railway convoy, when fate unexpectedly gave a helping hand: on 20 May, on the marshy left bank of the Bug, a German rocket fell without exploding. The local Home Army patrol camouflaged it and put it in a place for safe keeping, and instantly notified Warsaw.[35]

A commission of specialists promptly appeared on the Bug and began to dismount the complex mechanism, which numbered 25 000 parts. The most important were described and photographed, the radio receiving and transmitting apparatus bearing the number 0984 was preserved intact and a little smouldering liquid was set aside, which after analysis turned out to be simply oxidised water in a highly-concentrated state. It was initially assumed that this was the fuel driving the rocket, but it was later established that it was the liquid driving the pump that pressed the fuel into the engine. The entire find was transported to Warsaw, where a Research Commission in conjunction with the Economic Council produced a report entitled *Special Report 1/R, nr. 242.* It included a text of 4000 words, eighty photographs, twelve drawings, a sketch of the polygon in Blizna and a comparison of exploded rockets. It was completed with eight original parts of the rocket and three annexes.[36]

The report together with the rocket parts was to be sent immediately to London, but a delay ensued, caused by the extremely difficult operation bearing the cryptonym *Most* (Bridge). This consisted in landing a heavy Dakota – a transport plane sent from the Italian base in Brindisi – at a secret airfield in Poland. It was only on 25 July that all the most important factors of the operation – fine weather, a secret airfield and its cover – could be successfully co-ordinated, and operation *Most* was carried out. Together with several other people an envoy of the Home Army intelligence flew to Italy with the report and a bag containing the most important parts of the rocket. By 28 July he was already in London and handed over the important package to an authorised Polish officer from Bureau VI. After the report had been decoded everything was promptly handed over to British scientific intelligence.[37]

It so happened that a week or so earlier British Intelligence had received for inspection important parts of a V–2 that had been launched from Peenemünde, had fallen in southern Sweden on 13 June and had then got into the hands of the Allies. In the rocket was found a broken radio apparatus, adapted to remote control, and the British experts came to the conclusion that the Germans had already solved this difficult problem and that rockets would be exceedingly dangerous. Fortunately the radio apparatus removed from the rocket obtained in Poland was only capable of receiving and transmitting signals, without any steering capacity. This was the chief merit of the Polish discovery, as it was now apparent that the German weapon was not all that advanced.[38]

INVASION OF THE CONTINENT

At 2 a.m. on 6 June the first Allied parachutists landed on French soil having been dropped several kilometres inland. There were about 20 000 of them, and other 70 000 soldiers sailed at the same time to the coasts of Normandy as the principal striking force. They were to seize the landing-bridgeheads and open the way for the invasion of the continent, for which 2 million soldiers of various nationalities had been prepared, together with 1200 warships including battleships, 4000 transport ships, 7500 immediate support planes plus 3500 bombers, which could either be used in direct battle, or else fly over the German Reich in order to carry out further strategic bombings.[39]

The Allies had an overall superiority in the air, but landing on a fortified coastline was a very difficult operation and could have failed had it not been for the German's faulty assessment of the Allies' place of attack. The Germans failed to use their reserves in time, and three weeks later the Allies already had half a million soldiers in France and as many tonnes of supplies. Hitler attached considerable importance to the Western Front, about which he made a very telling remark: 'Unless the invasion is repelled we have lost the war'. But he was unable to change the course of events.[40]

1ST POLISH ARMOURED DIVISION AT FALAISE

The time came for the 1st Polish Armoured Division to go into action. Crossing the Channel took place without obstacles, and they harboured at the artificial port near Arromanches, and on 1 August Polish soldiers found themselves back on French soil after four years. Then, after the surrender, though defeated, they were still full of hope as they made their way in small groups, unarmed, to Great Britain. Now they returned fully armed and strong, organised in a splendid modern fighting division, and yet in their hearts they were afraid for the future of their country to which, on the warpath, they so badly wanted to return.

The division formed part of the Second Canadian Corps within the Canadian army, and almost immediately found itself in battle. The Germans were still trying counter-attacks, so as to strike at the flank of the American army, as it proceeded northwards. The Canadian Corps received the order to paralyse this manoeuvre and to strike at the Germans in the direction of Falaise.[41]

The night attack of 7–8 August, preceded by a great bombardment of British aircraft and artillery fire, was not a success. The fault lay with the bombers, which had dropped their charges either too far or too close, causing damage to their own. The German fortifications turned out to be better, and better defended, than had been assumed, and the German tanks *Panther* and *Tiger*, with their magnificent 88mm guns, whose missiles pierced a Sherman armour-plate from a distance of 2km, showed their considerable value in open terrain. The Polish division fought well and withstood its baptism of fire, and its commanders gained in experience, but the first losses made themselves felt – 656 men killed and wounded, and sixty-six tanks lost.[42]

Over the next several days a new operation was planned, which was launched on 14 August from the departure-points that had been gained in the first attack. The main attack fell on the Canadian divisions, which were considerably helped by British and American airforce. On 15 August the entire German defence position in the valley of the river Laison was in the hands of the Canadians, who were aiming in the direction of Falaise. The Germans were in retreat, General Patton's army reached the neighbourhood of Argentan, to the south-east of Falaise, and the possibility presented itself of totally surrounding the withdrawn German divisions. The operation of encircling the enemy was entrusted to the Polish and Canadian armoured divisions, which meant shifting from west to east, in the direction of Trun.[43]

While the division's first sally into battle had been exceptionally difficult, full of various failures, and had been crowned by a mediocre result, this second venture presented a totally different picture. Certainly, experience had been gained, but independently of that, luck also played its part. The division seized the bridge on the river Dives and the neighbouring fords, which were accessible even to tanks. This made it possible to march in a south-to-east direction, towards Trun, and allowed for freedom of movement, so important for an armoured division, which despite its heavy arms was a swift-manoeuvring unit. On 17 August the commander of the Canadian Corps brought an order from Montgomery that the division should proceed further and make for Chambois, 7km to the south-east of Trun. It would not be isolated, as the Canadian 4th Armoured Division was setting off from the north, and the Americans had already occupied Argentan to the south. It was a hard task, as reconnaissance had shown that the march was threatened from the east by the German 2nd Armoured Division.[44]

For many hours, between 19 and 21 August, a ceaseless battle was waged in a narrow strip between Chambois and Vimoutiers in order to check the German retreat. The division had also to resist attack from the east, as the Germans were trying to destroy the Polish unit and open the threshold. The toughest day was 20 August when the German 21st Armoured Division attacked Polish positions from the east and the detachments of the Eleventh Armoured Corps from the north. The fate of the battle was in the scales. With the help of the Canadian 4th Armoured Division all the German attacks were repulsed and the battle was coming to an end. Some small groups still appeared here and there, but anyone who could get through, did so, or else joined the long columns of prisoners.[45]

On balance the Falaise 'sack' ended in the only partial success of the Allies, for it encircled 60 000 Germans, and 40 000 escaped nevertheless to the east, but in the first place part of their detachments were already there before the snare closed in on them, and in the second, the Polish division responsible for that operation was the only deciding factor in the success. Before taking up its positions which closed the 'sack', it had to fight for them, and at the same time the American army of General Patton, which was active more to the south, in the direction of Argentan, was held up and left a gap through which many thousands of Germans escaped. This was because the Allied Command had earlier established the strips of terrain that would separate the individual armies from one another. The strip between the 12th Group of the American army and the 21st Group of the British army passed over 10km to the south of Argentan; and General Patton, an exceptionally aggressive commander who was ever thrusting forward nevertheless had to comply with the orders of his chief, General Bradley, and hold back. A number of considerations, including matters of prestige and American–British animosities weighed upon the decisions that led to an incomplete success.[46]

The division's losses were considerable, amounting to 325 killed, including twenty-one officers, 1002 wounded, including thirty-five officers, and 114 missing. The overall figure of 1441 men represented about 10 per cent of division figures, and in the detachments of the line attained 20 and even 30 per cent. Percentage wise these losses were higher than those of the Second Corps in the battle of Monte Cassino, yet at the same time could not be exploited with similar effect for Polish propaganda purposes, as the division had acted within the Canadian corps, to which the ultimate success was mainly attributed. German losses were difficult to evaluate, as some were due to the Air Force and other Allied detachments; however 5113 prisoners were registered, with one general and 136 officers, fifty-five tanks, forty-four guns, thirty-eight armoured cars and 207 motor vehicles, not to mention light weapons and horse vehicles. These figures naturally do not encompass the main task of the division which was to break up the German withdrawal, and which resulted in thousands of Germans being taken into captivity and leaving countless stocks of battle equipment behind.[47]

POLISH AIR FORCE AND NAVY

Polish fighter-pilots, who had been through suitable reorganisation and rearming, also took part in the invasion of the Continent. Of the field ports created by the British and intended for swiftest possible transportation to France, two – Nos. 131 and 133, – were exclusively Polish and created fighting grouping No.18. Field landing site 135 was added to this grouping: it comprised non-Polish squadrons, but came under the command of a Pole, Group Captain Gabszewicz. The grouping's task was to cover the landing operation, and the squadrons carried out several such flights each day. In the course of two days alone, from 6 to 8 June, it shot down thirty planes. On 11 June three Polish squadrons – Nos. 302, 308 and 317 – experienced the great emotion of landing on French soil at provisional airfield No. 131, in Normandy.

In the middle of he July the Air Force fighter groupings acting in conjunction were disbanded and individual wings were directly subordinated to the great fighter group. Group Captain Gabszewicz took over Wing 131, which protected the great battle in Normandy with the participation of a Polish armoured division, and took part in the battle of Falaise. There were victories but there were also losses, mainly from anti-aircraft artillery fire. Squadrons carried out fifty sorties a day. Later the Wing was active on the Belgium–Holland frontier, and was stationed near Ghent.[48]

One week after the beginning of the invasion, starting from 13 June, London came under fire of flying bombs, – V–1, – and fighter-planes, predominantly *Mustangs*, undertook the defence. By nose-diving it was possible to overtake and shoot down a V–1, as its speed did not exceed 500km an hour. Polish squadrons, those that had remained in the British Isles and two from field landing-site 133, withdrawn from the Continent on 9 July and enlisted in the air defence of Great Britain against the flying bombs, also took part in this action. Between 13 June 1944 and 29 March 1945 (end of German fire), the attainments of these squadrons were as follows: Squadon 306 – 60 V–1; Squadron 315 – 53 V–1; Squadron 316 – 74 V–1. This amounted to 10 per cent of the 2000 bombs that were shot down. These squadrons however did not only defend the Isles, but also carried out flights over the Continent, in collaboration with the land troops. A similar task was also fulfilled by Squadron 307, which covered the landing operation near Arnhem.

All in all in 1944, Polish fighters in the West shot down 100 planes for sure, as likely as not eight more, and damaged twenty-four others. Squadron 315 distinguished itself with the most, with forty-five shootings to its credit.[49] In the period of the invasion two Polish Bomber Squadrons, 300 and 305, were also active, carrying out raids over the Reich and destroying communication networks, fuel reservoirs and airfields. Britons also served in Squadron 305, which was always commanded by a Pole; as also did Canadians, Estonians, and Norwegians, often officers who were senior both in rank and in age.[50]

At the time of the invasion the German fleet was already so weak that it could not oppose the power of the Allies, and only the torpedo boats tried their luck, thought almost without effect. In the night of 8 June five German destroyers left the port in Brest in an attempt to get at least as far as Cherbourg. They were spotted by air reconnaissance, and the 10th Flotilla of British destroyers split into two Squadrons, 19 and 20, set out to intercept them. Number 20 was led by the Polish *Błyskawica* (Lightning), and *Piorun* (Thunderbolt) also belonged to it. This division joined battle with the Germans, and *Lightning* hit the enemy vessel *ZH*, which was leading the formation, several times. Another British destroyer sank it by torpedo attack. After this battle the Germans made no further attempt to go out to sea, and for the first time in several years patrol tasks could be carried out along the French coastline in broad daylight, the only threat being that of the rather ineffective German batteries on the coast.[51]

20 'Tempest'; Communists' Manifesto, the Attempt on Hitler's life, Italy, 'Bridges'

After the battles of the 27 Volhynia Division of the Home Army, the next contact with the Red Army took place in the regions of Wilno and Nowogródek, in the next phase of 'Tempest'. Home Army partisan squads, the only Polish units on that territory, had already been active there for a long time and had been trying to co-operate with similar Soviet units, with varying rates of success. Several anti-German actions had been agreed upon, but had ended with the unexpected departure of the temporary allies from the scene of battle. The Soviet soldiers behaved as if they were on their own land; several times the situation led to the treacherous arrest of Polish officers and to Polish units being wiped out. At the beginning of 1944 an order dispelling any remaining doubts was found beside the body of a Soviet commissar from the Czapajew Unit:

> At 7 a.m. on December 1st Polish legionaries ('partisans') are to be disarmed. Their arms and papers are to be confiscated and the men and the arms are to be sent to the Polish camp Milaszewski, near the village Nestorowicze, in the Iwieniecki district. If the 'partisans' offer any resistance while being disarmed they are to be shot out of hand.[1]

Despite this threat and many other difficulties – for the Germans were, after all, still in control of the land – the Commandant of the Wilno District of the Home Army, Lieutenant-Colonel Aleksander

Krzyżanowski (*Wilk*), managed, in the summer of 1944, to gather together quite considerable forces amounting to about 6000 soldiers. He attended a briefing in the Home Army Headquarters on 12 June and there received the order that he was to head the forces of the Wilno and Nowogródek districts, and to attack Wilno as soon as the eastern front was close enough. This order altered the principle in force up till then, that fighting in large towns was to be avoided, although in Warsaw it had very soon been realised that if they were not captured, even just a short time before the Red Army crossed, the political effect of 'Tempest' would not be achieved.[2]

Wilk's forces consisted of three partisan groups situated a short distance from the city and a clandestine battalion within Wilno, but the attack carried out during the night of 6–7 July was not successful. The Polish units did not possess any heavy weapons and the Germans had been preparing to defend the city and had surrounded it with concrete reinforcements. Within a few hours, however, Soviet units appeared, communications were set up and thanks to the artillery and tanks, the battle took a different turn. The Germans defended themselves fiercely but on 13 July they withdrew from Wilno, blowing up the waterworks, power station, radio station and all bridges. Most of the churches and monuments were saved; although it had been blackened by fire, the famous picture of the Madonna in the historical Ostra Brama gateway remained unscathed.[3]

The liberated city experienced great joy when the Polish troops appeared on its streets and placed soldiers to guard the most important places. The Soviet authorities did not intervene for two days and did not hamper free movement about the city, especially in the northern part. During this time Lieutenant-Colonel Krzyżanowski was invited to meet the Commander of the 3rd Byelorussian Front, General Ivan Czerniachowski. He presented himself as *General Wilk* and was well-received. Political problems were not discussed and his proposal was accepted that the Poles should raise an infantry division and a cavalry brigade with Soviet arms and that they should make for the front.[4]

By 15 and 16 July the initially good relations were already beginning to break down. The Soviet authorities were creating various difficulties and *Wilk* received a further invitation to visit General Czerniachowski in Wilno on 17 July with the additional request that he should take all the officers on his staff with him. At the same time a briefing was to take place in the village of Bogusze for the Brigade Commanders and lower-ranking officers, and the

Polish units near Wilno were to be inspected by Soviet officers. All these instructions were a deceitful stratagem; *Wilk* and his officers were arrested, and the detachments trying to hide in the Rudnicki Forest were almost entirely surrounded and disarmed. In all, about seventy officers and over 6000 soldiers were arrested and taken to the camp near Miedniki, and later to Kaluga. Only a few, under pressure, reported to Berling's army. The officers were taken first to the Wilno prison and later to Riazan.[5]

Several hundred soldiers from the Home Army Nowogródek District, who had not taken part in the battle for Wilno and a few from near Wilno who had managed to avoid the Soviet trap, gathered under the command of Lieutenant-Colonel Kalenkiewicz (*Kotwicz*), the new Commandant of the Nowogródek region. At the last briefing, in the heart of the Rudnicki Forest he presented his plan:

> I want to get out of the operational area of the Soviet armies in order to cross to the rear of the retreating Germans; after crossing the German front I intend to continue the battle against the Germans from the forests of the Białystok area. If we are surrounded by Soviet armies and if they intend to disarm us, we shall fight.[6]

The march began at once, but the Soviet decision to disarm all Polish forces was ruthless. Kalenkiewicz was pursued by a motorised squad which could have been escaped in the forests but not in open country. The Polish column was divided into several smaller detachments; Kalenkiewicz himself, at the head of several cavalry units, pushed westward hoping to reach the Białystok forests. On 21 August the Soviet pursuit caught up with him near the forester's lodge at Surkonty. Many of the attackers were killed, but Kalenkiewicz and all but one of his officers and uhlans fell. The Russians had captured an armed position and thirty-two corpses.[7]

'TEMPEST' NEAR LWÓW

When once the fundamental decision had been altered within plan 'Tempest' and the battle for Wilno had been carried out, the same process took place in Lwów. The First Ukrainian Front, commanded by Marshal Ivan Koniev, was approaching the town inside which there were four German infantry divisions and one armoured. The

Commandant of the Home Army Lwów District, Colonel Władysław Filipkowski (*Janka*), had about 3000 poorly-armed soldiers at his disposal. These forces attacked the city on the night of 22–23 July, when the Red Army was already engaged in combat and when joint action with it might have a chance of success. After three days Lwów found itself in Polish and Soviet hands. Like Wilno it experienced a moment of freedom and also like Wilno it was rapidly overtaken by new events. On 25 July Colonel Filipkowski was invited to meet the Commander of the Front. There he offered to create a full Polish division; the offer was accepted, but two days later the Soviet authorities categorically demanded the disbanding of the Home Army units. Seeing that no resistance was possible, the District Commandant gave the relevant command and was himself taken, with several officers, to Żhitomir and later to a prison in Kiev. After him, the Government Delegate, who had come out of hiding, was arrested in Lwów and the remaining officers and other ranks were incorporated into General Berling's First Army. Some managed to go into hiding.[8]

It was particularly difficult to carry out 'Tempest' in Polesie since the Germans had broken up the Home Army underground there in 1943, by making arrests. Help from outside was essential and the Home Army High Command appointed a new Commandant for the District, a parachutist, Lieutenant-Colonel Henryk Krajewski (*Trzaska*). He created a force of about 3000, which was quite well-armed, thanks to the fact that arms had been carefully stored away since 1939.

After local confrontations with the Germans in June and July, the division made contact with the Red Army. Agreement could not, however, be reached on joint action while on the other hand, pressure to comply with General Berling's orders grew day by day. At the end of July the thrust of the Soviet units forced the division to cross the Bug. Krajewski hoped to join up with the Home Army forces there, but came to the conclusion that they had in fact been disarmed. He decided to march in the direction of Warsaw, where fighting was about to begin, but he had to demobilise 2000 soldiers, and only 1000 of the best-armed were to make their way in eight groups to the capital. This attempt was unsuccessful; many more soldiers had to be demobilised and only 200 continued the march, but Soviet units stopped and disarmed them. The officers were taken to prison in Kiev and the soldiers to Majdanek camp near Lublin, which they left only under General Berling's orders.[9]

The disarming of the Home Army units after joint tactical operations with the Red Army, the imprisonment of the officers and the forcing of soldiers into General Berling's army provided the clearest proof of what political stance Stalin had decided to take as regards the army and the underground administration dependent upon the Polish government in London. However, these acts took place to the east of the Curzon Line and for that reason Warsaw, in constant touch with London, considered that 'Tempest' must be continued as it was not known how the Soviet authorities would behave to the west of that line. The Poles did not recognise it, but they had to ascertain what situation would arise as the political moves of the government in London depended upon that. Besides, it was impossible to cease fighting the retreating Germans under any circumstances. Therefore 'Tempest' was continued and the Home Army High Command in Warsaw sent signals to London from the field. There they still expected the Western Allies to support the Polish side at last. A signal reached Warsaw from Lwów, from the District Commandant, the Government Delegacy there and the political representatives:

> We call for an allied commission, we beg for intervention on behalf of the imprisoned Home Army members and the Delegacy, who have been extremely badly-treated.

Mikołajczyk tried to do this. He demanded that a British military mission be sent to the field of combat but Churchill wanted Stalin's agreement to this and he, of course, refused to give it. The Home Army leadership also was still expecting changes in the attitude of the West and so sent a telegram to the local districts: 'Our political question is being dealt with; for the moment you cannot count on any help, but patience and endurance are essential'.[10] 'Tempest' therefore moved to the west of the Bug.

'TEMPEST' NEAR LUBLIN AND NEAR BIAŁYSTOK

Polish hopes, however, that the Russians would behave differently to the west of the Curzon Line turned out to be unfounded. In the middle of July divisions of the Home Army were mobilised in the Lublin area and under Colonel Kazimierz Tumidajski (*Marcin*) they took a series of towns from the Germans. The Soviet commanders profited from this help but when the fighting had ended, Colonel

Tumidajski and many other officers were arrested and the soldiers were either thrown into Majdanek camp or incorporated into General Berling's army.[11]

The 'Tempest' action ended in the same way in the Białystok District, where the local commander of the Home Army units, Colonel Władysław Liniarski (*Mścisław*), already aware of what had happened near Wilno, did not carry out full mobilisation. All those who did gather were arrested and disarmed by the Russians.[12]

It was to the west of the Bug that all this happened, on land which even Stalin considered purely Polish, land which after the war he never questioned as belonging to the Polish state. The Government in London was at once informed of these events and had to take them into consideration when making its next political moves.

ESTABLISHMENT OF THE POLISH COMMITTEE OF NATIONAL LIBERATION AND ITS MANIFESTO

The Soviet pressures on the Home Army forces to subordinate themselves to General Berling's army were precisely synchronised with its movement westward and its firm entrenchment on Polish soil. By now it had support, in the political home front, which had crystallised and unified conclusively during the previous weeks. A few months earlier the situation had looked different, vast differences of opinion had existed between the Polish Workers' Party in Poland and the Union of Polish Patriots in Moscow with relation to a future Poland and in order to discuss them a delegation from the Polish National Council presented itself in the Soviet capital in May 1944. Talks began not only with the Union of Polish Patriots but also with Stalin, and the Ambassadors of Great Britain and the United States. At the beginning of July a second delegation came to Moscow from the Polish National Council, in which the chief member was General Michał Żymierski. Further talks took place, under pressure from Stalin who wanted to create a political body which in the near future would become a rival to the Polish Government in London. He did not want to go too far; he was counting on the Allies in the West, so what would emerge had to be of a temporary nature. Nobody dared to question Stalin's authority at all, so on 21 July the joint forces of the Polish National Council and the Union of Polish Patriots created the Polish Committee of National Liberation. Osóbka-Morawski from Poland headed it, but its deputies were Wanda Wasilewska and Andrzej Witos from Moscow; of the fifteen committee members, ten came from the Union of Polish Patriots and only five from the Polish National Council, so in the first battle for power the communists in Russia won the day.[13]

Immediately the next day the Polish Committee of National Liberation issued a manifesto in Moscow, the main purpose of which was to gain the widest possible popularity among the Polish masses. It was therefore considerably less radical than might have been expected. The largest group in society was the peasantry, so they had to benfit most after the communists had taken power. There was no talk of collective farms, the Germans, traitors and the owners of estates over 50hectares were to be dispossessed. But the latter were to be paid larger sums, especially if they could prove their patriotism.

In industry only the German factories would be nationalised; the others would come under provisional state management but the owners would be paid compensation. Small and medium-sized workshops and businesses would remain in private hands. In the political field, the manifesto promised a return to the constitution of 1921, which was very liberal and democratic, and would remain in force until the first general election. Promises about the general availability of science and education, and the rebuilding of the country were an important question. As regards the frontiers, the manifesto repeated the Soviet attitude that the Polish eastern border must have an ethnic basis (and so would correspond to the Curzon Line), while in the west Poland must take the lands on the Oder and Baltic from the Germans. The manifesto also contained the usual patriotic phraseology and formulae about friendship with the Soviet Union and the Red Army.[14]

The manifesto was issued in Moscow but a few days later the Polish Committee of National Liberation flew to Chełm, in the Lublin district, which was already in Red Army hands. There were not enough suitable people in Chełm for any sort of work but fourteen departments, corresponding to ministries, were created. On 27 July the Polish Committee of National Liberation was very greatly strengthened by Stalin, who signed an agreement with it, giving it control in the liberated Polish territories to the west of the Bug. On 1 August the Committee moved to Lublin, which had just been liberated, and made further efforts to gain some sort of foothold in society.[15]

THE ATTEMPT ON HITLER'S LIFE

In the West, after the invasion of the continent, the war also began to enter a decisive phase. Practically nobody in the German High Command believed in victory any longer, despite Goebbels' noisy propaganda about secret weapons. The flying bomb (V–1) raids on London had already begun on 13 June, a week after the invasion of Northern France; those who were in the know were aware that a rocket attack (V–2) was going to begin any week, but this did not alter the realistic assessment that the war was lost. This state of affairs forced the *Schwarze Kapelle* to make one more attempt to destroy Hitler, for if they were successful there were hopes that the Western Allies would decide to negotiate an immediate cease-fire with the Germans and change their attitude towards their Soviet partner. If that had in fact happened, the entire distribution of forces in central Europe would have undergone a change which would have fundamentally affected the fate of Poland and her borders.

On 20 July Colonel Claus Schenk von Stauffenberg placed a bomb in the 'Wolf's Lair', Hitler's field quarters in eastern Prussia, during a military briefing. The bomb exploded but by a miracle Hitler was saved, and in Berlin Goebbels was able to control the situation. The conspirators were executed by firing squad, by cruel hanging or took their own lives; mass arrests began in Germany, and the Nazis remained in power. Hopes, although very feeble, for a cease-fire in the West and for a change in the course of events, now definitely disappeared.[16]

THE SECOND POLISH CORPS IN ITALY

The victory of the Second Polish Corps at Monte Cassino opened the way to Rome and on 4 June, forty-eight hours before the landing in France, the American Fifth Army entered the Eternal City, with no resistance from the Germans. Field Marshal Kesselring believed that the Italian capital should not be fought over because of its great value to world culture, and despite Hitler's orders he considered it 'an open city'.

After its tough action and heavy losses, the Polish Corps needed some time to change equipment and reorganise those units that had suffered most. Unfortunately it had no reserves; General Alexander did not believe that those Poles who had been captured and incorporated by force into the Wehrmacht could fill these gaps and he wanted to reorganise the Corps into an infantry division, strengthened by armoured units. The commander of the Corps was strongly opposed to this and stood his ground, as he considered that he must be allowed to act independently. Not long afterwards he was proved right over the question of reserves from the prisoner-of-war camps.[17]

At the end of May the Corps received a new task. The Indian divisions that had until then been active on a stretch of the Adriatic, had to be transferred to the central section of the Front and Poles were to take their place. The outward move began on 15 June and two days later General Anders took command of the whole section in the Pescara region. He not only had his own corps under his command but also two British artillery regiments, an armoured regiment, many units of sappers, liaison and anti-aircraft, as well as a whole Italian corps. His numbers were up to strength but they were poorly-equipped, especially in transport. The initial task consisted of securing the middle strip of the roads linking Pescara and Aquila, by which the right wing of the Eighth Army received supplies, but before it could be started there was a change in plans. A new order was issued that the pursuit of the retreating Germans should be organised and the port of Ancona taken as quickly as possible. This was absolutely essential as the Allies had already moved far to the north. Ancona was to fulfil this role on the Adriatic and Livorno was to do likewise on the other side of the Italian peninsula.[18]

The change of order and the new task did not come at a good time for the corps as it needed rest and time to reorganise, and above all it had no means of transport for moving units and providing them with sufficient supplies. There was also a serious problem with those sappers who had been taken to the Rome section; and the terrain was difficult, as a belt stretched between the eastern slopes of the Appenines and the Adriatic, 25–40km wide and crossed by a large number of rivers. The retreating Germans blew up all the bridges and mined the roads; these all had to be repaired, which delayed the march of the tired units, and it was to have been a rapid pursuit. They moved forward, however, and on 1 July, after several days of marching and combat, reached the Musone river; they crossed it in several places and the eight-day battle for Loreto began. The victorious outcome enabled the troops to take up good positions before the attack on Ancona began.[19]

General Anders' plan anticipated that the port town would be taken by an outflanking movement from the west, while a pretence that the main attack was going to take place on the coast was maintained.

The attack started in the early morning of 17 July and after one day of battle it ended in almost complete success. Only the 6th Brigade of Rifles, which had had to struggle over hard terrain and cross the river Musone, was late in circling round from the north; it reached the coast a few hours too late and that allowed the Germans to withdraw a part of their forces. In the afternoon of 18 July the 14th Regiment of Uhlans entered Ancona, the port of which had escaped destruction. Almost 3000 prisoners and a lot of equipment were taken, but their own losses were heavy: thirty-four officers and 150 other ranks died, a further 116 officers and 1850 other ranks were wounded. The commander of the Eighth Army, General Leese, valued the Polish victory highly; it had brought about the rapid capture of an important port, which solved the supply problem.[20]

'BRIDGES'

The Allied victories in Italy also made it possible considerably to improve air communications with Poland, and the dropping of parachutists and supplies. Immediately after the southern part of the country had been captured, the reorganisation was begun of bases which were important to the British as they significantly reduced the distance to countries of importance to them, Greece and Yugoslavia in particular.

The problem of Poland had already become an embarrassment to the Western Allies. They did not want to help the Poles to amass arms for a possible uprising but they were still interested in sabotage and diversion, and for that reason the Polish base began to move to Brindisi on the Adriatic, 450km to the south-east of Rome, as early as October 1943.[21]

After a long period of flights, cryptonym *Intonation*, which came to a halt at the end of April 1943, a new period began under the cryptonym *Riposta*. Its beginning dated formally from 1 August, in Great Britain, but few flights were carried out from there. The transfer later took place and important operations began in spring 1944, from Italy. The Polish special duties Flight No. 1585 was also moved there and joined British Wing No. 334, which had the same special designation.

All flights to Poland from Great Britain were abandoned after these transfers and the two routes, over Denmark and over Sweden, were completely forgotten. New routes from Brindisi to southern Poland were marked out. Route no. 3 ran over Lake Balaton, skirted Budapest from the west and made for the Tatra Mountains. The distance to Cracow in one direction was 1000km, to Warsaw a further 450km. Route no. 4 left Budapest from the west side and reached Poland to the east of the Tatra. It was the same distance from the base as route no. 3. Route no. 5 passed even further to the east, over Albania and aimed directly for Lwów; the distance was 1100km.[22]

The transfer of the base to Italy and the resultant delay, political considerations and the appalling spring weather greatly weakened the operations. While *Riposta* was being carried out, from 1 August 1943 to 31 July 1944, 300 drops were promised but barely 205 were accomplished, while Poland was expecting as many as 500 operations. 146 parachutists were dropped (135 soldiers, ten political couriers and one woman), 286 tonnes of supplies, over 16 million dollars in banknotes and gold, 6.5 million German marks and over 40 million Polish occupation zloties. Sixteen planes and crews (five Polish and eleven British), four parachutists, 13.4 tonnes of supplies and over 1 million dollars were lost. Unfortunately the Home Army did not receive sufficient arms during its most crucial period of action.[23]

Some very complicated operations, cryptonym *Most* (Bridge), were also carried out from Brindisi. Night landings were to be made at a secret landing place in occupied Poland; people were to be transported in from the West, and politicians and emissaries were to be taken out in the opposite direction. The most difficult problem on the spot was that of finding a suitable landing place, which had to be about 1km in length and breadth, to allow for a sudden change in wind direction; it also had to have a hard flat surface, so that the wheels of the plane would not sink more than a few centimetres, and the surrounding area had to be clear of high trees and chimneys. Of course the landing place had to be in a part of the country where the occupying forces were not too numerous and where the vast partisan organisation could provide sufficient security.

The light signals marking the landing place were different from those used when parachute drops were made. Stable lamps were placed around the edges of the landing area, at distances of 75m; the side from which the plane was to approach the landing place against the wind was marked by three green lights and the opposite side with similar red lights. The direction of the landing was indicated by two paraffin flames at a distance of between 1 and 2km from the green lights. A runway officer was in command of the personnel manning the secret landing strip, and answerable to him were those in charge of the lights, the radio operators and the commander of two units providing armed cover; one of these guarded the landing place, and the other the take-off routes.[24]

Radio communication was important since the landing place had to maintain contact with the base which sent the plane, according to an established plan, cryptonym *Jodoform*. Everything was of importance in these complicated operations: not just the overall danger, but also any sudden change in the weather – any rain or snow or a strong wind from the wrong direction. All this caused extra complications, especially as the distance was about 1000km in one direction and the operation would last many hours.

Finally the question remained of what plane would be suitable to make the flight to Poland, land on an ordinary field and take off from it again. The heavy bombers, Liberators, Lancasters and Halifaxes, were out; the Lysander, which was indeed light and was used for flights into France, but which was not far-reaching enough, was also excluded. The choice fell on the American transporter, the Dakota, which had two engines and weighed only 11000kg.[25]

The distance to Poland, even from southern Italy, was so great, however, and the landing operations so complicated that only three were carried out, a negligible amount in comparison with the 112 landings in France. The first flight took place on the night of 15–16 April 1944, and it was treated as an experiment, carrying only post and two passengers into Poland. Four people were brought out, the landing place used was near Bełżyce, not far from Lublin. The second flight took place faultlessly on 29–30 May; only six minutes elapsed from the moment of touch-down on the *Motyl* landing strip near Tarnów to the moment of take-off.[26]

The last two-way operation, on 25–26 July, was the most important for it took three important people out of Poland: Tomasz Arciszewski (*Tom*), appointed by the political underground as the successor to the President of the Polish Republic; Jerzy Chmielewski (*Rafał*), taking parts of the V–2 and a report about it to London; and Józef Retinger (*Salamander, Brzoza*). His presence in Poland and his return to the West demand a special note.

From the moment that General Sikorski was taken from France to Great Britain, after the western front was broken, he became the

Polish premier's inseparable companion (except on that last, tragic journey) and he played quite an important, though still unexplained, role in Polish affairs. In spring 1944, a period of hot, political activity, when he was already 56 years old, he decided to parachute into Poland without any prior experience and when he landed, on 3–4 April, he injured his leg. Officially, he had been sent by the Polish Ministry of Internal Affairs and Premier Mikołajczyk knew of his journey, but in fact he was most probably in Churchill's confidence. His whole trip was shrouded in great secrecy and he entered the plane wearing a mask. He held talks in Poland with a number of people from the underground and was most likely seeking a *modus vivendi* between the Polish Underground State and the communists. He was to return to the West by the quickest route and the plane in *Most* landing no. 2 was expected to take him back. For inexplicable reasons, however, he did not reach the landing place in time and the cart carrying him also overturned; Retinger fell into icy water and lost the use of his legs. He had to wait for *Most* no. 3 and returned to London via Italy in a bad condition, still with almost no power in his legs. Nothing came of his mission.[27]

21   The Warsaw Uprising

DECISION TO FIGHT

In the original version of Operation 'Tempest' fighting in large cities was not contemplated. This had been changed and fighting had taken place for Wilno, Lwów and Lublin, but it did not mean that the Home Army would also fight for Warsaw. The Germans had plundered the Polish capital, cultural relics and works of art had been carried away, monuments and historical buildings destroyed, but the city with more than a million inhabitants still remained. The archives, museums, libraries were still there and they ought to be preserved for future generations. The population ought also to be protected as far as possible and therefore, in March 1944, Warsaw was excluded from Operation 'Tempest'. The Home Army units were to help the civilians when the city passed from German into Soviet hands and were themselves to evacuate to the West and there stand up to the Germans.[1]

This logical attitude, however, started to crumble under the influence of the failure of Operation 'Tempest'. the Prime Minister, Mikołajczyk, hoped to make political capital out of it, but without success. The Red Army was marching forward, Poland was changing hands, the Home Army divisions were fighting the Germans and co-operating with the Soviet commanders – and all this was happening without echo, because the Western leaders had already sealed the fate of Poland and had no intention of changing their decisions.

In the occupied country, as well as in London, the leaders appreciated the value of a fight for Warsaw, but they were not united in their opinions as to what should be done. In the HQ of the Home Army opinions were divided in relation to Soviet Russia and her behaviour in the event of an uprising. If the military commanders, politicians and Government Delegate in Warsaw had difficulty in reaching a common decision, the differences in London were even greater. Mikołajczyk was still trying to be active politically and considered the fight for Warsaw as his last trump in the dialogue with

276

the West, hoping also that an agreement with Moscow was still possible. Sosnkowski, as always irresolute and undecided, one day was in favour of fighting, another day strongly against it. He was definitely opposed to any discussion with the Russians and in his opinion Mikołajczyk's plans to go to Moscow were the first steps towards treason. This divergence of opinions was clearly shown in the dispatches sent to Warsaw by both leaders. Their dualism made the difficult situation of the underground leaders in Warsaw still worse and confirmed their conviction that, when the moment of decision would come, they would be left alone, to decide by themselves.[2]

SOSNKOWSKI IN ITALY AND MIKOŁAJCZYK IN MOSCOW

During this heated period, when at any moment the situation could demand decisions, General Sosnkowski decided to go to Italy for a round of courtesy visits, inspections and presentation of medals. All these functions were only a pretext. Premier Mikołajczyk planned to go to Moscow in a desperate attempt to change Stalin's attitude towards Poland and Sosnkowski considered this as a step towards treason. If, under pressure from Churchill, the Polish premier should capitulate in Moscow and accept a compromise, the Polish Commander-in-Chief, among his soldiers, would refuse to obey his own Government.[3]

Before leaving London Sosnkowski sent a signal to the Home Army commander with an enigmatic opinion for and against an uprising in Warsaw. This made no impression on the underground political and military leaders, they were accustomed to this tone from the Commander-in-Chief and accepted the fact that they themselves would have to decide on any further action. The majority of the officers of the HQ of the Home Army did not trust Russia and did not believe that an uprising would be successful.[4]

Unexpectedly the initiative was taken by General Okulicki who had left Russia with General Anders, but did not stay with him and volunteered for service in occupied Poland. He had jumped on the night of 21–22 May 1944 and reported to the HQ of the Home Army, bringing with him a personal letter from General Sosnkowski with the nomination to the post of one of General *Bór's* deputy commanders. He had enjoyed the full confidence of the Commander-in-Chief and before his jump into Poland had had a long conversation with him. On 21 July he put his point of view to General *Bór* and his Chief of

Staff, General Pełczyński, and they both accepted his arguments. They were carried out in two ways.

The first was strictly military. In their retreat from Russia, the Germans were making use of every large town as a stronghold, especially if it stood on a river, in order to prolong their resistance. They could be expected to do the same in Warsaw, which was not only a big city, but an important communications centre. If it were destroyed, it would suit them admirably. But if a Soviet attack on the city were supported by a rising within it, the battle would be shortened and the destruction of Warsaw averted. Not all the officers of the HQ of the Home Army accepted this point of view; some of them advised against attempting to co-ordinate a rising in Warsaw with the expected attack by the Russians, as they doubted their good faith, to say nothing of the fact that there was no liaison with them. But finally the purely military argument was accepted.[5]

However it was not the most important one. In 1939 Poland's situation had appeared completely desperate, no-one could have imagined that the Poles would beat the Germans, allied with Russia; yet Poland had gone to war and fought single-handed, though she had allies in the West. Then for five years an underground state and army were built up in preparation for the day when the Poles could hurl themselves on the enemy and drive him from Polish soil. That day was now at hand. The Germans were about to evacuate Warsaw. After all the years of preparation and subversion, resistance and hope, was the city now to change hands without any recognition of the fact that it was Polish? This problem was also connected with clarifying the very complicated political situation and pressing Stalin to show his cards. So far there were only acts of hostility against Polish underground forces by the Red Army, but these had all taken place in territory which the Russians regarded as their own. It was not clear what the Russians would do to the Home Army and the Polish political authorities in Warsaw, in territory to which they laid no claim.[6]

Next day the decision of the three Generals was accepted by the HQ of the Home Army and by the Government Delegate. General *Bór* also referred this important problem to the Central Committee of the Council of National Unity, in the presence of its Chairman and the Government Delegate, and obtained unanimous acceptance.[7] The men who made these important decisions in Warsaw, were aware of the fact that there had been an attempt on Hitler's life. The German dictator had survived, but this attempt was the best proof of the difficulties inside the Third Reich and the chances that it could collapse any time. They were also aware of what had happened at Wilno and of the fate of *General Wilk* and his soldiers, but this would not have restrained them in their decisions. Wilno was situated to the east of the Curzon Line and there were foundations for hope that the Russians would behave differently on the Vistula. So the underground leaders decided to begin a fight for the capital without consulting London and as a result a dispatch was sent by General *Bór* on 25 July to the Polish Staff in England:

> We are ready to fight for Warsaw at any moment. Participation of the Parachute Brigade would have immense political and tactical effect. Please make arrangements so that Warsaw airfields can be bombed at our request. Will inform you of time fixed for outbreak.[8]

Before this dispatch reached London, the Polish Government was aware that it had lost control over events in occupied Poland and that the authorities in Warsaw would decide for themselves if and when they would begin the fight for the capital. Mikołajczyk was in favour of this action, because he expected to gain some trump cards as the result of it. He tried to secure approval for the decisions made in Warsaw and therefore his Government, on 25 July, passed a resolution:

> The Council of Ministers has decided to empower the Government Delegate to take every decision required by the speed of the Soviet offensive, in case of need, without prior consultation with the Government.[9]

Next day the Government gave its consent to Mikołajczyk's journey to Moscow. This was no new matter, but it was well that it had received the Government's *placet* since there were differences of opinion and some of those in the know were aware that General Sosnkowski's departure for Italy was connected with it. The Prime Minister went to Moscow under strong British pressure, but this time it was well-founded. Poland had no diplomatic relations with Russia, but the latter was now a decisive factor on Polish territory and this fact had to be reckoned with. Stalin had agreed to a meeting with the Polish Premier and this opportunity could not be wasted, although he held almost no trump cards in negotiations with the Soviet dictator.

But in politics there are no lost causes until they have been confirmed by the facts. Mikołajczyk, without making any concessions or agreeing to the Curzon Line, might obtain from Stalin if not a promise at least some information as to how he intended to behave on the Polish territory to the west of the River Bug. There was much difference of opinion in the Polish camp on this question: some argued that there would be no Poland at all, but only a Soviet republic; others expected certain Soviet concessions; there were even those who counted on positive intervention by the Western Allies. It was a courageous journey, proving that Mikołajczyk was well aware of his duty as Polish Premier and did not flinch from it. On the airfield itself, on 26 July, he was handed an encoded dispatch from General *Bór* saying that Warsaw was prepared to fight.[10]

The decisions taken in Warsaw and in London were, of course, closely connected with events on the front. From 23 June, when the 1st Byelorussian Front moved forward on the central sector, Marshal Rokossowski had smashed the German forces and achieved several successes. His divisions, together with the Polish First Communist Army, had captured Lublin and on 25 July crossed the Vistula at Puławy. Further to the north they captured Garwolin and at Magnuszew had made a second crossing of Poland's largest river. It looked as if the capital would be partly encircled from the south.[11]

The German authorities had started evacuation in the spring, moving depots and army magazines and even some factories to the west, but now the haste became panic. All public offices, even the Gestapo, were on the move, German families were gathering at the railway stations, between 23 and 25 July all departure roads were crowded. Suddenly, on 26 July, part of the administration returned and next day, through the loudspeakers, it was announced that 100 000 men had to report themselves for work on fortifications. It was obvious that Warsaw was to be defended.[12]

SOVIET ENCOURAGEMENT

At the same time Communist propaganda became louder and louder each day. In its underground papers and leaflets the Home Army was attacked for its passivity and the Home Army soldiers were encouraged to move to the People's Army where they would get a chance to fight the Germans. In the second part of July this propaganda was strengthened by the Soviet radio, which through the station *Kościusz-*

ko, speaking in Polish, started to call on the population of Warsaw to take up arms against the occupants. In the last days of July this propaganda was already very aggressive:

> Warsaw already hears the guns of the battle which will soon bring her liberation. Those who have never bowed their heads to the Hitlerite power will again, as in 1939, join struggle against the Germans, this time for a decisive action.
>
> The Polish Army, trained in the USSR, now entering Polish territory, is now joined to the People's Army to form the Corps of the Polish Armed Forces – the armed core of our nation, in its struggle for independence... For Warsaw, which did not yield, but fought on, the hour of action has already arrived.

The above text was intercepted on 29 July and the next day the station *Kościuszko* broadcast a much more clamorous appeal:

> Citizens of Warsaw! To arms! The whole population should support as one man the National Council and the underground army. Attack the Germans, prevent the plan of destroying public buildings. Help the Red Army in its efforts to cross the Vistula.

Even the most sceptical had started to believe that the capture of Warsaw by the Red Army was only a matter of days.[13]

During the last days of July Home Army units were already mobilised and had gathered in many secret places all over the city. The officers of the HQ met daily and observed events on the front. The Soviet armoured units were advancing unopposed in the region of Otwock, on the south-east outskirts of Warsaw, and Soviet aircraft were in the skies above the capital. On 31 July, at 5 p.m., Colonel Antoni Chruściel, the Commander of the Home Army in Warsaw, arrived at the secret HQ of General *Bór* and reported that Soviet tanks had captured Radzymin. Some hours earlier a radio communiqué from the German command had given out that the Russians had started a general attack on Warsaw from the south-east. At the same time General *Bór* received a dispatch from London that Premier Mikołajczyk had gone to Moscow. There was a chance of an agreement with the Russians and to synchronise action between the Home and the Red Armies. There were only two Generals, Pełczyński and Okulicki, with General *Bór* at that time, as well as Colonel Chruściel and Janina Karaś (secret liaison), but the Home

Army commander decided to act. He sent for the Government
Delegate and when the latter arrived and gave his consent, General
Bór turned to Colonel Chruściel and said: 'Tomorrow, at 5 p.m.
precisely, you will start operations'.[14]

POLISH AND GERMAN STRENGTH

Even assuming that the Red Army would take advantage of the
uprising and try to capture the city as soon as possible, the insurgents'
strength was insufficient. Colonel Chruściel had at his disposal in
Warsaw about 30 000 soldiers and a further 10 000 around the city.
All of them belonged to the Home Army, except for 800 members of
the National Armed Forces and 500 of the People's Army. It might
perhaps have been enough, but they were very poorly equipped.
They had twenty heavy and ninety-eight light machine-guns, 1386
rifles, 604 machine-pistols, 2665 pistols, 50 000 hand-grenades, two
anti-tank guns, two Piats and twelve anti-tank rifles. These figures are
taken from the statistics for February 1944, but after this date some
equipment had been sent to the east, to the fighting units of the
Home Army. During the fighting, as the result of drops, the
insurgents gained thirteen mortars, 150 light machine-guns, 230 Piats,
300 machine-pistols, 950 pistols and over 13 000 hand-grenades, but
all these quantities were small in comparison with the enemy's
armament.[15]

The strength of the German forces fluctuated. They were reinforced on 20 August and on some days were as many as 40 000 men.
They consisted of:

Police	8 000
Party units (SS, SD, SA)	2 000
Waffen SS	5 000
Airmen	6 000
Vlasov's[16] Army	4 000
Wehrmacht (sentry and military schools' battalions, car park attendants, some reserve units)	15 000
	40 000

They were well-armed, possessing artillery, tanks and planes, and
their combat value and determination, especially of the *Waffen SS*,
airmen and police, as well as the party units, were highly regarded.[17]

EFFORTS TO SECURE AID AND NEGATIVE SOVIET ATTITUDE

Immediately on 1 August, the Government Delegate and the Home Army Commander sent a dispatch to London, reporting that fighting had begun. On the same day they sent a second message to the Prime Minister and Commander-in-Chief, demanding that they would arrange an immediate Soviet attack on the city. Unfortunately, even before this dispatch was sent, the Soviet guns had fallen silent and Soviet aircraft disappeared from the sky. There was no liaison at all with the Red Army, there were no diplomatic relations with the Soviet Government, Mikołajczyk had only just arrived in Moscow and the Western Allies had not been informed about the planned uprising in Warsaw. It was even worse: when General *Bór* on 25 July sent his signal to London, he did not know the technical possibilities of the Air Force and that his demand for the bombing of targets near Warsaw was unrealistic. Nor did he know that the same applied to dropping the Parachute Brigade and that the Polish Government, together with the Polish Commander-in-Chief, at the beginning of June, had decided that the Brigade would take part in the invasion of Northern France. The problem of the Polish Air Force was no better. The only Polish air unit which was capable of aiding Warsaw was No. 1586 special duties Flight, stationed at Brindisi.[18]

In this situation the Poles started a hastily improvised action to urge the Allies, and above all the British, to send the utmost possible help to the capital. First of all Ambassador Raczyński made representations on behalf of the Polish Government. He was received by the Under-Secretary of State, Sir Alexander Cadogan, who reported his request direct to Churchill. The following afternoon, on 3 August, the Ambassador saw the Prime Minister and handed him a letter from President Raczkiewicz, who also sent another letter to the King, George VI, and a telegram to President Roosevelt. Jan Kwapiński, Mikołajczyk's deputy, saw Eden; General Kopański wrote to and saw General Ismay; Generals Kukiel and Tatar tackled other military personages. Individual politicians also tried to use their contacts and influence. On 6 August General Sosnkowski at last returned from Italy and immediately began his own intervention, mostly in the form of letters. He wrote to Marshal Sir Alan Brooke, the Chief of the Imperial General Staff; to Air Marshal Sir Charles Portal; to General Maitland Wilson, the Allied Commander in the Mediterranean area, and to the Secretary of State for Air, Sir Archibald Sinclair. The demands were three: immediate assistance for Warsaw by air drops, recognition of the Home Army soldiers as combatants and pressure on Russia to alter her attitude to the uprising and to give it help.[19]

At that time Premier Mikołajczyk was already in Moscow. He had arrived there on 30 July, but was not received by Stalin until 3 August. He wanted to come to an agreement on four main points:

1. The establishment of lasting Polish–Soviet relations based on co-operation against Germany.
2. The securing of an agreement about the taking over of the administration of the liberated Polish territories (after Stalin's agreement with the Polish Committee of National Liberation this issue was no longer topical).
3. The establishment of the Polish Government as soon as possible in Poland, augmenting it with members of the Polish Workers' Party, and to hold a democratic election quickly. A further important point was the demand for immediate help for fighting Warsaw.

Stalin promised to undertake to drop arms into the city, but pushed aside the other points, arguing that Mikołajczyk must meet the representatives of the Polish Committee of National Liberation. There were two meetings, but they did not produce any significant results. The Committee demanded the abrogation of the 1935 constitution and the establishment of a new government in which they would have fourteen of the eighteen members.

Several days passed before Stalin received Mikołajczyk again on 9 August. Once more he promised aid for Warsaw, but when, after a completely fruitless visit, the Polish Premier returned to London, a dispatch from Moscow was waiting for him:

> Now, after probing more deeply into the Warsaw affair, I have come to the conclusion that the Warsaw action is a reckless adventure, taken without the knowledge of the Soviet command... So the Soviet headquarters have decided to dissociate themselves openly from the Warsaw adventure since they cannot assume any responsibility for the Warsaw case.[20]

This was the result of the intervention with Stalin, but with Churchill it had produced an immediate effort. In the early morning of 3 August Air Marshal Sir John Slessor, the Commander of the Air Force in the Mediterranean area, received an emergency signal from London about the uprising in Warsaw. The British Government considered the matter important and urgent. Drops were to be started at once if it was technically possible.

SUPPLY FLIGHTS FROM ITALY AND ONE FLIGHT BY US AIR FORCE

Slessor had at his disposal the Polish special duties Flight No. 1586 and the British Squadron No. 148, but in his opinion the task was almost impossible. The distance from Brindisi to Warsaw was 1500km, the August nights were short and those planes which had not been shot down over the Polish capital would have to return to their bases by day, over Hungary and Yugoslavia. There the heavy bombers would be an easy target for the German fighters. He had a lot of sympathy for Poland and understood Stalin's political game and the Warsaw tragedy, but he had to defend his soldiers and gave in only under the most severe pressure. During several nights only Polish volunteers flew to Warsaw, against the opinion of their British commander.

The night sorties to the fighting city (see Table 21.1) were an epos of heroism, technical difficulties, every possible intervention, erroneous and groundless accusations and Soviet treachery. Two opinions should be quoted here of Poles who knew the problem from their own experience. General Ludomir Rayski, the pre-war Commander of the Polish Air Force, an experienced pilot, who himself made five flights to Poland during this time, two of them to Warsaw, reported as follows:

> The crews return in aircraft holed like sieves. Even their parachutes are so shot to pieces that they would be useless if needed...
> In operations over Germany the losses are 3–5 per cent, in operations over Poland more than 30 per cent... The crews sent lately are young, newly-trained airmen, used to instrument flying. All the flights to Poland require skilled navigation by landmarks. They depend wholly on this and are the very opposite of instrument flying... From the Polish point of view this is a suicidal waste of airmen.

The views of Squadron Leader Eugeniusz Arciuszkiewicz, commander of 1586 Flight during the uprising, who himself flew over Warsaw, are quoted in the following message (20 August 1944):

TABLE 21.1. Flights and drops during the Warsaw rising

Drops on Warsaw, Kampinos Forest and Kabacki Woods from 1 August to 2 October 1944

	Took off					Mission carried out					Lost					Warsaw		Kampinos and Kabacki Woods	
	Polish	British	S. African	American	Total	Polish	British	S. African	American	Total	Polish	British	S. African	American	Total	Dropped	Picked up	Dropped	Picked up
1 4.8	7	7	—	—	14	3	—	—	—	3	—	5	—	—	5	2	2	1	1
2 8.8	3	—	—	—	3	3	—	—	—	3	—	—	—	—	—	3	3	1	1
3 9.8	4	—	—	—	4	4	—	—	—	4	—	—	—	—	—	—	—	—	—
4 12.8	5	6	—	—	11	4	3	—	—	7	—	—	—	—	—	7	5	4	4
5 13.8	4	4	20	—	28	3	2	4	—	9	—	2	—	—	2	9	5	—	—
6 14.8	5	6	15	—	26	2	3	8	—	13	1	3	4	—	8	11	10	—	—
7 15.8	3	4	—	—	7	3	2	—	—	5	—	—	—	—	—	—	—	2	2
8 16.8	5	4	9	—	18	2	2	3	—	7	2	2	4	—	8	—	—	5	5
9 17.8	4	—	—	—	4	1	—	—	—	1	—	—	—	—	—	—	—	7	7
10 18.8	2	5	—	—	7	—	—	—	—	—	—	—	—	—	—	1	—	1	1
11 20.8	4	—	—	—	4	3	—	—	—	3	1	—	—	—	1	—	—	—	—
12 21.8	4	—	—	—	4	2	—	—	—	2	—	—	—	—	—	—	—	2	1
13 22.8	2	—	—	—	2	—	—	—	—	—	—	—	—	—	—	—	—	2	—

	Date																		
14	23.8	3	—	—	—	3	2	—	—	—	2	—	—	—	—	—	—	—	2	—
15	24.8	6	—	—	—	6	6	—	—	—	6	—	—	—	—	—	—	—	6	4
16	25.8	7	—	—	—	7	4	—	—	—	4	—	—	—	—	3	—	—	4	—
17	26.8	5	—	—	—	5	—	—	—	—	1	3	—	—	—	2	1	—	—	—
18	27.8	4	—	—	—	4	1	—	—	—	2	2	—	—	—	4	1	—	2	1
19	1.9	7	—	—	—	7	2	—	6	—	9	3	1	1	—	5	7	—	2	—
20	10.9	5	4	—	11	20	1	—	—	—	1	1	—	—	1	1	1	—	2	2
21	13.9	2	—	—	—	2	1	—	—	—	1	—	—	—	—	5	7	—	—	—
22	18.9	—	—	110	—	110	—	—	—	107	107	—	—	—	2	2	107	19	—	—
23	18.9	—	5	—	—	5	—	3	—	—	3	—	—	—	—	—	—	—	3	—
24	21.9	—	5	—	—	5	3	—	—	—	3	—	—	—	—	—	—	—	—	1
Total		91	55	50	110	306	47	17	21	107	192	17	13	9	2	41	149	44	43	27

Notes: All aircraft which crashed while landing are included in the table.

 1. Aircraft crashed while landing. 3 drops outside Warsaw.
 5. Also 2 'blind' drops outside Warsaw.
 6. 1 aircraft crashed while landing.
 8. 2 aircraft crashed while landing.
 9. Only 7 packages were picked up.
10. 1 'blind' drop outside Warsaw.
11. 1 aircraft crashed while landing crew saved.
12. From 1 drop on Kampinos 12 packages were picked up.
17. 1 aircraft crashed while landing.
19. 1 drop outside Warsaw.
20. There is no confirmation that Warsaw picked up 5 drops.
22. 1 aircraft landed completely shot up.
23. The aircraft turned back on the way.

The commander of 1586 Flight informed me to-day that in the present state of the anti-aircraft defence of Warsaw and, as experience has shown, precision drops from the height of 600–800 ft are impracticable. In his opinion sending aircraft to Warsaw in practice amounts to the loss of aircraft and crews without any guarantee of supplying the troops in the capital.[21]

But the above opinions were not heeded and the Polish airmen continued their flights over Warsaw, unfortunately for the most part without success.

HOME ARMY UNABLE TO HELP WARSAW FROM OUTSIDE

Only during the first few days, thanks to the surprise attack, were the insurgents able to take the initiative and some of their attacks on German strongholds were successful. But the Germans were able to hold on to all their military barracks, offices and important factories, which were guarded by the army. By 4 August the insurgents' impulsion had already weakened, their command had ordered them to confine themselves to defence only, and the Germans, using tanks and aircraft, were taking offensive action. To secure free transit from east to west they captured the Kierbedź bridge and some of the streets leading to it. The whole city was cut into separate districts, the insurgents' actions were restricted to defence, with some sporadic attacks and local successes. From the very beginning the German units, together with Vlasov's soldiers left no illusions as to what would happen to the population if they finally won: mass executions, rape, driving a human chain in front of their tanks, setting houses on fire.[22]

On 14 August the Home Army Commander issued an order that the Districts which were carrying out Operation 'Tempest' should change their plans and start to march towards Warsaw in full strength. The first to react was the District Radom which had mobilised about 30 000 soldiers in two infantry divisions and co-operated with the Red Army, helping it to take two bridgeheads on the Vistula at Magnuszew and Baranów. The command selected 5000 of the best-equipped soldiers and ordered them to march towards Warsaw, but the German defence on the River Pilica was so strong that the units had to abandon this operation and return to local fighting. The Home

Army partisan units in the Kampinos Forest had also tried to break through to Warsaw, but without success.[23]

POLITICAL EFFORTS TO FIND A COMPROMISE WITH USSR

Mikołajczyk's trip to Moscow, having helped to make clear the Soviet position and its attitude towards the Polish Committee of National Liberation, gave occasion to formulate a Polish point of view, which could be a basis for the settlement of Polish–Soviet relations. The problem was very serious, because half of Poland was already in Soviet hands and Warsaw desperately needed help. The Government in London had already prepared an appropriate five-point statement. The first point concerned the formation of the Government in free Poland and presumed that apart from the four major parties, the Polish Workers' Party would also be included; the second concerned diplomatic relations with the Soviet Union as well as the free elections and a new constitution; the third, the continued war against Germany with the support of numerous alliances; the fourth express-ed the view that in the east Poland should retain the economic and cultural centres; the fifth point dealt with the Government's war work. The majority of the Government accepted this statement, but the representatives of the Polish Socialist Party put forward their own text which precluded any eastern losses as well as any co-operation with the Polish Committee of National Liberation. In such a situation the Government had no option and on 22 August sent both state-ments to fighting Warsaw – the government statement as text *A* and the Socialist as text *B*.[24]

Between 28 and 30 August the Council of National Unity discussed the two statements and after heated debates unanimously accepted the Government declaration with nine amendments. These con-cerned the behaviour of the Red Army on Polish territory, the release of all Polish citizens arrested by the Soviets, endorsement by the Western Allies of the Polish Soviet compromise, and recognition of the reconstructed Polish Government, both by the Western Allies and the Soviet Union. The politicians in Warsaw were critical of the governmental statement and did not accept any resolution; the Commander of the Home Army categorically rejected it as being 'utter surrender'. On 31 August the Council of Ministers in London unanimously accepted text *A* with the amendments of the Council of National Unity. Discussions and exchanges of views still continued and objections were raised by political parties. However, what was important was that the Council of National Unity in Warsaw and the Government in London accepted the same text.[25]

SURRENDER OF OLD TOWN AND SOVIET DROPS

The second half of August saw the converging German attack on the Old Town which, although defending itself to virtually the last standing house, was still utterly ruined and passed into German hands on 1 September. The insurgents got into the city centre by going through the sewers. The loss of the Old Town as well as the capture by the Germans of the ruins of the ghetto created a break in the fragile chain of Polish defence. The Germans were now able to direct more of their forces against the city centre. By now this was the third phase of the uprising which consisted only of defence beyond the limits of human endurance. However, the Home Army Command still remained hopeful that a Soviet attack would take place; they sought contact with the Red Army and suppressed all thoughts of capitulation. The Germans also were taking into account the possibility of a Soviet attack and thus in the first days of September captured the riverside area, between the Kierbedź and Poniatowski bridges.[26] On 30 August the Governments of the United States and Great Britain declared that they would recognise the Home Army as 'an integral part of the Polish Armed Forces'. This recognition applied to all members of the Home Army and was a warning to the Germans. On 18 August the German Commander, SS General Erich von dem Bach-Zelewski, put forward a proposition of surrender with a guarantee of combatant rights and the Warsaw leaders began to consider the possibility of the fighting coming to an end. During the first days of September the Council of National Unity considered this problem and contacted the Home Army Commander as well as the leaders in London. The first contact with the Germans took place on 8 September when they agreed to the evacuation from Warsaw of a group of civilians. Von dem Bach repeated his proposal of honourable surrender but before it could ever be considered, the atmosphere in the capital improved. Sounds of battle from the east side of the Vistula were heard. On 10 September the Red Army launched an attack which lasted until 15 September and concluded with the take-over of the whole district. At the same time, overnight on 13–14 September, the first Soviet air-drops of arms and food took place.

Two days later, on 16 September, in the Czerniaków district, near the Poniatowski Bridge, an infantry battalion of the First Polish Communist Army landed. The following day, near Żoliborz, there was a further landing of infantry units. There were now distinct possibilities of Soviet aid and all thoughts of surrender were put aside.[27]

US AIR FORCE BIG FLIGHT

Apart from the instructions he had sent to Italy, to Air Marshal Slessor, Churchill turned his eyes eastward. It had been decided at Teheran that to the west of the River Bug, there would be an independent Poland. Stalin had signed this, so there was no reason why he should not offer his help to Warsaw. On 12 August Churchill appealed for the first time to the Russian dictator to aid the fighting city and allow Western planes to land on Soviet airfields. Two days later the British and Americans made a joint appeal. On 16 August the American ambassador received a curt refusal, and on the same day a similar answer went from Stalin to Churchill. To make their attitude perfectly clear, the Russians added that they would not even permit the use of their airfields by damaged Allied aircraft with wounded on board. The Western leaders did not give up and on 20 August addressed a further, sharply-worded message to Stalin on the question of landings. A peremptory 'No' came two days later.[28]

Churchill lost his patience and was in favour of overriding Stalin's refusal and informing him that the planes would land on Soviet airfields, but he could not do this without Roosevelt's agreement, and the latter refused to reply jointly in this sense. He too was indignant, but he did not want to add to the tension, bearing in mind that he still needed Soviet help against Japan.

Besides the flights from Brindisi in which Polish, British, Canadian and South African crews took part, the Polish authorities had tried to secure American help. A large airlift with thousands of containers full of arms, ammunition and medical supplies could have redressed the balance of forces. Before mid-August, after some intervention, the Americans agreed to the use of their powerful Eighth Air Force of Flying Fortresses (B-17) stationed in Britain. Preparations were begun, but the operation was impossible without Soviet permission. The colossal machines, flying by day only, required a fighter escort and would have had to land behind the Russian lines. The Americans had a base at Poltava, 2500km from Britain, but Russian permission had to be sought for every single flight.

In the hope of Soviet agreement, preparations were pushed forward. The Polish Section of SOE was faced with an unprecedented problem, because the Americans were willing to provide only the planes, crews and a fighter escort. Each Fortress, with a crew of ten, could take twelve containers. As it was proposed to send 110 Fortresses the Section had to find 1320 of the giant metal cigars, weighing 100kg each.

The 1320 containers were loaded with:

Sten guns	2976 with ammunition
Bren guns	211 with ammunition
Piats	110 with shells
Revolvers	545 with ammunition
Gammon grenades	2490
Hand grenades	4360
Plastic expl.	17523 lbs.
Instantaneous detonating fuses	59492 yards
Safety fuses	9536 yards
Detonators	21990
Tins of meat	23520
Tins of biscuits	2016
Tins of margarine	2016 lbs.
American rations	5820
American milk rations	5820
Medical equipment	12 containers

At long last, on 12 September, after many interventions, telephones and telegrams, the Russians agreed to the landing. The weather was bad, but at last, on 18 September, the great armada took off. It started despite local fog and made for southern Denmark, escorted by seventy fighters. In Warsaw the weather was fine, but the burning city was engulfed in heavy clouds of smoke. The insurgents were fighting with their last vestiges of strength, it was thirty-four days since they had received a single drop from the West. They had ceased to expect any, so the appearance of a colossal air armada was met with indescribable enthusiasm. Two days earlier some landings took place from the other side of the Vistula. Was there still a chance for a change of fortune for the fighting capital?[29]

Unfortunately Warsaw was already mostly in German hands; the insurgents were occupying only small and widely-spread enclaves, the containers fell far and wide and many of them were collected by the enemy. As a result, of the drop of 1284 containers the Home Army safely picked up only 228 of them, and 32 more had to be fought for. The hopes raised by the landings from the other side of the Vistula also were not fulfilled, as they were liquidated by the Germans in a couple of days. The Soviet drops also were only in a small proportion successful, as they had no parachutes and suffered destruction on landing.

CAPITULATION

On 2 October, after exceptionally bloody fighting that had lasted longer than anyone had anticipated, and was marked by German atrocities, Warsaw had to capitulate. The agreement contained the clause that all the Home Army soldiers and all other formations subordinated to the Uprising Command would be protected by the Geneva Convention of 27 July 1929 concerning prisoners-of-war. Further the agreement said that the whole population must evacuate the city and leave it empty.[30]

SUMMARY OF RESULTS AND LOSSES

The huge Warsaw effort unfortunately ended in defeat from the military and political point of view. First of all the Polish capital, a city of over 1 million inhabitants, was almost completely destroyed and under the ruins were buried historical relics and art collections of priceless value. That which was not destroyed during the fighting by artillery fire and bombs, was later demolished by special German units which systematically blew up and set on fire whole streets. The exact figures of the losses among the civilian population will never be known, but it is estimated that between 150 and 200 000 lost their lives. The insurgents lost more than 10 000 killed and 5000 missing, almost certainly also dead. 7000 were severely wounded. All of them belonged to the best, the most dedicated of the young Polish generation. 20 000 of the insurgents were supposed to go into German captivity as prisoners-of-war, together with General *Bór* and his Command, but German sources quote only 11 668 and they are presumably right. Many soldiers, at the last moment, had decided to stay with the civilian population. The German losses, according to their own sources, were 10 000 killed, 7000 missing and 9000 wounded, and were higher than the Polish losses, when soldiers alone are taken into consideration. The percentage of losses of both belligerents altogether was very high.[31]

The military defeat was the more painful for the Poles as once again they had to surrender to the Germans, when on the other side of the river stood the victorious opponents belonging to the Allied camp. They were on the eve of victory and had at their disposal a mass of modern military equipment and millions of soldiers.

However what was even more painful and had greater consequences was the political defeat. It went deeper and further than even the most negative forecasts of the pessimists. The only positive result was that it proved to the whole world how wrong were the decisions undertaken in Teheran and just how untrustworthy an ally the Soviet Union was. At Teheran both Western leaders agreed to shift Poland westwards, but at the same time, together with Stalin, they decided that Poland would be independent and self-governing. Taking Warsaw as his prime example, the Soviet dictator brutally showed how he understood the agreement and how he saw the future Poland. The attitude of their Soviet partner offended both Churchill and Roosevelt; however they did not draw any conclusions from it and left Poland at his mercy.

Each defeat, especially when it is as painful as the tragedy of Warsaw, always leaves a taste of bitterness, a wave of criticism, a trail of sorrow and reproach, claims and accusations. In the early days all this is very emotional.

Looking back on the whole question through the perspective of the years, remembering the historical significance of the Warsaw uprising and the heroism of the young soldiers and airmen, remembering the suffering of the population and the destruction of a large city, it is important to realise that everything that happened was the result of earlier political decisions. Once the Western leaders had abandoned Poland to Stalin, Warsaw found herself in a situation in which victory was impossible.

The tragedy of the city should not, however, lead to unfounded accusations concerning the help sent by air from the West. Some of these accusations were addressed to Air Marshal Slessor who opposed the flights and forbade them, thereby reducing the aid to Warsaw. The facts and figures should be examined.

The Air Marshal had at his disposal the Polish special duties Flight No. 1586, the British Squadron No. 148 and two further Squadrons of Liberators, the British No. 178 and the South African No. 31, both specially withdrawn from flights over the south of France. Only these units, specially rebuilt, could reach Warsaw and return to their bases.[32]

Out of sixty nights of the uprising, from 3 August (when Slessor received orders to commence the sorties) to 2 October, twenty-five were lost because of bad weather and on twelve more there was a full moon, so that flights were banned. During the remaining twenty-three nights sorties were carried out to the maximum possible limit of the number of crews and aircraft. A look at the table of sorties shows that from 15 August onwards the drops on Warsaw did not reach the insurgents. Even if sorties had been undertaken during the forbidden periods, they would only have increased the losses, which were colossal, with no gain to the fighting city. The cessation of the sorties after 21 September was due only to very bad weather.[33]

From the Italian base 196 Polish, British and South African aircraft took off, but many turned back half way or even earlier. Only forty-two managed to reach Warsaw and drop supplies. To achieve this small result thirty-nine planes were lost – more then 90%! Of these forty-two drops the insurgents picked up only twenty-five. Another forty-three drops were made also on the Kampinos Forest and the Kabacki Woods, but they had no serious significance for Warsaw. Of the eighteen Polish crews that flew over Warsaw during the uprising, only two survived this period, so that 160 per cent of the establishment of the special duty Flight, together with the reserve, was lost. The British and South African percentage of loss was even greater, for altogether twenty-two crews were lost. The Americans in their great operation lost only two planes and eleven airmen, but they flew under privileged conditions and the effect of their drop, made from a great height over a small area of the city still in Polish hands, was minimal (see Table 21.2). Out of 1284 containers only 228 were picked up by the insurgents, and even this figure is not certain. Altogether in Warsaw and the Kampinos Forest 100 tonnes of supplies were picked up: 80 tonnes of arms and ammunition and 20 tonnes of food and medical equipment.[34]

Existing documents confirm that the Second Soviet Armoured Army was thrown back on 3 August by the German Armoured Corps which on 28 July passed over by rail via Warsaw to the eastern bank

TABLE 21.2 *Airmen who flew to aid Warsaw, the number shot down and their subsequent fate*

	Poles	British and South Afr.	Americans	Total
Number that flew	637	735	1 110	2 472
Number shot down	112	133	11	256
Survivors of those shot down	34	7	—	41

Note: Of the 112 Polish airmen whose planes were shot down, 78 were killed, 28 were taken prisoner and 6 reached Home Army units, after baling out. Similarly 7 British and South African airmen were saved. After baling out, they fell in with Home Army units.

of the Vistula and gave support to the German Ninth Army. Its task was the defence of German positions from Warsaw to Dęblin and Puławy, preventing any crossing of the Vistula, especially to the south of the capital which would have allowed the Red Army to surround it. The Soviet defeat at Okuniew due east of Warsaw, undoubtedly delayed, if only for several days, the possibility of a Soviet attack and a rapid capture of the city. According to contemporary German data, purely professional, in no way propaganda, the Russians were massing army units there. 'The use of such forces shows that the enemy places great importance on crossing the Vistula and taking Warsaw, all the more so when the Vistula presents the last serious barrier before the German frontier'.[35]

Thus one must reject the post-war explanations of Rokossowski, Zhukov and Shtemenko that the German victory prevented any earlier Soviet attack and was only possible on 10 September, when an eastern suburb, Praga, came under Russian fire. Again one has to look into the records of the German Ninth Army: 'Day after day, when German action in this region aimed at the destruction of the III Soviet Armoured Corps, was already over, Moscow radio stations spoke of strong German thrusts to the east of Praga and dressed up these claims with details of battles which from beginning to end were complete lies'.[36] Had Stalin really intended to help Warsaw, he would not have refused the Allies the right to land on their airfields and the Red Army would not have disarmed the Home Army units marching to the capital's rescue. The landings at Poniatowski and Kierbedź Bridges, the airdrops over Warsaw which amounted to 40 tonnes of arms and ammunition as well as 15 tonnes of food, and the agreement for the American armada to land near Poltava – all these gave an impression of wanting the capital's agony to continue rather than offering definite aid.[37]

It appears likely that this aid would have been completely different had the leadership of underground Poland not decided to pursue the fight for Warsaw. Appeals by Soviet radio for the capital's population to show the Red Army their support during the crossing of the Vistula, would have been capitalised by the People's Army whose leadership gave orders to take over important sites in such a situation. There was an applicable proclamation of the communist National Council on 30 July and discussion on welcoming the Soviet forces and the take-over of power in the city by the communists. Only then when it was certain that the Home Army would at any moment begin the struggle to free the capital, did Bierut and Gomułka leave Warsaw and move to the eastern bank of the Vistula.[38]

RECAPITULATION AND CONCLUSION

From the beginning of the conspiracy the underground army leaders, with the backing of the politicians, thought of a general uprising, having both planned and prepared for it. Had favourable conditions allowed an all-Polish boost, there would have been struggles for all the towns. As a general uprising did not take place and only a 'Tempest' was ordered, the decision to save the towns was the right one. The course of events, however, forced an alteration to these decisions; Wilno, Lwów and Lublin were fought for and finally the difficult decision to fight for the capital was taken. In the political situation of the time it was the correct decision, but nobody could later say that he was not aware of the tremendous risks involved. The venture was complete improvisation, both militarily and politically. It was impossible in ten days to prepare the capital for the fight and there was no possibility of securing enough outside aid. After Teheran it was known that Poland would be left alone to deal with her eastern neighbour. There were no diplomatic relations between the Polish Government and Moscow, and the Home Army had no links with the Red Army. It was a very difficult, virtually hopeless situation, caused by the politics of the Western powers, but that was no secret. Even under such conditions the fight for the capital should have taken place, but was it right to count on Russian aid?

With this complex and unfavourable background all the insufficiencies of earlier Polish planning, mutual decisions and information came to the fore. In occupied Poland the situation did not look too bad, because although there were certain drawbacks, there was also a certain correct co-operation between the Council of National Unity, the Government Delegacy and the Home Army Command. The decision to fight for the capital was undertaken in unison, however it immediately transpired that underground Warsaw was not aware of the Western political decisions or of the technical limitations in the air. This is best illustrated by General *Bór's* signal of 25 July demanding the Parachute Brigade and bombing of airfields around Warsaw. This was repeated in the signal of 8 August. In his other messages as well as in the appeals of underground politicians to Western leaders it was plain that they knew nothing of the Teheran decisions.[39]

The responsibility for this state of affairs lay with London where the situation was worse than in underground Warsaw. Between the Government and the Premier on the one hand and the Commander-in-Chief on the other there lay a vast chasm, a divergence of opinion on basics. While Mikołajczyk was doing all he could to get support from Western leaders and decided on a visit to Moscow, General Sosnkowski was in opposition to everything and everybody. As Commander-in-Chief he not only had the right but the duty to give Warsaw the order 'to fight or not to fight'; he gave no such order. As he could reasonably have expected the uprising to erupt, he should have confirmed the technical possibilities of coming to Warsaw's aid; he never did so. The most critical days were approaching and at any hour he could have been needed at his post. He was not there, but had gone to Italy. At a crucial period for the uprising he issued his controversial Order No. 19. In it he stated that in 1939 Poland had resisted the German attack because she was persuaded to do so by the British Government. He continued by strongly criticising the insufficient aid for fighting Warsaw, without taking into account what was technically possible.[40]

This Order is a document which best shows the confusion of ideas and the tangled web of correct but overdue reflections alongside a complete misrepresentation of facts and military–political realities. It was the reason for Sosnkowski's dismissal by the President of Poland under pressure from the Polish and British Governments. This took place on 30 September and the same day the nomination for Commander-in-Chief was given to the Home Army Commander, General Tadeusz Komorowski (*Bór*) who was to take up his new post and new responsibilities as soon as he found himself at the seat of the President and Government.[41]

One must accept that the decision to fight for Warsaw would have taken place even had the underground leaders known of the decisions taken at Teheran. This does not, however, alter the fact that the Government and the Commander-in-Chief were responsible for the lack of information, as well as the lack of definite warning about the technical possibilities of the Western Allied Air Forces. The aim of the struggle was a final effort by Poland to tell the world that she was fighting for the freedom to which she had a right, an effort to awaken the conscience of the West responsible for the Polish tragedy. This was partially successful. The Western leaders were moved and for the first time lost patience with Stalin. The evidence of an enemy historian is of great importance and value. The German, Hans von Krannhals, at the very beginning of his book on the Warsaw Uprising has included the following: 'Here and nowhere else the "Cold War" between East and West commenced'.[42]

Unfortunately neither Roosevelt's nor Churchill's anger had any further consequences.

22 Polish Units in Further Combat; Conference in Moscow

LIBERATION OF PARIS

At the same time as Warsaw was hopelessly fighting for its very existence, events in the West were taking a very different turn. After his defeat at Falaise, von Kluge was removed from command and committed suicide probably because he was also involved with the *Schwarze Kapelle* and the attempt on Hitler's life. He was succeeded by Field Marshal Walther Model.

On 15 August the Americans with French units landed in southern France. Two days later General Patton reached the Seine, north-west and south-east of Paris. At that moment the French capital rose with the same aim as Warsaw had done: to liberate the city with their own hands. Street fighting began, and Hitler ordered that Paris must be destroyed, if necessary by bombardment. However the military commandant of the city, General Dietrich von Choltitz, ignored the dictator's order. General Eisenhower had had different plans but he adjusted them to the new situation and accepted General de Gaulle's suggestion that the capital be liberated as quickly as possible and that at the vanguard of the Allied forces entering Paris should be General Jacques Leclercq's 2nd French Division. On 24 August, after a week of fighting, Paris was free. The following day de Gaulle arrived in the capital and took over provisional rule.[1]

1ST ARMOURED DIVISION IN FRANCE AND HOLLAND

After Falaise the 1st Armoured Division, having had a few days rest, gave chase to the retreating Germans towards Abbeville and Ypres. It was nearly a triumphant march of the Polish soldiers who were

300

enthusiastically greeted by the liberated French towns. The actions against the Germans were not so tough and bloody as before. Abbeville, St Omer, Cassel, historic Ypres and Ghent were captured, the last two on Belgian soil. In under twenty days the Division had advanced nearly 500km, suffered only small losses and had taken 4000 prisoners and much equipment. After the battle for Antwerp undertaken with the British, in mid-September, the Divison found itself on Dutch territory. In front of the Polish tanks was Breda, the capital of the Catholic part of Holland.[2]

After further fighting and a period of defence, between 6 and 26 October, a large-scale Allied operation began with the aim of capturing the beautiful town. The Germans, expecting the attack to come from the west and south-west, had strengthened their positions there and had dug a massive anti-tank trench. If the attack had been launched in that direction, the battle would have been tough and the Allies would have used their Air Force and massed artillery with the result of seriously damaging the town. Wanting to avoid this, General Maczek prepared a plan of attack from the east and began his manoeuvre on 27 October, concluding it with great success. After four days the town was free. The main task had been accomplished and the Division took up positions in Breda for the winter. This was essential after the loss of 367 killed and 1325 wounded, especially in the rifle companies whose effective strength was reduced to 60 per cent. The only reinforcements were Poles, German POWs, surrendering voluntarily.[3]

The stay in Breda was one long period of receptions and pleasure. The gratitude and hospitality of the Dutch surprised the Polish soldiers, who did not expect such joyful enthusiasm from what they regarded rather as a cold nation. The whole division received honorary citizenship of the town. At each step warm friendship, nearly love, was shown, as victorious troops were treated in their own country. The Dutch have remained faithful in their gratitude and friendship. Many years have passed and the graves of Polish soldiers are still looked after by schoolchildren. The parishes cultivate Polish traditions and care for Polish mementoes.

ARNHEM AND THE 1ST PARACHUTE BRIGADE

All Polish military formations fighting outside Poland experienced the same hardship of fighting on foreign soil while Warsaw was reaching for its last reserves to avoid defeat. The same fate was to overtake the Independent Parachute Brigade, which for purely technical reasons could not be flown into Poland and was placed by the Polish Government at the disposal of the British who were planning an attack on northern France.

The use of the Polish paratroopers was not foreseen in the first phase of the invasion of the continent, as they had still to be equipped for use in the second phase. The moment came when the first phase was completed, when the invasion forces had a strong hold on northern France, and when the Western Allies especially the senior commanders began to believe that the European war could be brought to an end in 1944.

In mid-September, Field Marshal Montgomery, whose forces were now east of the Somme and had taken Brussels and Antwerp, came up with a detailed plan. The main assault was now to have been directed against the Ruhr, the industrial centre of Germany. However it was covered by the Siegfried Line from the Swiss frontier to Belgium, but not covering the German–Dutch border. Montgomery proposed that instead of a frontal attack due east, an assault be made through Holland, by-passing the Siegfried Line from the north and then turning south against the Ruhr. The whole plan would have to encompass two operations: the parachute forces would have to gain control of the bridges and canals in Holland, whilst the land forces would attack from the south. Their task would be to reach Eindhoven and Nijmwegen, joining up with the American airborne forces, pressing on to Arnhem to reach the British and Polish parachutists. General Eisenhower accepted the plan and put at Montgomery's disposal two American airborne divisions: the 82nd and 101st.[4]

The plan was good, but the speedier conclusion of the war was probably not the only aim. One week after the invasion of France the first flying bombs, the V-1, fell on London, and caused serious damage. Unpleasant though this was, it was not especially dangerous since the bombs could be held up by means of barrage balloons, anti-aircraft artillery and fighters. However the German secret weapons did not end at this. On 8 September the first V-2 rockets fell on London. They caused not only serious damage but great consternation. The British feared the rockets most as they flew with great speed in the stratosphere and there was no defence against them. The following day Montgomery received alarming news on this subject. He requested an immediate meeting with Eisenhower and within twenty-four hours presented his plan of attack on Holland with the additional information about the rockets. He received Eisenhower's agreement. For London it was of great importance as it was from Holland that the Germans launched the V-2 rockets. The speedy capture of that country would cancel the threat. Northern France and Belgium were already in Allied hands and the range of the rockets was not more than 320km.[5]

The quickly-prepared operation began on 17 September. Both American airborne divisions took their objectives in Eindhoven and Nijmwegen. The Thirtieth British Corps gained contact with them after four days but its further advance was halted by minefields and a strong German defence. This had disastrous consequences, as further north at Arnhem the situation was critical. First, there were two SS Panzer divisions in the area. They were to undergo reorganisation but were still excellent combat formations. It is still uncertain whether Montgomery received news about this but either he ignored it or his intelligence failed. The fact is that the 1st British Airborne Division was dropped, but not on the most important bridge on the Rhine, near Arnhem but more than 10km further. The element of surprise was lost, though the first battles were successful. Part of Arnhem was captured, as was a bridgehead across the Rhine. However by the following day German superiority made itself felt. The next day, in the framework of the second echelon, part of the Polish Parachute Brigade arrived by glider formation, and the second part the following day. It brought heavy arms, anti-aircraft artillery, radio stations and signal equipment. Only on 21 September did the main bulk of the Brigade take off from Britain in 114 planes, but it was ordered by the British Command to turn back. Sixty-one planes received the order and returned, the rest continued and dropped 1067 paratroopers, among them the commander, General Sosabowski.[6]

The incomplete Brigade landed south of the Rhine, near Driel, being under German fire even during the landing. The situation was bad. Arnhem was in German hands and the British division on the opposite side of the Rhine, in Oosterbeek, was completely surrounded. It was necessary to form a base of defence to prevent being pushed back from the positions held as British land forces were coming from the south, and at the same time to cross the river and bring relief to the encircled division. There were only few boats, though during the night, suffering heavy losses, sixty soldiers managed to reach the other bank. Earlier General Sosabowski had made contact with General Urquhart, the overall Commander, after having sent an officer who swam the river. The following night, thanks to the boats supplied by the most forward units of the Thirtieth Corps, further forces of the battalion with anti-tank guns and part of Brigade HQ were got across. On 23 September the remainder of the Brigade which two days previously had been turned back, was dropped some distance from Driel. It reached the town by foot and began to cross the river, but with little result; the German fire was too strong. On 25 September the order was given that all forces fighting north of the Rhine were to cross to the south, link up with the Poles in Driel and together head south. Only 2163 soldiers of the British division with 140 Poles crossed the river.

The operation was a failure. The Arnhem bridge remained in German hands until April 1945; 1200 men were killed and 3000 captured. The Polish Brigade lost forty-nine killed (four of them officers), 159 wounded (twelve of them officers) and 173 missing (sixteen of them officers). Unfortunately this élite Polish formation, prepared for the most modern warfare, did not taste the joys of victory. Moreover it fought with the knowledge that at the same time Warsaw was dying.[7]

SECOND POLISH CORPS IN ITALY

After the capture of Ancona the Second Corps had a respite, whilst new combat tasks were allocated to the Polish soldiers. In front of them the Allies had the next German fortifications, known as the Gothic Line, from Pesaro on the Adriatic to La Spezia on the other side of Italy, which had to be broken. The main assault was to be undertaken by the Eighth Army on either side of Florence. The Fifth American Army was to gain control of the Pistoia area, whilst the Poles were, through their activity, on the Adriatic to pretend that an attack would be launched there, against the German defensive line.

The central attack in the mountainous and difficult terrain against strong German opposition, failed. It was decided to change the plan and break the line on the Adriatic where the terrain was flatter and with Ancona as a supply base. The task of the Second Corps changed. It was to push the Germans across the Metauro river and prepare a starting-point for the Canadian and British Corps. After heavy artillery, armoured and infantry fighting the task was accomplished between 19 and 22 August.

Eighth Army Command deployed its forces in such a way that the British Fifth Corps was on the left western flank, the Canadian First

Corps was in the centre and the Polish Second Corps on the Adriatic. Its task was to reach the Fogila river, by-pass Pesaro from the west and capture the hills sprawling north-west of the town. The battle began on 23 August and lasted to 2 September, when the Gothic Line was finally broken and the Second Corps ended its three-months fighting along the Adriatic. Its losses were 288 officers and 3403 men killed and wounded.

After a good respite the Polish Corps was moved to the western flank of the Eighth Army, where the terrain was mountainous, with bad roads. There it was to advance along the Santa Sofia–Galeata–Forli axis. The fighting was difficult but with results and by mid-December the Eighth Army reached the Senio river whilst the Second Corps took Faeza. Losses amounted to forty-three officers and 627 men killed, and 184 officers and 2630 men wounded. Only thirty-three men were missing, probably in German captivity.[8]

Beside directing military operations the Corps Commander was also concerned with politics and flew several times to London. Both he and his troops feared that under the pressure being brought to bear by the Allies and in the newly-created situation, the Polish Government might agree to territorial concessions towards Russia. The majority of soldiers of the Second Corps came from the eastern lands and in their minds a compromise was unthinkable. Their fears proved groundless.

In this period reinforcement of the Corps became a possibility, as over 40 000 Poles were in Allied hands. They were prisoners-of-war from the German army who had surrendered on the battlefields or came from German prisoner-of-war camps in France, recently liberated. A certain number of Poles reached France having escaped from internment in Switzerland. The Allied command decided that 20 000 Poles from the German army would be transported from southern France to Italy and placed at the disposal of the Polish authorities. General Anders also put forward a proposal that all Polish land forces should be joined under his command. Nothing came of this. The arrival of prisoners from France enabled the organisation of three new brigades. During the winter the Corps limited its actions to the minimum necessary for defensive purposes.[9]

GENERAL OKULICKI – NEW HOME ARMY COMMANDER

After the capitulation of Warsaw and before General *Bór* and his staff went into German captivity, he issued his last radio order on 3

October to district commanders in which he said: 'I nominate as my successor in the underground citizen *Niedźwiadek*'.

This was the new pseudonym of General Okulicki, who had been kept in reserve as Commander of the Home Army, in case the uprising failed. He had not taken part in the uprising and had preserved total anonymity, only replacing the Chief of Staff, who was wounded, for a few days. Now, on 3 October, he left Warsaw together with its civilian population, escaped from the convoy to Germany and eventually arrived in Radom where the District HQ of Home Army was located. There, with the support of the local network, he started the arduous task of rebuilding the shattered Command.[10]

General *Bór's* last radio order was received in London, where General Kopański, who performed the duties of Commander-in-Chief, wondered how to interpret it. It could refer to the Home Army command, but it could likewise concern the new underground organisation *'Nie'* that was currently being planned, and which was to be created in the event of the Soviets taking over the entire country. The situation was exceptionally difficult, the more so as the new Commander-in-Chief, General Komorowski, had been made prisoner and could not perform his duties.

The first news to be received by London from Poland was a signal from General Okulicki, dated 6 October. The following day Okulicki sent a second signal in which he stated that he had left Warsaw on the orders of General *Bór* 'with the task of assuming command over all underground activities in Poland under both German and Soviet occupation'.[11] This was concrete information, though it failed to clarify what was the general scope for action in Poland, so General Kopański decided to send a reliable man to the occupied country. The situation was critical, for with the fall of Warsaw the HQ of the underground state had also been shattered.[12]

The choice fell on Group Captain Roman Rudkowski (*Rudy*– Redhead) who had already made one parachute jump into Poland in January 1943, and had returned by 'Bridge' No. 2. His next descent was carried out in the night of 17–18 October, and the Group Captain found his way to Okulicki in Czestochowa, the new HQ of the Home Army. From there he sent a dispatch to London: 'There is monstrous chaos and lawlessness in the districts... Poldek (i.e. Okulicki) is the only man in such a situation. I am sure he will manage to curtail the anarchy if you give him the authority of *Bór* and inform the districts accordingly.'[13]

Unfortunately this swift and accurate assessment did not evoke so swift a reaction from London. The President of the Polish Republic procrastinated with the nomination of Okulicki, as he wished for a consensus of opinion, so meanwhile the reconstruction of the echelons of the shattered underground army in Poland was considerably hampered. Work was carried on in extraordinarily primitive conditions, many underground commanders did not want to recognise General Okulicki as their new leader, and it was imperative to establish contact with the Government Delegation, which was located in Cracow.[14]

A particularly difficult problem was the continuation of action 'Tempest' in central and western Poland, which were still under German rule. Radom District had two infantry divisions under arms, comprising a total of about 7000 soldiers, and could at any moment summon a further 30 000 from the underground, if only equipment could be found for them. Cracow District was halved, as the Red divisions had halted on the banks of the river Wisłoka. However the part that was still under German occupation formed an Operational Group, amounting to some 3500 soldiers. The Cracow Cavalry Brigade operated by means of independent detachments. Silesia district was also mobilised, with the aim of setting up two divisions, of which only the first ultimately came into being.

Both were mobilised in the area of Cracow District, as Silesia was annexed to the Reich and therefore had no such possibilities. Finally Łódź District launched into action during the period of the Warsaw Uprising, mobilising a total of 1200 soldiers, and several partisan detachments. All these units were poorly equipped and were waiting for drops. The period of autumn rains and winter was approaching, and general supplies were in a bad way, hence a tangible lowering in morale that had already been undermined by the disaster of Warsaw. General Okulicki visited these detachments, giving them moral encouragement, but he often encountered difficulties stemming from his unclarified position of commander.[15]

CONFERENCE IN MOSCOW

The disaster of the Warsaw Uprising shattered the Poles in London and considerably weakened the position of Premier Mikołajczyk who placed his political hopes in the fighting force of the Home Army. He now no longer had this last trump, and could count only on pressure from the Allies on Stalin to alter his stance on the Polish issue. Chances were minimal, for the Soviet dictator had attained all he wished for, he had the Polish Committee of National Liberation in his pocket, and on 1 August he exchanged diplomatic representatives with the Committee although he did not yet consider it to be the Polish Government, and had no cause for hurry. Churchill however still entertained the hope that he would strike some sort of bargain, and that some small concessions on the part of the Soviets would persuade the Polish Government to compromise. He attached much importance to a renewal of Polish–Soviet discussions and he obtained Stalin's agreement to issue a fresh invitation to the Polish Premier.

Mikołajczyk arrived in Moscow on 12 October, and the first joint meeting took place on the following day. Apart from the Premier, Tadeusz Romer, Minister for Foreign Affairs, and Stanisław Grabski. member of the National Council, took part on the Polish side. The British were represented by Churchill, Eden and Archibald Clark-Kerr, the British Ambassador in Moscow. Stalin was accompanied by the Soviet Ambassador in London, Fyodor Gusev, and by Molotov, who was in the chair. The American Ambassador, Averell Harriman, was there in the capacity of observer.[16]

The basic problem of the whole conference and of all additional discussions and meetings was the Polish–Soviet frontier, which was to adhere to the Curzon Line or, something the Russians would rather forget, the Ribbentrop–Molotov line of 1939. This matter had already been decided in Teheran, but had not yet been formally promulgated, emendations and changes were not impossible, and Churchill sought a formula that the Polish delegation would swallow. Following his suggestion the Poles could accept the proposed frontier 'on practical grounds' in order to facilitate further discussions with the right to appeal in the future to a peace conference. Before the Polish delegation had time to adjust to this proposal, Stalin butted in with the claim that this was unacceptable to the Soviet Union and that Polish acceptance of the Curzon Line must be expressed forthwith. There could be no question of such an agreement, as in the first place the Polish delegation did not have the authorisation of the whole Government. Second, no Polish Government could hope to stay in office after taking such a decision. Churchill aimed nevertheless at an understanding, and in a number of separate discussions resorted to every kind of persuasion – including shouting, to convince Mikołajczyk. On his way to Moscow the Polish Premier obviously knew that an agreement would only be possible at the price of a compromise, so after the sharpest exchange of views with Churchill he proposed a new formula: if Russia agreed to return Lwów and the oilfield of Borysław to Poland, he would endeavour to convince his Government of the need to accept the rest of the Curzon Line. He was in a position to make this proposal, as he already had the agreement of his Government and of the Council of National Unity for such a solution. Churchill immediately took the proposal to Stalin, who rejected it out of hand.[17]

The British Premier made a new proposition. If 'the Polish Government were prepared to recognise the necessity of accepting the Curzon Line as the basis of a future Polish–Russian frontier', Poland would receive a joint British–Soviet guarantee of her new territory. This variation did not catch on either: all possible arguments concerning the frontier had been exhausted, and there remained only to discuss the future Polish Government. The British however wanted to gain something and prepared the formulation that 'the Polish Government of National Unity under the chairmanship of Premier Mikołajczyk would be created without delay on the territory freed by the Russian armies'. This was a purely theoretical proposal, which had no chance of being realised, for when Mikołajczyk met Bierut, the latter testified quite simply, 'We have assumed responsibility for a democratic Poland and must therefore have a majority of 75 to 25 per cent in the government'.[18]

The only hope for the Polish Premier was now President Roosevelt. In June 1944, in Washington, he had promised Mikołajczyk that he would help Poland to keep Lwów, Drohobycz and Tarnopol and the American principle was not to accept territorial changes before the end of war. Mikołajczyk now wanted to find out what position Roosevelt adopted and whether he acceded to Stalin's demands.[19]

A letter was sent on this subject to Ambassador Harriman, but it was only after Roosevelt was elected for the fourth time, that the Ambassador handed the President's letter to Mikołajczyk.

1. The Government of the United States of America 'stands' unequivocally for a strong, free and independent Polish state, with the untrammelled right of the Polish people to order their internal existence as they see fit.
2. In regard to the future frontiers of Poland, the American Government will voice no reservations if a mutual agreement is attained between the Governments of Poland, the Soviet Union

and Great Britain, including the proposed compensation for
Poland at the expense of Germany. In so far as the United States
guarantee of any specific frontiers is concerned I am sure you will
understand that in accordance with its traditional policy this
Government can make no such guarantee.[20]

MIKOŁAJCZYK'S RESIGNATION

After this clarification it became apparent that there were no longer
any possibilities of carrying on the negotiations with Stalin, who had
all the trumps in his hand, was no longer under pressure from the
Western leaders, and could in no way be forced into making
concessions. Churchill and Roosevelt gave it to be understood with
increasing clarity that Polish claims were unjustified, and emphasised
that the Poles were jeopardising their alliance with Russia and the
hopes of some Poles that the Russians could be induced into making
concessions by sheer force were treated as folly. Mikołajczyk's
situation was becoming more and more difficult, for even whilst
attempting some concessions he had attained nothing, and his own
Government considered that he had gone too far with these
concessions. He himself was beginning to understand that his role as
Premier was coming to an end, as he had sought a practical solution
and the majority of Polish opinion considered that symbolic
resistance in the given situation was the only proper attitude. On 24
November the Polish Premier offered his resignation.[21]

ARCISZEWSKI AS NEW POLISH PREMIER

On 29 November the President of the Polish Republic entrusted the
function of creating a new Government to Tomasz Arciszewski – one
of the oldest and most meritorious members of the Polish Socialist
Party, who had come to the West via Bridge No. 3 – as Poland's
nominee for the next President. This nomination put an end to the
period of attempts at establishing diplomatic relations and normalis-
ing matters at issue with Russia, with certain concessions on the
Polish side. Mikołajczyk did what he could to achieve this aim; he
had the support of the occupied country and of his Government to
make concessions on the question of the Polish–Soviet frontier; Stalin
had rejected them, and now the new Polish Premier had no intention

of returning to these matters. On 7 December he delivered a speech over the radio to Poland, in which he emphasised that good neighbourly relations with Soviet Russia were of supreme importance to Poland, and expressed the hope that these would be achieved, though he did not promise any concessions on the Polish side.[22]

This stance caused a further isolation of Poland and the Polish Government to such an extent that the British for a time hesitated as to whether they should recognise it. The British Ambassador in Moscow argued that Stalin would see the acceptance of Arciszewski's Government as a direct confrontation, but Churchill did not accept this view; the Government was recognised. However in a letter of 3 December to Stalin the British Premier expressed the opinion that he would not stay long in office. The attitude of President Roosevelt, who had been elected for the fourth time, was less extreme. He had free hands after the elections and wanted to take a more active part in the Polish question; he did not however intend to go any further than he had suggested in his letter to Mikołajczyk on 17 November. This was made manifest in the declaration of the new Secretary of State, Edward Stettinius, Jr, on 18 December, in which it was repeated that the United States did not recognise frontier changes that had occurred during the war, but that at the same time they would endorse the joint settlement of these matters by Poland and Russia before the peace conference. A new element was the declaration that the United States would offer economic help to all countries destroyed during the war, and that help would also include Poland.[23]

President Roosevelt also tried to distract Stalin from his decision to recognise the Polish Committee of National Liberation as the provisional Polish Government, but to no avail. On 1 January 1945, on the strength of the resolution of the National Council, the Polish Committee of National Liberation was transformed into the 'Provisional Government of the Republic of Poland', and was formally recognised by Russia five days later.[24]

BRITISH MILITARY MISSION IN POLAND

It was only on 21 December that the President of the Polish Republic signed the nomination of General Okulicki as Commander of the Home Army, and the signal with this news was received in Częstochowa during the Christmas period. The General had previously received several dispatches from London, concerning the matter of sending a British Military Mission to Poland. The Polish Government had been trying to obtain the sending of this mission since the spring of 1944, and after the initial refusal had obtained an agreement at the beginning of July. It was important for Poles to have Western observers who could rectify the numerous Soviet lies about the Home Army and the activities of communists, and Churchill wanted to have his own men there.

Mikołajczyk was just on his way to Moscow and there were hopes of some understanding and therefore on 2 August, when the Uprising was already in progress, the following dispatch was sent to the Commander of the Home Army:

> On the subject of the Military Mission the English are making preparations, and they foresee two possibilities: (a) when an understanding is reached with Moscow, the Mission will depart for the territories taken over by the Soviets. Part of the expedition will go through Moscow, part by plane straight into the field; (b) if no understanding is reached, they want to send the Mission to one of the partisan detachments on the German side. To be sent by plane by means of a drop or landing.[25]

In Warsaw this stirred up hopes of a serious British commitment to the cause of the Uprising, but they were not to materialise. Worse than that, Churchill wanted Stalin's agreement for despatching the Mission, and Stalin obviously refused. Two months went by and the capital had to surrender, before the British Government decided, under considerable Polish pressure, to send the Mission without Soviet agreement. Unfortunately bad weather hampered the proceedings, and when it improved Mikołajczyk handed in his resignation and Churchill wondered whether there was any point in sending his observers to Poland without any prospect of a compromise. After prolonged hesitation, the Mission was finally given the green light at the beginning of December.

On the night of 26–27 December, three British officers, a Polish officer–interpreter and a British communications sergeant made a parachute jump to the outpost near Radomsko. The Mission, which received the cryptonym *Operation Freston*, was headed by Colonel D. T. Hudson. All were in full uniform and equipped with small arms.[26]

There is no document that fully represents the instructions received by Colonel Hudson before his parachute jump into Poland, for his two discussions with Churchill were held confidentially, and the Colonel refused to divulge their contents. His report after his return to Great Britain also makes no revelations, so one has to rely on the document sent on 21 October by the head of Bureau VI to Colonel Perkins, the head of the Polish Section of the SOE, which sent the Mission on its way.

1. The Mission's chief task is to observe the activities of the Home Army and report upon its situation, plans, attitude and needs to its chiefs in London.
2. The Mission has the additional task of reporting on the relations between the Home Army, other partisan groups and the Soviet Army. The Mission must endeavour to put right the relations between these units and the Home Army.
3. The Mission is answerable to its British chiefs in London, but in the underground sphere it will be assigned to the Home Army.[27]

The execution of these instructions proved to be impossible, as there was a lack of goodwill on the part of the Home Army's opponents and, in a later phase, of the Soviets. The Mission however established contact with partisan detachments of the Home Army and with the local population, circulating over the small territory and keeping well out of German hands. On 3 January a meeting took place with General Okulicki in Zacisze, a small manor-house situated in the forests near Radomsko. In the situation as it stood the General was opposed to the sending of the Mission, as there was nothing for it to see. The period of the great Home Army thrust in action 'Tempest', when large Polish units, organised and armed in the underground, had come into open battle with the Germans and sought the co-operation of Red divisions, was now over. Warsaw had fallen even as the Red Army stood on the opposite bank of the Vistula, and many months had been wasted in procrastinating and haggling over whether or not to send some British observers. And now that the Polish Underground State was in ruins, when the large units had been demobilised, when it was difficult even to ensure the safety of the British officers, these belated and untimely observers had arrived from the West.

A meeting, however, was essential, and the Polish point of view had to be represented yet again. In his report Colonel Hudson presented the silhouette and statement of the General:

He gave the impression of a man of integrity, calm and certain of his opinions. After a short review of the existing situation he concluded that 'after beating the Germans the British and Americans would have no other alternative, but to stand up to Soviet aggression'.[28]

It was the heart of winter and none of those present at the meeting supposed that great changes would take place in the course of the next few days. On 12 January, however, the last great Soviet offensive was launched.

23 The Last Soviet Offensive; Dissolution of the Home Army; Yalta

THE LAST SOVIET OFFENSIVE

The Germans still presented a significant power disposing of 300 divisions, but they had to fight on three fronts, West, East and South; thousands of bombs were landing on the Reich; its industry was severely impaired, and human reserves were exhausted. For that reason the Soviet winter offensive met with no great resistance, and the Red divisions advanced swiftly. On 17 January the ruins of Warsaw were seized with the participation of the First Army; on 19 January the Germans left Cracow which yet again avoided destruction and on 23 January the Soviet divisions were already on the Oder, on German soil. During this offensive Marshal Rokossovsky was no longer leading the 1st Byelorussian Front. He had been transferred to the leadership of the 2nd Byelorussian Front, which was attacking further to the north, towards Pomerania, and beyond to Szczecin and Świnoujście. His place was taken by Marshal Georgy Zhukov, who was heading straight for Berlin in attack.[1]

Nearly 200 000 soldiers took part in this offensive, in units of the First Polish Army subordinate to the Department of National Defence of the Polish Committee of National Liberation, and operationally to the Soviet leadership. On the strength of an order dated 20 August 1944, and issued by the head of this department, General Michał Żymierski, the Second Army began to be organised. Unlike the Polish Armed Forces in the West, which were always short of recruits, the units formed by the communists on Polish territory were in a considerably better position. They could benefit from conscription and also, in part, from Home Army soldiers who were enlisted into the ranks either by force or else under threat of deportation into the heart of Russia. Apart from the desire to create

315

the greatest possible armed forces, which strengthened the position of the communists both with regard to Polish society and to Russia, it was also a matter of depriving the terrain of its young element, which viewed the new Soviet occupation with disfavour, and was prone to put up resistance.

When the last Soviet offensive was launched, the First Army comprised more than 93 000 men: five divisions of infantry, one cavalry brigade, four artillery brigades and other branches. It also possessed 172 tanks, 1213 cars and 118 planes. As from 4 October 1944, its command was taken over from General Berling by General Władysław Korczyc who on 18 December handed it over to General Stanisław Popławski. After gaining control of Warsaw the army went over to the second echelon, ensuring the join-up of the 1st and 2nd Byelorussian Fronts. However within the new offensive it again found itself in the first echelon and it attacked in the direction of the Pomeranian Rampart fortifications on the northern wing of the 1st Byelorussian Front. Its armoured brigade was detached in March and subordinated to the 1st Soviet Army Armoured Guard, and took part in the seizure of Gdynia and Gdańsk. In the first half of March its forward units were already starting the fight for Kołobrzeg. Somewhat later the 1st and 2nd Armoured Divisions were already on the Bay of Szczecin.[2]

The Second Polish Army, put together in haste at the beginning of 1945, included 4968 officers and 51 343 men, and had five infantry divisions: the 5th Saxon, 7th Lusatian, 8th Dresden, 9th Dresden and 10th Sudetian. There were moreover two brigades of anti-tank artillery – the 9th Dresden and the 14th Sudetian – and a division of anti-aircraft artillery, as well as a brigade of sappers. At the beginning of February the army was reinforced with the 16th Soviet Armoured Brigade. Initially General Świerczewski was in command of the army, only to hand it over after a short spell of time to General Popławski, and then take it over again. In the organisation period it was exclusively under Polish command, and after the launch of the January offensive it was tranferred to the region of Warsaw, Kutno, Łódź and Piotrków, and the 10th Armoured Division, being in reserve, moved over to Cracow and Katowice. On 20 February the whole army, like the First Army, was under the orders of the commander of the 1st Byelorussian Front as a part of the second front echelon. On 20 March a basic change took place, for the army was subordinated to the commander of the 1st Ukrainian Front, with the addition of a Soviet Armoured Corps numbering 268 tanks. It then counted almost 90 000 soldiers and was regrouping to the North of

Wrocław. At the beginning of April it was in the first Front echelon with the task of taking part in the Berlin operation.[3]

The Soviet winter offensive was a great shock for the West, which did not expect the attack before the early spring, but Stalin had no intention of waiting. As already decided, a conference was going to be held in Yalta in the course of the next few weeks, at which the proposals agreed in Teheran were to be resolved. The Soviet dictator, being himself both treacherous and cunning, trusted no-one and although everything had already been promised to him, he preferred to put his contracting parties before the accomplished facts. He had been promised Poland, but preferred to have her in his pocket before coming to the conference table.

DISSOLUTION OF THE HOME ARMY

The offensive was also a great shock for General Okulicki, who was in Cracow at the time, meeting the Government Delegate. They both returned in haste to Częstochowa, which was already in Soviet hands. The General now faced the most difficult decision in his life. He was in favour of fighting, particularly on home ground, and had led the fight from the first days of the September campaign through underground warfare, arrest, Lubyanka prison, the Polish army in Russia, and a parachute jump back into Poland. He had rejected an easy career in the West, lived through the hell of the Warsaw Uprising and had attained the highest honour he could expect: he had been made commander of the Home Army. With the greatest difficulties, he had recreated the HQ, gathered elements of command in his own hands and, now that the occupants had changed, he had to tell his soldiers that all their previous fighting had come to an end. His Order was issued on 19 January 1945:

Officers and men of the Home Army!

This is the last order I shall issue to you. From now on, your activity and energies are to be devoted to the restoration of the full independence of the Polish State and the protection of its population from destruction.

You must strive to be the leaders of the nation and to bring about the independence of the Polish State. In this endeavour, each and every one of you must be his own commander.

In the conviction that you will carry out this order and remain eternally loyal to Poland, to facilitate your work in the future, I hereby, with the authority of the President of the Republic, release you from your oath and disband the Home Army.

I thank you in the name of the Service for the devotion you have shown up to this moment. I profoundly believe that our sacred cause will triumph and that we shall meet once more in a truly free, unoccupied Poland.

May our country live long in freedom, independence and happiness!

The Commander of the Armed Forces in Poland.[4]

This decision was confirmed in a radio speech of the President of the Polish Republic on 8 February. It began as follows: 'Now that the German invader has been driven out of Poland by the Red Army, armed activity on our national territory has ceased and the detachments of the Home Army are dissolved'.[5]

The order was issued, but this did not mean that thousands of Home Army soldiers would easily and automatically be demobilised. The tough years of war and occupation had marked the hearts and souls of millions of people too deeply for them to be suddenly foregone at the mere issuing of an order. It would have been very difficult, almost impossible, even if the war had ended in victory, but what was to be expected in a situation where the country had simply changed one occupant for another? Society was totally disorientated and in the grips of chaos, still shattered by the events of war that had succeeded one another at great speed, and torn by differences of view as to the new political situation. Operation 'Tempest' had been very limited during the winter months, but a certain number of detachments still stuck to the villages and forests, and now that there were no more Germans and the order had been given, they were expected to show up and lay down their arms. Some of them, about 50 000, behaved accordingly and were arrested and deported to the East, others buried their arms and quietly scattered to their places of residence, without revealing their adherence to the Home Army. The latter were fiercely pursued by the NKVD, which would have had considerable difficulties had it not been for the Poles working in the state security department.

For many months now they had been observing their political opponents, from whom they were to take over the government of the country; they now had an easy way to dispose of them. With the help of denunciations the Soviet authorities, aided by the Polish militia arrested thousands of officers and soldiers of the Home Army and deported them into the heart of Russia. Thus began the reign of terror, in one respect worse even than the German one, as Polish society had then been united, whereas now it was torn in internecine strife.[6]

The most serious problem was however caused by those soldiers of the Home Army who did not disclose themselves nor lay down arms, but remained in the underground as partisans and were resolved to carry on the fight, this time with the Soviet occupant and the Polish security forces. They had no connection with the new underground military organisation bearing the cryptonym NIE (*Niepodległość*–Independence) at the head of which stood General Emil Fieldorf (*Nil*), and the formation of which had been announced by General *Bór* in a cable to General Sosnkowski dated 26 November, 1943.

> In the event of a second Soviet occupation, I am preparing in the greatest secrecy a nuclear skeleton network commanding a new secret organisation for your use, General. I shall report the particulars after concluding my decisions on this matter. At all events it will be a separate network, not connected with the wider organisation of the Home Army, which has been largely deciphered by elements in Soviet service.[7]

The purpose of the new organisation was not day-to-day fighting. It was planned in the very long term, and had a purely staff character. Surviving detachments of the Home Army knew nothing about it, but for the new communist Polish administration and the NKVD a distinct connection existed between it, the still-functioning underground and General Okulicki. He was in an exceptionally difficult situation, for he had to explain to his ex-subordinates the need to stop the fight and come out into the open, whilst at the same time he was still in hiding, being constantly sleuthed, as were the Government Delegate and politicians, by the new occupants.

A further complication, purely political, was caused by the resignation from the premiership of Stanisław Mikołajczyk, whose place was taken by Tomasz Arciszewski. The Peasant Party was opposed to his political line, as it considered that mere protests were not enough: they were being lodged in London, whereas in Poland a new reality had come into being, and some solutions had to be sought in agreement with Soviet Russia. This did not alter its negative attitude to the 'new government' imposed by Russia. The Party demanded the return of Mikołajczyk to the Cabinet and threatened to leave the Delegation of the Government and Council of National Unity, which were still in existence.[8]

Detachments of that part of the NSZ, which had not subordinated themselves to the Home Army, found themselves in a specific and highly difficult situation. Basically their command had been opposed to operation 'Tempest' and coming out of hiding, but in the terrain of Lwów and Lublin districts several of their detachments had taken part in the capture of these cities by the Home Army. These detachments had ceased to exist, but others were still strong to the west of the Vistula, mainly in the province of Kielce, and had to be prepared for the worst, for they had to their credit fighting with the People's Army, and now the Red Army was on the march, the ally of Polish communists. On 11 August 1944, the Chief Command of the NSZ organised the formation of a larger unit, which was given the name of '*Świętokrzyska* – Holy Cross Brigade'. It included about 700 well-armed soldiers and was ready for the march westwards. The unexpected Soviet offensive had surprised the Brigade, which was wintering at a number of points in the district of Miechów. Immediately after the front had set out the Brigade quickly assembled itself, filling its ranks and, now 850 soldiers strong, it started its march to the west, in the direction of Silesia and thereafter to Czechoslovakia, benefiting from the friendly neutrality of the German units. This was achieved on the strength of discussions with the local German front commanders, and of a promise that the Polish group would not attack Germans and whilst on the march would avoid larger cities. In the second half of January the Brigade found itself on German soil, and in February it reached Czechoslovakia. After covering some 600km it vanished into the forests in the vicinity of Prague. It was then cut off from its higher command, which had remained in Poland, and from its political chiefs, who had made off for the west via Vienna. Finally, on 6 May, just before the end of the war in Europe, the Brigade established contact with American detachments.[9]

CONFERENCE IN YALTA AND POLISH REACTION

In this difficult and tragic period for Poland, the previously announced Conference of the three powers took place in Yalta between 4 and 11 February 1945. Just as in Teheran, no one else was represented there, and Stalin repeated his manoeuvre *vis-à-vis* Roosevelt and won him over to his side by offering this dying man the role of chairman. The fact that the Western Allies had agreed to so important a conference taking place on Soviet soil was a proof, a pointer, towards the victory of the Red dictator.

The conference was the continuation of the negotiations in Teheran, and was to give form to resolutions of the earlier discussions. A number of general matters were therefore settled there, such as the structure of the organisation of United Nations, the partition of Germany into occupational spheres, concessions that China must offer Russia, and a few others. The Soviet Union received the Baltic states and gained a basic zone of influence in Bulgaria, Czechoslovakia, Hungary, Romania and, of course, in Poland as well as in a certain area in Austria and Yugoslavia. The conference however made a very solemn declaration that free elections would take place in all these countries, and that democratic governments would be installed.

Poland was discussed at length, and a resolution was passed which is Point 6 in the general resolution of the conference:

We came to the Crimea Conference resolved to settle our differences about Poland. We discussed fully all aspects of the question. We reaffirmed our common desire to see established a strong, free, independent and democratic Poland. As a result of our discussions we have agreed on the conditions in which a new Polish Provisional Government of National Unity may be formed in such a manner as to command recognition by the three major Powers. The agreement reached is as follows:

A new situation has been created in Poland as a result of her complete liberation by the Red Army. This calls for the establishment of a Polish Provisional Government which can be more broadly based than was possible before the recent liberation of Western Poland. The Provisional Government which is now functioning in Poland should, therefore, be reorganized on a broader democratic basis with the inclusion of democratic leaders from Poland itself and from Poles abroad. This new Government should then be called the Polish Provisional Government of National Unity.

Mr Molotov, Mr Harriman, and Sir A. Clark Kerr are authorized as a Commission to consult in the first instance in Moscow with members of the present Provisional Government and with other Polish democratic leaders from within Poland and from abroad, with a view to reorganization of the present Government along the above lines. The Polish Provisional Government of National Unity shall be pledged to the holding of free and unfettered elections as soon as possible on basis of universal suffrage and secret ballot. In these elections all democratic and anti-Nazi parties shall have the right to take part and to put forward candidates.

When a Polish Provisional Government of National Unity has been properly formed in conformity with the above, the Government of the USSR which now maintains diplomatic relations with the present Provisional Government of Poland, and the Government of the United Kingdom and the Government of the United States will establish diplomatic relations with the new Polish Provisional Government of National Unity, and will exchange Ambassadors, by whose reports the respective Governments will be kept informed about the situation in Poland.

The three Heads of Government consider that the Eastern frontier of Poland should follow the Curzon Line, with digressions from it in some regions of five to eight kilometres in favour of Poland. They recognize that Poland must receive substantial accessions of territory in the North and West. They feel that the opinion of the new Polish Provisional Government of National Unity should be sought in due course on the extent of these accessions and that the final delimitations of the Western frontier of Poland should thereafter await the peace Conference.[10]

These resolutions showed some appearances of caring for the Polish question. In the event it was however a total victory for Stalin, and it met with a categorical protest from the Polish Government in London; in Poland however, which was now completely in Soviet hands, the question was seen differently. On 21 February the Council of National Unity met near Warsaw with the participation of the Government Delegate, and although all present were depressed by the Yalta decisions, they tried to look positively at the sitution that had come into being. It was understood that Poland would lose almost 50 per cent of her territory and that the basis of the new government would be people completely dependent on Moscow. They relied, however, on the point of the Yalta decision that mentioned free elections. When this was carried out the communists would suffer defeat, and the government of Poland would be in the hands of representatives of independent Polish political parties. Seeing this as its last hope, the Council passed a resolution in which, *inter alia*, the following was said:

> The Council of National Unity expresses the conviction that the decisions of the Crimean Conference taken without the participation or consent of the Polish State...impose new, arduous and unjust sacrifices on Poland. The Council of National Unity, whilst protesting against the unilateral decisions of the Conference, is however obliged to comply with them, seeing in them a chance of saving the independence of Poland, the avoidance of further impoverishment of the Polish nation and a chance of creating the basis for organizing our own forces and for conducting a future independent Polish policy.
>
> The Council of National Unity does this in the conviction that Western allies of Poland and the USSR alike in the name of the principles of the Atlantic Charter and of democracy that they profess, will respect the true independence of Poland, and that the USSR will refrain from all interference in her internal affairs.

In its subsequent points the Council expressed its opinion regarding the frontiers, expecting that in the east they would come into direct negotiations with Russia, and that in the west they would be based on the Nysa and the Odra, and include the annexation of Eastern Prussia to Poland. The Government of National Unity should in the first place be taken over by London and the Council of National Unity, as representing the country, with Mikołajczyk as premier.[11] The Council had admittedly made a considerable compromise in recognising Yalta, but at the same time its resolution was again on the optimistic side, without any basis in reality.

An exceedingly difficult situation had developed, as the government of Arciszewski was still continuing to reject any form of compromise, even though it would have liked to come to an agreement with the Soviets, and the party supporting him in Poland differed in views as to what should be done next. The Peasant Party considered that it was possible to come out of hiding and launch an attempt to form a Provisional Government of National Unity, others were determinedly opposed to this. In Warsaw, in the district of Praga, a Provisional Government was already functioning with

Osóbka-Morawski as Premier, though recognised only by the USSR and it already had a certain amount of power, based on Soviet strength. Leaders of the main political parties together with the Government Delegate and General Okulicki were still hiding in the villages, suburbs and outskirts of Warsaw, mainly in Milanówek. These people were constantly followed by the NKVD and the security forces of the Provisional Government, who would set up traps; arrests were daily. Radio contact with London was still maintained but it was becoming increasingly difficult.

ARREST OF SIXTEEN LEADERS OF THE UNDERGROUND

In the first half of March, 1945, the Government Delegate and General Okulicki received via underground channels identical envelopes, dirty and crumpled through having passed through several hands, but still unopened, as the wax seals had not been broken. Inside they found identical letters written in Russian and dated 6 March. These were invitations signed by Pimyenov, Colonel of the Guard, proposing a meeting with the representative of the Command of the 1st Byelorussian Front, General Ivanov, which 'can and unconditionally should decide what is doubtful to resolve quickly by other means. Mutual understanding and trust will allow us to decide very important matters, and avoid embitterment'. At the end of the letter was a guarantee of personal safety.[12]

Both leaders immediately discussed the problem and both were at a loss. They had no doubt but that this was a Soviet ruse; on the other hand a refusal to attend the meeting would make it easier for the Soviets to repeat their accusation that the underground authorities were sabotaging all hopes of an understanding. General Okulicki had to refuse, as he had already been in contact with the head of Staff in London, General Kopański, and had been instructed not to come out of hiding, further reinforced by orders from General Anders, but Delegate Jankowski was in a different situation. He represented a political line, maintained permanent contact with parties, had to reckon with their opinion and therefore, through an intermediary, he allowed several meetings with Colonel Pimyenov. Only the PPS hung back. The Delegate himself also met up with the Soviet Colonel and came to the conclusion that a general meeting would have to be agreed upon. In this conversation he was distinctly told that General Okulicki could not be absent from the representation of the underground, and that the Soviet authorities accept the condition of the representation being previously taken to London to come to an agreement with the government.[13]

Politicians attached high hopes to these conversations and especially the possibility of flying to London, but General Okulicki had no doubts that it was trickery. He knew the Soviet methods, had already been in Soviet hands, had spent many months in the Lubyanka and knew that by coming out of hiding he was stepping along the same road. There was however little else he could do. He could use the pretext of General Anders' order and refuse to take part in the meeting, but then he would be reproached with persistently putting obstacles to a settling of relations with the Russians. There was even a terrible accusation of cowardice, which he could dismiss with a shrug of the shoulders, but could he allow himself with the same gesture to reject even the slightest chance of Soviet goodwill? He believed in fighting, and strove to fight throughout the war years, but now he could fight no longer. His task was to demobilise the army over which he had command. All he could do was sacrifice himself in a last attempt to save the nation and the country.

On 25 March a joint sitting of the National Council of Ministers and the Council of National Unity took place with General Okulicki, at which it was decided to arrange a meeting with the Soviet General. The Colonel acting as go-between was given the names of the people intended for the meeting. They were already partly-known to the Soviet authorities, as several weeks previously the British government, concerned for the safety of these people, had obtained them from the Poles and passed them on to Moscow. Obviously this was not the only source from which the NKVD drew its information, the underground was in its last days and had already been deeply penetrated by agents of the Provisional Government in Warsaw.[14]

On 27 March the three most eminent representatives of Poland's Underground, Delegate Jan Stanisław Jankowski, the chairman of the Council of National Unity Kazimierz Pużak and the last Commander of the Home Army, General Leopold Okulicki, set off for the headquarters of the Command of the 1st Byelorussian Front in Pruszków. They were met by General Ivanov, who promised to prepare a meeting with Marshal Georgy Zhukov. The next day the following representatives of political parties came along: Adam Bień (Peasant Party), Stanisław Jasiukowicz (National Party) and Antoni Pajdak (Polish Socialist Party), members of the National Council of Ministers and Kazimierz Bagiński (Peasant Party), Jozef Chaciński

(Labour Party), Eugeniusz Czarnowski (Democratic Party), Kazimierz Kobylański (National Party), Stanisław Michałowski (Democratic Party), Stanisław Mierzwa (Peasant Party), Zbigniew Stypułowski (National Party), Franciszek Urbański (Labour Party), and Jozef Stemmler (interpreter). They were joined by Aleksander Zwierzyński (National Party) who had been arrested several days beforehand. None of them flew to London and no-one met the Commander of the front. They were all arrested and in two groups, first Jankowski, Pużak and Okulicki, two days later the rest of them. They were transported to Moscow and imprisoned in the Lubyanka.[15]

Just before setting off for the meeting with the Russians General Okulicki had had a conversation with Colonel Jan Rzepecki, Head of the Bureau of Information and Propaganda of the HQ of the Home Army, who had returned from a German prisoner-of-war camp. He handed over his function to him. After informing London about this, Rzepecki received from General Anders, in agreement with the President of the Polish Republic, the confirmation of his function with the title 'Delegate of the Armed Forces in Poland'. In the area of personnel, legislation and discipline he had the same rights as the Home Army Commander enjoyed, but the network under his command functioned differently. He had to inform London about the situation in Poland, protect society and conspiratorial organs under his command by eliminating exceptionally pernicious individuals, help in the transfer of money, post, necessary materials and men, and carry out propaganda activities among General Zymierski's soldiers.[16]

In the new situation it very soon became apparent that the organisation *Nie*, which had started functioning with caution, would come into collision with the underground activities, would cause conflict with the political parties and would lead to numerous arrests, as it had already been decoded by Soviet intelligence. Therefore on 15 April Colonel Rzepecki sent a signal to London with the suggestion that General Anders should dissolve *Nie*. The proposal was accepted, and the organisation formally ceased to exist.[17]

SECOND POLISH CORPS AND 1ST ARMOURED DIVISION

Unlike the conference in Teheran, the results of which had been kept secret, the decisions of Yalta were instantly communicated to the

Polish Government and openly published. They were therefore known also to the Polish Armed Forces. It was most bitterly felt by the Second Corps, which for the vast majority consisted of inhabitants of the eastern lands of Poland that had been taken over by Russia. Moreover almost all the soldiers of the Corps had lived through deportation to the Soviet Union and knew the style of life there, and the methods of government. General Anders reacted immediately by sending a cable to the President of the Polish Republic with the spontaneous suggestion of withdrawing the Corps from fighting. He also wrote on this matter to the Commander of the Eighth Army. Later the General had several conversations on this issue with General Alexander and General Clark, who tried to mitigate the harshness of these political decisions by showing understanding for the Polish drama. The General's departure for London and the discussion of the situation in the Polish political milieu consolidated the view that the army must carry on fighting. A new duty fell to the commander of the Second Corps, as on 26 February the President of the Polish Republic entrusted to him the function of Commander-in-Chief.[18]

In the spring a new Allied offensive was launched in Italy, and the Second Corps took part in this. On account of his new function General Anders was in London, but on 6 April he joined the Corps to lead it into its last battle. The plan was to outflank the Germans from east and west, so as to destroy their forces before they withdrew beyond the river Pau. The Eighth Army, together with the Second Corps, was to move in from the east, in the direction of Ferrara, the Fifth American Army from the west, in the direction of Parma, by-passing Bologna and aiming further north to Verona. The Polish Corps was reinforced by a British Armoured Brigade and several other units and, together with its own two newly-formed Infantry Brigades, constituted a considerable force.

The attack was launched on 9 April and after heavy fighting, after crossing several rivers and routing the German forces, the main battalion of the Corps was the first, on 21 April, to enter Bologna. Fighting still went on for several days, the Allies crossed the river Pau and occupied a number of towns. German resistance was now in vain, and on 28 April, in the main quarters of the Allies in Caserata, the German plenipotentiaries signed the act of capitulation of their armies in Italy. The war road of the Second Corps had come to an end, distinguished by numerous victories, of which Monte Cassino was the greatest. Table 23.1 shows the losses for the period of fighting.[19]

TABLE 23.1   *Casualty figures for the Second Polish Corps*

	Officers	Men
Killed	174	2023
Wounded	614	8123
Missing	9	255

After the conclusion of war operations in Europe, when the armed forces of the fighting nations began to demobilise, the Second Polish Corps did not reduce, but expanded. Soldiers who had finally got out of captivity, from internment, from Nazi concentration camps, from occupied territory, came from Germany, France, Switzerland and Poland, with the desire to don uniforms just once more. The numbers in the Corps soon reached 112 000 soldiers. This led to troubles with the British authorities, who had difficulties in delivering supplies. Moreover they knew full well that there could be no question of any further war in Europe, while Polish hearts still nurtured some dim flame of unfounded hope that something might unexpectedly be changed. Families also joined the Corps, and within a short time over 10 000 civilian persons had collected. The Corps' Command was situated in Ancona, the divisions were billeted to the south of the town, on the Adriatic, and further south still, near Brindisi, in Barletta and Triani, camps were set up for the families and for those who could no longer be squeezed into the ranks. A new phase of Corps activity began: graves were arranged for the dead, cemeteries were established, but the chief concern was for the living. Primary and secondary schools were set up, numerous Polish uniforms appeared in Italian universities and publishing activities were launched (among which was the birth of the Paris *Kultura*). Newspapers were initiated; there was an excellent theatre; sports developed – a whole little Poland was created.[20]

News of the Yalta decisions had also shattered the 1st Armoured Division, but there the awareness of the necessity to carry on the fight with the Germans was widespread. The beginning of aggressive action on Dutch territory coincided more or less with the negotiations in the Crimea. The Polish division again found itself within the

Second Canadian Corps; it was reinforced by a battalion of Belgian Parachutists and a Canadian regiment of light artillery and was to proceed northwards, along the Dutch–German frontier, towards a distant target, the German port of Emden. In the course of operations the destination was changed to Wilhelmshaven.[21]

The distance between Breda and the region of concentration amounted to 250km, and the division covered this distance in an 18-hour march. It was already April when the division's last military operation was launched; it was considerably easier than earlier ones, as the Germans were no longer offering very strong resistance. More significant fighting took place between 19 and 29 April when the marshy terrain around the river Leda had to be cleared of the enemy. In this period the Polish soldiers experienced highly emotional moments as on the German side of the frontier, nearby – in Niederlangen – a camp of women and soldiers of the Home Army who had been brought there after the Warsaw Uprising was freed. The division reached Wilhelmshaven in the first days of May and launched the attack on the defence belt of the port, when on 4 May a cease-fire was announced on that front. Two days later division units manned Jever, Neudenburg and Wilhelmshaven, where, symbolically, the act of German capitulation was received.[22]

In the whole period of its operations, from August 1944 to May 1945, the 1st Armoured Division took into captivity 2200 officers and over 50 000 men, destroyed 260 tanks and guns on tram-tracks, 310 anti-tank guns, thirty armoured cars, and shot down thirteen planes and nine V-1 flying bombs. The division's losses amounted to 304 officers and about 5000 men; and 240 tanks of the Cromwell and Sherman type, twenty-two cannon, ninety-six troop-carriers, seventy-one lorries and 300 radio stations.[23]

The division found itself in a symbolic role in defeated Germany, as it took part in the occupation of that country. The British authorities, knowing that there were many thousands of Polish ex-concentration-camp prisoners, prisoners of war and deportees to forced labour handed the town of Haren on the river Ems in northern Freesia over to the division. All the inhabitants were evacuated, the name was changed to Maczków, and for two years, under the care of the division, it was ruled by a Polish administration, which organised primary and secondary schools, theatres, publishing firms and periodicals. It was a small but exclusively Polish enclave on the territory of defeated Germany.[24]

PARACHUTISTS, AIR FORCE AND NAVY

The 1st Independent Parachute Brigade also took part in the occupation of Germany. After the battle of Arnhem it returned to Great Britain and was reorganised, with further recruiting of Poles who had been prisoners-of-war of the Germany army. The Brigade was kept in a state of alert, as it was intended to transfer it to the continent to take control of the isolated point of German resistance in Dunkirk. However, when it landed in Ostend on 8 May it was the day after the German surrender. The brigade was directed towards Cleve, and a little later was transferred to the region of Bersenbrueck, near Meppen, where the 1st Armoured Division was stationed. In matters of tactics and garrison the Brigade took orders from the Division Commander, and thus two major Polish units took over a considerable area of German territory as occupational powers. Apart from these duties the Brigade, no less than the Division, took care of the many thousands of Poles who had been driven into this inhospitable territory by the war. The settlement of Emmerich, where the Polish transit camp was situated, was given the name *Spadochronowo* (Parachuting).[25]

In the last months of the war the Polish Air Force in the west and the south was increased by only one Squadron – No. 663 – which was formed in Italy in September 1943, but went into active service only at the beginning of the following year. Its task was to co-operate with the artillery of the British Eighth Army, of which the Second Corps formed a part. The flying activities of fighter squadrons were limited by then, as the Germans had no petrol and restricted their flights to the minimum. Between 16 December 1944, and 5 January 1945, the last, unexpected counter-offensive of the Germans took place in the Ardennes, and was initially successful on account of the surprise element and also the bad weather, which prevented the Allied airmen from going into action. When, a few days later, this became possible, flights of bombers took part in bombing the supply-line of Field Marshal von Runstedt, and the Polish Fighter Wing 131 took part in their cover. On 1 January by way of retaliation the Germans attacked the Allied air bases in France and Belgium, and destroyed eighteen Polish fighters in Ghent airport, mainly from Squadron 302, killing two pilots. On their return from battle the two remaining Polish Squadrons, 308 and 317, attacked the Germans and shot down eighteen planes. It was one of the last serious encounters with the Luftwaffe in the West. In 1945 Polish fighter planes shot down thirty-six machines, of which one third was the work of Squadron 308.[26]

The Polish Bomber Squadrons 300 and 305 functioned more intensively, as the Allies were aiming at ending the war in Europe in the shortest possible time, and undertook a major bombardment of the Third Reich. In the middle of February 1945, Squadron 300, using Lancasters, took part in the great raid on Dresden, and on 25 April took part in the attack on Hitler's mountain residence of Berchtesgaden in the Bavarian Alps. It was its last military sally. Squadron 305, equipped with Mosquito planes, was among the 10 000 bombers which on 22 February set out to paralyse communications throughout Germany. The Squadron's last military expedition was its night-time attack on 25–26 April on German transports in the region of Westerland–Flensburg–Neuhaus, in the northern part of the country.[27]

The approaching end of the war in Europe also restricted the operations of the small Polish Navy. Its chief task was the cover of great transatlantic vessels (*Queen Elizabeth, Ile de France, Sobieski*) as they entered and left ports transporting the army from the Western hemisphere. Polish vessels also functioned in Norwegian waters, and the destroyer *Garland* was active in the Mediterranean.[28] All in all, over the period of the war as a whole, the Polish Navy covered more than 1 million nautical miles, carried out 1162 patrols and operations, took part in 787 convoys, attacked seagoing vessels seventy-three times and submarines 211 times. Six vessels were destroyed, two submarines were sunk and nine damaged, and seventeen planes were shot down. Its own losses included two submarines – *Jastrzab* (Hawk) and *Orzeł* (Eagle) – two destroyers – *Grom* (Thunder) and *Orkan* (Hurricane) – and the cruiser *Dragon*.[29]

FIRST AND SECOND ARMIES IN FIGHT WITH GERMANS

On 11 April, the Second Army, led by General Świerczewski, found itself on the eastern bank of the Neisse, on a sector of front that was 30km wide. It formed the nucleus of the grouping that provided cover for the left wing of the 1st Ukrainian Front, whose main forces were to march on Berlin. The Army's task was to break through the German defence and press forward in the direction of Dresden. The offensive was launched on 16 April and after a few days brought positive results. But a hiatus occurred between the divisions heading

for Budziszyn and Dresden and the divisions that were situated more
to the north, near Bad Muskau.

German armoured units (among them Hermann Göring's Division) entered this gap, split the Army in two parts, and tried to get to
the rear of the front line. Heavy fighting ensued, and considerable
losses were incurred on both sides. General Świerczewski withdrew
his main forces from the Dresden area and sent them to the region of
the German break-in. He succeeded in holding back the enemy's
march in the region of Budziszyn and towards the end of April a new
front line was formed between Kamenz, Doberschutz and Dauben.
The Second Army was able to start preparing for an offensive in the
direction of Prague. There were considerable losses. Together with
the Russian First Corps they amounted to 20 160 killed, wounded
and missing, and 205 tanks and armoured guns lost. Over 20 000
Germans were killed, 550 prisoners taken, and 314 tanks and 135 guns
and armoured cars destroyed.[30]

In the first half of April 1945, the First Army, commanded by
general Popławski, in the Baltic, carried out a swift manoeuvre to the
south, marched some 170km to the vicinity of the Oder, about 50km
to the north-east of Berlin. Its task was to break through the German
defence, cross over the Oder and march on Sachsenhausen, to the
north of Berlin, and further on to the Łaba, so as to encircle the
German capital. On 16 April the offensive set off, and a few days
later it reached its targets. On 30 April the First Army broke through
the defence on the Havella Canal, and its First Armoured Division
was transported to Berlin, where it took part in street fighting. Other
divisions of the Army went further to the west; on 3 May they
reached the Łaba and established contact with the American Ninth
Army. The losses of the First Army were considerable – 2958 officers
and men were killed, and 9427 were wounded.[31]

HITLER'S SUICIDE AND THE END OF THE WAR IN EUROPE

During the Battle of Berlin, which was one of the last chords of the
war in Europe, on 30 April in a bunker beneath the Chancery of the
Reich, Adolf Hitler took his life. Seven days later Germany surrendered unconditionally.

24 Conference in San Francisco; Provisional Government of National Unity; Testament of Fighting Poland; End of the War

CONFERENCE IN SAN FRANCISCO

On 25 April 1945, as the last shots were fired in Europe, a conference opened in San Francisco that was to give rise to the United Nations Organization. The problem was first touched on at the meeting of the representatives of the great powers in Dumbarton-Oaks, near Washington, between 21 August and 7 October 1944. The United States, Great Britain, Russia and China there put forward the project to create an international security organisation. Its main organ would be a Council consisting of eleven members, five of whom – the United States, Great Britain, Soviet Russia, China and France – would have a permanent place there, while the remaining six would be elected for a period of two years by the General Assembly. The problem was discussed again at Yalta, where the structure of the new organisation was established; and now, although the war was still on, the conference was attended by representatives from forty-five (later even forty-nine) countries. A couple of weeks previously, on 12 April, President Roosevelt had died, his place was automatically taken by vice-president Harry Truman, and everyone awaited his appearance with considerable interest, wondering what political line he would follow.[1]

The new international body was to replace the Leage of Nations, which had ceased to exist in 1940 and had been an imperfect institution; but what succeeded it was worse. After the First World War the idealism of President Wilson of the United States was a driving force towards justice and real freedom for all. Now, however, the United Nations Organization rose from the morass of opportunism and capitulation *vis-à-vis* the great powers, who retained the right of veto. The supremacy of Soviet Russia made itself particularly felt : it had entered the war as Hitler's ally, and had finished up as a leading representative of the victors' camp, striving brutally towards its own political aims.[2]

At the conference that was to decide about the new post-war world there was unfortunately no place for a Polish delegation. This was because the resolutions of Yalta concerning the Provisional Government of National Unity had not been carried out. It was perfectly obvious that as this new Government did not exist the Polish Government should be invited from London as it was recognised by all except Soviet Russia. No such logic was however binding at the time, Stalin had recognised the Polish Committee of National Liberation and now Molotov was demanding that this group of people subservient to Russia should be invited. This time the Western Allies voiced their objection, but they did not manage to impose their point of view, and were unable to ensure the inclusion of a representative of the legal Polish Government. They were, notwithstanding, hostile towards that Government and demanded that it change its attitude and accept Yalta, for they expected that this would level out the differences between Poles and facilitate the formation of a Government of National Unity. In this they failed though they managed to make Mikołajczyk himself alter his stance. Being no longer Premier, he made the following declaration on 15 April:

> In order to avoid all doubts as to my attitude, I wish to declare that I accept the decisions taken in the Crimea concerning the future of Poland, her sovereign, independent position, and the creation of a provisional government to represent national unity.[3]

This declaration caused an instant reaction on the part of the Polish Government, which in a communiqué of the Polish News Agency, dissociated itself from the declaration. There was no question of an understanding, and now a new problem presented itself that made the already embittered situation even more complex. Dispatches arrived from Poland about the sixteen representatives of the Underground, headed by General Okulicki and the Government Delegate, who had set out for discussions with the Russians and had not returned. This news was passed on to the British, who were most disturbed by it as they had themselves given those people's names to the Russians in order to ensure their safety. Eden had meetings with Molotov in San Francisco, so on 3 May in the course of luncheon with Stettinius, the American Secretary of State, he touched on the matter and received the reply 'They were arrested on a charge of diversionary activities against the Red Army'.[4]

The Western leaders, already accustomed to Soviet aggressiveness and their disregard for the given word, had nevertheless not expected so outrageous an act, and they instantly reacted. The American and British delegations both issued a declaration that in such a state of affairs they suspended discussions on Polish matters. President Truman reacted particularly sharply, by categorically demanding of Molotov that the Yalta resolution concerning Poland be carried out. Unfortunately Roosevelt's political bequest gave him no real chance of winning, matters had gone too far. Moreover, without any international experience, he could not measure up to the far-sighted Stalin. The first anger slowly abated, they all returned to the negotiation table and the conference proceeded without Polish representation.[5]

TRIAL IN MOSCOW

In Moscow affairs were meanwhile developing normally, according to the Soviet manner. Straight after the Underground leaders were brought to the Lubyanka an investigation was started, but the prisoners were not told what it was all about, nor what the Soviet authorities were aiming at. Some of the arrested men already had some experience. Kazimierz Pużak had spent many years under the tsarist regime in the dungeons of Shlisselburg, Kazimierz Bagiński had also tasted tsarist prisons, Aleksander Zwierzyński had landed in the Lubyanka straight from another Soviet prison, and General Okulicki was there for the second time in several years. Every night they were called out for interrogation and kept for hours in the harsh light of electric bulbs, then escorted back to their cells, then brought back before their interrogators, and asked about the minutest details of Underground activity. They were asked trick questions, startled by sudden changes of tone. Finally after eleven weeks of interrogation the situation was clarified. Each of the prisoners was served an indictment, of which the main point was the accusation that 'the Polish Underground was preparing a plan for a military offensive against the USSR in conjunction with Germany'.[6]

The indictment listed every conceivable 'crime' committed by the accused, and moreover presented a picture of the real state of affairs that was going to exist in Poland. The Home Army and the Council of National Unity were called illegal organisations, and their leaders were accused of possessing armed detachments, arms caches, broadcasting stations, printing presses and clandestine premises.

The absurdity of the accusation of collaboration with Germany from a state that together with Hitler had invaded Poland in 1939 and shared out the territory was obvious. To call Polish underground organisations operating on her own territory 'illegal' sounded grotesque and was an echo of Goebbels' propaganda, but the chances of defending logic and justice were nil. The prisoners had been driven to the very limits of physical and nervous resistance, some had succumbed to the constant pressure and confessed to crimes they had never committed, or else had accepted the insidious line of argument; and that was all the Soviets wanted. Who could prevent the show trial, in the eyes of the world, at which the 'Polish criminals' would confess to collaboration with the Germans?[7]

On 21 June all the accused were transported to the HQ of the Soviet Trade Unions, which was situated in a beautiful old palace of the tsarist period, with a large reception hall. This is where the Soviet show trials were held, where Rykow, Bucharin, Kamieniev and other eminent communists were tried and condemned, where General Tukhachevsky was condemned to death at a secret trial. The choice of this hall pointed to the inclinations of the Soviet authorities, and indicated what would be the fate of the accused Poles. The College of the Highest Military Court of the USSR consisted of General W. Ulrich and two colonels. The prosecutors were General N. Afanasy-ev and Councillor of State R. Rudenko. The hall was filled mainly by the military. Many foreign correspondents had come, and the organisers had invited representatives from the American, British and French embassies.

The accused were entitled to a defence *ex officio*, and this was granted; but the Government Delegate, Jan Stanisław Jankowski, Zbigniew Stypułkowski and General Okulicki, who had learned Russian in the Lubyanka, decided to present their own defence. Okulicki was the chief defendant, as the Soviet authorities were anxious to discredit the entire Home Army. Although debilitated by the interrogations and suffering from a heart complaint, the General had to muster all his strength to defend a cause that was being forcibly presented here in a false light and vilified. He obviously had none of the possibilities of a defendant in a normal court of law, and he was refused the right to call the witnesses to which the indictment referred. These were senior officers of the Home Army, commanders of the Eastern Districts: General Ludwik Bittner, Colonel Władysław Filipkowski, Colonel Jan Kotowicz, Lieutenant-Colonel Aleksander Krzyżanowski, and Colonel Kazimierz Tumidajski. Okulicki demanded a confrontation, wanted to ask them a series of questions, as on their territories there had been instances of encounters with Soviet partisans who endeavoured to disarm Polish partisans. It was there that the Red Army had encircled the larger Polish units that co-operated with it tactically in the fight with the Germans. The court shirked the issue on the grounds of technical difficulties, *inter alia* the bad weather – even though the trial took place in June – and refused to bring along witnesses from Soviet prisons.[8]

The prosecutors had no such difficulties. Their witnesses, brought out of prison without exception in the last stage of exhaustion and suitably prepared, in answer to every question and sometimes without being asked, adduced hundreds of facts – of which they claimed to be the eye witnesses – to prove that the Home Army had attacked Soviet detachments and representatives of the Soviet administration. Amid the monotony of confessions from grey-faced, tortured people, the young face of a Home Army telegraph operator shone like a ray of bright light against the black background. Her accusers had made the mistake of keeping her for too short a time in prison. Her girlish beauty, her melodious, regional accent, her clear and open statement concerning the activities of the Home Army without any self-abasement or contrition, created a considerable impression on all present. The court had her swiftly removed.[9]

On the fourth and last day of the trial, after the speeches of the prosecutors and the defence who in no way diminished the accusations, but merely the defendants and by that same token their deeds, General Okulicki spoke. He did not screen himself, but simply defended the cause he had served and the army he had commanded. This was the climax of the trial as the accused – against the tradition of Soviet courts – was not availing himself of his right to speak in order to express contrition, admit his persecutors were right and beg them for mercy. He was exhausted by interrogations and by illness, he was no speaker, he had no legal experience, he was using a foreign language, but the entire hall listened to him in silence and concentration:

> This is a political trial... its object is to blacken the Polish underground movement... The truth is that the Polish underground is endowed with moral credit as a result of its fight against the Germans. No-one can deny this, or bring any evidence to show that the Polish underground did not fight the Germans for five long years... In accusing us of collaborating with the Germans, you are impugning our honour. To accuse the 300 000 soldiers of the Home Army is to accuse the whole Polish nation... The Warsaw rising... was a heroic struggle and in no way justifies political reprisals... During the trial the prosecution has presented in a lurid fashion certain shocking accusations of terror. In so doing it has cast a slur on the Home Army, which it has portrayed in a despicable light. I requested that certain witnesses might be summoned – the commanders of the Home Army areas, districts and divisions concerned – so that I might question them before the court and discover the true cause of such useless and harmful activities. These men were in command at the time and they must know what happened. Unfortunately I was not enabled to question them... What is my opinion of Polish–Soviet relations? I will give it, not for the purpose of justifying myself to the court... I must declare that I feel no hostility whatever towards the Soviet Union. My actions were not hostile, nor were they inspired by hostility. I acknowledge that they were inspired by distrust of the Soviet Union... That distrust was not born during this war; it has existed for centuries. We lived as an independent State for only twenty years. We have not forgotten the 123 years of slavery imposed on us from the east, from Tsarist Russia... My actions were not aggressive but defensive. I know that the Polish people sincerely desires friendship with the Soviet people. And I should regard myself as a criminal of the first order if I did not desire it too, on the inviolable condition that Poland's independence is preserved.
> This is – *conditio sine qua non*.[10]

The General's speech made a great impression, but it could not change what is the normal procedure in Soviet Trials. He was sentenced to ten years imprisonment, the Delegate Jankowski to eight, Bień and Jasiukowicz to five, Puzak to one and a half, Bagiński to one, the rest to several months. The court counted the months of investigation as part of the sentence to be served, so some of the accused were instantly released.[11] These were mild sentences for this type of Soviet political trial; its aim, however, was achieved. By condemning the Polish leaders for alleged activities against the Red Army the Soviet authorities were at the same time displaying the 'magnanimity' that a powerful state could afford.

PROVISIONAL GOVERNMENT OF NATIONAL UNITY

While the trial of the underground leaders was going on discussions were also being conducted in Moscow with a view to creating a Provisional Government of National Unity. Unfortunately, when the Western powers yet again yielded to Soviet pressure and limited themselves to protesting on behalf of the sixteen arrested members of the underground, their fate was pre-empted and Stalin was given a completely free hand to realise his plans. President Truman admittedly made one further gesture and sent Harry Hopkins to Moscow for discussions with Stalin, but he could hardly have made a worse choice. In the first place he was at the end of his physical tether, and in the second he represented the same viewpoint as the late President Roosevelt, namely that the world should be divided between the United States and Russia, together with the decline of the British Empire and the compliance of other states. He soon came round to the view that in order to bring the Poles round to 'unity' one should break British resistance, sacrifice the accused leaders and agree that the Polish Underground should be represented by people chosen by Stalin.[12]

Negotiations began in Moscow on 17 June at the initiative of the American and British Ambassadors and of Molotov. Władysław Kiernik of the Peasant Party; Zygmunt Żuławski of the Polish Socialist Party; Professors Stanisław Kutrzeba and Adam Krzyża-nowski; and Henryk Kołodziejski, director of the library of the pre-war Parliament, came from Poland. Only the first two genuinely belonged to the political underground; the two professors had never been seen in any political role before, and Kołodziejski had presumably been chosen because he was one of the eminent Freemasons, thanks to which he exerted considerable influence, and was also known for a sobriety of opinion that bordered on opportunism.[13]

Mikołajczyk had already come round to the Yalta standpoint. He still had hopes of reaching some acceptable compromise, and so he came to Moscow in the company of Jan Stańczyk, a member of the Polish Socialist Party, and Antoni Kołodziej. He was a member of the Sailors' Union and his sole qualification was that he favoured Stalin's concept of a future Poland. The PKWN were represented by Bolesław Bierut, Władysław Gomułka, Edward Osóbka-Morawski and Władysław Kowalski. Soviet stage-management neglected nothing and in no way infringed Stalin's line; and Stalin wanted to show the whole world that he alone had the power of decision in Polish affairs. The contrast was overwhelming: the men who had dared to conduct an independent policy for Poland and to oppose Moscow were now in the dock, while those who obeyed the dictator were taking part in the banquet at the Kremlin. It was a particularly hard pill for Mikołajczyk to swallow, as he believed in the possibility of an advantageous compromise with Russia. On that same day, 21 June, and at almost the same hour as the sentences were being passed on the leaders of the Underground, the Provisional Government of National Unity was brought into existence. Osóbka-Morawski was made Premier, Gomułka and Mikołajczyk Vice-Premiers, and Mikołajczyk's group received only four out of twenty-one ministries. It had happened exactly according to the forecast made by Bolesław Bierut when he met Mikołajczyk in Moscow in October 1944. The 'Government of National Unity' assumed a farcical form: Stalin's victory was total. Several people connected with Mikołajczyk were also admitted among the 444 members of the National Council, which was headed by Bolesław Bierut.

On 27 June the new government landed at Warsaw airport. Large crowds were waiting – but only for Mikołajczyk, who enjoyed considerable popularity in the country, and with whose person and policies the weary society connected great hopes.[14]

LAST ASSEMBLY OF THE COUNCIL OF NATIONAL UNITY

After the arrest of the Sixteen and the initial state of bewilderment, yet another attempt to rebuild the Government Delegacy was undertaken by Stefan Korboński. Of the underground members who had remained free he played the most eminent role as the director of the department for Home Affairs and head of the KWC, so on 7 April he summoned a meeting in Warsaw. It was attended by representatives of parties belonging to the Council of National Unity and after a discussion Korboński was entrusted with the functions of temporary representative of the Government Delegacy. It was also decided to rebuild the Chief Commission of the Council, and even the Council itself. A signal on this subject was sent to London, and on 11 April a confirmation of the decision was received. The time had now come for the arduous reconstruction of the underground authorities, so that the country could voice its opinion on events that were now taking place in rapid succession. Twice, on 24 April and 3 May the re-established Council of National Unity passed resolutions addressed to the representatives of nations assembled in San Francisco, in which it expressed the hope that the Polish nation's right to an independent existence would not pass unrecognised. Also of importance was the appeal launched on 17 May to the Polish nation, in which was stated their sincere intention of having good relations with Soviet Russia, but on the basis of Polish independence. It furthermore appealed to the Polish nation to apply itself to the rebuilding of the country independently of offering resistance to the communist rule, and not to allow itself to be provoked into armed conflict and to returning to the underground. The Plenipotentiary of the Government and the Delegate of the Armed Forces in Poland expressed themselves in similar terms, and called upon the soldiers of the Home Army who were still in hiding in the forests in their partisan detachments to give up the fight and return to a normal life.[15]

These activities went on for several weeks, but when the sentences were passed in the Moscow trial and when the Provisional Government of National Unity appeared in Warsaw, fundamental changes had to take place in the underground. The trial had caused great indignation and depression, and had shattered hopes of any help from the West, but Mikołajczyk's arrival reawakened these hopes. His participation in the new Government seemed to indicate some chance of free elections which it was hoped would be under the supervision of the Western powers. It was desirable to take part in these elections, which could dramatically alter the situation, so it was imperative to come out of the underground and join the open political fight. Moreover, the Council of National Unity was considerably weakened, as it had been deserted by the Peasant Party, which had given its unconditional support to Mikołajczyk's policy.[16]

THE TESTAMENT OF FIGHTING POLAND

On 27 June, at the same time as the Government created in Moscow was landing at Warsaw airport, the Council of National Unity was assembling in Cracow under the chairmanship of Jerzy Braun, from the Labour Party. Representatives of the PPS, SN, SP , Democratic Union, *Racławice* and *Ojczyzna*, took part in the meeting. It was also attended by the stand-in for the Government Delegate, Stefan Korboński, a member of the Peasant Party, who that same day handed over his functions to the chairman of the Council. The situation was discussed, and a joint decision was taken to cease underground activities. These had to be concluded by a manifesto, and a few days later the text of the manifesto was ready. It was made public on 1 July 1945, and ended with the *Testament of Fighting Poland*. It contained the following postulates:

1. The Soviet army and the Russian political police should leave Polish territory.
2. Political persecution should be halted, of which the following would be proof:
    (a) release of those condemned and imprisoned in the Moscow trial;
    (b) amnesty for political prisoners and for all Home Army soldiers and so-called 'forest detachments';
    (c) return of Poles deported into the heart of Russia and abolition of concentration camps which recalled the grim methods of German totalitarianism;
    (d) abolition of the police system as manifest in the existing so-called Ministry for Public Safety;
3. Unification and granting of independence to the Polish Army through:
    (a) Polonisation of officer corps in the army of General Rola-Żymierski;
    (b) return in arms of Polish forces from abroad;
    (c) amalgamation on equal footing of Polish forces in Europe, and the one-time Home Army with General Żymierski's army.
4. To put an end to the economic devastation of the country by the occupational authorities.
5. To allow all Polish democratic parties to take part in the elections.

6. To ensure the independence of Poland's foreign policy.
7. To create a full territorial, socio-economic, and cultural–educational self-government.
8. To nationalise big capital holdings and organise a just distribution of social revenues.
9. To ensure for the working masses the joint management and control of the whole national economy, and material conditions that would guarantee family welfare and the cultural development of the individual.
10. Freedom for the working class to fight for its rights within a free trade union movement.
11. A just realisation of the agricultural reform and control by the nation of the resettlement operation of the regained territories in the West and in Eastern Prussia.
12. To base universal and democratic schooling and education on the moral and spiritual principles of the civilised heritage of the West and of Poland.

In warranting the fight for this programme in an open political arena, the democratic parties of the Council of National Unity express the hope that the Provisional Government of National Unity will strive towards a democratic Poland and will erase the differences and quarrels that have so far divided various groups within Polish society.

Until this design is made manifest in deeds, there can be no permanent detente in internal relations, and many members of Underground Poland will be forced to remain in hiding, without any hostile intentions regarding the Government, but simply from fear for their own safety.

For its own part Fighting Poland asserts that it is not aiming at provoking a war between the democracies of the West and the Soviet Union, on which the Government press claims that 'the Londoners are basing their political calculations'.

A new war would inflict such terrible wounds on the Polish nation that it is the wish of all Poles to reach an understanding between Poland and Russia, likewise between England, America and Russia on the road to peace. If this understanding is to be long-lasting, it will not suffice to restore trust to Poland's relations with Russia. The Polish nation is a member of the great family of Central European nations, of the Western Slavs in particular, with which it is linked through its geopolitical position and its historic past, and it wishes to enter into the closest possible political, economic and cultural partnership with them.

We express the hope that it is possible to reach an understanding with Russia on this basis, and that it will put an end once and for all to Polish–Russian enmity, which goes back to the reactionary politics of the Tsars, and replace it with mutual respect, trust and friendship for the good of both nations, of Europe and of all of democratic mankind.

The Council of National Unity[17]

After the manifesto, which was passed unanimously, the Council decided to dissolve the Government Delegacy and it also dissolved itself.[18] This was the last act of the Underground State of Poland, and five days later, on 5 July 1945, the Governments of the United States and of Great Britain recognised the Provisional Government of National Unity in Warsaw and withdrew their recognition of the legal Polish Government which had been formed in accordance with the Polish constitution and was resident in London.[19]

POTSDAM CONFERENCE

The war in Europe had ended, but Japan was still fighting and moreover not all European problems had been settled, including that of Poland's western frontiers.

A new international conference was held in Potsdam near Berlin between 17 July and 2 August, 1945, at which 'the Great Three' met yet again. There was one basic change in its make-up, as the new American leader, Harry Truman, came instead of President Roosevelt, who had died. The British side was still represented by Churchill, but he appeared in the company of deputy Prime Minister Clement Attlee, the leader of the socialists. Immediately after the end of the war in Europe a general election was to be held in Great Britain, and it was not yet known who would win. To the amazement of the world Churchill lost the elections, and in the second phase of the conference Britain was represented by the leader of the Labour Party.

The conference could develop in a totally unexpected direction, as several days before it opened the Americans had carried out the first successful explosion of the atom bomb, and Truman had an incredibly powerful weapon in his hands, but he was a completely new man in the international arena, and could not so much as think of a sudden change in policy for the USA.

During the conference the three leaders discovered that Japan had proposed to Sweden the role of mediator in negotiations that could put an end to the war, so this problem was at the top of the agenda. Japan did not yet know that the Americans had the atom bomb, but its situation was so desperate that it did not categorically reject the ultimatum that was issued. Japan was to hand over all territories acquired in the course of the war, punish war criminals, come to terms with American occupation and accept these conditions without any reservations: it was unconditional surrender. A number of matters connected with the occupation of Germany were also settled.

The question of Poland's western frontiers, previously discussed behind the scenes, was regulated on 24 July in the presence of representatives of the Provisional Government of National Unity, whom Truman had invited to participate. The Polish delegation consisted among others of B. Bierut, chairman of the Polish National Council, Premier E. Osóbka-Morawski, Vice-Premiers', W. Gomułka and S. Mikołajczyk and the Minister of National Defence, General M. Rola-Żymierski.

Hitler's Germany was defeated, the country was to come under long-term occupation and pay vast war compensation, but the victors could not agree as to the future of the German nation. Great Britain and the United States did not wish to oppress Germany unduly, nor to shift its frontier too far into the west, as they expected that in the future Germany could be a partner in their strife with Russia. Stalin likewise did not wish to go to extremes as this would mean automatically driving Germany into the arms of the British. At the same time however he understood full well that the more the Poles obtained in the west and north at the expense of Germany, the more they would be dependent on him. A political contest was played behind the scenes as the official negotiations were taking place. The Polish delegation insisted on the greatest possible territorial compensation, upon which point there was no disagreement, though Mikołajczyk could see the danger latent in these demands. However after the heinous German rule, which had not only caused millions of human victims but had also deeply wounded Poland's national pride, no Polish politician could adopt any other stance.

The final decision of the three powers established Poland's western frontier along the Oder and the Neisse in Lusatia, together with Szczecin and a small area of territory on the western side of the town. In the north Poland received Gdańsk and part of Eastern Prussia. At the same time it was decided that all Germans would be evacuated from the territories allotted to Poland. The conference moreover reaffirmed that free elections were to be held in Poland at the earliest possible date, and that the Red Army was to leave Polish territory. On the question of German compensation it was decided that the Soviet Union would settle this on Poland's behalf, and pay 15 per cent of its own share. This decision was very disadvantageous for Poland.[20]

The ultimatum issued to Japan was not accepted, and President Truman was faced with an exceptionally tricky problem. A continuation of the war and the necessary landing on the Japanese islands could cause the death of millions of American and Japanese soldiers. The war could be terminated more swiftly, but only through use of the atomic bomb. The President had British support in this matter, but the decision belonged to him alone. He took the decision, and on 6 August the first bomb was dropped on Hiroshima. Three days later a second one was dropped on Nagasaki. They were the only two bombs in the possession of the United States at the time, and neither failed. Destruction was so terrible that on 14 August Japan accepted conditions for surrender, thereby marking the end of the Second World War.[21]

Poland in August 1945

Notes

INTRODUCTION

1. *Mały rocznik statystyczny*, pp. 10 and 39.
2. Ibid, p. 26.
3. Ibid, pp. 148–51.
4. A. Polonsky, *Politics in Independent Poland, 1921–1939*, p. 490. Also W. Stachiewicz, 'Przygotowania wojenne w Polsce, 1935–39', *Zeszyty historyczne*, no. 40, pp. 78–122.
5. W. Stachiewicz, pp. 11–18.
6. J. Joll, *Europe since 1870*, p. 374.
7. Polonsky, pp. 397–8.
8. Ibid, pp. 446–7.

1 THE OUTBREAK OF WAR

1. Joll, *Europe since 1870*, p. 368.
2. *Polskie Siły Zbrojne w Drugiej Wojnie Światowej*, vol. I, part 1, pp. 46–7.
3. N. Williams, *Chronology of the Modern World, 1763–1965*, p. 566.
4. *Polskie Siły Zbrojne*, vol. I, part 1, p. 48.
5. Ibid, p. 58.
6. Ibid, p. 54.
7. V. Mastny, 'The Czechoslovak Government-in-Exile during the World War II: an Assessment', p. 5. (Lecture given in London, October 1977).
8. *Polskie Siły Zbrojne*, p. 56.
9. E. Raczyński, *The British–Polish Alliance*, p. 14.
10. J. C. Fest, *Hitler*, p. 586.
11. *Polskie Siły Zbrojne*, pp. 93–106. Also Raczyński, *British–Polish Alliance*, p. 19.
12. *Nazi–Soviet Relations, 1939–41*, pp. 5–6.
13. J. Garliński, *Intercept*, pp. 28–45.
14. *Documents on Polish–Soviet Relations*, vol. I, p. 40.
15. Fest, *Hitler*, p. 595.
16. Raczyński, *The British–Polish Alliance*, pp. 21–2.

2 THE SEPTEMBER CAMPAIGN IN POLAND

1. *Polskie Siły Zbrojne*, p. 113.
2. Stachiewicz, 'Przygotowania wojenne w Polsce', pp. 157–8.
3. *Polskie Siły Zbrojne*, table VI.
4. Ibid, p. 292. Also Polonsky, *Politics in Independent Poland*, p. 494. Also Izydor Koliński, *Regularne jednostki Wojska Polskiego (lotnictwo)*, pp. 9 and 59.
5. Stachiewicz, 'Przygotowania wojenne w Polsce', p. 79.
6. *Polskie Siły Zbrojne*, tables II–XIV.
7. Ibid, sketch no. 24, between pp. 416–17.
8. *Polskie Siły Zbrojne*, pp. 448 and 465. Also Karl Ploetz, *Auszug aus der Geschichte*, p. 1354; and Polonsky, *Politics in Independent Poland*, p. 494.
9. *Polskie Siły Zbrojne*, pp. 434–5.
10. Ibid, vol. II, pp. 17–18.
11. Ibid, pp. 16–17. Also Czesław Madajczyk, *Polityka III Rzeszy w okupowanej Polsce*, vol I, pp. 37–8.
12. *Polskie Siły Zbrojne*, vol. II, pp. 13–14.
13. Ibid, p. 13.
14. Ibid, vol. I, p. 85.
15. Ibid, vol. II, pp. 5–9.
16. Ibid, pp. 9–11.,
17. Bohdan Wroński, *Poza krajem – za Ojczyznę*, p. 47. Also *Encyklopedia II wojny światowej*, p. 463.
18. *Polskie Siły Zbrojne*, vol. II, pp. 564–605.
19. Ibid, pp. 544–63.
20. *Encyklopedia*, pp. 96–7. Also Władysław Pobóg-Malinowski, *Najnowsza historia polityczna Polski*, vol. III, pp. 52–5.
21. Basil Liddell Hart, *History of the Second World War*, p. 18.
22. Ibid.
23. Peter Calvocoressi and Guy Wint, *Total War*, p. 100. Also Ploetz, *Auszug aus der Geschichte*, p. 1354.
24. Polonsky, *Politics in Independent Poland*, p. 499. Also Liddell Hart, *History of the Second World War*, pp. 18–19.
25. Pobóg-Malinowski, *Najnowsza historia polityczna Polski*, p. 59.
26. *Documents on Polish–Soviet*, vol. I, pp. 46–7. Also *Polskie Siły Zbrojne*, vol. III, p. 3.
27. Ibid, p. 40.
28. Pobóg-Malinowski, *Najnowsza historia*, pp. 57–9. Also Polonsky, *Politics in Independent Poland*, p. 501.
29. Pobóg-Malinowski, *Najnowsza historia*, p. 61.
30. *Encyklopedia*, pp. 670–1.
31. Ibid, p. 670.
32. Ibid, pp. 285 and 670. Also Ploetz, *Auszug aus der Geschichte*, p. 1355.
33. *Documents on Polish–Soviet*, vol. I, p. 68.
34. Calvocoressi and Wint, *Total War*, p. 101.

3 THE PARTITION OF POLAND

1. *Documents on Polish–Soviet*, pp. 52 and 59–61.
2. Aleksander Bregman, *Najlepszy sojusznik Hitlera*, 4th edn, p. 73.
3. The German parliament, 1871–1945.
4. Madajczyk, *Polityka III*, pp. 66–72.
5. Ibid, pp. 38 and 46.
6. *Polskie Siły Zbrojne*, vol. III, pp. 10–11.
7. This was a declaration opting for German nationality giving certain privileges.
8. *Polskie Siły Zbrojne*, vol. III, pp. 11–17.
9. Władysław Bartoszewski and Zofia Lewinówna, *Righteous among Nations*, p. xix.
10. *Das Generalgouvernement*, Reichshandbuch von Karl Baedeker, p. xxviii (the end of 1942).
11. Madajczyk, *Polityka III*, pp. 99–100.
12. Ibid, pp. 102–4.
13. *Polskie Siły Zbrojne*, vol. III, pp. 20–8.
14. Józef Garliński, *Fighting Auschwitz*, pp. 12–14.
15. Bartoszewski and Lewinówna, *Righteous among Nations*, pp. xvii–xxii.
16. Vidkun Quisling (1887–1945), the prime minister of the Norwegian government in 1940 under the German occupation. Hanged in 1945, the symbol of collaboration.
17. Madajczyk, *Polityka III*, pp. 96–7.
18. *Polskie Siły Zbrojne*, vol. III, p. 29.
19. *Documents on Polish–Soviet*, pp. 69–70.
20. Ibid, p. 65. Also Madajczyk, *Polityka III*, p. 31.
21. *Polskie Siły Zbrojne*, vol. III, pp. 36–7.
22. Aleksander Wat, *Mój wiek*, vol. I, pp. 262–70.
23. *Polskie Siły Zbrojne*, vol. III, p. 37.
24. *Armia Krajowa w dokumentach*, vol. I, pp. 106–8. Also Wat, *Mój wiek*, pp. 265–80.
25. *Polskie Siły Zbrojne*, vol. III, pp. 33–4.
26. Ibid.
27. Ibid, p. 34.
28. Wacław Grubiński, *Między młotem a sierpem*, pp. 16–20.
29. Williams, *Chronology*, p. 570.
30. Pobóg-Malinowski, *Najnowsza historia*, pp. 103–6.
31. Bregman, *Najlepszy sojusznik Hitlera*, pp. 104–5.
32. Margareta Buber, *Under Two Dictators*. Also Bregman, *Najlepszy sojusznik Hitlera*, p. 90.
33. Tadeusz Bór-Komorowski, *The Secret Army*, p. 50.

4 THE UNDERGROUND UNDER GERMAN AND SOVIET OCCUPATION

1. *Armia Krajowa w dokumentach*, vol. I, pp. 1–3. Also Stefan Korboński, *Polish Underground State*, pp. 22–3.

2. *Armia Krajowa w dokumentach*, vol. I, pp. 3–4.
3. Ibid, pp. 31–6.
4. Korboński, *Polish Underground State*, pp. 24–5.
5. *Armia Krajowa w dokumentach*, vol. I, p. 22.
6. Ibid, p. 62.
7. Ibid, p. 61.
8. Ibid, p. 62.
9. Ibid. Also Korboński, *Polish Underground State*, p. 109.
10. *Armia Krajowa w dokumentach*, vol. I. p. 61.
11. The Third or Communist International. It was founded in 1919 in Moscow for the organisation of the revolutionary forces of the world. It dissolved itself in 1943.
12. *Armia Krajowa w dokumentach*, vol. I, p. 61. Also Korboński, *Polish Underground State*, p. 115.
13. Korboński, *Polish Underground State*, p. 64.
14. This name was taken over from a secret organisation formed by Poles in 1397 in Pomerania for self defence against Teutonic Knights.
15. Józef Garliński, 'Konferencja w Belgradzie', *Zeszyty Historyczne*, vol. 34, p. 19.
16. Ibid, pp. 5–6. Also *AK w dokumentach*, vol. I, pp. 65 and 346.
17. Bronisław Krzyżanowski, *Wileński Matecznik, 1939–1944*, pp. 15–20.
18. Ibid, p. 20. Also *AK w dokumetach*, vol. I, p. 226.
19. Garliński, 'Konferencja', pp. 21–2.

5 POLISH GOVERNMENT AND ARMY IN FRANCE

1. *Constitution of the Republic of Poland*, 24 April 1935, pp. 10 and 16.
2. Pobóg-Malinowski, *Najnowsza historia*, pp. 72–3.
3. Wroński, *Poza krajem*, pp. 16–17 (quotation from a letter of the Polish Foreign Minister, Józef Beck, to the new President at the beginning of October 1939).
4. Pobóg-Malinowski, *Najnowsza historia*, p. 97.
5. Wroński, *Poza krajem*, p. 18.
6. *Armia Krajowa w dokumentach*, vol. I, pp. 4–5 and 10.
7. Ibid, pp. 10–21.
8. J. Garliński, *Poland, SOE and the Allies*, pp. 34–5.
9. J. Garliński, *Między Londynem i Warszawą*, pp. 15–17
10. *Armia Krajowa w dokumentach*, vol. I, p. 148.
11. Garliński, *Między Londynem i Warszawą*, pp. 12–17.
12. E. Duraczyński, *Stosunki w kierownictwie podziemia londyńskiego, 1939–1943*, p. 41.
13. *Polskie Siły Zbrojne*, vol. III, p. 53.
14. *Armia Krajowa w dokumentach*, vol. I, pp. 221–2.
15. Duraczyński, *Stosunki w kierownictwie*, p. 23.
16. Wroński, *Poza krajem*, p. 19.
17. Ibid, p. 28.

18. O. Tuskiewicz, *Polskie Siły Powietrzne na Obczyźnie*, pp. 1–7.
19. Wroński, *Poza krajem*, p. 23.
20. Ibid, pp. 23–4.
21. Ibid, p. 24.
22. Williams, *Chronology*, pp. 570 and 572.
23. Liddell Hart, *History of the Second World War*, p. 59. Also *Encyklopedia*, p. 364.
24. *Encyklopedia*, pp. 285–6. Also J. Cynk, interview, 6 June 1981.
25. S. Kopański, *Wspomnienia wojenne, 1939–1945*, pp. 108–110.
26. Wroński, *Poza krajem*, pp. 47–8.

6 THE CHURCH

1. C. Madajczyk, *Polityka III Rzeszy w okupowanej Polsce*, vol. II, pp. 176–7.
2. Ibid, pp. 177–8. Also D. J. Dunn, *The Catholic Church and the Soviet Government, 1939–1949*, p. 41.
3. Madajczyk, *Polityka III*, p. 178.
4. Option to German nationality.
5. *Le Saint Siège et la Situation religieuse en Pologne et dans les Pays Baltes, 1939–1945*, vol. 1, p. 6.
6. Madajczyk, *Polityka III*, pp. 179–80.
7. M. Broszat, *National sozialistische Polenpolitik, 1939–1945*, p. 174. Also Madajczyk, *Polityka III*, pp. 182–6.
8. *Le Saint Siège*, pp. 392–8.
9. Madajczyk, *Polityka III*, pp. 186–7.
10. Ibid, pp. 188–9.
11. Ibid, p. 189.
12. Ibid, pp. 190–1.
13. Ibid, p. 212.
14. Ibid, p. 191.
15. Ibid, pp. 189 and 194–5.
16. Dunn, *The Catholic Church*, pp. 1–15 and 35.
17. Ibid, pp. 41–2.
18. Ibid, pp. 51–3 and 74.
19. Ibid, p. 54. Also A. Wat, *Mój wiek*, part I, p. 285.
20. *Le Saint Siège*, vol. I, pp. 100–117, 128, 160, 191, 287. Also Dunn, *The Catholic Church*, pp. 51–4.
21. Dunn, *The Catholic Church*, pp. 49–51.
22. Ibid, p. 62.
23. *Le Saint Siège*, vol. I and II, pp. 423, 437, 491, 548, 564.
24. Dunn, *The Catholic Church*, pp. 45–6.
25. Ibid, pp. 46–7.
26. Ibid, p. 58. (*New York Times*, 25 December 1939).
27. *Le Saint Siège*, vol. I, pp. 117–18, 158, 168, 277–8.
28. Dunn, *The Catholic Church*, p. 72.

29. Madajczyk, *Polityka III*, pp. 197–8.
30. Dunn, *The Catholic Church*, pp. 57 and 195.
31. Ibid, pp. 87–90.
32. Madajczyk, *Polityka III*, pp. 20–8.

7 THE COLLAPSE OF FRANCE; THE POLISH GOVERNMENT IN LONDON

1. Calvocoressi and Wint, *Total War*, p. 114.
2. Ibid, p. 117. Also Chapman, *Why France Collapsed*. pp. 337–49.
3. Liddell Hart, *History of the Second World War*, pp. 67–71.
4. Ibid, pp. 70–2.
5. Calvocoressi and Wint, *Total War*, p. 121.
6. Ibid, pp. 122–3.
7. Ibid, pp. 120–3. Also Chapman, *Why France Collapsed*, p. 212.
8. Wroński, *Poza krajem*, pp. 35–6.
9. Ibid.
10. Ibid,
11. Ibid, pp. 38–9.
12. Ibid, pp. 37–8.
13. Tuskiewicz, *Polskie Siły Powietrzne*, part II, pp. 7–9. Also Jerzy Cynk, interview, 6 June 1981.
14. Tuskiewicz, *Polskie Siły Powietrzne*, part II, p. 10. Also *Encyklopedia*, p. 286.
15. Liddell Hart, *History of the Second World War*, pp. 62–3. Also Wroński, *Poza krajem*, pp. 33–4 and 44.
16. Wroński, *Poza krajem*, pp. 43–4.
17. Ibid, p. 46.
18. *Armia Krajowa w dokumentach*, vol. I, p. 259.
19. Garliński, 'Konferencja w Belgradzie', *Zeszyty historyczne*, vol. 34.
20. Ibid.
21. *Armia Krajowa w dokumetach*, vol. I, pp. 262–4.
22. Garliński, *Fighting Auschwitz*, p. 16.
23. Bartoszewski and Lewinówna, *Righteous among Nations*. p. xxi.
24. *Documents on Polish–Soviet*, vol. I, pp. 96–7. Also Williams, *Chronology*, p. 572.

8 THE REBUILDING OF THE POLISH ARMY IN GREAT BRITAIN; THE POLISH AIR FORCE

1. *Polskie Siły Zbrojne*, vol. II, part 1, pp. 223–5.
2. Wroński, *Poza krajem*, pp. 62–3.

3. Tuskiewicz, 'Organisation', p. 6, and 'Polish Fighters in Great Britain', pp. 3–6.Also Wacław Król, *Polskie dywizjony lotnicze w Wielkiej Brytanii, 1940–1945*, pp. 138–9 and 167–8.
4. Len Deighton, *Fighter*, pp. 49–50.
5. Ibid, pp. 297–8.
6. Tuskiewicz, 'The Battle of Britain', pp. 5–7.
7. Ibid, p. 9.
8. Ibid, pp. 10–13. Also Calvocoressi and Wint, *Total War*, pp. 140–3.
9. Mastny, 'Czechoslovak Government-in-Exile', p. 9.
10. 'Proceedings of a Conference on Britain and European Resistance, 1939–45, St Antony's College, Oxford, 1962.
11. Garliński, *Poland, SOE and the Allies*, pp. 55–62.
12. Garliński, *Między Londynem i Warszawą*, pp. 22–4.
13. *Polskie Siły Zbrojne*, vol. III, p. 232.
14. Garliński, *Poland*, p. 148.
15. *Polskie Siły Zbrojne*, vol. III, pp. 230–1.
16. Ibid, pp. 232–3.
17. Ibid, pp. 231–6.
18. Ibid. Also *AK w dokumentach*, vol. I, a map on the end of the volume.
19. *Polskie Siły Zbrojne*, vol. III, p. 232.
20. Chester Wilmot, *The Struggle for Europe*, p. 60.
21. Bregman, *Najlepszy sojusznik Hitlera*, p. 111.
22. Calvocoressi and Wint, *Total War*, pp. 146–7.
23. *Polskie Siły Zbrojne*, vol. II, part 1, pp. 219–20.
24. Calvocoressi and Wint, *Total War*, pp. 152–3.
25. Kopański, *Wspomnienia wojenne*, pp. 132–4.
26. Liddell Hart, *History of the Second World War*, pp. 188–20.
27. Kopański, *Wspomnienia wojenne*, pp. 141–2.
28. *Polskie Siły Zbrojne*, vol. II, part 1, pp. 216–17. Also *AK w dokumentach*, vol. I, a map on the end of the volume.
29. Garliński, *The Swiss Corridor*, p. 33.

9 THE GERMAN ATTACK ON USSR AND THE UNEASY POLISH ALLIANCE WITH RUSSIA

1. Karl Lüönd, *Spionage und Landesverrat in der Schweiz*, vol. II, p. 55. Also *Encyklopedia*, pp. 649–50.
2. Calvocoressi and Wint, *Total War*, pp. 173–4. Also *Encyklopedia*, p. 650.
3. Winston S. Churchill, *The Second World War*, vol. III, pp. 331–2.
4. *Documents on Polish–Soviet*, vol. I, p. 108.
5. Ibid, p. 118.
6. Ibid, p. 130.
7. *Polskie Siły Zbrojne*, vol. II, p. 2, pp. 46–7.
8. *Documents on Polish–Soviet*, vol. I, pp. 141–2.
9. *Polskie Siły Zbrojne*, vol. II, p. 2 and pp. 50–1.

10. Ibid. Also *AK w dokumentach*, vol. II, p. 24.
11. *Armia Krajowa w dokumentach*, vol. I, pp. 368–9. Also Korboński, *Polish Underground State*, pp. 42–3.
12. *Armia Krajowa w dokumentach*, vol. II, pp. 1–2, 6–8 and 14.
13. Ibid, p. 14.
14. Ibid, pp. 42–3.
15. Calvocoressi and Wint, *Total War*, p. 333.
16. *Documents on Polish–Soviet*, vol. I, pp. 147–8.
17. *Polskie Siły Zbrojne*, vol. II, p. 2 and pp. 245–53.
18. Ibid, pp. 220–7.
19. Ibid, p. 226.
20. Ibid, p. 224.
21. Władysław Anders, *An Army in Exile*, 6th edn, pp. 62–6.
22. *Polskie Siły Zbrojne*, vol. III, p. 2, pp. 54–5.
23. *Documents on Polish–Soviet*, vol. I, pp. 231–43.
24. Ibid, pp. 231–43.
25. Ibid, p. 246.
26. *Polskie Siły Zbrojne*, vol. II, pp. 2 and 59.
27. Pobóg-Malinowski, *Najnowsza historia*, p. 209.

10   THE POLISH UNDERGROUND STATE

1. *Polskie Siły Zbrojne*, vol. III, p. 108. Also *Das Generalgouvernement*, p. xxviii.
2. Michael R. D. Foot, *Resistance*, pp. 259–69 and 272–8.
3. *Walka o dobra kultury, Warszawa 1939–1945*, vol. II, pp. 407–17.
4. *Armia Krajowa w dokumentach*, vol. I, p. 220. Also Władysław Sieroszewski, 'Z działalności Wojskowego Sądu Specjalnego', *Najnowsze Dzieje Polski*, viii, pp. 121–8.
5. Ibid.
6. Madajczyk, *Polityka III*, vol. II, pp. 148–9.
7. Ibid, pp. 142–6.
8. Czesław Wycech, *Z dziejów tajnej oświaty w latach okupacji, 1939–1944*, p. 64. Also Jerzy Michalewski, 'Relacja o Delegaturze Rządu', *Zeszyty Historyczne*, no. 26, p. 80.
9. Ibid.
10. Wycech, *Z dziejów*, p. 64. Also Madajczyk, *Polityka III*, vol. II, p. 160.
11. Madajczyk, *Polityka III*, vol. II, pp. 150 and 158–9.
12. Ibid, p. 153.
13. Ibid, pp. 153–4.
14. Wycech, *Z dziejów*, pp. 88–90. Also Władysław Kowalenko, *Tajny Uniwersytet Ziem Zachodnich w latach 1940–1944*, pp. 10–93.
15. Wycech, *Z dziejów*, p. 92.
16. Madajczyk, *Polityka III*, vol. I, p. 230 and vol. II, pp. 161–2.
17. Ibid, vol. II, pp. 134–5.
18. Stanisław Marczak-Oborski, *Teatr czasu wojny, 1939–1945*, pp. 238–46. Also Madajczyk, *Polityka III*, vol. II, pp. 134–5.

19. *Walka o dobra kultury*, vol. II, p. 421.
20. Madajczyk, *Polityka III*, vol. II, pp. 129 and 134–6.
21. Marczak-Oborski, *Teatr czasu wojny*, pp. 138–73 and 190–91.
22. Ibid, pp. 190–1 and 246–7.
23. Ibid, pp. 244–50. Also Madajczyk, *Polityka III*, vol. II, p. 138.
24. Ibid. Also Marczak-Oborski, *Teatr czasu wojny*, pp. 244–50.
25. Madajczyk, *Polityka III*, vol. II, pp. 140–1.
26. Marczak-Oborski, *Teatr czasu wojny*, pp. 239–47.
27. Madajczyk, *Polityka III*, vol. II, pp. 120–1.
28. Ibid, p. 123.
29. *Walka o dobra kultury*, vol. I, pp. 8 and 20–104.
30. Ibid, pp. 20–104.
31. Madajczyk, *Polityka III*, vol. II, p. 125.
32. Władysław Chojnacki, *Bibliografia zwartych druków konspiracyjnych wydanych pod okupacją hitlerowską w latach 1939–1945*, pp. 12–13.
33. Madajczyk, *Polityka III*, vol. II, pp. 166–7.
34. Lucjan Dobroszycki, *Centralny katalog polskiej prasy konspiracyjnej, 1939–1945*, pp. 35 and 168–9.
35. Ibid, pp. 60, 87, 98 and 109. Also J. Garliński, *Polska prasa podziemna (1939–1945) w zbiorach londynńskich*, p. 3.
36. Garliński, p. 3.
37. Dobroszycki, *Centralny katalog*, pp. 6–9.
38. Ibid, p. 11.
39. *Polskie Siły Zbrojne*, vol. III, pp. 482 and 499.
40. *Armia Krajowa w dokumentach*, vol. II, p. 199.
41. Jerzy Michalewski, 'Relacja', *Zeszyty Historyczne*, no. 26, pp. 77–86.
42. Stefan Korboński, *Polish Underground State*, pp. 72–3.
43. S. Korboński, *Fighting Warsaw*, p. 170. Also *Polskie Siły Zbrojne*, vol. III, p. 55.
44. Jerzy Pilaciński ('Lech'), *Narodowe Siły Zbrojne*, pp. 81–2 and 138–9. Also Korboński, *Polish Underground State*, pp. 104–9.
45. Aleksander Wat, *Mój wiek*, vol. I, pp. 281–98. Also Korboński, *Polish Underground*, p. 110.

11   FURTHER WAR DEVELOPMENTS AND POLISH PARTICIPATION

1. John Costello and Terry Hughes, *The Battle of the Atlantic*, pp. 1–6.
2. Calvocoressi and Wint, *Total War*, pp. 331–2.
3. Costello and Hughes, *Battle of the Atlantic*, p. 218.
4. Ibid, pp. 194 and 305.
5. Garliński, *Intercept*, pp. 76–80, 92–3 and 137–8.
6. Ibid, pp. 164–6.
7. Marian Żebrowski, *The History of Polish Armoured Units, 1918–1947* (in Polish) p. 229.
8. Tadeusz Lisicki, *Polish Technical Achievements* (in Polish).

9. *Polskie Siły Zbrojne*, vol. II, part 2, pp. 402–4.
10. Edward R. Stettinius, Jr, *Lend-Lease*, pp. 9, 92 and 135–6.
11. Garliński, *Poland, SOE and the Allies*, pp. 63–70.
12. Ibid, pp. 79–81 and 88–92.
13. *Polskie Siły Zbrojne*, vol. II, part 2, p. 467.
14. Garliński, *Poland*, p. 183.
15. Tuskiewicz, 'Organisation', p. 7. Also Król, *Polskie dywizjony*, pp. 77–8.
16. Tuskiewicz, 'Bombers in Great Britain', (in Polish), p. 4. Also author's correspondence with the Ministy of Defence.
17. *Polskie Siły Zbrojne*, vol. II, part 2, pp. 152–61. Also Kopański, *Wspomnienia wojenne*, pp. 157–68.
18. Kopański, *Wspomnienia wojenne*, p. 171.
19. Ibid, pp. 181–202.

12 THE POLISH ARMY IN RUSSIA AND ITS EVACUATION

1. *Polskie Siły Zbrojne*, vol. II, pp. 2 and 259–60.
2. Anders, *An Army in Exile*, pp. 98–100.
3. Ibid.
4. *Polskie Siły Zbrojne*. vol. II, pp. 2, 60–2 and 270.
5. Anders, *An Army in Exile*, pp. 113–22.
6. *Polskie Siły Zbrojne*, vol. II, pp. 2, 277–8 and 299.
7. Ibid, pp. 278–83.
8. Polonsky, *The Great Powers and the Polish Question*, 1941–45, pp. 23 and 109.
9. *Polskie Siły Zbrojne*, vol. II, pp. 2 and 66, note 13.
10. Ibid, pp. 67–8 and 289.
11. Ibid, pp. 291–2.
12. Ibid, p. 295.
13. Ibid. Also Anders, *An Army in Exile*, pp. 57–8 and 129.
14. S. Kot, *Listy z Rosji do gen. Sikorskiego*, pp. 178–9. Also H. Zatorska, *Wanda Wasilewska*, p. 56.
15. Protocol by N. Giedronowicz, 13 October 1942.
16. Zbiniewicz, *Armia Polska w ZSRR*, pp. 14–15.
17. Ibid, p. 15.
18. *Dokumenty i materiały do historii stosunków polsko-radzieckich*, vol. VII, pp. 222–3.
19. Ibid, p. 220.
20. Ibid, p. 237.
21. *Polskie Siły Zbrojne*, vol. II, p. 284. Also Zbiniewicz, *Armia Polska w ZSRR*, pp. 15–16.
22. Zbiniewicz, *Armia Polska w ZSRR*, p. 22.
23. Ibid, pp. 14 and 22.
24. Ibid. p. 17.
25. *Polskie Siły Zbrojne*, vol. 2, pp. 2 and 70–1. Also Urszula Muskus, *Długi most*. The author, an employee of an outpost, was arrested in

1942, separated from her small children and spent fourteen years in prisons and camps.
26. Anders, *An Army in Exile*, p. 129.
27. *Documents on Polish–Soviet*, p. 427–8.
28. *Polskie Siły Zbrojne*, vol. II, pp. 2 and 72–4.
29. Ibid, p. 74.
30. *Polskie Siły Zbrojne*, vol. II, pp. 2 and 75.

13   THE PLIGHT OF THE POLISH JEWS

1. Bartoszewski and Lewinówna, p. xix. Also Madajczyk, *Polityka III*, vol. II, p. 324.
2. Madajczyk, *Polityka III*, vol. II, pp. 310–16.
3. Gerald Reitlinger, *The Final Solution*, pp. 40–1.
4. Madajczyk, *Polityka III*, vol. II, pp. 294–343.
5. Ibid, pp. 329–30.
6. Bartoszewski and Lewinówna, pp. xxii–xxvii.
7. Ibid, pp. xxxii–iii.
8. Ibid, p. xix.
9. Ibid.
10. Józef Garliński, *Fighting Auschwitz*, pp. 34–56 and 84–93.
11. Bartoszewski and Lewinówna, p. xliii.
12. Ibid.
13. Ibid, pp. xxx–xxxi.
14. Madajczyk, *Polityka III*, vol. II, p. 320.
15. Bartoszewski and Lewinówna, pp. xxxiii–v and liii.
16. Madajczyk, *Polityka III*, vol. II, pp. 310–12.
17. Bartoszewski and Lewinówna, p. lvi.
18. Ibid, pp. lvii–viii.
19. Ibid, pp. lxi–lxiv.
20. *Armia Krajowa w dokumentach*, vol. II, pp. 500 and 506–7.
21. Bartoszewski and Lewinówna, p. lxv.
22. Ibid, p. lxvii.
23. Ibid, p. lxvi.
24. Ibid, p. lxviii. Also Madajczyk, *Polityka III*, vol. II, p. 327.
25. Madajczyk, *Polityka III*, vol. I, pp. 228–31.
26. Ibid, vol. II, pp. 310–12.
27. Ibid, p. 323.
28. Bartoszewski and Lewinówna, p. lxix.
29. Gerald Reitlinger, *The Final Solution*, pp. 542–3.

14   THE POLISH ARMY IN THE MIDDLE EAST AND CRISIS IN LONDON

1. Calvocoressi and Wint, *Total War*, pp. 364–5.
2. Ibid, pp. 360–2. Also *Polskie Siły Zbrojne*, vol. II, p. 2 and pp. 309–14.

3. Calvocoressi and Wint, *Total War*, p. 367.
4. Liddell Hart, *History of the Second World War*, pp. 438–9.
5. André Brissaud, *Canaris*, pp. 112–15.
6. Calvocoressi and Wint, *Total War*, pp. 398–9.
7. M. E. Hohenlohe, report of meeting with Dulles, Berlin, 30 April 1943 (documents, department VI *RSHA*).
8. Heinz Höhne, *Canaris*, p. 482.
9. Joachim Fest, *Hitler*, p. 665.
10. *Polskie Siły Zbrojne*, vol. II, pp. 2 and 299–308.
11. Ibid, pp. 312–17.
12. Kopański, *Wspomnienia wojenne*, pp. 270–1. Also *Polskie Siły Zbrojne*, vol. II, pp. 2, 75 and 321.
13. Leon Mitkiewicz, *W Najwyższym Sztabie Zachodnich Aliantów*, pp. 14–15.
14. *Polski Słownik Biograficzny*, vol. 108, p. 57.
15. *Armia Krajowa w dokumentach*, vol. II, pp. 295–6.
16. Ibid, pp. 461–2.
17. Korboński, *Polish Underground State*, pp. 112–13.
18. *Armia Krajowa w dokumentach*, vol. II, pp. 369–71.
19. *Polskie Siły Zbrojne*, vol. II, pp. 2 and 79.
20. *Zbrodnia katyńska w świetle dokumentów*, 3rd edn, p. 85.
21. Ibid, pp. 86–7. Also *AK w dokumentach*, vol. II, pp. 491–2 and 501–3.
22. *Zbrodnia katyńska*, p. 88.
23. Ibid.
24. Ibid, pp. 90–1.
25. Calvocoressi and Wint, *Total War*, pp. 341–4.
26. *Zbrodnia katyńska*, pp. 94–5, 96–112, 144–53 and 157–200.
27. *Documents on Polish–Soviet Relations*, vol. I, pp. 533–4.
28. Ibid, pp. 537–8.

15 POLISH COMMUNISTS IN USSR

1. *Documents on Polish–Soviet*, vol. I, pp. 534–6.
2. Zbiniewicz, *Armia Polska w ZSRR*, p. 37.
3. Ibid, pp. 32–4.
4. Ibid, pp. 35–7. Also Włodziemierz Sokorski, *Polacy pod Lenino*, pp. 8–11.
5. Zbiniewicz, *Armia Polska w ZSRR*, pp. 49–53.
6. Ibid. Also Sokorski, *Polacy pod Lenino*, p. 11.
7. Zbiniewicz, *Armia Polska w ZSRR*, pp. 50–1.
8. Ibid, pp. 36 and 45–6.
9. Ibid, pp. 46–8.
10. Ibid, pp. 53–8.
11. Ibid, p. 61.
12. Ibid.
13. Sokorski, *Polacy pod Lenino*, pp. 11–12 and 20.
14. Zbiniewicz, *Armia Polska w ZSRR*, pp. 65 and 73.

15. Ibid, pp. 39–41.
16. Ibid, pp. 186–6. Also *Encyklopedia*, p. 433.
17. Zbiniewicz, *Armia Polska w ZSRR*, pp. 120–8.
18. Ibid, pp. 138–41.
19. Ibid, pp. 142–4.
20. Ibid, pp. 146–8. Also Sokorski, *Polacy pod Lenino*, pp. 64–74.

16 UNDERGROUND FIGHT IN POLAND; ARREST OF GENERAL
   ROWECKI; DEATH OF GENERAL SIKORSKI

1. *Polskie Siły Zbrojne*, vol. II, pp. 2 and 84. Also Williams, *Chronology*, p. 586.
2. *Armia Krajowa w dokumentach*, vol. III, pp. 24–5.
3. J. Garliński, *The Swiss Corridor*, pp. 84–97.
4. *Polskie Siły Zbrojne*, vol. III, pp. 114–20.
5. Ibid, pp. 158–9.
6. Ibid, pp. 323–5. Also *AK w dokumentach*, vol. II, p. 236.
7. *Polskie Siły Zbrojne*, vol. III, pp. 329–35.
8. A. Horodyski-Kotecki, 'Podziemny przemysł zbrojeniowy', pp. 6–7.
9. K. Czerniewski, 'O prawdę historyczną', pp. 386–91.
10. Garliński, *Poland, SOE and the Allies*, pp 97–8.
11. Ibid, p. 98.
12. Ibid.
13. Ibid, pp. 146–8 and 235–6.
14. *Polskie Siły Zbrojne*, vol. III, p. 462.
15. Ibid, pp. 466–7.
16. Ibid, pp. 533–8.
17. Ibid, pp. 529–30.
18. Ibid, pp. 527–9.
19. Ibid, p. 524.
20. *Encyklopedia*, pp. 23–7. Also *Zeszyty do historii Narodowych Sił Zbrojnych*, vol. III, pp. 51–6.
21. *Polskie Siły Zbrojne*, vol. III, pp. 458–9.
22. Ibid, pp. 459–60.
23. K. Bogacki, 'Konspiracyjna łączność Armii Krajowej', *Dziękuję Wam Rodacy*, str. 126–7.
24. J. Srebrzyński, "Zagadnienia łączności krajowej", *Dziękuję Wam Rodacy*, pp. 62–7.
25. *Armia Krajowa w dokumentach*, vol. II, pp. 20–1.
26. Garliński, *Hitler's Last Weapons*, pp. 47–52.
27. M. Protasewicz, letters to the author: 19 November 1975 and 12 April 1976.
28. David Irving, *The Mare's Nest*, pp. 98–114. Also Walter Dornberger, *V-2*, pp. 119–20.
29. Bernard Zakrzewski, 'Aresztowanie gen. Grota', *Stolica*, 21 and 28 July and 4 August 1957.
30. Anders, *Bez ostatniego*, pp. 144–5.

31. Ibid, pp. 148–9.
32. *Polskie Siły Zbrojne*, vol. II, pp. 2 and 85.
33. Ibid, pp. 86–7. Also David Irving, *The Death of General Sikorski, Accident*, pp. 77–113 and 185–94.
34. R. W. Thompson, *Generalissimo Churchill*, pp. 232–3.

17 DIFFICULTIES WITH COMMUNISTS; 'TEMPEST'; TEHERAN

1. *Polskie Siły Zbrojne*, vol. II, pp. 2 and 88.
2. J. Zarański, *Świadek wydarzeń*, pp. 41–66.
3. Kopański, *Wspomnienia wojenne*, pp. 300–1.
4. Calvocaressi and Wint, *Total War*, pp. 478–9.
5. *Armia Krajowa w dokumentach*, vol. III, p. 43.
6. *SPP*, personal file of General T. Komorowski.
7. *Armia Krajowa w dokumentach*, vol. III, pp. 68 and 93–4.
8. Ibid, pp. 126–7.
9. Mitkiewicz, *W Najwyższym Sztabie*, pp. 28 and 78–86.
10. Ibid, pp. 104–12.
11. T. Pełczyński, 'Geneza i przebieg Burzy', *Bellona*, vol. 3/48, pp. 7–8. Also *AK w dokumentach*, vol. III, pp. 188–9.
12. Ibid, pp. 182–5.
13. *Polskie Siły Zbrojne*, vol. III, p. 555.
14. Pełczyński, pp. 8–9.
15. Ibid. Also *AK w dokumentach*, vol. III, pp. 209–13.
16. Pełczyński, 'Geneza i przebieg Burzy', pp. 9–10.
17. *Polskie Siły Zbrojne*, vol. III, pp. 145–8.
18. Ibid, pp. 149–57 and 167–8. Also Pilaciński, *Narodowe Siły Zbrojne*, pp. 149–57.
19. Calvocoressi and Wint, *Total War*, p. 344. Also Duraczyński, *Stosunki w kierownictwie*, p. 254.
20. Zbiniewicz, *Arma Polska w ZSRR*, p. 170.
21. *Polskie Siły Zbrojne*, vol. II, pp. 2 and 91.
22. *Armia Krajowa w dokumentach*, vol. III, pp. 156–7, 179, 208–9, 215 and 222–8.
23. Astley, *The Inner Circle*, p. 121.
24. *Documents on Polish–Soviet*, vol. II, pp. 97–8.
25. Calvocoressi and Wint, *Total War*, p. 347.
26. *Documents on Polish–Soviet*, vol. II, p. 84.
27. Ibid, pp. 85–6.
28. Ibid, pp. 96–101. Also Calvocoressi and Wint, *Total War*, p. 345.
29. *Polskie Siły Zbrojne*, vol. II, pp. 2 and 91.

18 SECOND POLISH CORPS IN ITALY; OTHER POLISH
FORMATIONS

1. Calvocoressi and Wint, *Total War*, pp. 378–80.
2. Liddell Hart, *History of the Second World War*, pp. 447–75.
3. Calvocoressi and Wint, *Total War*, p. 512.
4. Anders, *An Army in Exile*, pp. 175–6.
5. Ibid, pp. 176–8. Also *Polskie Siły Zbrojne*, vol. II, pp. 2 and 335–6.
6. *Polskie Siły Zbrojne*, vol. II, pp. 2, 340–1 and 349–50.
7. Anders, *An Army in Exile*, pp. 191–2.
8. Ibid, pp. 185–6.
9. Calvocoressi and Wint, *Total War*, pp. 514–15.
10. Ibid, p. 515. Also Garliński, *Poland, SOE and the Allies*, p. 29.
11. *Polskie Siły Zbrojne*, vol. II, pp. 2, 118 and 126.
12. S. Maczek, *Od podwody do czołga*, pp. 141–7.
13. W. Biegański *et al.*, *Polski czyn zbrojny w II Wojnie Światowej*, p. 220.
14. S. Sosabowski, *Najkrótszą drogą*, pp. 158–64.
15. Ibid, pp. 167–80.
16. Tuskiewicz, 'Organizacja', p. 7. Also Król, *Polskie dywizjony*, pp. 123 and 357.
17. Tuskiewicz, 'Lotnictwo myśliwskie', pp. 23 and 27–31.
18. Tuskiewicz, 'Lotnictwo bombowe. 6–8.
19. Ibid, pp. 9–10.
20. *Polskie Siły Zbrojne*, vol. II, pp. 2 and 530–2.
21. Ibid, pp. 547–58.
22. Ibid, pp 559–67.
23. Wroński, *Poza krajem*, p. 159.
24. Ibid.
25. *Polskie Siły Zbrojne*, vol. II, pp. 2 and 451–60.
26. S. Liberak, *Témoignages*, pp. 29–30. Also SPP, file nos.5,2,8, document 8927, 30 September 1942.
27. Liberak *Témoignages*, pp. 31–3. Also Garliński, *The Swiss Corridor*, pp. 115–18.
28. *Polskie Siły Zbrojne*, vol. II, pp. 2 and 118.
29. Kopański, *Wspomnienia wojenne*, pp. 296–7.

19 NEW DEVELOPMENTS IN POLAND; MONTE CASSINO;
FALAISE; TEMPEST

1. Polonsky and Drukier, *The Beginnings of Communist Rule in Poland*, p. 10.
2. Ibid, pp. 10–11.
3. *Polskie Siły Zbrojne*, vol. III, pp. 60–1. Also Korboński, *Polish Underground State*, p. 103.
4. *Polskie Siły Zbrojne* vol. III, pp. 65–8.

5. Ibid, pp. 68–9.
6. Ibid, pp. 69–74. Also Korboński, *Polish Underground State* pp. 103–5.
7. Ibid, p. 45.
8. *Documents on Polish–Soviet*, vol. II, pp. 123–4, 132–4 and 138–9.
9. *Polskie Siły Zbrojne*, vol. III, pp. 566–7.
10. Ibid, pp. 584–6.
11. T. Sztumberk-Rychter, *Artylerzysta piechurem*, pp. 202–3. Also T. Klimowski, an interview, 15 January 1967.
12. *Arma Krajowa w dokumentach*, vol. III, pp. 392–4.
13. Ibid, pp. 398–9.
14. Ibid, pp. 402–3.
15. Ibid, pp. 594–9.
16. *Encyklopedia*, pp. 432–3. Also Zbiniewicz, *Armia Polska w ZSRR*, p. 331.
17. *Encyklopedia*, p. 31.
18. Ibid, p. 491.
19. Ibid, pp. 30–1
20. Calvocoressi and Wint, *Total War*, pp. 509–10.
21. Ibid. Also Liddell Hart, *History of the Second World War*, pp. 529–30.
22. Anders, *Bez ostatniego*, p. 163.
23. Ibid, pp. 163–4.
24. Ibid, p. 165.
25. Ibid, pp. 170–4.
26. Ibid, pp. 175–6.
27. Ibid, pp. 176–7.
28. Ibid, pp. 178–80.
29. Ibid, 180–2.
30. Ibid, pp. 182–3.
31. *Armia Krajowa w dokumentach*, vol. III, p. 457.
32. Garliński, *Hitler's Last Weapons*, pp. 150–1.
33. Lord Cherwell was a German by descent and his name was Lindemann.
34. Garliński, *Hitler's Last Weapons*, pp. 60–1.
35. Ibid, p. 152.
36. Ibid, p. 159.
37. Polish Underground Movement, 1939–45 Study Trust, file *Special Report 1/R, no. 242*. Also Reginald Jones, report written in August 1944 on V–2. Also M. Wojewódzki, *V–1, V–2*, pp. 463–73.
38. Crossbow Committee, Meeting, 31 August 1944.
39. Calvocoressi and Wint, *Total War*, p. 515.
40. Ibid, p. 514.
41. Maczek, *Od podwody do czołga*, pp. 150–1.
42. Ibid, pp. 151–6.
43. Ibid, pp. 156–7.
44. Ibid, pp. 158–62.
45. Ibid, pp. 165–6.
46. Ibid, pp. 181–5. Also Calvocoressi and Wint, *Total War*, p. 519.
47. Maczek, *Od podwody do czołga*, pp. 180–1.
48. Tuskiewicz, 'Polish Air Force Abroad', *Fighters*, pp. 46–66.

49. Wroński, *Poza krajem*, p. 192.
50. Ibid, pp. 193–4.
51. Ibid, pp. 163–7. Also Cajus Bekker, *Hitler's Naval War*, p. 364.

20 'TEMPEST' COMMUNISTS' MANIFESTO, ATTEMPT ON HITLER'S LIFE, ITALY, 'BRIDGES'

1. *Armia Krajowa w dokumentach*, vol. III, pp. 292–3.
2. J. Ciechanowski, *The Warsaw Rising*, pp. 205–6.
3. J. Garliński, *Między Londynem*, pp. 73–4 and 80.
4. *Armia Krajowa w dokumentach*, vol. III, p. 560.
5. R. Korab-Żebryk, *Epilog, Wileńszczyzna 1944*, pp. 43–74.
6. *The Unseen and Silent*, p. 187.
7. Ibid.
8. H. Pohoski, 'Wspomnienia', 1968, Polish Underground Movement, 1939–45 Study Trust, file Okręg Lwów.
9. *Wierny*, a report: '30 Poleska Dywizja AK', Polish Underground, file Okręg Polesie.
10. *Polskie Siły Zbrojne*, vol. III, p. 628.
11. I. Caban and Z. Mańkowski, *Związek Walki Zbrojnej i Armia Krajowa w Okręgu Lubelskim, 1939–1944*, vol. I, pp. 169–82.
12. *Polskie Siły Zbrojne*, vol. III, p. 622.
13. Polonsky and Drukier, *The Beginnings of Communist Rule*, p. 22. Also W. T. Kowalski, *Wielka Koalicja, 1941–1945*, vol. II, pp. 273–81.
14. Polonsky and Drukier, *The Beginnings of Communist Rule*, p. 23.
15. *Encyklopedia*, pp. 486 and 490.
16. Royce, Zimmermann and Jacobsen, *20 Juni 1944*, p. 120.
17. Anders, *An Army in Exile*, p. 222.
18. Ibid, pp. 221–2 and 224–5.
19. Ibid, pp. 226–9. Also Biegański *et al.*, *Polski czyn zbrojny*, pp. 566–70.
20. Anders, *Bez ostatniego*, pp. 230–2.
21. Garliński, *Poland*, pp. 140–2.
22. Ibid, pp. 142–3.
23. Ibid, pp. 145–8.
24. Ibid, pp. 157–9.
25. Ibid, pp. 155–6.
26. Ibid, p. 160.
27. Ibid, p. 162. Also Korboński, *Fighting Warsaw*, pp. 296–301.

21 THE WARSAW UPRISING

1. A. Borkiewicz, *Powstanie Warszawskie 1944*, pp. 9–10. Also *Polskie Siły Zbrojne*, vol. III, p. 651.
2. Ciechanowski, *The Warsaw Rising*, pp. 349–52.

3. K. Sosnkowski, *Materiały historyczne*, pp. xxiv–xxv. Also Kopański *Wspomnienia wojenne, p. 314.* Also Babiński, 'Powstanie Warszawskie', *Zeszyty historyczne*, no. 6/1964, pp. 59–60.
4. *Armia Krajowa w dokumentach*, vol. III, p. 505.
5. Ciechanowski, *The Warsaw Rising*, pp. 255–6.
6. Ibid, p. 257. Also Garliński, interview with the General Bór-Komorowski, *Tydzień Polski*, 1 August 1964.
7. Korboński, *Fighting Warsaw*, p. 180.
8. Bór-Komorowski, *The Secret Army*, pp. 222–7. Also *Polskie Siły Zbrojne*, vol. III, p. 658.
9. Ciechanowski, *The Warsaw Rising*, pp. 352–3.
10. Z. Zaremba, *Wojna i konspiracja*, p. 253.
11. *Polskie Siły Zbrojne*, vol. III, pp. 694–6.
12. Ibid, pp. 697–8.
13. Bór-Komorowski, *The Secret Army*, pp. 230–1.
14. Ibid, pp. 232–3. Also *Polskie Siły Zbrojne*, vol. III, p. 710.
15. Ibid, pp. 676, 678–9 and 693–4. Also J. Zawodny, *Nothing but Honor.* p. 210.
16. The Soviet General Andrey Vlasov was taken prisoner by the Germans, went over to their side and undertook to raise an army from Soviet prisoners-of-war. They distinguished themselves by great cruelty. Vlasov was taken prisoner by the Americans and handed over to Russians. After a short trial he was hanged in Moscow in 1946.
17. *Polskie Siły Zbrojne*, vol. III, p. 687. Also Zawodny, *Nothing but Honor*, p. 211.
18. Garliński, *Poland*, p. 185. Also *AK w dokumentach*, vol. IV, p. 31.
19. Garliński, *Poland*, pp. 187–8.
20. S. Mikołajczyk, *The Pattern of Soviet Domination*, pp. 78–90.
21. L. Rayski, an interview (Flights over Warsaw), London, 11 February 1968. Also J. Slessor, *The Central Blue*, pp. 615–19.
22. *Polskie Siły Zbrojne*, vol. III, pp. 711–13. Also Borkiewicz, *Powstanie Warszawskie*, pp. 304–15.
23. *Polskie Siły Zbrojne*, vol. III, pp. 632–46, 751 and 791.
24. *Armia Krajowa w dokumentach*, vol. V, pp. 165–70.
25. Ibid, vol. IV, pp. 208–9, 213–214, 221–3, 237–8, 240–1 and 248–50.
26. *Polskie Siły Zbrojne*, vol. III, pp. 714–715.
27. Ibid, pp. 717–18. Also *AK w dokumentach*, vol. IV, pp. 250–1.
28. Ibid, pp. 108–9, 134–5 and 195–7.
29. Garliński, *Poland*, pp. 199–200.
30. *Polskie Siły Zbrojne*, vol. III, pp. 870–3.
31. H. von Krannhals, *Der Warschauer Aufstand, 1944*, pp. 214–15. Also J. Matecki, 'Dziennik działań niemieckiej 9 Armii', *Zeszyty historyczne*, no. 15, p. 128.
32. Garliński, *Poland*, pp. 190–1.
33. Ibid, p. 205.
34. Ibid.
35. Matecki, 'Dziennik działań', p. 79. Also Garliński, *Intercept*, p. 178.
36. Matecki, 'Dziennik działań', p. 79.

41. *Armia Krajowa w dokumentach*, vol. IV, pp. 416–17.
42. Von Krannhals, *Der Warschauer Aufstand*, p. 5.

22   POLISH UNITS IN FURTHER COMBAT; CONFERENCE IN MOSCOW

1. Calvocoressi and Wint, *Total War*, pp. 519–21.
2. Maczek, pp. 187–97.
3. Ibid, pp. 202–9.
4. Calvocoressi and Wint, *Total War*, pp. 523–4.
5. Garliński, *Hitler's*, p. 179.
6. Sosabowski, *Najkrótszą drogą*, pp. 231–2. Also Calvocoressi and Wint, *Total War*, pp. 524–5.
7. Ibid, p. 535. Also Sosabowski, *Najkrótszą drogą*, pp. 236–60.
8. Anders, *The Army in Exile*, pp. 254–91.
9. Ibid, pp. 291–305.
10. Garliński, *Poland*, pp. 210–11.
11. Ibid, p. 212.
12. Ibid.
13. Ibid, p. 213.
14. Ibid.
15. Garliński, 'Piechota', pp. 34–40.
16. *Documents on Polish–Soviet*, vol. II, p. 405. Also Zarański, *Świadek wydarzeń*, pp. 57–8.
17. Mikołajczyk, *Pattern of Soviet Domination*, p. 111.
18. Zarański, *Świadek wydarzeń*, pp. 61–4. Also Polonsky, *The Great Powers*, pp. 36–7 and 220–1.
19. *Documents on Polish–Soviet*, vol. II, pp. 443–4.
20. Ibid, pp. 468–9.
21. Ibid, p. 417. Also Mikołajczyk, *Pattern of Soviet Domination*, pp. 117–18.
22. *Documents*, pp. 488–9.
23. Ibid, pp. 485–6 and 497–8.
24. Ibid, pp. 495–505. Also Mikołajczyk, *Pattern of Soviet Domination*, pp. 119–20.
25. *Armia Krajowa w dokumentach*, vol. IV, p. 33.
26. Garliński, 'Między Londynem', p. 107.
27. Ibid, p. 114.
28. Hudson, 'Report of the British Observer to German-occupied Poland'.

23 THE LAST SOVIET OFFENSIVE; DISSOLUTION OF THE HOME
ARMY; YALTA; THE END OF WAR IN EUROPE

1. Kowalski, vol. III, pp. 18–20.
2. *Encyklopedia*, p. 35.
3. Ibid, pp. 39–41.
4. Garliński, *Poland*, p. 221.
5. Ibid.
6. *Armia Krajowa w dokumentach*, vol. V, pp. 250–5. Also Korboński, *Polish Underground State*, pp. 211–12.
7. *Armia Krajowa w dokumentach*, vol. III, p. 210. Also S. Kluz, *W potrzasku dziejowym*, pp. 40–1.
8. Korboński, *Polish Underground State*, pp. 213–14.
9. Z. Siemaszko, *Narodowe Siły Zbrojne*, pp. 143,145,153–67.
10. *Documents on Polish–Soviet*, vol. II, pp. 520–1.
11. Ibid, pp. 532–3.
12. *Armia Krajowa w dokumentach*, vol. V, p. 323.
13. Ibid, pp. 346–7.
14. *Documents on Polish–Soviet*, vol. II, pp. 528 and 542.
15. *Armia Krajowa w dokumentach*, vol. V, pp. 357–8. Also Korboński, *Polish Underground*, pp. 216–19.
16. *Armia Krajowa w dokumentach*, vol. V, pp. 359–60 and 406–7.
17. Ibid.
18. Anders, *An Army in Exile*, pp. 247–261.
19. Ibid, p. 235. Also Wroński, *Poza krajem*, p. 116.
20. Anders, *An Army in Exile*, pp. 287–8.
21. Maczek, *Od podwody do czołga*, pp. 226–7.
22. Ibid, pp. 226–36.
23. *Polski czyn zbrojny*, p. 652.
24. Maczek, *Od podwody do czołga*, p. 245.
25. *Polscy spadochroniarze*, pp. 356–62.
26. Biegański *et al.*, *Polski czyn*, pp. 662–5. Also Król, *Polskie dywizjony*, pp. 365–7.
27. Biegański *et al.*, *Polski czyn*, pp. 665–70.
28. Ibid, pp. 697–8.
29. Wroński, *Poza krajem*, p. 167.
30. *Encyklopedia*, p. 68.
31. Ibid, pp. 65–8.

24 CONFERENCE IN SAN FRANCISCO; PROVISIONAL
GOVERNMENT OF NATIONAL UNITY; TESTAMENT OF
FIGHTING POLAND; END OF THE WAR

1. A. Bregman, *Dzieje pustego fotela*, pp. 7–8.
2. Ibid, pp. 8–11.
3. *Documents on Polish–Soviet*, vol. II, p. 564.

4. *Armia Krajowa w dokumentach*, vol. V, pp. 399–401.
5. Ibid.
6. *Sprawozdanie sądowe*, p. 31. Also Stypułkowski, *Invitation to Moscow*, p. 309.
7. Ibid, pp. 301–12.
8. Ibid, p. 274. Also Garliński, *Poland*, p. 231.
9. Stypułkowski, *Invitation to Moscow*, pp. 322–3.
10. *Sprawozdanie sądowe*, p. 270.
11. Ibid, pp. 269–78.
12. Bregman, *Dzieje pustego fotela*, pp. 169–71.
13. Korboński, *Fighting Warsaw*, pp. 457–9.
14. Mikołajczyk, *Pattern of Soviet Domination*, pp. 146–7. Also Korboński, *Polish Underground State*, pp. 234–5.
15. Korboński, *Polish Underground State*, pp. 223–6. Also *AK w dokumentach*, vol. V, pp. 367–8 and 421–3.
16. Korboński, *Polish Underground State*, pp. 225–7.
17. *Armia Krajowa w dokumentach*, vol. V, pp. 482–4.
18. Korboński, *Polish Underground State*, p. 232.
19. *Armia Krajowa w dokumentach*, vol. V, pp. 484–5.
20. Mikołajczyk, *Pattern of Soviet Domination*, pp. 153–7. Also Polonsky and Drukier, *Beginning of Communist Rule*, pp. 120–1.
21. Churchill, *The Second World War*, vol. VI, p. 553. Also Williams, *Chronology*, p. 598.

Bibliography

ARCHIVAL SOURCES

1. Archives

Bundesarchiv-Militärarchiv, Freiburg, West Germany.
General Sikorski Historical Institute, London.
Polish Underground Movement, 1939–45, Study Trust, London.
Public Record Office, London.

2. Unpublished documents, reports, statements and letters

Crossbow Committee (CBC) (44) Meetings: 14 July 1944, 18 July 1944, 10 August 1944, 31 August 1944 (Public Record Office).

Cynk, Jerzy, an interview, London, 6 June 1981.

Garby-Czerniawski, Roman, an interview, London, 13 July 1978.

Hudson, D. T. 'Report of the British Observer to German-occupied Poland, 26 December 1944', Polish Underground Movement, 1939–45, Study Trust, file: British Military Mission.

Jones, Reginald Victor, report on V–2, written in August 1944; copy in author's possession.

Klimowski, Tadeusz, an interview, London, 15 January 1967.

Lisicki, Tadeusz, an interview, London, 5 November 1981.

Mastny, Vojtech, 'The Czechoslovak Government-in-Exile during the World War II: an Assessment'. Lecture given during a conference on Government Exiled in London during the Second World War, London, October, 1977.

Mirewicz, Rev. Jerzy, an interview, London, 27 February 1982.

Areas and Districts of the ZWZ/AK (in Polish), file No 4497/B II, Polish Underground Movement, 1939–45, Study Trust.

Pociski rakietowe (Special Report 1/R, no. 242, 12 July 1944. Files of the VIth Bureau of the Polish General Staff. Polish Underground Movement, 1939–45, Study Trust.

Pohoski, Henryk, Memories (in Polish), 1968, Polish Underground... file, 'Okręg Lwów'.

Report No. 79, 1 March 1941 – 1 September 1941, Commander of the ZWZ, Polish Underground...., file 3.3.1/3.

'Proceedings of a Conference on Britain and European Resistance, 1939–1945', St Antony's College, Oxford, 1962.

Protasewicz, Michał, letters to the author, 19 November 1975 and 12 April 1976.

Rayski, Ludomir, an interview (Flights over Warsaw), London, 11 February 1968.

Tuskiewicz, Otto, 'Polish Air Force Abroad' (roneo) London 1947.
Wilkinson, P. A., letter to the author (The Polish Section of SOE), London, 12 February 1968.
Wiśniowska, Halina (primo voto Szymańska), authorised interviews, London, 14 June 1979, 28 August 1979 and 13 February 1980.

BOOKS AND ARTICLES

Anders, Władysław, *An Army in Exile* (London: 1949).
Armia Krajowa w dokumentach, 1939–45 (London, 1970–81) vols I–V.
Astley, Joan Bright, *The Inner Circle* (London, 1973).
Babiński, Witold, 'Odpowiedzialność Naczelnego Wodza', *Wiadomości* (London: 2 March 1952). 'Pokłosie dyskusji', *Zeszyty historyczne* (Paris: no. 16/1969). 'Powstanie Warszawskie', *Zeszyty historyczne,* (Paris: no. 6/1964).
Bartoszewski, Władysław and Lewinówna, Zofia, *Righteous among Nations* (London: 1969).
Bekker, Cajus, *Hitler's Naval War* (London: 1974).
Biegański, Witold et al., *Polski czyn zbrojny w II wojnie światowej (walki formacji polskich na zachodzie), 1939–1945* (Warsaw: 1981).
Bogacki, Konrad, 'Konspiracyjna łączność Armii Krajowej', *Dziękuję Wam Rodacy* (London: 1973).
Borkiewicz, Adam, *Powstanie Warszawskie, 1944* (Warsaw: 1964).
Boyle, Andrew, *The Climate of Treason* (London: 1980).
Bór-Komorowski, Tadeusz, *The Secret Army* (London: 1953).
Bregman, Aleksander, *Dzieje pustego fotela* (London: 1948); *Najlepszy sojusznik Hitlera* (London: 1980).
Brissant, André, *Canaris* (London: 1973).
Broszat, Martin, *National Sozialistische Polenpolitic, 1939–1945,* (Stuttgart: 1961).
Buber, Margareta, *Under Two Dictators* (London: 1952).
Caban, Ireneusz and Mańkowski, Zygmunt, *Związek Walki Zbrojnej i Armia Krajowa w Okręgu Lubelskim, 1939–1944,* (Lublin: 1971).
Calvocoressi, Peter and Wint, Guy, *Total War* (London: 1974).
Cave Brown, Anthony, *Bodyguard of Lies* (New York: 1975).
Cazalet, Victor, *With Sikorski to Russia* (London: 1942).
Chapman, Guy, *Why France Collapsed* (London: 1968).
Chojecki, Władysław, *Bibliografia zwartych druków konspiracyjnych wydanych pod okupacją hitlerowską w latach 1939–1945* (Warsaw: 1970).
Churchill, Winston, *The Second World War* (London: 1950) vols I–VI.
Ciechanowski, Jan, *The Warsaw Rising* (London: 1974).
Costello, John and Hughes, Terry, *The Battle of the Atlantic* (London: 1977).
Czapski, Józef, *On Inhuman Land* (London: 1965).
Czerniewski, Kazimierz, 'Jeszcze o produkcji polskich stenów', *Polska technika w walce z okupantem* (Warsaw: 1966). 'O prawdę historyczną w publikacjach o konspiracyjnej produkcji broni w okresie okupacji', *Kwartalnik Historyczny,* year LXXXVI, Polska Akademia Nauk (Warsaw).

Das Generalgouvernement, Reichshandbuch von Karl Baedeker (Leipzig: 1943).

Deighton, Len, *Fighter* (London: 1979).

Dobroszycki, Lucjan, *Centralny katalog polskiej prasy konspiracyjnej, 1939–1945* (Warsaw: 1962).

Documents on Polish–Soviet Relations, 1939–1945 (London–Melbourne–Toronto: 1961–7) vols I and II.

Dokumenty i materiały do historii stosunków polsko-radzieckich (Warsaw: 1973).

Destiny Can Wait (The Polish Air Force in the Second World War) (London: 1949).

Domańska, Regina, *Pawiak* (Warsaw: 1978).

Dornberger, Walter, *V–2* (London: 1958).

Dunn, Dennis, *The Catholic Church and the Soviet Government, 1939–1949* (Columbia, USA: 1977).

Duraczyński, Eugeniusz, *Stosunki w kierownictwie podziemia londyńskiego, 1939–1943* (Warsaw: 1966); *Wojna i okupacja* (Warsaw: 1974).

Edwards, Bob and Dunne, Kenneth, *A Study of a Master Spy (Allen Dulles)* (London: 1961).

Encyklopedia II Wojny Światowej (Warsaw: 1975).

Fest, Joachim, *Hitler* (London: 1977).

Foot, Michael R. D., *Resistance* (London: 1976).

Garliński, Bohdan, 'Fünf Jahre in der Schweiz', *Polen und die Schweiz* (Solothurn: 1945).

Garliński, Józef, 'Decyzja podjęcia walki o Warszawę', an interview with General Bór-Komorowski, *Tydzień Polski* (London, 1 August 1964). *Hitler's Last Weapons* (London: 1978); *Intercept, Secrets of the Enigma War* (London: 1979); *Fighting Auschwitz* (London: 1975); 'Konferencja w Belgradzie', *Zeszyty historyczne*, no. 34 (Paris: 1975); *Poland, SOE and the Allies* (London: 1969); *The Swiss Corridor* (London: 1981).

Generał Sikorski, Premier i Naczelny Wódz (London: 1981).

Grubiński, Wacław, *Między młotem i sierpem* (London: 1948).

Hawes, Stephen and White, Ralph, *Resistance in Europe, 1939–1945* (London: 1975).

Hinsley, F. H., *British Intelligence in the Second World War* (London: 1979–82). vols I and II.

Hitler, Adolf, *Mein Kampf* (London: 1939).

Horodyski-Kotecki, Aleksander, 'Podziemny przemysł zbrojeniowy' *Polska technika w walce z okupantem* (Warsaw: 1966).

Höhne, Heinz, *Canaris* (London: 1979).

Interim Report of the US Congressional Select Committee (Washington: 1952).

Irving, David, *The Death of General Sikorski, Accident* (London: 1967); *The Mare's Nest* (London: 1964).

Joll, James, *Europe since 1870* (London: 1978).

Kluz, Stanisław W., *Potrzasku dziejowym* (London: 1978).

Koliński, Izydor, *Regularne jednostki Wojska Polskiego (lotnictwo)* (Warsaw: 1978).

Kopański, Stanisław, *Wspomnienia wojenne, 1939–1945* (London: 1961).

Korboński, Stefan, *The Polish Underground State, 1939–1945* (New York: 1978); *Fighting Warsaw* (London: 1956).

Kot, Stanisław, *Listy z Rosji do gen. Sikorskiego* (London: 1955).

Kowalenko, Władysław, *Tajny Uniwersytet Ziem Zachodnich w latach, 1940–1944* (Poznań: 1946).

Kowalski, Włodzimierz, *Wielka Koalicja, 1941–1945* (Warsaw: 1976–7) vols I, II and III.

Krannhals, Hanns von, *Der Warschauer Aufstand, 1944* (Frankfurt am Main: 1962).

Król, Wacław, *Polskie dywizjony lotnicze w Wielkiej Brytanii, 1940–1945* (Warsaw: 1976).

Krzyżanowski, Bronisław, *Wileński matecznik, 1939–1944* (Paris: 1979).

Le Saint Siège et la Situation religieuse en Pologne et dans les Pays Baltes, 1939–1945 (Rome: 1967) vols I and II.

Liberek, Stanislas, *Témoignages* (Sion: 1978).

Liddell Hart, Basil, *History of the Second World War* (London: 1970).

Lüönd, Karl, *Spionage und Landsverrat in der Schweiz* (Zürich: 1977).

Maczek, Stanisław, *Od podwody do czołga* (Edinburgh: 1961).

Madajczyk, Czesław, *Polityka III Rzeszy w okupowanej Polsce* (Warsaw: 1970) vols I and II.

Mały Rocznik Statystyczny (Warsaw: 1939).

Marczak-Oborski, Stanisław, *Teatr czasu wojny* (Warsaw: 1967).

Markert, Werner, *Polen* (Cologne, Graz: 1959).

Masterman, John C., *The Double-Cross System in the War of 1939 to 1945* (London: 1973).

Matecki, Józef, 'Dziennik działań niemieckiej 9 armii', *Zeszyty Historyczne* no. 15 (Paris: 1969).

Michalewski, Jerzy, 'Relacja', *Zeszyty Historyczne* no. 26 (Paris: 1973).

Mikołajczyk, Stanisław, *The Pattern of Soviet Domination* (London: 1948).

Mitkiewicz, Leon, *W najwyższym sztabie zachodnich aliantów, 1943–1945* (London: 1971).

Moczulski, Leszek, *Wojna Polska* (Poznań: 1972).

Moravec, František, *Master of Spies* (London–Sydney–Toronto: 1975).

Muskus, Urszula, *Długi most – moje przeżycia w Związku Sowieckim, 1939–1956* (London: 1975).

Nazi–Soviet Relations, 1939–1941 (the documents of the German Foreign Office) (Washington: 1948).

Pełczyński, Tadeusz, 'Geneza i przebieg "Burzy"' *Bellona*, 21 and 28 July, 4 August 1949.

Pilaciński, Jerzy, *Narodowe Siły Zbrojne* (London: 1976).

Piszczkowski, Tadeusz, *Między Lizboną a Londynem* (London: 1979).

Ploetz, Karl, *Auszug aus der Geschichte* (Würzburg: 1968).

Pobóg-Malinowski, Władysław, *Najnowsza Historia Polityczna Polski, 1864–1945* (London: 1960) vol. III.

Polonsky, Antony, *Politics in Independent Poland, 1921–1939* (Oxford: 1972); *The Great Powers and the Polish Question, 1941–1945* (London, 1976).

Polonsky, Antony and Drukier Bolesław, *The Beginnings of Communist Rule in Poland, December 1943 – June 1945* (London: 1980).

Polscy Spadochroniarze (London: 1949).

Polski Słownik Biograficzny (Warsaw: 1981) vol. 108.

Polskie Siły Zbrojne w Drugiej wojnie Światowej (London: 1950–75) vols I, II and III.

Popiel, Karol, *Generał Sikorski w mojej pamięci* (London: 1978).

Prawdzic-Szlaski, Janusz, *Nowogródczyzna w walce, 1940–1945* (London: 1976).

Pużak, Kazimierz, 'Wspomnienia', *Zeszyty Historyczne*, no. 41 (Paris: 1977).

Raczyński, Edward, *The British–Polish Alliance* (London: 1948); *In Allied London* (London: 1962).

Reitlinger, Gerard, *The Final Solution* (London: 1971).

Renauld, P., 'La machine à chiffrer "Enigma"' *Bulletin triméstrial de l'Association des Amis de l'École supérieure de Guerre*, no. 78 (France: 1978).

Reports of Congress of the United States of America, 1945–75

Royce, Hans, Zimmermann, Erich and Jacobsen, Hans-Adolf, *20. Juni 1944* (Bonn: 1961).

Rzepecki, Jan, *Wspomnienia i przyczynki historyczne* (Warsaw: 1956).

Schellenberg, Walter, *The Schellenberg Memoirs* (London: 1956).

Seale, Patric and McConville, Maureen, *Philby, the Long Road to Moscow*, (London: 1973).

Shtemenko, Sergey *Jeszcze o sztabie generalnym w latach wojny* (Warsaw: 1976).

Siemaszko, Zbigniew, *Narodowe Siły Zbrojne* (London: 1982).

Slessor, John, *The Central Blue* (London: 1956).

Sokorski, Włodzimierz, *Polacy pod Lenino* (Warsaw: 1971).

Sosabowski, Stanisław, *Najkrótszą drogą* (London: 1957).

Sosnkowski, Kazimierz, *Materiały historyczne* (London: 1966).

Speer, Albert, *Inside the Third Reich* (London: 1971).

Sprawozdanie sądowe w sprawie organizatorów, kierowników i uczestników polskiego podziemia na zapleczu Czerwonej Armii na terytorium Polski, Litwy oraz obwodów zachodniej Białorusi i Ukrainy. Rozpatrzonej przez Kolegium Wojskowe Sądu Najwyższego ZSRR, 18–21 czerwca 1945 roku (Moscow: 1945).

Srebrzyński, Józef, 'Zagadnienia łączności krajowej', *Dziękuję Wam Rodacy* (London: 1973).

Stachiewicz, Wacław, 'Przygotowania wojenne w Polsce, 1935–1939', *Zeszyty historyczne*, no. 40 (Paris: 1977).

Stettinius, Edward E., *Lend-Lease* (New York: 1945).

Strzembosz, Tomasz, *Odbijanie i uwalnianie więźniów w Warszawie, 1939–1944* (Warsaw: 1972).

Stypułkowski, Zbigniew, *Invitation to Moscow* (London: 1957) vols I and II.

Sztumberk-Rychter, Tadeusz, *Artylerzysta piechurem* (Warsaw: 1966).

Szumowski, Tadeusz, 'Po upadku Pragi', *Kierunki*, nos 20 and 21 (Warsaw and Cracow: 1968).

The Report of Jürgen Stroop (Warsaw: 1958).

Thompson, R. W., *Generalissimo Churchill* (London: 1973).

Tuskiewcz, Otto, 'Działania na korzyść Armii Krajowej', *Skrzydła*, no. 20/493 (London: 1 November 1946).
Ustawa konstytucyjna z dnia 23 kwietnia 1935 (London: 1941).
The Unseen and Silent (London: 1954).
Walka o dobra kultury, Warszawa, 1939–1945 (Warsaw: 1970) vols I and II.
Wat, Aleksander, *Mój wiek* (London: 1977).
Williams, Neville, *Chronology of the Modern World, 1763–1965* (London: 1973).
Wilmot, Chester, *The Struggle for Europe* (London: 1959).
Wojewódzki, Michał *V–1, V–2* (Warsaw: 1975).
Wroński, Bohdan, *Poza krajem – za Ojczyznę* (Paris: 1975).
Wycech, Czesław, *Z dziejów tajnej oświaty w latach okupacji, 1939–1944* (Warsaw: 1964).
Zarański, Józef, *Świadek wydarzeń* (London: 1968).
Zaremba, Zygmunt, *Wojna i konspiracja* (London: 1957).
Zatorska, Helena, *Wanda Wasilewska* (Warsaw: 1977).
Zawodny, Janusz, *Nothing but Honor* (London: 1978).
Zbiniewicz, Fryderyk, *Armia Polska w ZSRR* (Warsaw: 1963).
Zbrodnia katyńska w świetle dokumenotów (London: 1982).
Żebrowski, Marian Włodzimierz, *Zarys historii polskiej broni pancernej, 1918–1947* (London: 1971).

PERIODICALS

Bellona (quarterly), London.
Biuletyn Stowarzyszenia Techników Polskich w Wielkiej Brytanii (quarterly), London.
Bulletin triméstrial de l'Association des Amis de l'École Supérieure de Guerre (appears three times p.a.), France.
Dzieje najnowsze (quarterly), Warsaw, Wrocław, Cracow, Gdańsk.
Kierunki (weekly), Warsaw-Cracow.
Kultura (monthly), Paris.
Kwartalnik Historyczny (quarterly), Warsaw.
Monitor Polski (irregular), Paris.
Najnowsze dzieje Polski (quarterly), Warsaw.
New York Times (daily).
Piechota (quarterly), London.
Polska technika w walce z okupantem (monthly), Warsaw.
Skrzydła (monthly), London.
Tydzień Polski (weekly), London.
Wiadomości (weekly), London.
Zeszyty do historii Narodowych Sił Zbrojnych (yearly), Chicago.
Zeszyty Historyczne (quarterly), Paris.

Index

382 *Index*